LAW
BY
NIGHT

GLOBAL AND INSURGENT LEGALITIES,
edited by Eve Darian-Smith and Jonathan Goldberg-Hiller

LAW
BY
NIGHT

JONATHAN
GOLDBERG-HILLER

———

DUKE UNIVERSITY PRESS

Durham and London 2023

Printed in the United States of America on acid-free paper ∞
Project Editor: Bird Williams
Designed by Matthew Tauch
Typeset in Garamond Premier Pro by
Westchester Publishing Services.

Library of Congress Cataloging-in-Publication Data
Names: Goldberg-Hiller, Jonathan, 1958 author.
Title: Law by night / Jonathan Goldberg-Hiller.
Other titles: Global and insurgent legalities.
Description: Durham : Duke University Press, 2023. | Series: Global and
insurgent legalities | Includes bibliographical references and index.
Identifiers: LCCN 2023013168 (print)
LCCN 2023013169 (ebook)
ISBN 9781478025351 (paperback)
ISBN 9781478020530 (hardcover)
ISBN 9781478027454 (ebook)
Subjects: LCSH: Night—Social aspects. | Nightlife—Social aspects. |
Sociological jurisprudence. | Night—History. | Night riding (Racial violence) |
BISAC: LAW / General Classification: LCC GT3408. G653 2023 (print)
LCC GT3408 (ebook)
DDC 306.4—dc23/eng/20230615
LC record available at https://lccn.loc.gov/2023013168
LC ebook record available at https://lccn.loc.gov/2023013169

Cover art: Jon Rollins, *Schedule*, 2020. Acrylic, enamel, silkscreen
ink, charcoal, graphite, ballpoint pen, masking tape, copy paper,
sketchbook paper, and newsprint on canvas, 60 in. x 48 in. Cour-
tesy of the artist.

To my students

CONTENTS

ACKNOWLEDGMENTS

I am deeply grateful for the generosity of so many colleagues and friends who helped me in the writing of this book. Davina Cooper was instrumental in the first efforts to transform a rough idea into the set of studies comprising this work. We sat together on the beach in Kailua composing a list of what seemed like unexplored intersections of law and night, thinking we might write together from this list. Later, I asked to write the project alone, which she supported. Although the book today looks quite different than we sketched it then, it retains a kernel of those first imaginative surveys. Austin Sarat's encouragement in the earliest stages of writing allowed me to trust my hunch that these explorations could contribute a new angle to sociolegal studies, and it gave me the initial courage I needed to work in new and unfamiliar areas.

Noenoe Silva helped nourish the project from beginning to end during many years of beautiful hikes in the Koʻolau mountains, long discussions over early versions of various chapters, and royal commands to delete as the Queen of Concision. This book also takes its shape from the careful reading of exploratory drafts, and the encouragement and direction to pull more clarity out of dark obscurantism by Brenna Bhandar, Davina Cooper, Eve Darian-Smith, Carolyn Eichner, Kennan Ferguson, Jairus Grove, Cressida Heyes, Sankaran Krishna, Charles Lawrence III, Marisela Martinez, Renisa Mawani, Neal Milner, Samson Opondo, Gitte du Plessis, Avi Soifer, Alberto Toscano, and several anonymous reviewers. I have also benefited from generous commentary, suggestions, and novel ideas from Jeannine Bell, Kathy Ferguson, Lois Harder, Didi Herman, Katharina Heyer, David T. Johnson, Catherine Kellogg, Mona Lynch, Mari Matsuda, Kunal Parker, George Pavlich, Michael J. Shapiro, and Mariana Valverde.

Courtney Berger contributed beneficial organizational and intellectual guidance, and the title for the book. She is the consummate editor. My appreciation also goes to the staff at Duke University Press, whose professionalism in preparing this book exceeds what an author could wish for.

Many ideas for this book were presented and tested with academic audiences at the Universities of Hawai'i, Wisconsin–Milwaukee, Alberta, British Columbia, Edinburgh, and Simon Fraser University, and at meetings of the Law and Society Association and the Association for the Study of Law, Culture, and the Humanities. I am grateful for the discussions that followed.

All sustained writing depends on gentle reminders to stay engaged with life away from the desk and library, made all the more vital and difficult during the recent years of quarantine and the horrors of emergent neofascism. I am especially thankful for the love and friendship of my partner, Alexandra French, and from others not named above, including Ann-Marie Brege, Peter Reagan, the Potluck group, the driveway dinner gang, the William Morris Cup Society, and my siblings, Betsy, Ben, Elissa, and Adam. All of you brought light and laughter, thankfully interrupting my efforts to stare too hard into dark corners.

Finally, I want to express my gratitude to my graduate students, past and present, who have repeatedly shown me the infectious joys of encountering new ideas. I dedicate this book to them.

INTERRUPTIONS

Continuity is one of the postulates of positive law: permanent as well as general, legal rule is a sun that never sets. —**Jean Carbonnier**

If it were self-evident and in the heart, the law would no longer be the law, but the sweet interiority of consciousness. If, on the other hand, it were present in a text, if it were possible to decipher it between the lines of a book, if it were in a register that could be consulted, then it would have the solidity of external things: it would be possible to follow or disobey it. Where then would its power reside, by what force or prestige would it command respect? In fact, the presence of the law is its concealment. —**Michel Foucault**

The values of the day become the obsessions of the night.
—**Andrea Dworkin**

Lon Fuller's iconic and enduring 1949 article, "The Case of the Speluncean Explorers," has greeted thousands of students in their first course in legal theory. In this fictional story of anthropophagy set far into the future, Roger Whetmore is eaten by his fellow spelunkers after the cave they were exploring collapsed, blocking their exit for thirty-two days. Eventually realizing that their rescue would be delayed far beyond the limit of their provisions, the cavers agreed that, by lot, one man would be killed in order to nourish the rest. Whetmore had proposed this solution, and when he lost the cast of the dice—despite his last-minute bid for a delay and expressed withdrawal from the procedure—he was dispatched and consumed. In the fictional reconstruction of the case, the trial court convicted the remaining cavers of murder and sentenced them to hang, but both jury and judge pleaded for executive clemency, acknowledging the inequities of the statutory laws and professing their sympathies for these explorers' cruel fate. The divergent opinions rendered by the several appellate justices that comprise the allegory tell the conflicting stories constructible by mid-twentieth-century jurisprudence. Students are left scrambling to follow the paths of legal reasoning: Was this murder, necessity, or a simple matter of freedom to contract?

While many have debated and extended Fuller's review of the philosophical landscape, making it a veritable "cave drawing for the ages," few have delved into the meaning of this cave for legal thought and pedagogy.[1] What is so compelling about a dark and remote cavity for legal theory? Perhaps one answer lies in what the cave means for law's relation to time. Fuller situates the case in the year 4300, but the cave is a cultural symbol of prehistoric origin against which the progress of law to re-create social norms is measured. Justice Keen, ventriloquizing the sociological jurisprudence of Roscoe Pound, intimates a parallel with Plato's allegory of the cave:[2] "I wish to emphasize once more the danger that we may get lost in the patterns of our own thought and forget that these patterns often cast not the slightest shadow on the outside world."[3] This Platonic cave seems to situate the justices themselves, as they each seek to articulate rationales avoiding oracular obscurity. The transcendence of this dark past and concern for law's proper dominion—both symbolized by the cave—draw many of the justices to a central metaphor of light: statutes must be interpreted with the "light of . . . evident purpose" (Justice Foster, Justice Tatting), the light of "human realities," or the light of "common sense" (Justice Handy).[4] The manifold and divergent formal, moral, and popular means of construing the meaning of Whetmore's death in the cave constitute the miasmic darkness from which the law must drag itself into the visible realm of public life.

And yet the persistent metaphors of light, so central to legal discourse in our day (consider, here, the terminology of "bright-line tests," "blue sky laws," and "bargaining in the shadow of the law," as well as constitutional "penumbras" and zones of twilight), ironically seem to reinforce an imminent, lurking darkness, whether it be the dark ages of the past eclipsed by the Enlightenment and modern law, or formal public law writing over the violent cave of the night.[5] The cavernous gloom of night brings us face to face with the physical needs and precarities associated with the body; Whetmore is all of us and, perhaps in gruesome Freudian logic, *in* all of us as well. "The Case of the Speluncean Explorers" is a textual echo of Sigmund Freud's story of legal and symbolic origin—the killing and eating of the primal father—and Whetmore's cannibalized body drives the search for jurisprudence attentive to the primal violence it will conceal and transcend.[6]

Hidden within the gloom of the cave, Whetmore might be less the vulnerable everyman and more the *Other*: the "dangerous" or disadvantaged individual taken by surprise in the dark so that others may live better or sleep peacefully, the one who has "whet" others' appetites for political or economic power. Law privileges the powerful in this critical, alternative source for jurisprudence, unable or unwilling to account for what happens in the dark shadows, especially to the weak. This alternative inquiry— exploring the relations of power and darkness in their material and rhetorical manifestations sustaining or transforming social hierarchy—is the focus of this book. I seek to paint diverse pictures of legality at night in order to think anew the contribution of law to racial and gender hierarchies, to colonial relations, and to the positioning of the most socially vulnerable and precarious among us.

This chapter's epigraph by Michel Foucault challenges us to paradoxically locate law's concealment if we are to find law's real power, a speluncean task of discovery that requires deferring law's presence, or searching for a law gone dark. In his *History of Madness*, Foucault suggests that what has escaped history is frequently metaphorized as night. He claims that his intellectual return to the historical moment of the split between reason and madness, of "sense from senselessness . . . will allow that lightning flash decision to appear once more, heterogeneous with the time of history, but ungraspable outside it, which separates the murmur of dark insects from the language of reason and the promises of time."[7]

Perhaps because Fuller had heard these dark, murmuring creatures, recently quieted in the fresh defeat of European fascism and its vast legal exceptionalism that Western legal theory had to explain and refute, his tale seems to presage later twentieth-century critical jurisprudence that has embraced the philosophical idea that there always is an element of the nonlaw sequestered within the law.[8] This includes Fuller's own morality within and beyond law, Jacques Derrida's mythic and theological "mystical foundation" of the law, Slavoj Žižek's "obscene 'nightly' law" that necessarily parallels and infuses the public law, Walter Benjamin's originary violence that founds or sustains a legal order, Robert Cover's field of pain and death on which the law is repeatedly inscribed, Giorgio Agamben's and Carl Schmitt's sovereign exception at the heart of law, and Alain Badiou's nonlaw as law, to name a few.[9]

The cave (and the dark fears and threats beyond law it represents) is metaphorical and allegorical, but it is not only rhetorical. Law's split between enlightened reason and the darkened cave of cannibal madness is not so distant that it must bear a vast historical search for origins. Discovering the cavernous darkness as an alibi for a necessary legal enlightenment need look no further than the celestial cycles of night and day and their sociological and sociolegal qualities. Like others, I claim in this book that law has not outrun its dark interiors, but I find these not only in their figurative tropes—the legal, philosophical, and racial rhetoric of darkness, blackness, sleepiness, and shadow—but also in the material and sociological consequences for law and legality of our organic bodies needing sleep, of the persistence of civilian and police vigilantism and terroristic interracial violence at night, of the curfew that imposes a lethal nocturnal order, and of the ways night and darkness are used by the disadvantaged to create sustaining legal ideas and political action. Night is a time of excessive absence, a parajudicial experience whose meanings for legal order and governance are too often ignored by legal scholars.[10] Night, I suggest, is our speluncean cave, an evanescent center to thought about law. What happens at night and under darkness resembles Plato's *pharmakon*, which is simultaneously medicine and poison: a disordered and violent set of seemingly lawless encounters that nonetheless serves as the provocation to law—its protections and its violence—but also a stimulus to law's forgetfulness, the decaying memory of what is left unwritten in its books.

Night wasn't always absent in the law. Ancient legal norms regarding self-defense explicitly permitted extraordinary action after dark. Mosaic law, for example, immunized from retributive blood feud any homeowner who killed while defending his house from a burglar at night.[11] The English common law absorbed this norm, constricting the crime of burglary, which Sir William Blackstone called "nocturnal housebreaking," only to the hours of night; theft or robbery in a domicile by day made violators appear "deranged" rather than criminally culpable.[12] Other crimes were made exceptional if they occurred at night. Early medieval sanctuary laws and practices allowed protection for homicides, but canon law forbade eligibility for "public thieves and 'nocturnal destroyers of fields.'"[13] The revolutionary Haitian Constitution of 1801 protected the nocturnal home absolutely: "The residence of any person shall constitute an inviolable asylum. During night-time, no one shall have the right to enter therein unless in case of fire, flooding or upon request from within. During the day, authorities shall have access for a particular objective determined either by a law or by an order issued by a public authority."[14] Students in the early European Renaissance were admonished not to study the law at night. As Peter Goodrich recounts, "Night . . . was the time of fantasy or imaginings, of images and women, and all were perceived as threats to the capacity, probity, and reason of law, for 'night always comes on with the mind disturbed.'"[15] In Roman law and its incorporation into medieval European law, contracts and wills made at night were suspicious, if not void.[16] Law took explicit account of night, even framing it in criminal terms: "Nighttime in the eighteenth century was defined not in terms of the setting of the sun but according to the law against burglary."[17] Kings in Europe and elsewhere performed an intricate political theater to project their everwakefulness so that the law could be imagined to remain perpetually in place, allowing their subjects to safely sleep after dark.[18] In postbellum America, Black men and women were banned from the streets at night in some cities, and from the entire environs of "sundown" towns through the twentieth century.[19] The homeless regularly faced bans on sleeping and were subject to particularly disruptive treatment at night. As these many historical fragments suggest, night had a distinct history that affected and was affected by the law. Night had its own crimes, its own dangers, and its distinctive ways of knowing.

In more contemporary times, night may appear to lose its distinctive character. Streetlights pierce the urban darkness, work continues around the clock, and electronic surveillance persists, unimpeded by obscurity in a way that optical observation is not. Increasingly quantified and studied, sleep has to some degree become a politically cultivated means for assuring daytime alertness in public transportation and schools, and a key to securing diurnal citizenship.[20] The connections among night and sleep, economic and public worlds, give support to what Gilles Deleuze has called societies of control, in which the disciplinary "environments of enclosure," such as factory, school, and family, have melted away into the smooth spaces and times of governance through continuous means.[21] It is easy to agree with the historian of night A. Roger Ekirch, who "imagine[s] a time when night, for all practical purposes, will have become day—truly a twenty-four/seven society in which traditional phases of time, from morning to midnight, have lost their original identities."[22] For Eric Santner, this is our Kafkaesque "life-world that has itself come to resemble a kind of office that never goes dark."[23]

I take a different tack in this book, rejecting the future anterior expectation that night, culturally opposed to the aspirations of day, is destined for irrelevance. Instead, I emphasize the periodic darkness that persists in our lifeworlds and the forms of legal governance and social violence that the oscillation between night and day enables. While contemporary governance has indeed sutured many aspects of night to day, night has not been entirely colonized, to use Murray Melbin's popular terminology.[24] Much as in early modern times, sociological and geographic boundaries matter today for nocturnal strategies of authority, with consequences for racial hierarchies and gender violence, as I explore in the chapters to follow. Not all people live nights in the same fashion, or suffer night's disabilities and gain its advantages in equal manner, making night a time for social and political struggle. Cultural meanings that situate night as a time of danger and form what Robert Williams called a "contrapuntal space" remain potent, legitimating violence on and resistance by those who are culturally designated as threats.[25] The physiological need for sleep is the object of biopolitical efforts to harness, control, and render it useful for economy and social order, but the defense of sleep is also a site for conflict where and when the state and biopower appear to falter. Foucault famously argued that our thinking about law cannot fully shake the philosophies and theologies of the Middle Ages, and to the extent that night once explicitly mattered to law and legal thought then, I argue, we will find that it still matters today.[26]

To understand what night means for our thinking about, and varied experiences with, law and legality, I suggest that we must find multiple ways to look deeply into what has been hidden in the cave of the night. Martin Heidegger argued that there is no light without, first, an opening into which it can shine: "Outward appearance, however, is a manner of presence. No outward appearance without light—Plato already knew this. But there is no light and no brightness without the opening. Even darkness needs it. How else could we happen into darkness and wander through it?"[27] I elevate histories, philosophies, cultural works, and sociology—the panoply of sociolegal devices—that can reveal this opening and permit scholarly wandering through the darkness. While disciplinary studies of night are still in their infancy, brought together they offer a scaffold from which to scrutinize Foucault's paradox of the law's concealment as its ultimate presence. The assembly of various perspectives on law's authority at night exposes the intricate contingencies that constitute legality, what Michel Foucault, Giorgio Agamben, Gilles Deleuze, Davide Panagia, Roberto Esposito, and others have called the *dispositifs*—or the arrangements and apparatuses—of governance.[28] For Agamben, *dispositif* refers to "a set of practices, bodies of knowledge, measures, and institutions that aim to manage, govern, control, and orient—in a way that purports to be useful— the behaviors, gestures, and thoughts of human beings."[29] *Dispositifs* do this work, according to him, by capturing living beings through subjectivities produced within the struggles over their capture. These subjectivities are not totalizing, in Deleuze's reading, and "the productions of subjectivity escape from the powers and the forms of knowledge of one social apparatus in order to be reinserted in another, in forms which are yet to come into being."[30] *Dispositifs*, therefore, can change philosophical orientations from what Deleuze calls the Eternal toward the creative production of the new.[31] They also break our philosophical attachments to the state as the sole authority for law, and as the central organizer of violence and power.

The *dispositif* is a mainstay, by other terms, in many corners of Anglo-American sociolegal studies, such as inquiries into the "mobilization" (or citation) of law by social movements, and research into legal consciousness designed to ascertain law's many possible meanings. Michael McCann, for one, emphasizes a "decentered" view of law with behavioral significance only where, and when, it interacts with other institutional forces that together comprise the elements of social control. Decentered law means "not only that law is pluralistic and relatively independent of the state, but that its role in sustaining traditional hierarchies, and hence in structuring potential strategies of resistance, varies significantly among different terrains of social struggle. As such, attention to tactical options concerning the particular sites, terms, and timing of struggle are an important concern for analyses of legal mobilization."[32] One important finding of the legal consciousness literature is that the various orientations that people consciously (or unconsciously) take to the law (resisting it, aligning themselves "before" it and the power it purports to hold, or treating law mostly as a game to be strategically maneuvered with particular skills) reveal the myriad ways that law infiltrates and extends other dynamics of power.[33] These plural orientations to law "reveal the amazing capacity of law to roll with the punches, exhibiting a kind of Zen flexibility that strengthens rather than diminishes its power."[34] One key to understanding the varied significance of legality is law's importance for individual identity. According to David Engel and Frank Munger, "Not only does identity determine how and when rights become active, but rights can also shape identity. . . . Rights may influence identity by altering how individuals perceive themselves or by changing how they are perceived or treated by others, bringing about a new perspective on who one is and what one expects. The self, so constituted, acquires an identity that can, under certain circumstances, lend itself to the perception that he or she is being treated unfairly—that rights are being violated."[35] Similar to the theory of the *dispositif*, it is subjectivity that is mutually constituted by and in legal relations, affirming some ways of being and energizing some experiences of becoming.

An important implication of these philosophical and sociolegal perspectives for this book is that there may be no "theory" of night that can be abstracted from its temporal contributions to various *dispositifs*. Indeed, if Deleuze and the sociolegal scholars are right, one consequence of *dispositifs* or a decentered view of law is that there are no universals, a somewhat ironic way to examine modern legal phenomena that are ideologically driven by their universality. Unlike a Hegelian historicism of reason, or a liberal affirmation of the growth of individual liberty emerging from the darkness of traditional authority, thinking in terms of *dispositifs* takes us to an aleatory and transitory history intertwined with present possibilities.[36] A night of many stars, perhaps, more than a day with its singular sun.

LAW AND TIME

Attention to the variability of law is not new. By dissolving the Marxist and functionalist claims for the social and historical utility of law, critical scholars have drawn attention to the plural forms of legal and normative ordering, the divisions between sovereign/juridical and biopower, the cerebral gap essential to legal aesthetics, the historical significance of the opposition to legal rights, and the fields of pain and death with which the law is inevitably entangled. This pluralist orientation has reimagined the rule of law to be pointillist, as in a painting by Georges Seurat, its granularity offering contingent contributions to governance.

Recent studies of legal temporality have converged with this picture. The various orientations to time within legal discourse are no longer as monolithic as the poet W. H. Auden once satirized:

> Law, says the judge as he looks down his nose
> Speaking clearly and most severely,
> Law is as I've told you before,
> Law is as you know, I suppose,
> Law is but let me explain it once more,

Law is The Law . . .
Law is the clothes men wear
Anytime, anywhere,
Law is Good morning and Good night.[37]

The orientations to past precedent ("as I've told you before") as well as to future consequence, the distant horizons of the common law's "time immemorial" as well as beliefs in the constitutional framers' historically fixed thought-worlds, are all temporalities that frequently mix into "a technique of faith" illustrated by what Oliver Wendel Holmes called "the path of the law," an Enlightenment temporal flow by which "history, in illuminating the past, illuminates the present, and in illuminating the present, illuminates the future" in Benjamin Cardozo's interpretation.[38] This autochthonous, synoptic temporality that makes modern law appear "anytime, anywhere," in Auden's words, is undercut by recent anthropological and historical scholarship that has located the source of law's myth of continuity in the abrupt encounters with colonialism and its temporal "othering," uncovering an imperial "politics of time."[39]

Legal and social time have the potential to diverge, one driver of this political reality. Within Western law it is possible to find a linearity by which progress is given meaning and a cycle of return through which iterative regularity reconciles community with the past, as well as the complex interactions between both.[40] Similar temporal mixtures infuse the political constitution of sovereignty, particularly the reconciliation of the medieval king's two bodies, one corporeal, finite, and cyclically replaceable, and the other institutional and enduring.[41]

Of course, legal discourse and doctrine have always declared their own sense of time—as once did the monarch. Glimpsed in the irony of "all deliberate speed" that facilitated white resistance to the *Brown* court's demands for an end to racial segregation in education, in the adherence to past precedent, and in the persistent rule of *res judicata* that affixes temporality to legal decisions, legal discourse controls the time frames by which it orders itself and makes itself authoritative in other discursive domains. For example, Kunal Parker has shown how the nonhistorical "time immemorial" that authorized the common law tradition provided a dynamism for legal development that kept law proximate to democratic values.[42] This temporal openness, understood as the commonality between life and law, anticipates the event that lies beyond structure, the disruption that makes legality discontinuous and ultimately political.

It is surprising that in this constellation of diverse temporal orientations, another discontinuity, that of the cycles of night and day, which have played a much more significant role in what we might call legal literature, is so frequently overlooked by legal scholars interested in questions of temporality and governance. Few have drawn sociolegal attention to what H. G. Wells intimated when he wrote in *The Island of Doctor Moreau* that the hybridized "beast people" who were forced to live by human norms under a law decreed by the doctor "broke the Law only furtively and after dark; in the daylight there was a general atmosphere of respect for its multifarious prohibitions."[43] Likewise, it is the hanging of Herman Melville's Billy Budd at the very instant of dawn that seals the metamorphosis in which "innocence and guilt . . . in effect changed places."[44]

In the chapters that follow, I approach the natural oscillation between night and day as a constant generator of legal pluralism in order to think about the contexts in which this daily rhythm may contribute to governance.[45] I don't think that it is the quantity of law that is altered at night; the idea of the quantum of legality is a remnant of behaviorist sociolegal thought.[46] Yet behaviorism gets some things right: using tools designed for knowing law in daytime, perhaps we understand very little about how to think about law at night, how to collect useful data, or how to comprehend how the state "sees" after dark.[47] These epistemological uncertainties mark the limits of abstract legal doctrines about time, and they magnify the significance of the body with its own circadian rhythms and experiences of nocturnal vulnerability. Not knowing what is in store as darkness falls and the state's vision wanes enhances the experiences of anticipation, another form of legal temporality requiring our attention. This sense of anticipation is different from the delay attendant on—or even integral to— the legal process.[48] The shifting between nocturnal and diurnal governance may encourage a vigilant waiting for daybreak, or, for others, an embrace of the obscurity of darkness.

Attention to the daily interruptions in fields of legal organization, the institutional shifts attributable to darkness, and the mobilization of human vulnerabilities generated by the needs for sleep and security at night furthers the aims of critical legal pluralism that seeks to disrupt the state's "monist" monopoly over law and its attendant rationalism and idealism.[49] For Margaret Davies, pluralism "describes a situation in which incommensurable terms coexist in a comparative space."[50] The understanding of law as a plural experience began within anthropological thought about the (sometimes colonially enforced) persistence of Indigenous legal norms in

Africa and elsewhere but rapidly became applied to other social contexts.[51] Critical legal pluralism champions the discrete separation of legal norms, which is a direct challenge to the ideology of legal centrism.[52] In Desmond Manderson's words, "Pluralism welcomes incoherence. . . . There is a trust in disorder here and an attraction to the small-scale, contingent, and even contradictory workings of what Clifford Geertz called 'local knowledge.'"[53] Strong forms of legal pluralism may coexist with weaker ones, permitting state law to be seen as fundamentally "singular plural," a conceptual cohesion, akin to the *dispositif*, that remains fragmentary in practice and divergent in experience.[54]

The political theology of the two bodies of the medieval European king suggests that the state and, paradoxically, its commitment to a unitary concept of sovereignty have long been invested in performances around plural temporalities. Attention to the ways that the state has always had to invent and adapt to other *dispositifs*, particularly to account for nightfall, allows a recognition of the state's own febrile basis for claiming a persistent rule of law. For instance, South Vietnamese rule, for which the Americans fought during the 1960s, persisted and was intensified only during daylight in many peasant hamlets that their enemies, the Viet Cong, controlled after dark.[55] How distinct is this alternation outside wartime? Perhaps more than we recognize, violence at night by state officials and a willful "blindness" to private enforcers of social hierarchies legitimated by the dark shore up law and legal order as much as these performances during the day.

WHAT HIDES AT NIGHT?

The movement of night to day, as its own *dispositif*, should be understood contingently and ambivalently, producing various subjectivities. Nocturnal *dispositifs* interrupt those of the day, encouraging some advantaged by legal order to believe in the seamless continuity of the law and others to wait patiently for the dawn, desired to offset the threats and vagaries of the night, or to sleep peacefully, only to wake again in a familiar world.[56] Foucault calls this vigil for the morning "after evening" for its indebtedness to what has come before. In contrast, others orient themselves "before morning," approaching night as an opportunity for political and social novelty, an occasion—regularly repeated or singular—to challenge spatial boundaries, thwart legal norms, or simply escape the agents of enforcement.[57] Both orientations are linked to distinctive cultural experiences of night that couple night to law. One is the rather intuitive idea that night is a more dangerous time than day. Fear raises concerns for law's effective control of social and community threats in the dark. The other cultural idea is often recognized obliquely, if at all: that night contains the potential for experiencing and reconstructing notions of equality, sometimes confounding social and legal status through the production of new legal meanings corresponding to shared needs for resting, sleeping, defying boundaries, avoiding authority, even dreaming. Both cultural ideas, I argue, can contribute to violence by activating a politics of fear and by threatening the social hierarchies that appear by day, authorizing not just legal authority but extrajudicial force. One promise of the study of night is a greater understanding of how this violence operates in and is legitimated by the dark.

BUMPS IN THE DARK

In many but not all cultural ontologies, the darkness of night condenses fears for personal and community security, the waning influence of rationality, and the limited capacity of political institutions.[58] This set of fears, sometimes psychologized as nyctophobia, has a long genealogy. In the European Middle Ages, "darkness play[ed] an important symbolic role as a metaphor of pagan obscurantism—deviancy, monstrosity, diabolism."[59] Witches and werewolves, who played benevolent roles in some peasant societies, were accused by the church of subverting social, moral, and legal orders at night, sleeping with the Devil, as well as committing theft and other maleficence.[60] The ecclesiastical accusation of witchcraft and the interrogation of accused women stoked legal development in Europe, including the nature of trials and the adoption of the Roman law, which was integrally concerned with the improprieties of magic.[61]

Sorcery was not the only danger of the night that produced legal order. In the sixteenth and seventeenth centuries, European cultural authorities helped spread the idea that "the night is perilous for the body and the soul, it is the threshold of death and of hell."[62] Nightwalkers, who de facto violated formal and unofficial nocturnal curfews, were targeted as a threat to social order. Matthew Beaumont observes that "nightwalking seems to have functioned as a sort of floating signifier used by the authorities to criminalize or ostracize any errant, irritating or undesirable activity after dark."[63] Policing practices, including the night watch, emerged as a response to nightwalking, thieves, and other nocturnal threats and dangers. Even rudimentary street lighting was thought to reduce the dangers of the night, and law quickly stepped in to mandate the carrying of lanterns by passersby and watchmen (and in colonial America, enslaved and free Black people) to expose their presence.[64] Today fears of witches have given way to concerns for urban "light pollution," but night continues to be perceived as a dangerous time for the law-abiding, and illumination—perhaps incorrectly—as one key to personal security at night.[65] So significant has been the association of fear of crime and night that Ekirch has suggested that day may be thought of as the time of civil law, night its replacement by criminal sanction.[66]

Despite the obstacles of crime control, the night was and remains for many a time of freedom and community, reminding us that the fears of nocturnal crime and calamity are not anthropological but were and are produced politically.[67] In the shadows of the streetlamps and beyond sight of the watchmen, night in early modern Europe remained for some "a time for conviviality, intimacy, experimentation, excitement and spectacle."[68] While urban areas were transitioning away from sovereign prohibitions on nocturnal movement and toward *dispositifs* of regulated control of nighttime activity in the late seventeenth century, a process the historian Craig Koslofsky calls "nocturnalization," rural communities in Europe reflected a different pattern, balancing entertainment and sociality with fears of disorder at night.[69] Public houses and spinning bees, respectively, brought adults and courting youth together after sunset.[70] Even sleep in early England was patterned with social interruptions. The waking interregnum between "first" and "second sleep" was a time for social and sexual intercourse, quiet meditation, and private prayer, suggesting that night was not a time solely given over to the defense against threats.[71] However, night provided an opportunity to commit acts of petty—and not so petty—crime and to anonymously reproach one's neighbors.[72] Yet Alain Cabantous has shown that the most dangerous time in sixteenth- and seventeenth-century France was most likely at dusk, rather than in the darker hours of night.[73]

Both church and state increasingly tried to discipline nocturnal life, privileging the activities of "respectable" bourgeois citizens over youth in the city and struggling "to *clear* the rural night of its traditional activities . . . and create an ordered time largely empty of activity."[74] By the seventeenth century, this control of the night involved curfews and laws against the sinfulness of carnal activity and security dangers after dark. Although the laws may have been mostly symbolic, public and ecclesiastical authorities nonetheless sought to actively govern by augmenting fear of immoral and criminal behavior.[75]

The fueling of fears is still a tool for governance today and, in many ways, continues to focus on the night.[76] In the protests following the killing of George Floyd by a police officer in 2020, violence by police and protesters flared after dark, prompting calls by worried authorities to respond even more aggressively.[77] Fears of disorder play distinctively on sociologically divergent groups. For example, enslaved people, who often made community, conspiracy, and flight at night, were often warned of nocturnal dangers (a menace made real by vigilantes).[78] Movie theaters were once considered by elites to be too dark, and thus too dangerous for middle-class and white patrons, and were lightened accordingly, while films avoided offensive darkened scenes in the early twentieth century.[79] Today Black men are most often misidentified as the source rather than target of nocturnal threats.[80] Women are conditioned to feel, and report on, extensive fear for their safety in public at night, even while they are statistically most endangered in their homes.[81] While night still draws many out of doors, at some level most people in Western societies live nights differently than days, and insecurities (as well as respect for insecurities that others may hold) about criminals, cars, animals, vigilantes, the supernatural, and the dark make for a collective nocturnal anxiety. Night is a time-space, for the geographer Robert Shaw, "in which we are more open, more uncertain, more tentative and perhaps more vulnerable."[82]

Cultural and philosophical associations of night with fear are legion.[83] "Sable Night, mother of Dread and Fear," wrote William Shakespeare.[84] His Theseus exclaims, "In the night, imagining some fear/ How easy is a bush suppos'd a bear!"[85] Rudyard Kipling confirmed the emotional potency of the dark: "Comes a breathing hard behind thee—snuffle-snuffle through the night—/ It is Fear O little hunter, it is Fear."[86] For Edgar Allan Poe, the night has its own populace, bringing forth "every species of infamy from its den."[87] These links between night and fear are "primitive" and intrinsic for Claude Lévi-Strauss and Sigmund Freud.[88] Friedrich Nietzsche mused in his aptly named *Daybreak* that the ear is the organ of fear and could only have evolved at night.[89]

The politics of fear projects blame, and blame lubricates violence at night, most often against the weakest members of society rather than those posing the greatest threats.[90] The idea that the night holds dangers beyond the normal abilities of the state to control becomes a potent excuse for emergency powers, but rarely in a discrete format. Not every night brings a curfew, but every night authorizes the power of the police hunt, often unencumbered by surveillance through cell-phone and body cameras symbolically promising restraint.[91] Not every night calls for a posse comitatus, but night helps hide the identities of vigilantes and provides excuses for lone gunmen "standing their ground" against racialized threats, as well as opportunities for domestic abusers to quietly punish and torture their partners through the denial of sleep. Every night *is* an emergency, normalized to some degree by the *dispositifs* of nocturnal power: the police and private authorities working hard to build and repair the social hierarchies that appear flimsy in the daylight, often justified by a nocturnal foundation of fear. Gabriel Naudé illustrates how this inversion of law, which he called the *coup d'état*, positions the political night before, and not following, day:

> In these *master strokes of State*, the Thunderbolt falls before the Noise of it is heard in the Skies. . . . Prayers are said before the Bell is rung for them; the Execution precedes the Sentence; he receives the Blow that thinks he himself is giving it; he suffers who never expected it, and he dies that look'd upon himself to be the most secure; all is done in the Night and Obscurity, amongst Storms and Confusion, the Goddess *Laverna* presides, and the first Grace requested of her is this,
>
> Make me a Saint and Just to human Sight,
> But wrap my Cheats in Clouds, and Crimes in Night.[92]

Cheats and crimes reveal law as carnivalesque, the coups d'état of night underwriting the day of legal reason.

EQUALITY AT NIGHT

> Help me to shatter this darkness,
> To smash this night,
> To break this shadow
> Into a thousand lights of sun,
> Into a thousand whirling dreams
> Of sun!
> —**Langston Hughes**

The experience of fear at night becomes a source for imagining not only retribution and transgression but also forms of nocturnal equality through which legal norms and social hierarchies can be rearranged or leveled.[93] Elias Canetti opens his masterful work on crowds and the equality that they facilitate with the seminal nocturnal fear of being touched in the dark. "In the dark," he begins, "the fear of an unexpected touch can mount to panic."[94] Canetti draws an affective link between this nightly fear and the transformation of crowds, where jostling and touching become a comfort when confronting the wolves of the night. Murray Melbin, who pioneered the sociology of night, noted something similar. "Aware that they are out together in a dangerous environment, people identify with each other and become more outgoing. The sense of safety that spreads over those together at night in a diner or in a coffee shop promotes camaraderie there."[95] Beyond the shop, the streets themselves are never fully controlled by illumination, observation, and the discourses of danger. Michel de Certeau writes of the tactical skill of using the dark, analogized to a Roman driver, "ceaselessly recreating opacities and ambiguities—spaces of darkness and trickery—in the universe of technocratic transparency."[96] In the antebellum South, despite the expansive exertions of slaveholders and police who effectively controlled the day, "every Southern city had its demimonde, and regardless of the law and the pillars of society, the two races on that level foregathered more or less openly in grog shops, mixed balls, and religious meetings. Less visibly, there thrived 'a world of greater conviviality and equality.' Under cover of night, 'in this nether world blacks and whites mingled freely, the conventions of slavery were discarded, and . . . the women of both races joined in.'"[97] As Langston Hughes poetically observes, night is a time for shattering oppressive norms, for transgression, for reordering and enchanting the world. Night makes "revolution against the archetypal," and darkness is not just preserved alongside illumination but cultivated for these other insurgent values.[98]

The shared need and preparation for sleep may also require overcoming nocturnal fears. Jean-Luc Nancy writes that "night is the wilderness of fears" and sleep "presupposes the fear of night has been conquered."[99] Certainly, not all have the freedom to experience a good sleep, as I explore in later chapters. Nonetheless, the universal periodic need for sleep constitutes a rhythmic equality distinguishing itself from the inequalities of day, even where it is not fully actualized. For Nancy, "all nights are equal. All equally suspend the time of difference, the time of differentiations of all kinds, like that of speech, of food, of combat, of travel, of thought."[100]

Sleep once rehearsed a symbolic leveling. The historian A. Roger Ekirch writes that in the eighteenth century, "a French priest noted, 'The Prince hath no advantage over his subjects, when they are both asleep.' In bed, kings forswore their crowns, bishops their miters, and masters their servants. 'Sleep hab no Massa,' affirmed a Jamaican slave proverb."[101] Sleep and the night, in essence, expressed a shadow *dispositif* of sovereignty in which all were equal, because equally vulnerable. The expansion of extreme penalties for nighttime crimes in the seventeenth and eighteenth centuries suggests that "despite the steadily rising powers of the state, nighttime defied the imposition of government authority."[102] Historically, then, nighttime was not without laws, as it remains law bound today, but those laws then, and frequently today, may seem more fragile in the night due to the desire for alternative social orders and the reality or imagination of limited state capacity. The resultant sense of increased vulnerability not only permits other forms of sociality but also leaves sanctioned space for extrajudicial vigilantism.

What other kinds of equality are expressed at night? Martin Jay has shown the ways vision has long been critical to the iconography of political equality through his study of the artworks of Jacques-Louis David and the ever-seeing Masonic Eye that French revolutionaries used as a symbol of equality following the destruction of the monarchical center of power.[103] And yet vision is also instrumental in discerning social inequalities at a distance. Darkness renders these significations difficult or inoperative, obscuring the markers of clothing, age, gender, and color; night historically brought a relaxation of otherwise strict sartorial and social rules.[104] Freedom from labor and social scrutiny meant "night revolutionized the social landscape."[105] Jacques Rancière emphasizes that this revolution emerges from where the temporalities of work and rest are shaken off by those workers who lucubrate and in so doing share equally with the bourgeois aesthetes the world of imagination:

> It is not day but night that is involved here, not the property of others but their "chagrin," their invented sorrow that contains all real sorrows. It is not knowledge of exploitation that the worker needs in order "to stand tall in the face of that which is ready to devour him." What he lacks and needs is a knowledge of self that reveals to him a being dedicated to something else besides exploitation, a revelation of self that comes circuitously by way of the secret of others: that is, those intellectuals and bourgeois people with whom they will later say . . . they want to have nothing to do.[106]

One important implication of Rancière's history is that night should not be subsumed under the empire of sleep and work, especially for those seeking social and political justice. Where Maurice Blanchot recognizes that too often "sleep belongs to the world; it is a task. We sleep in accord with the general law which makes our daytime activity depend on our nightly repose," Rancière responds that night holds an aesthetic and epistemological equality freeing it from the social and material inequalities of the day for those who can seize its other opportunities: "The inventors, the poets, the lovers of the people and the Republic, the organizers of the cities of the future, and the apostles of new religions. The worker needs all of these people, not to gain scientific or scholarly knowledge of his condition, but to entertain and maintain his passions and desires for another world. Otherwise the constraints of labor will level them down to the mere instinct for survival and subsistence, turning the worker brutalized by work and sleep into the servant and accomplice of the rich people bloated with egotism and idleness."[107] The enhanced possibility of aesthetic imagination at night creates an equality but at the same time, and integrally, a possible resistance that comes from reimagining the world, "not as a specific single world but as a conflictive world: not a world of competing interests or values but a world of competing worlds."[108]

For some, the night has always held another world of pleasure allowing for new encounters that frequently escape legal and other forms of order. The feminist philosopher Hélène Cixous observes, "What is outside of us during the day takes place within us during the night."[109] Henri Lefebvre parallels this embodiment with his theory of spatiality: "Space is divided up into designated (signified, specialized) areas and into areas that are prohibited (to one group or another). It is further subdivided into spaces for work and spaces for leisure, and into daytime and night-time spaces. The body, sex and pleasure are often accorded no existence, either mental or social, until after dark, when the prohibitions that obtain during the day, during 'normal' activity, are lifted."[110] The lifting of prohibitions may become a strategy for male power; Simone de Beauvoir observes, "In the shadows of night man invites woman to sin. But in full daylight he disowns the sin and the fair sinner."[111] Darkness also permits less patriarchal forms of sexuality to thrive. Urban night life has been critical to various youth cultures, identities, and personal growth, sometimes ordered by night economies promoted by governments and businesses, leading to exclusions based on class, ethnicity, and gender.[112] But night also allows for the development of social networks among people whose diurnal differences are no longer preeminent, allowing a new commonality or equality to emerge. With the loss of sanction, new and experimental forms of life emerge and express what Elisabeth Anker has recently extolled as "ugly freedoms."[113] Night and darkness long provided cover for illicit public homosexual liaisons, for example. Prosecutions of homosexuality in the late Middle Ages in Florence were directed by a committee known as "Officials of the Night."[114] Hundreds of years later, London's "Night Czar" was appointed in 2016 to help protect smaller nocturnal venues, particularly those catering to sexual and other minorities.[115]

In this book I explore the tensions between the fears that create a collective wariness at night and the pleasures of an equality that many can indulge—often against other "officials of the night"—only at night. The interests of some in retaining social hierarchies that are legally governable by day but more easily flattened at night (absent intensified nocturnal strategies) suggest that our attention to these temporal cycles may provide insight into what supplements we should append to our understanding of sociolegal phenomena. We can also gain access to those inequalities that are exacerbated by darkness and night, for example, the modes of security that allow some to sleep well because others are prevented from doing the same, and the nocturnal strategies used to struggle for power.

METAPHOR AND MATTER

What does it mean to write about night when thinking about the law? As well as a daily terrestrial phenomenon, night is complexly metaphorical and idiomatic across many cultures, reflecting various "nightly practices."[116] Although administrative rules, such as those for aviation or driving, technically define night's beginning and its end, for most other endeavors night is understood in a practical and variable manner.[117] Often, it is night's effects—such as darkness and quiet, the closing of financial and judicial offices, somnolence and sleep, the start of the graveyard shift or the end of the workday, the affect of fear and the expectation of caution, the desires for love or sex—that give night its sensibility, even in courts of law. While night is a culturally defined period of time, it is also deployed to signify the clarity of distinction ("like night and day," lacking daylight between this and that), the lack of or singularity of encounter ("like ships in the night," "one-night stand"), the inaccessible ("night of oblivion," "left in the dark," the Dark Ages), death (that "good night"), the sketchy ("fly by night"), and other idiomatic meanings. Legal metaphor, enchanted by the Enlightenment, stresses light, clarity, and visibility, but it sometimes extols its reason through tensions that emphasize darkness and finality (e.g., the permanence and indubitability of "black letter" laws or the value of leaving a matter "in the constitutional shade").[118]

In this book I treat night as a real, terrestrial time when the sun is below the horizon, as well as a trope. We know that not all nights are dark, that not all shadows hide their lurking occupants, that not all reason is illuminated, that not all sleep occurs after the sun goes down, and that dawn and dusk complicate the binary of night and day. Nonetheless, common associations of night with darkness and danger, obscurity and incapacity, sleep or fatigue, can be mobilized without undue justification to excuse inattention, to explain actions based in fear or doubt, and to distinguish self-defense from murder. At the same time, as I have argued, darkness can be cultivated as a kind of freedom and pleasure in itself and a source for community that law would otherwise protect; here, it may escape the edict of the law or promote new associations of law and life, what we commonly call *legality*. We sing of dancing in the dark; we dim the lights to improve the mood and enliven social gatherings. Some assemble ritually in the dark nights before solstice or Easter sunrise ("faith sees best in the dark," wrote Søren Kierkegaard) or retreat into darkness to meditate.[119] Some freedom at night is only won by hiding from legal authority. How should we account for this variability in social practice and meaning when accounting for night as metaphor?

The French *noir* can be translated as "dark" or "black," and this entanglement of meanings—separated and compartmentalized in English yet equally attributable to night—perhaps explains the attention paid by French philosophers to subtle distinctions otherwise obscured by Enlightenment ideals. François Laruelle writes, "Black is without opposite. . . . Black is anterior to the absence of light . . . [it] is the Radical of color, what never was a color nor the attribute of a color, the emotion seizing man when affected by a color."[120] Dark can be made light, but black resists such efforts. Black absorbs light, radiating none, making it unlike other colors. For Nicola Masciandaro, who ponders Laruelle's "Radical," black is omnipresent and impenetrable, "the vision of something whose presence is nothing other than the form of its own non-visibility."[121] Like the black letter of law, this black stands beyond reproach. Unilluminated, neither is it "sighted, imagined or known."[122] Black retains its secret status, exceeding "the dialectical opposition light defines it by."[123] From this dialectical perspective, black is not the same as darkness, which may be an evanescent property of night, but black is always anterior to shadow. "Black is the Void of the colors," writes Alain Badiou, that which we cannot know (such as the nameless, formless god of Genesis, who creates the universe and only then separates the night from the day), or that which we do not know but infer (such as the black hole and dark energy, neither of which can be seen, but both of which can be known).[124] When we name torture centers *black sites*, we play with this secret form where, despite knowing about them (they are not disavowed), we know nothing of them.[125] In this playful sense, as Badiou shows, black spontaneously fissures, revealing not dialectical synthesis but dialectical fecundity where one divides into two. Black is the flag of anarchy with its vision of reconciliation, as well as the barbarity of fascism and nihilism, he observes.[126]

Daylight and vision disperse dark spaces and interrupt some of the dividing power of black. Revealed to scrutiny (perhaps by "sunshine laws"), black sites no longer emanate their secret valence of power. Badiou recalls various games in his youth played strictly in the dark; one rule was "there could be no daytime trace of the dark."[127] Not all traces can or need be erased or made secret to hold their spell. Black's void is productive of power in multiple registers. Maurice Blanchot's concept of the *other night*—not the night of darkness but the black night without stars that we cannot reach but can glimpse in our dreams—expresses his aesthetic inspiration, a lightless source for artistic light.[128] Emmanuel Lévinas contrasts this with the long tradition of critical philosophy's homage to the sun: "Art is light. Light from on high in Heidegger, making the world, founding place. In Blanchot it is a black light, a night coming from below—a light that undoes the world; leading it back to its origin, to the over and over again, the murmur, ceaseless lapping of waves, a 'deep past, never long enough ago.' The poetic quest for the unreal is the quest for the deepest recess of that real."[129] In a parallel manner, the legal theorist Niklas Luhmann argues that law's opacity vis-à-vis other systems of meaning—its closed character and impenetrability—is paradoxically what makes it "open" to other social systems. As identity *and* difference—an "operatively closed communicative system"—law orients communication toward itself (its formalism and rulemaking) and external meanings (its value for other systems) simultaneously, speaking effectively from its blackness.[130] Black's fecundity, identified by these philosophers, reveals the potential to think

seeing challenging. One task of this book signaled by my metaphor is to attend to what it means to know both facts and norms at night, to plot a nocturnal jurisprudence. Night disturbs surveillance, changes access to legal institutions and policing, and yet does not attenuate law. How we know or imagine law at night is also related to its ontology. For Michael Serres, night secures our realities, even where we must find other ways to know them. "Darkness does not betray, nor does shadow: in them a thing remains a thing, veiled or not, visible or not, always accessible through touch. Fog betrays, completely fills the environment with potential things. Whether they are objects or vapours—we cannot tell. Night unsettles phenomenology, mist disturbs ontology. Shadow reinforces the distinction between being and appearance, mist blurs it. Thing or veil, being or nonbeing, that is the question."[139] Pursuing law at night by reading its shadows, I suggest, deepens our senses of law's power while refiguring its ontology to account for its concealment.

I search for law's power in the chapters that follow in three major ways. The first is an exploration of law's contribution and response to nocturnal subjectivity. Night, I suggest, leads us to rethink what it means to be a legal subject endowed with rights and entitled to "access" the law. In chapter 1 I consider the sleeper—whom we all become for hours per day—whose unconscious life lacks the agential qualities of reason and responsibility that law demands. Sleep is not only a biological impediment to the rationality presumed by the legal person. It also interrupts the vigilance that the law presumes, punctuating our ability to actively grasp (and remain grasped by) the law. The ancient legal principle of equity, *Vigilantibus non dormientibus jura subveniunt* (Laws aid the vigilant, not the sleepy), uses the exception of sleep to metaphorically tie vigilance to a notion of diligent (legally ordered) timeliness: one caught "sleeping on one's rights" forfeits the entitlement to litigate them.[140] For law to take greater account of sleep requires a means for thinking its social basis: our dependency on and duties to others that guarantee sufficient security for sleep. Sleep takes us, I argue, to a more collective, more expansive idea of legal subjectivity, and because some sleep poorly so others may sleep more securely, the politics of sleep also reveals new ideas of justice commensurate with this new legal subject.

Nocturnal struggles for power raise a second alteration to our understanding of legality's contingent relationship with other social dynamics. Robert Cover has argued that law's relationship to violence is modulated by an assemblage of deed, role, and word.[141] Legal violence destroys the shared moral world, he argues, and the feelings of revulsion caused by doing violent deeds are attenuated by this assemblage: the division of roles permits judges to act conscientiously, solely with words, and apparently with clean hands as jailers and executioners do the violence that they authorize, assured that they act as cogs and not as morally culpable agents. Night upsets this *dispositif.* Darkness inhibits some aspects of representation; words may pierce the night, but signs of order are less tangible or rendered invisible. In this obscurity, roles may diverge from the text of law: police may more easily become the authors of law, and vigilantes may assume their own enforcement roles. The night, therefore, exposes us to the ways that law operates without the full force of its compensatory schemes of representation. Night is often when violence becomes more pronounced, but it is also where other means can be deployed to take account of what happens in the darkness, means that are reincorporated into schemes of legal order.

These themes are explored in chapter 2, where I present a history of American interracial violence to illustrate the ways that law and vigilantism enable the rights of white individuals to bear arms, while concomitantly disarming Black people. I show how the persistent duty of disarmament, which I identify as one of the main functions and meanings of the militia, has frequently operated at night, when Black men and women have asserted freedom of movement and have thus been identified as dangerous to white interests. The militia is a core republican concern, but I argue that the political philosophy of republicanism, so influential in American institutional development, never had a theory of the night that could account for this nocturnal politics, allowing violence to persist without adequate critique. I link the history of controlling the night to contemporary police and vigilante killings of Black people, which I show have a previously overlooked temporal dimension.

The desire for law and legal order—its mobilization by individuals and by social movements—is also enhanced and modified by the uncertainties and the emergencies of nights, a third direction for inquiry. This condition of emergency is officially declared and enhanced in the case of the curfew, when normal rules permitting movement and sociality are suspended, most often at night. Chapter 3 explores the political function of the curfew. Although curfew has frequently been deployed in colonial efforts at Indigenous pacification, and has been extended to control youth and stabilize urban racial violence, little has been written about how curfew works. Curfew establishes a brief and temporary form of sanctuary, and I argue that this temporality works to augment the power of law through the creation of desire for law's certainty and more predictable forms of violence manifest in the day. I link the premodern curfew to its modern forms in this chapter, seeking to understand what role the night plays in the efficacy and political limits of this emergency technique, and I explore its role in contemporary critical theory and political theology about emergency.

Even without an official designation of curfew, behavioral norms restricting and altering nocturnal movement often diverge from those practiced in daylight. The Enlightenment promised transparency, rationality, and generality, all qualities attributable to law and imagined as disseminating light. The appeal of these values is not necessarily self-evident, especially for those who have historically been disadvantaged by legal norms and by restricted legal subjectivity. Chapter 4 is a study of feminist activism nominally designed to "Take Back the Night." I ask what this politics, oriented against the persistent problem of violence against women, enacts with its nighttime marches. Unlike much other feminist and identity politics generally, nocturnal protests perform an opposition to Enlightenment norms and institutions, as well as representation generally as they target the law's inadequate protection of women from men. Rather than rejecting law, tout court, I argue this activism asserts a new property relationship: a desire to "take back" and possess what has been stolen, metaphorized as the night. I explore what this property in night can mean and what it portends for women's safety. I use this analysis to explore the contemporary value and the limits of feminist theory expounded by Andrea Dworkin, who was an early proponent for Take Back the Night activism. This chapter is a study of one way in which night, opposed to Enlightenment norms, is valuable for political ends.

Although this book tries to "see" night in our legal relations, the common scholarly neglect of night is also associated with a paucity of specific attention to day.[142] The tradition of legal scholarship that attends to metaphorical and analogical reasoning—both indebted to images of light—indirectly gives homage to day. Chapter 5 concludes the book by relating the analogy of night to its rhetorical and ontological status in the law. Using the important work of Derrida, who has written on the significance of the heliotrope, the centralizing image of the sun integral to all metaphorical thinking, I ask what it might require to bring night back into legal thought. This question requires us to attend to the propagation of Enlightenment metaphors that dominate legal reasoning. The deconstruction of the heliotrope makes day explicit while leading to a greater understanding of the significance of law's dark places, permitting us to better account for the violence and freedom of night. Finding night and law's concealment, as Foucault suggests, is the key to locating law's power.

CHAPTER ONE

IS THERE A RIGHT TO SLEEP?

A drunken and drowsy tyrant is soon despised and attacked; not so he who is temperate and wide awake. —**Aristotle**

Even the strongest must sleep at times and, when asleep, loses temporarily his superiority. This fact of approximate equality, more than any other, makes obvious the necessity for a system of mutual forbearance and compromise which is the base of both legal and moral obligation. —**Herbert Lionel Adolphus Hart**

The insecurity of night, which is everyone's daily concern, is nonetheless made into an uneven sociological terrain. While some live in gated communities with private police enforcing quiet and ensuring empty streets at night, others occupy (usually urban and non-white) neighborhoods strewn with violence, the police perceived as agents of a hostile state. In these areas, "violence is used to punish wrongdoers, to take over new territories, and to intimidate enemies," and as a consequence "adults and children alike live in a perpetual state of aggression, insecurity, and fear," a Hobbesian existence amplified after dark.[1] The perception of household safety has been shown to be strongly associated with quality of sleep, physical health, and educational success, negatively affecting many within poorer, non-white neighborhoods.[2] There, sleep is secured through the moral economy of violence, which is made easier for some by shelter (though not women denied sleep by their abusers) and more difficult for those forced to "sleep rough" in the face of violence from gangs as well as state authorities who deny sleep as a means of social control.[3] Immigrant children held at the

United States' southern border by authorities can be denied soap, blankets, and adequate sleep.[4] There is, seemingly, no right to sleep.

Is a right to sleep inconceivable? Precolonial Hawaiian legal norms did express the right to sleep as a central concept cohering sovereign responsibility and power. The Hawaiian historian Samuel Kamakau, writing in the mid-nineteenth century, maintained that Kamehameha I (1736–1819), who forcefully unified the archipelago in 1810, had a *kumukānāwai*, or constitution, which was the *Kānāwai Māmalahoa*, or the Law of the Splintered Paddle.[5] Kamakau wrote that the young Kamehameha's encounter with several fishermen who had severely beaten him with a paddle led him to proclaim the law several years later when his tormentors were brought before him for punishment: "Let the old men, the old women and the children sleep [in safety] on the highway."[6] With these words Kamehameha declined to put his attackers to death. For Kamakau, this constitution was a law "promising life."[7] For contemporary legal and political scholars, it can be generalized as a legal norm "protecting even the most defenseless from oppression by those with more power and authority," while being performative of the sovereign's mana and authority.[8]

This idea of authority emergent from and named for the experience of physical vulnerability suggests—and I can only speculate here, as much more work needs to be done—that Kamehameha's authority was more than the sovereign power of decision to take life or let live.[9] The image of the sleeping body in the *Kānāwai Māmalahoa*—understood through the story of the attacking fishermen to simultaneously refer to the *Mōʻī*'s (king's) sacred body—meant that legitimate power was complexly intertwined with the rights to sanctuary while traveling and exposed, including the rights to take refuge and receive absolution from legal punishment in or beside the designated sanctuaries and persons called *puʻuhonua* that continued in Kamehameha's reign.[10] The recitation of vulnerable people sleeping in open sanctuary in the crystalline kernel of the law expressed the kingdom's affirmative power to "make live," a power shared with and ensured by the *aliʻi* (nobles) and *kāhuna* (professional experts with related religious duties) responsible for/as the *puʻuhonua*.[11]

Although I draw ideas of authority from the confluence of sleep and sovereignty in this chapter, I very cautiously allude in the text and notes above to the political dynamics of authority under Kamehameha in concepts belonging to a critical European-focused political theory. In doing so, my goal is limited to showing some overlap between aspects of European and Hawaiian *dispositifs* of authority, particularly the reciprocal binding of the weakest and most vulnerable to the powerful. Yet, while the analogous European ties were often predicated on the extralegal granting of mercy that redounded to sovereign and ruling-class interests—a European governing process imputed to Hawai'i by Sally Merry—it is significant, I believe, that law and sanctuary were explicitly understood by Kamakau and others to uphold life, a general and decidedly biopolitical principle of *ali'i* governance made concrete by the concerns over the ravages of Western disease.[12]

This political concern for life is emphatically less prominent in the ongoing colonial context in Hawai'i. The lack of conceptual continuity today is signaled by the legal reception of the persisting—or at least reinvented—*Kānāwai Māmalahoa.* The Hawai'i state constitution (ca. 1959) includes the Law of the Splintered Paddle,[13] translating the Hawaiian word *moe* as "lie" rather than "sleep" (both meanings are commonly found in the original Hawaiian).[14] This contemporary refusal and suppression of protected sleep as a central norm is evident in Hawai'i's jurisprudence. Despite the echo of the old language and efforts to seek sanctuary in its name, courts in Hawai'i have discarded its older meanings and joined courts elsewhere in rejecting any right to sleep or protest at night, especially in public places, while the Honolulu City Council—with impunity—has recently enacted "sit-lie bans" against homeless people sleeping by the side of the city streets.[15]

It is interesting to speculate what law might look like were rights to and care for sleep constitutive of or at least more prominent among legal norms today. These norms persist within some colonially subordinated contemporary societies, such as the Walpiri of northern Australia, who arrange sleep communally through arrangements (often outdoors) that spatially position some to assume the duties of care for the others, who are then able to sleep more soundly despite the collective vulnerability to wild animals and human threats.[16] This has at least a literal resonance with Michel Foucault's conception of pastoral power in which the devoted leader, as shepherd, protects their flock. "Everything the shepherd does is geared to the good of his flock. That's his constant concern. When they sleep, he keeps watch."[17]

In Euro-American history, nocturnal pastoral power may have played a role in the development of legal authority. The night watch, sometimes "less ... a police force than ... a collection of local keepers of the peace," roamed the cities of medieval Europe and colonial America, sometimes enforcing curfews but always offering visual and aural assurances of urban peace to those lucky to be indoors.[18] Watchmen "were the eyes of the sleeping public," offering a paradoxical vigilance: they were imaginary surrogate eyes but were effective against real nocturnal dangers only when silent and dressed down in common clothes, harder for ne'er-do-wells to avoid.[19] This paradox perhaps expresses a conundrum or contradiction of nocturnal vigilance: an impossible effort to see in the dark and be seen seeing. With street lighting lessening this paradox, the night watch frequently developed into an armed police force with interests extending beyond sleep and security.[20]

In the United States, policing was also spurred by the need to control and hunt enslaved people—a "cynegetic" form of power that Grégoire Chamayou has argued to be antithetical to pastoral governance, which often expressed itself at night.[21] Surveillance of Black people—by both officials and vigilantes—has continued long after the migration of freed persons to northern cities within their racially segregated neighborhoods.[22] Might a return to a more pastoral concern for sleep orient us toward a law more attentive to individual and social—including racialized—precarity as well as offer a democratic avenue for resistance?

This chapter addresses several issues related to this speculative search. As the introduction has argued, night was once more prominently a concern for Western law. What vestiges of this history remain unseen in the shadows of modern law? What are the expectations for the rational legal subject challenged by the biological imperative to sleep and by the security and darkness that sleep requires? If we conceive of rights at night, what kinds of radical equality does the sleeping subject express or demand? If night is not a time of pure lawlessness, nor simply under the control of daytime forces (a recovery from the day, a period of reproduction following a day of production), what kinds of justice can still be called on in the night, and who is awake to listen?[23]

SLEEP AND THE LEGAL SUBJECT

Modern legal theory often begins with some notion of the responsible subject, vigilant for its rights, culpable for intentional violations of the rights of others, endowed with responsibility and memory, hence "the right to make promises" in Friedrich Nietzsche's conception.[24] It comes as no surprise, then, to find acceptable criminal defenses for the violent, reckless, or drugged sleepwalker, or the "sexsomniac."[25] Where enslaved people had criminal subjectivity without legal personhood, the legal person today has no or limited criminal subjectivity while asleep.[26] In some critical occupations, such as airline pilot or train engineer, one has a duty to sleep, or at least a duty to remain off-duty so that sleep may come; yet this is not a right *to* sleep as much as it is a right for others to avoid the potential dangers of the sleepy.[27] This protective veil is consonant with attempts to develop and enforce laws against sleepy driving.[28] In all these examples, sleep is a problem to be managed, if not by criminal sanction or industrial regulation, then by medicine. That we *do* sleep suggests that our ideas of the legal person are already erasures of our unconsciousness.

If a right to sleep is to be meaningful, it will be necessary to critically reevaluate the legal image of the responsible subject in an effort to recover the erasure of sleep. It will also be necessary to expand the potential of rights to move beyond the liberal Lockean constraint of the rational subject and its protective shell of privacy that fails to empower those burdened by nocturnal social and political orders. In his influential *Essay Concerning Human Understanding* (1690), John Locke used the concept of the legal person to comprehend the bearer of rights and duties, rather than the body or the soul. The person was a purely "forensic term appropriating actions and their merit," belonging "only to intelligent agents capable of a law, and happiness and misery. This personality extends itself beyond present existence to what is past, only by consciousness, whereby it becomes concerned and accountable, owns and imputes to itself past actions."[29] Locke hoped for a "great day" in which "no one shall be made to [legally] answer for what he knows nothing of."[30]

My rejoinder to Locke's enduring influence rests on an accounting of the collective nature of sleep, a kind of "flesh" to which we have little conscious access but which, I argue, can reorient us to an expansive reimagination of the legal subject more attentive to the social precarities of those denied security for sleep and the freedom to move at night.[31] Two political and philosophical discourses can give some insight into the possibilities for a right to sleep. The first is phenomenology, which challenges the binary coding rationality/irrationality within law, repositioning the sleeper as a subject. Although Jean-Luc Nancy may be correct that "the sleeping *self* does not appear: it is not phenomenalized . . . sleep does not authorize the analysis of any form of appearance whatsoever," nonetheless phenomenology provides insight into the paradoxes of rationality and the importance of—perhaps, priority of—sleep for thinking the subject.[32] A second discourse that I rely on here is political theology that explores the legal valence of sleep, particularly the monarchical inheritance of the body in democratic society and the ambivalent biopolitics that results. I use this literature to speculate about the ways rights and law—parallel with Kamehameha's *Kānāwai Māmalahoa*—can embrace a richer vision of life, what I call with others an affirmative biopolitics. I link these two discourses by studying their confluence in our relatively unexplored ideas of legal vigilance, which have been genealogically connected to the ideas of timeliness and watchfulness that sleep and night both interrupt and make possible.

OF SOMNOLENCE AND EUROPEAN KINGS

The sleeping king, who demonstrated the impossibility of a continuously vigilant sovereign, was once a historical condensation point for concerns of Western political and legal theory, particularly the temporal continuity of power and authority. Ernst Kantorowicz, in his masterful study of the political theology of European medieval kings' dual bodies—one mortal and replaceable, the other enduring through its symbolic permanence—emphasizes the ritualized problems of royal succession. Illustrative of this problem is the use of an effigy at royal funerals, beginning in England in 1327 and France in 1422, representing the imperishable symbolic political investments over and against a body that would, predictably, expire. Kantorowicz writes, "The importance of the king's effigy in the funerary rites of the sixteenth century soon matched or even eclipsed that of the dead body itself. Noticeable as early as 1498, at the funeral of Charles VIII, and fully developed in 1547, at the rites held for Francis I, the display of the effigy was connected successively with the new political ideas of that age, indicating, for example, that the royal Dignity never died and that in the image the dead king's jurisdiction continued until the day he was buried."[33] While death posed one of the major issues for the symbolic continuity of state authority, as the effigy signified, Kantorowicz footnotes concern for the endurance of law when the king's parallel bodies collapsed in sleep: "Albertus Magnus [a twelfth-century German philosopher] demanded that the king be neither torpid nor sleepy, but be the 'living and vigilant Justice,' adding that the king was above the law because he was the 'living form of the Law.'"[34] This idea of *lex animata*—that the omnipresent king embodies the law—and the ideal of continuous vigilance that Eric Santner has recently called *rex exsomnis* had a long tradition.[35] Kantorowicz quotes one

Renaissance philosopher who expressed the vitality of this idea: "'I sleep and my heart, that is, my king watches.'" Kantorowicz adds, "The image was not uncommon."[36] Nor was it confined to European courts, as other scholars have observed.[37]

Kantorowicz and others have noted in work specifically concerned with royal sleep the symbolic significance of the French morning and coronation rituals of *Lever du roi*, in which one body of the king was acknowledged to sleep while the other remained ever vigilant.[38] The historian Richard Jackson sums up the French coronation ritual of 1610, which expressed this duality:

> Twice, the Bishop of Laon knocked on the door of the king's chamber and asked for "*Louys XIII. fils de* [son of] *Henry le Grand.*" Both times he was told, "*Il dort.*" [He sleeps.] The third time, the bishop asked for "*Louys XIII. que Dieu nous a donné pour Roy* [that God has given us as King]." Only then was the door opened to reveal the young monarch ready to be led to his coronation. In other words, the young Louis, the descendant of Henry IV as a man, was sleeping. The King, however, was not sleeping, and he was represented as ready for his coronation the moment he was called. The dialogue made a distinction between the corporeal king (Louis XIII) and the abstract kingship, which Louis embodied. . . . The door was opened to show that the King never sleeps, the King never dies.[39]

In addition to these rituals, there was a nightly concern to make the king's sleep legible for power. Jacques Derrida writes in regard to Louis XIV:

> The king's doctors looked after the king's body as two bodies at once. They were looking after the king's body both as the body of a respected, admired, venerated, feared, all-powerful, and omniscient God, and as the objective, objectified, coldly regarded and inspected body of an animal with irresponsible reactions (one cannot help but think of the role and discourse and sometimes the publications of such doctors at or after the death of our presidents of the Republic, Pompidou and Mitterrand). When I say that they were looking after and over the body of the king, I mean it literally since they kept vigil even over his sleep, when the king, supposed to see and know everything, to have all power and have everything, could no longer see them, his own doctors, seeing him.[40]

Derrida's recognition of the paradox of sleep—that the sovereign sleeper cannot maintain a vigil over themself—also realizes a supplement essential to the idea of legal power: here, the medical doctors and their practice of medicine.[41] Because even the sovereign self cannot act as agent in sleep, auxiliary sources of authority must step into the breach.

The premise of political theology—that "complex symbolic structures and dynamics of sovereignty . . . do not simply disappear from the space of politics once the body of the king is no longer available"—begs us ask how well this genealogical concern about a paradoxically vigilant sovereign travels to our day.[42] One of the earliest meanings of *vigil* was the ritualized observance of the evenings prior to church holidays, a time of watching and expectation.[43] The term *vigilante*, sharing the same etymological root, absorbed this nocturnal character. Vigilantism originally expressed the popular and democratic concern for doing justice. Only after a contest with the state for exclusive control of judicial violence did vigilantism furtively move to the night, where it could advance biopolitical projects maintaining racial and other hierarchies that the state preferred to obscure, many of which intentionally threaten the sleep of others.[44] (See figure 1.1 for a contemporary example.) The political vigil seems, in some manner, opposed to vigilantism as much as to the excesses of legal vigilance such as police killings, and these forms of protest are almost universally nocturnal (as the vigil over the king's sleep originally was).

Vigilance shares with surveillance an optic metaphor (e.g., keeping a lookout), but I suggest that the two ideas are only tangentially related. Building on Foucault's arguments about the asymmetries of panoptic power, surveillance has been shown by some scholars to be an assemblage of gazing powers in which the body is "broken down by being abstracted from its territorial setting and then reassembled elsewhere (a credit reporting database, for example) to then serve as virtual 'data doubles,' and also as sites of comparison."[45] These sites of comparison and the normative forms of knowledge produced by surveillance may be prompted by and advance racial and other biopolitical projects as well as being sites of struggle; although surveillance usually serves the power of the state, "sousveillance" that returns the gaze of authorities (such as bystander videos of police watching protesting crowds) may oppose these projects.

Surveillance may have been a modern technical response to the demands for sovereign vigilance—a temporally seamless expression of centralized power—but vigilance persists in the unique forms of knowledge that its own temporality requires. Vigilance is less a technological strategy

FIGURE 1.1 "You can sleep tonight knowing the Klan is awake!" 2014. *Source:* Slabaugh, "Klan Leaflets." Thanks to Jeannine Bell for sharing this image. The original Ku Klax Klan also played to the vulnerability of night. Consider this notice to an Arkansas sheriff in 1868: "We have come! We are Here! Beware! Take heed! When the black cat is gliding under the shadows of darkness, and the death watch ticks at the lone hour of night, then we, the pale riders, are abroad. Speak in whispers and we hear you. Dream as you sleep in the inmost recesses of your house, and, hovering over your beds, we gather your sleeping thoughts, while our daggers are at your throat." Trelease, *White Terror,* 55.

than a tactic, which Michel de Certeau understands to "vigilantly make use of the cracks that particular conjunctions open in the surveillance of contemporary powers. . . . When one examines this fleeting and permanent reality carefully, one has the impression of exploring the night-side of societies, a night longer than their day, a dark sea from which successive institutions emerge."[46] It is worth noting here the explicit and nearly paradoxical juxtaposition of vigilance and night that Certeau makes. Vigilance, as tactic, operates less with visibility and more as an intensive excitement of legal and other opportunities, and an urge to bring them close in the dark.

Tactics demand constant interpretation, and they are not just retained as weapons for the weak, as Certeau suggests, but also are an integral part of state and legal power. The demand for watchfulness, responsiveness, and promptness—the requirement that one not sleep on one's rights—makes the tactical use of the law and a willingness to see events through a temporally bounded legal screen a dutiful aspect of legal subjectivity. The state is also required to be watchful against enemies and other contingencies—to control "the night-side of societies" in Certeau's words—as was the king. We can see monarchical vigilance clearly echoed in the American concern for the automatic, nonelectoral mechanics of presidential succession, as well as in the demand for an executive's immediate availability for a reasoned response to nocturnal threats to national security, a theme once prominently featured in a 2008 campaign ad for Hillary Clinton suggesting it was she who could best protect sleeping children at 3 a.m.[47]

While perhaps necessary, the executive's ever-present red telephone and launch codes, as well as policies encouraging sleep deprivation of political detainees threatening state security, are insufficient guarantees for a good sleep.[48] For this reason, many of us still practice a medieval form of "shutting in" at night, acknowledging the limit to state capacity that the king's symbolic sleeplessness could not adequately hide (and that subversively rehearsed a discourse of equality against feudal and monarchical hierarchy). Yet Lisa Guenther has shown that solitary confinement—the ultimate shutting in, where there is almost no sociality—far from guaranteeing sleep, makes sleep horrifyingly difficult, revealing that sleep always has a degree of relationality and dependence.[49] Sleep is necessarily communal since the sleeper, royal or otherwise, cannot watch themself sleep, nor can sleep pleasantly come without some sense of being watched over (if only to secure the gates that shut others out). The duty to maintain vigilance, and the desire to sleep securely, suggests that sleep may be "naturalized" but is always a matter for collective governance.[50]

A VIGILANT SLEEP

Sleep is simultaneously a matter for the governance of the self. Maurice Blanchot adds that our consciousness of sleep is always already commanded; sleep politically conforms to the demands of the day: "There is between sleep and us something like a pact, a treaty with no secret clauses and according to this convention it is agreed that, far from being a dangerous, bewitching force, sleep will become domesticated and serve as the instrument of our power to act. We surrender to sleep, but in the way that the master entrusts himself to the slave who serves him. Sleeping is the clear action which promises us to the day. To sleep: admire this remarkable act of vigilance."[51] Blanchot's Hegelian imagery of the vigilant slave of sleep is ripe for dialectical reversal, something that Emmanuel Lévinas in his early work makes clear. For Lévinas, the pure facticity of being (the *il y a*, or "there is") is oppressive, which we sense most when we—like King Macbeth, who famously murders sleep—cannot sleep, lying exposed in the night.[52] "Submerged . . . , invaded, depersonalized, stifled. . . . The disappearance of all things and of the I leaves what cannot disappear, the sheer fact of being in which one participates, whether one wants to or not."[53] Insomnia is a vigilance, but it is devoid of objects or rhythm, lacking both a king who could symbolically watch our somnolent space and Sigmund Freud's oneiric guardian.[54] Trapped alone in our insomnia, we are revealed to a nocturnal eye. "In insomnia, it is the night itself that watches. It watches. In this anonymous nightwatch where I am completely exposed to being, all the thoughts which occupy my insomnia are suspended on *nothing*. . . . I am, one might say, the object rather than the subject of an anonymous vigilance."[55] In its anonymity, insomnia is a vigilance promising—or, perhaps, threatening—an escape from that daytime subjectivity experienced within our political and legal lives. If law demands a vigilance, insomnia is a vigilante, a greater vigilance with the potential for justice were we to heed its potential, as Lévinas argues in later work. And yet insomnia is painful, a condition from which we pray to be relieved.

To stop insomnia, Lévinas writes as if to emphasize our desire for deliverance, "a subject would have to be posited."[56] We do this by seizing a position in space and time (we make an "instant"), which then comes to constitute us: "The summoning of sleep occurs in the act of lying down. To lie down is precisely to limit existence to a place. . . . [S]leep is like entering into contact with the protective forces of a place. . . . *Consciousness comes out of rest, out of a position, out of this unique relationship with a place.*

Position is not added to consciousness like an act that it decides on; it is out of position, out of an immobility, that consciousness comes to itself."[57] This "nocturnal ontology" upends the legal notion that the awake, rational, self-vigilant being could ever comprise the totality of subjectivity; as Simon Wortham frames Lévinas's remarkable claim, "Sleep is the constitutive force or enabling limit found at the very origin of consciousness."[58] Might this originary subjection—prior even to the sovereign created by a ritualized sleep—be useful to rethink the legal subject?

If our own consciousness is in some fundamental manner constituted by sleep, we must acknowledge the paradoxes of intentionality and sovereignty posed for legal subjectivity when we must consciously will our own unconsciousness. Wortham writes, "Sleep is not taken by surprise (unlike that which causes us to faint), but instead prepares for itself, for its own coming, before itself and by itself. However, in this very same movement, sleep is tasked with outmaneuvering and overcoming the conscious 'me' who nevertheless courts it through controlled and sometimes elaborate gestures of invitation and submission."[59] How do we understand this notion of submission? To what are we submitting, and how might this differ from our submission to the law?

A LIVING SLEEP

The paradoxical idea of sleep as a willing of the lack of will is expressed in the general problematic of the legal person—a medieval atavism—that disturbs the idea of a simple legal subject. More than a Lockean forensics, Roberto Esposito rightly calls the legal person a *dispositif* owing to its always divided and assembled character.[60] Indeed, the *person*, Peter Goodrich reminds us, etymologically derives from *parson* and from the king, who is "parsonified."[61] Much like the dual living and symbolic bodies of the king and their divergent temporalities, the person is a theological, theatrical, and juridical effort to distinguish and separate rights from a broader conception of life.[62] The lack of a right to sleep seems an apt expression of this division: the legal person as the rational kernel is distinguished and separated from the sleeper, whose critical supplement to rationality is bound within another extralegal dimension, such as medicine, public health discourse, or policy.

If we consider the legal person as the full subject of rights, we may see that the subject, itself, is irreducibly doubled, as Étienne Balibar has shown.[63] Not simply the vessel for rights and duties, the subject is always, at the same time, "an individual or a person submitted to the exercise of a power, whose model is, first of all, political, and whose concept is juridical."[64] Balibar is less convinced that the modern citizen is a subject equivalent to the absolutist subject; in part, since the citizen is empowered to make law, modern subjects will their own obedience, but they no longer must respond to hierarchy. "Because of the dissymmetry that is introduced into the idea of sovereignty from the moment that it has devolved to the 'citizens': until then the idea of sovereignty had always been inseparable from a hierarchy, from an eminence; from this point forward the paradox of a *sovereign equality*, something radically new, must be thought."[65]

Can this egalitarianism of which Balibar writes, or lack of hierarchy, extend meaningfully to a sleeping subject? To the extent that we remain enslaved to sleep, our conscious will embedded as a homunculus in our unconscious rest, perhaps it is impossible to fully will our own obedience, or, at any rate, to do so in a manner that is any different than it was in hierarchical European societies. This is more than a simple matter of willful legislation, besides. Sleep is willed in its paradoxical manner, but it is also dependent on community to vigilantly provide or supplement the security of body and, in light of Lévinas, of place: conditions and contexts we cannot will. If we search for an analogy for the sleeping subject, perhaps we need to adhere to Esposito's argument that sovereignty is *not* and should not be at the center of our concerns. More overriding, in his mind, are the forms in which life is protected, forms that run through absolutist sovereignty as much as modernity. Glimpsed in the king's two bodies, where biology (the living body) overlaps with the juridical (the symbolic body signaling continuity), this is an *immunitary dispositif* where death unnervingly serves life: "A relationship of mutual functionality is established between the two bodies of the king: the individual body gives his mystical body its fleshy consistency, while the mystical body ensures stability and durability to the individual body. It makes his mortality immortal through a hereditary chain that plays the same role as the resurrection: it immunizes him through a separation from himself that makes his natural death the vehicle for his institutional survival."[66] Esposito makes worrisomely clear in his work that immunity that holds the reciprocal sovereign concerns for both life *and* death, and that extends through "chains of doubling" into the legal concept of persons protected from the demands of community, has the capacity for broader lethality within a postmonarchical "body politic."[67]

Although immunity is necessary to the preservation of our life, when driven beyond a certain threshold it forces life into a sort of cage where not only our freedom gets lost but also the very meaning of our existence—that opening of existence outside itself that takes the name of communitas. . . . [T]hat which protects the body (the individual body, the social body, and the body politic) is at the same time that which impedes its development. It is also that which, beyond a certain threshold, is likely to destroy it. To use the words of Walter Benjamin, one could say that immunization at high doses is the sacrifice of the living—of every qualified life, that is—for the sake of mere survival.[68]

This sacrifice is not limited to bodies politic thought at the level of abstraction of the nation-state but also extends globally today, often through the mechanisms of the corporation as a legal person.[69]

Sleep has compelling parallels to the immunity relationship, involving an intricate political dance of life and death. The ritualization of kingly sleep promised the continuity of authority and symbolically rehearsed the vigilance associated with law. This acknowledgment of the "daily resurrection from the little death of sleep" is still our almost religious commerce for the sake of consciousness as well as our renewed debt to community that provides sufficient security for sleep.[70] That this is an immunitary relationship is perhaps nowhere more palpable than in neoliberalism where responsibility for sustaining life is devolved as much as possible onto the individual. As Jonathan Crary and others have noted, this 24/7 neoliberal responsibility, bolstered by what Alan Derickson has noted to be the anti-sleep masculinist norms of work, has caused us to increasingly forsake the value and practice of sleep, making ourselves—and others—ill.[71] This personal willingness to forgo sleep, made necessary because there is no right to sleep, has dangerous social consequences, and it is monitored by a vast array of indicators quantitatively surveilling the nation's rates of sleep as well as its impact on student performance and critical enterprises. Yet state policy is also attentive to sleep as a field of pain and death. The prevention of sleep or its excess, whether through torture or psychological impediment, or via policies that deny sleep to the homeless and the refugee child and that ignore the security needs of the poor and Black people in the inner city, is a sacrifice of the living for some expectation of national health and strength.

How can law today, challenged by the sleepless neoliberal subject and by the immunitary responses targeting sleep for some, play a life-affirming role? How can there be a worthwhile right to sleep today as there seemed to be in Kamehameha's Hawai'i? Esposito has noted that rights are an increasingly superseded form of the immunitary *dispositif*. As Esposito argues, "It is clear that today we are no longer inside the immunitary semantics of the classic modern [Hobbesian] period. . . . The immunitary relationship between politics and the preservation of life was still mediated or filtered by a paradigm of order that was articulated in the concepts of sovereignty, representation, and individual rights. [Today,] however, that mediation diminishes in favor of a more immediate superimposition between politics and life."[72] Certainly, rights persist, but they attach not to lives and bodies as much as persons, and this *dispositif*, which reaches back to a Christian pluralization of the divine, parallels the immunitary tensions between community and individual. The person produces order by drawing conflict within, creating a hierarchy of parts akin to the Christian relationship between father and son, and in this tension helps constitute political subjectivity, "penetrating into the very consciousness of the individual."[73] As we have seen in the numerous immunities granted the sleeping miscreant, the legal person is defined as divided, and unity requires submission of one part to another, especially that which "risks evading their control or even being forgotten."[74]

THE *HATTON* CASE

One British effort to declare a right to sleep can help us think about the neoliberal limits to rearticulating the *dispositif* of the person, particularly the tactics of embedding this right in the legal concept of privacy and the deployment of the discourse of health as an affirmative biopolitics.

In the early 1990s, Ruth Hatton and several neighbors who lived near Heathrow Airport sued for relief from the noise and rumbling of night flights that were keeping them from falling and staying asleep. They took aim at a 1993 British government regulatory scheme that, in the name of environmental protection, had increased the number of early morning flights from the airport. The plaintiffs sued the government in the UK courts, and in 1994 the High Court declared the scheme in violation of the Civil Aviation Act. Several years later, the Court of Appeal reversed this decision, arguing that the government's economic interests outbalanced whatever rights that the complainants held, and the House of Lords dismissed a petition for further appeal. In 1997 Hatton's still sleep-deprived complainants took the case to the European Court of Human Rights. The central support for their legal claim was Article 8 of the Convention for the Protection of Human Rights and Fundamental Freedoms, which promises to "everyone . . . the right to respect for his private and family life, his home and his correspondence." Under that clause the applicants claimed that the ability to sleep is an intimate right.[75]

The United Kingdom, responding to the suit, argued that the case involved general matters of policy and that while sleep was important, the collective and individual interest in sleep must be weighed against economic interests. These concerns included the value of maintaining Heathrow as the busiest airport in the world, as well as the dependence of passenger comfort on continued nocturnal operations. Besides, they claimed, the government had already made significant efforts to mitigate the nocturnal nuisance via environmental regulation in accordance with a sleep study that was done in 1992.

The chamber judgment, rendered in 2001, ruled five to two that there had been a violation of Article 8. Although the chamber accepted the United Kingdom's argument that a balance needed to be struck between community concerns and individual rights (or, in Esposito's language, immunities), the judges also argued that the economic impact had not been quantified, nor the deficiencies in the 1992 sleep study rectified. "In the particularly sensitive field of environmental protection, mere reference to the economic well-being of the country is not sufficient to outweigh the rights of others."[76] In a separate opinion, one of the judges added that these rights were public health concerns: "Anyone who has suffered for a long period from noise disturbance such as to disrupt their sleep (or prevent them from getting back to sleep once awake) is well aware that the effects of this on the nerves and on one's physical and mental well-being are extremely unpleasant and even harmful."[77]

This decision came close to guaranteeing a right to sleep under the umbrella of a right to privacy. In 2003, however, on appeal by the United Kingdom to the Grand Chamber, which consisted of seventeen judges, including the officers of the court, this right was finally rejected. All but five dissenting judges found that the balance the United Kingdom sought was appropriate. Only where there is a direct and serious impact on individuals might an Article 8 privacy issue arise, they argued. In this case, the Grand Chamber found, sleep disturbances were not serious, and if some individuals were overly sensitive, "the fact that they can, if they choose, move elsewhere without financial loss [is] significant to the overall reasonableness of the general measure."[78]

The five dissenters were adamant that health is a basic human need that was denied by this decision. Although precedent dealt with interruptions of sexuality as grounds for finding a privacy violation, for the dissenters, "the point is not that the sexual life of the couple whose home reverberates with the noise of aircraft engines may be seriously affected. The thrust of our argument is that 'health as a state of complete physical, mental and social well-being' is, in the specific circumstances of this case, a precondition to any meaningful privacy, intimacy, etc., and cannot be unnaturally separated from it."[79] The essential preconditions of these rights necessitated, they claimed, a different balance of community interest and individual rights because of the "fundamental nature of the right to sleep, which may be outweighed only by the real, pressing (if not urgent) needs of the State."[80]

The failure to secure a right to sleep under norms protecting intimate life is significant in Lévinas's phenomenological ethics. If subjectivity depends on the sleeper securing a place in which to constitutively gather the self, then we become ontologically committed to place, forgetting the lessons of insomnia where we are always hostage to this otherness. Ethically, this impersonal, anonymous otherness turns us to the Other, whose place is uncertain and whose rights to place (as a portal to sleep) would be both an obstacle to hospitality and a violent commitment to borders, property, and even "human" being—to a belonging belying our own debt to otherness.[81]

The problem, of course, as Hawaiian law once recognized, is that the practical need for a secure place to sleep is a guarantee of life to those who have none and who therefore cannot claim a protected intimacy as did Hatton and her neighbors. Lévinas's philosophical denial of a right to place on account of our debts to placeless Others nonetheless reifies property and nation for those who now enjoy both, if only because, as the *Hatton* court recognized, Hatton could exchange her house for a quieter one without invoking any right or claim. Certainly, any right to sleep yoked to the security of place in one's own house would enhance the haves more than the have-nots, while making those without place a community nuisance to be further immunized against. Rights to sleep, imagined within the context of rights to intimate life, may simply augment the problems associated with the biopolitics of immunity where some sleep comfortably by making certain others do not.

BEYOND SLEEP AND LANGUAGE: TO A POLITICS OF THE SLEEPING BODY

What ethical possibilities can we find within the relationship of the sleeper to their conscious self, and how might this orient us to new legal opportunities beyond the biopolitical boundaries of privacy and health? It is not an easy task to find a dialogical relationship between the sleeping and the conscious self, as we know when unsuccessfully beseeching ourselves for sleep. In liberal and neoliberal regimes of governance, it is the rational and self-regulating part of the self that counts more than the spiritual or sleeping components, and that rational side, as we have seen, dominates the idea of the legal person. This emphasis is hard to shake, perhaps because of the ways we are embedded in language while awake, while the unresponsive sleeper is not. Even were the sleeper to coherently speak to their rational self, the problem of language may still impede ethical dialogue. Émile Benveniste's study of the personal pronoun demonstrates this problem. He noted, "It is in and through language that man constitutes himself as a subject, because language alone establishes the concept of 'ego' in reality, in its reality which is that of the being. . . . Consciousness of self is only possible if it is experienced by contrast. *I* use I only when I am speaking to someone who will be a *you* in my address. It is this condition of dialogue that is constitutive of *person*, for it implies that reciprocally *I* becomes *you* in the address of the one who in his turn designates himself as *I*."[82] Esposito notes that this dialectic of I and thou ethically reduces to a first-person perspective, unable to secure an ethical relation. Benveniste's dialectic "reveals the rhetorical character of all philosophies of the second person (from Martin Buber to Vladimir Jankélévitch and beyond), whose logics always remain within the status of the first person, despite their claims of surpassing it. . . . [T]he *you* only takes on meaning from the *I* that interpellates it, whether in the form of a command, an invocation, or a prayer. The 'two' is necessarily inscribed in the logic of the 'one,' just as 'one' always tends to split into 'two' in order to be able to mirror and recognize itself in its human or divine interlocutor."[83]

Ethical theories, such as Lévinas's, that rely on the third person are distinctive from those developed in light of an interlocutor because they escape this reductive problem of recognition and its institutionalized forms of political language. For Esposito, the impersonal third offers the hope of an "affirmative biopolitics," an alternative to the thanatopolitics of a ragingly immunized, hence genocidal twentieth century. This biopolitics is centered somewhere beyond the normative person in this impersonal space, and for Esposito, this is also beyond law. How well can the unconscious sleeper serve to develop such a politics, and must this politics necessarily eschew legal vigilance and rights?

Sleep, which comes to us all, is impersonal and nondialogical, a conundrum even to the internal dialogues that we call on to explain our nightly absences. Thomas Hobbes notes this at the beginning of *Leviathan* when he argues:

> It is a hard matter, and by many thought impossible to distinguish exactly between Sense and Dreaming. For my part, when I consider, that in Dreames, I do not often, nor constantly think of the same Persons, Places, Objects, and Actions that I do waking; nor remember so long a trayne of coherent thoughts, Dreaming, as at other times; And because waking I often observe the absurdity of Dreames, but never dream of the absurdities of my waking Thoughts; I am well satisfied, that being awake, I know I dreame not; though when I dreame, I think my selfe awake.[84]

Recognizing the limits of language and reason, Hobbes relies on the body to identify dream consciousness; while waking thoughts stem from external stimuli and the senses, dream consciousness results from "the agitation of the inward parts of mans body," about which we lack intimate or discursive knowledge.[85]

Hobbes's mechanical idea of the body is paralleled even within the phenomenological tradition. In one of the more beautiful and poetic passages about sleep, Maurice Merleau-Ponty writes:

> I lie down in bed, on my left side, with my knees drawn up; I close my eyes and breathe slowly, putting my plans out of my mind. But the power of my will or consciousness stops there. As the faithful, in the Dionysian mysteries, invoke the god by miming scenes from his life, I call up the visitation of sleep by imitating the breathing and posture of the sleeper. The god is actually there when the faithful can no longer distinguish themselves from the part they are playing, when their body and their consciousness cease to bring in, as an obstacle, their particular opacity, and when they are totally fused in the myth. There is a moment when sleep "comes," settling on this imitation of itself which I have

been offering to it, and I succeed in becoming what I was trying to be: an unseeing and almost unthinking mass, riveted to a point in space and in the world henceforth only through the anonymous vigilance of the senses. . . . The body's rôle is to ensure this metamorphosis. It transforms ideas into things, and my mimicry of sleep into real sleep.[86]

The imitation of the sleeping body metamorphosed into a real but "anonymous" sleeping body reveals the limits of a dialectical relationship to the self. We think of our own sleep, save the few dreams we translate as we wake, as delinguistified, paradoxically impersonal, even. We rarely think of ourselves sleeping without projecting ourselves as sleeper, as though we were impossibly watching ourselves sleep, nor do we find this lack of consciousness politically significant (along with Hobbes, who resisted oneiric prophetical movements of his time).[87] Merleau-Ponty's emphasis on mimesis as a key to sleep suggests, however, that we relate to this aspect of ourselves as in the third person: it is I who sleep, but I can only speak of myself in the twilight moment of falling into sleep as though I were "the sleeper," whom I must mimic but cannot implore, even if it is the other sleeper lying beside me. Unconsciously, nondiscursively, my body becomes asleep. We simultaneously embody the "I" and the "it"; sleep is our second body.

It may be politically significant to ask, Who is this sleeping body that we mime? If the body is the vehicle of our transit into sleep, it must also be a secure body, one unthreatened by physical surroundings or other people, a relaxed body, a watched body. But not only watched by us in the theater of our minds; our projected sleeping body must be watched by others in our imagination, for just like the sleeping king, we cannot extend our sovereignty to this vulnerable moment of being. Here a pure phenomenology fails: there is a political moment in our recognition that our impersonal sleeping body that we wish to immunize is a collective body, our immunity open to—indeed, dependent on—community (including but extending beyond those preyed on by this community). Put in other ways, there is continuity with the problem of the sleeping king, whose necessary sleep once impelled the rituals that symbolically told his subjects that he was ever vigilant, never asleep. The fiction of the sleepless king is what permitted some to sleep by internalizing something about their own bodies and the law (recollect the Renaissance-era quote above, "I sleep and my heart, that is, my king watches"). Recall, as well, that Freud argued that the law created by the killing and eating of the primal father was, in some sense, ingested and similarly held within.[88] In liberalism, where sovereignty has been devolved to the individual, sleep comes because something now more dispersed and now more theatrically mimed is analogously brought within the heart that watches. The question of who we mime, then, devolves to a particular (hence, political) idea of the body at rest. Far from a primordial task, sleep, as the *Hatton* case reveals, is complicated by the frenetic activity and ubiquitous communication of this shared body that disrupts daily patterns.

If the king is no longer there to watch within our hearts, what is this heart-felt substance at the center of this somnolent conundrum? Perhaps it is best understood as flesh. For Merleau-Ponty in his posthumously published work *The Visible and the Invisible*, the flesh is a concept that links body to world. Our bodies see and are seen, touch and are touched, making us subject and object, and yet more than these reflecting parts:

> There is encroachment, infringement, not only between the touched and the touching, but also between the tangible and the visible, which is encrusted in it, as, conversely, the tangible itself is not a nothingness of visibility, is not without visual existence. Since the same body sees and touches, visible and tangible belong to the same world. It is a marvel too little noticed that every movement of my eyes—even more, every displacement of my body—has its place in the same visible universe that I itemize and explore with them, as, conversely every vision takes place somewhere in the tactile space. There is double and crossed situating of the visible in the tangible and of the tangible in the visible; the two maps are complete, and yet they do not merge into one. The two parts are total parts and yet are not superposable.[89]

Flesh designates this unmerged space, what Merleau-Ponty called the abyss between body as sensible and sentient, a "presentation of a certain absence, . . . a prototype of Being, of which our body, the sensible sentient, is a very remarkable variant, but whose constitutive paradox already lies in every visible."[90] Taken up by Esposito, the flesh, lacking political configuration, is what resists incorporation and deconstruction.[91] Thus, while bodies are the "inside," immunized and protected, the flesh—with obvious connections to the Christian notion of divine incarnation—is "the space opened, uncovered, and lacerated by community."[92] Rather than a particular focus of power, as the body is for Foucault, the flesh for Esposito holds the potential for an affirmative biopolitics that takes place between norm and body.[93]

In absolutism the king's flesh secured the promise of life: larger than his bodily corpulence, the kingly flesh promised an impossibly excessive vigilance. For Santner, this paradoxical potential reveals that while the enjoyment of human life always remains intertwined with symbolic entitlements and investitures, there is a surfeit of life, a pressure that circulates as the flesh, binding "subjects to that [postmonarchical] space of representation that is the 'body politic.'"[94] These are the "royal remains" within the republican body: "With democracy the concept of the nation replaced the monarch and sovereignty was dispersed from the king's body to all bodies. *Suddenly every body bore political weight.*"[95] What the concept of the flesh tries to enable in this context is thinking the biopolitical migration from the king's two bodies into the people's two bodies, particularly in light of the uncertainties and potential failures of this process: the body corresponding to the fiction of the king's symbolic body (thought of as the People's dignity or race) and the subject created by sovereignty.

Flesh is, perhaps, that question of what now ecstatically, and I think vigilantly, links my body to another in what Fred Moten has called "a new analytic of sociality," not merely in a formal and abstract manner, which can be found in liberal black-letter law or the capitalist political economy that cannot guarantee obedience, but in such a manner that might guarantee meaning in light of the history of the monarchy's violent end.[96] This is the sentiment born of "the order of rituals and the legitimacy of ceremonies that cover over the absence of the father, the pure blankness that lies at the origin of law," sentiment that forms a political order and enchants "legal symbols and representations . . . real enough to live by, to bind the popular will, and warrant fidelity to law."[97]

In this enchanted world, of course, there is no guarantee of success. Santner seems to agree with Eugene Thacker on the necrological idea that the political body is haunted by falling apart, akin to Esposito's concern that the *dispositif* of immunity may collapse on itself in a thanatopolitical spiral to secure life.[98] The haunting by death of the body (royal and republican) is ambivalently imagined with the flesh that has the "capacity to split into sublime and abject, intoxicating and merely toxic, modalities."[99] Where the sublime aspects once ritualized the continuity of the king's office after his mortal death, Santner understands this excess energy in postmonarchical society to be expressed as both human libido and a "demand for work in excess of any apparent teleological order, work that keeps one busy beyond reason."[100]

Both of these psychosocial dimensions of the flesh that Santner pursues, I believe, are theorized as analogical responses to a cycle of the life and death of the king in which the concerns and fantasies of political continuity and dissolution were once symbolized, ritualized, and to some degree expiated by reference to and care for the royal mortal body. For this reason, Santner has no problem seeing these excess pressures colonizing the night. I have been arguing in this chapter that there are at least two symbolic systems of care corresponding to the temporality of sovereign succession, one of which is subordinated and overlooked in Santner's account and which I would like to recover here. This is the daily cycle of wake and sleep that was real for the king, and hence productive of the symbolic concerns that made his finite life span seem the largest temporal problem to be solved. Santner's praise for Jonathan Crary's 24/7 thesis of a modern world pressuring sleep to its limits fails to find this other temporality.[101] "Sleep, as Crary argues, would thus indeed seem to represent something like a final frontier where the exigencies of a 24/7 world—a world at some level unworlded or, as I have put it, decreated—run up against the recalcitrance of human embodiment. The paradox of a 24/7 environment would thus seem to be that only in sleep do we inhabit a truly human world, one not fully adapted to, (de) created for, the inhuman rhythms of 24/7 routines of work, consumption, connectivity, and vigilance."[102] While Santner's gesture toward the human and immunitized frontier of sleep against democratic vigilance leads him to a dream-filled psychoanalytic account of this fleshy problem of symbolic connection—an oneiric vigilance—it is, in the end, depoliticizing, demonstrated by his idea that sleep is itself merely human, as opposed to what Merleau-Ponty suggests: its own theatrical and mimetic world. If the promise of the concept of flesh is to help capture where biopolitics might offer positive political potentials, relegating sleep to a frontier uses a lethal colonial imagery, reproducing the problem that not all are considered human, that not all are permitted the human act of sleep.

I think we gain more by acknowledging that sleep is not purely "human" but is socially organized through a meaningful vigilance, and unevenly distributed through (sometimes violent) political arrangements. Sleep depends on a collective sense of care and protection by those included in the political community and even others, such as dogs, left outside. The sleeper, like the protective animal, has no evident legal subjectivity, no particular bodily form, but is, as Merleau-Ponty suggests, imagined and mimed to produce what it seeks. In sleep, I wish to argue, we have vigilant flesh. But, as unpracticed as we are, how can we rouse or address this somnolent substance?

Bonnie Honig has suggested, in her response to Santner's transposition of the king's two bodies into the people's two bodies, that both monarchy and democracy express a third body of the sovereign, which is a supplement to both the ecstatic features of the political-theological and the productive, calculative expressions of political economy.[103] Like all Derridean supplements, she argues, and not unlike Lévinas's ethical third, this one is generative and impure, "the source of the undoing of the very sovereign form and figure on which both theology and economy depend."[104] In monarchy, this third body is revealed in "the sanctuaries and refuges that vented sovereignty when it was more fleshed out."[105] In democratic society, it appears in a flesh that multiplies political possibilities, even where—indeed, sometimes especially because—it uses sovereign power to expand democratic opportunities, holding the possibility of "busy bodies busying themselves to undo or rework the demand to be a (certain kind of) busy body."[106] In Richard Sherwin's words, this reworking may be "the pulse of the flesh taken in the emanations of political and legal perturbation—protests, occupations, signs in popular culture of shared anxiety or shame or anger": flesh pursued as popular vigilance against hierarchical power as in political vigils, competing politically (and not humanistically) for the night.[107]

I am suggesting here, against Santner, that it is important to seize sleep as this kind of popular flesh and to render significant the forms of vigilance that sleep takes. This fleshly focus also holds the potential, I suggest, to take us beyond Esposito's concern that the law, upholding persons, relentlessly pursues an immunitary logic. Much as Kamehameha realized in his constitution, this third body of the flesh orients us to conceptually grasping sleep as sanctuary, not as collapse into the natural, and at the same time as the creative source of the political self. Perhaps law can advance an affirmative biopolitics by reformulating the legal subject in new ways compatible with the flesh. I argue in the following that the Supreme Court of India may have begun this effort.

RAMLILA AND THE COLLECTIVE SLEEPING SUBJECT

In *Re: Ramlila Maidan Incident v. Home Secretary* (2012), the Indian Supreme Court took up the challenge to constabulary violence against sleeping protesters in the Maidan, an enclosed public ground in Delhi, in June 2011. The public space had been legally secured for a three-week yoga training camp. Several days after the camp began, yoga guru Baba

Ramdev, who had been leading an anticorruption campaign, initiated a hunger strike. In response, the police revoked the permit to camp, and when the guru and about twenty thousand of his followers defiantly remained, more than a thousand police moved in just past midnight with tear gas and batons, killing one participant and injuring many others—particularly women and children—and destroying property.[108] The court ruled against the police, arguing that their violent action was taken arbitrarily and constituted an abuse of power. One of the more remarkable aspects of the opinion was the predicate for a right to sleep.

Dr. B. S. Chauhan, Justice, writing separately to underline the constitutional issues of liberty and freedom at stake in the case, presented the question before the court as one pitting police powers against the rights held by a unique legal subject: "The question is as to whether such an order [to disperse the crowd] stands protected under the restriction clause of Article 19 of the Constitution of India or does it violate the rights of a peaceful sleeping crowd, invading and intruding their privacy during sleep hours."[109] The "sleeping crowd" did not "prima facie reflect any apprehension of eminent [sic] threat or danger to public peace and tranquility" simply because it could not.[110] "It is believed that a person who is sleeping, is half dead. His mental faculties are in an inactive state."[111] Lacking mens rea—the ability to constitute a criminal intent—Justice Chauhan argued that "Aristotle, the great Greek philosopher has said that all men are alike when asleep. To presume that a person was scheming to disrupt public peace while asleep would be unjust and would be entering into the dreams of that person."[112]

The protection of the sleeping subject is more than a formal requirement for the court. Much like the *Hatton* dissenters, Justice Chauhan emphasized the ways in which sleep is a necessity that promotes health, happiness, and the quality of life, including mental sharpness, emotional balance, creativity, and vitality.[113] Sleep is so essential that "its deprivation would result in mental and physical torture both. . . . Sleep . . . is a self rejuvenating element of our life cycle and is, therefore, part and partial [sic] of human life. . . . Sleep is therefore, both, life and inherent liberty."[114] Indeed, in the opinion the legal right to sleep is fused to a vision of life greater than the promise of political rights.

If the right to sleep that this court pronounced is predicated on the collective subject of a sleeping crowd, another image of the sleeping body emerges. The attributed Aristotelian idea that all sleepers are alike, equally without status or legal personality, renders this body homogeneous—a mass of sleeping flesh.[115] Not severable due to sleep, these are persons-in-relation, all vigilant for the other, asserting a democratic pastoral power. This sleeping flesh asserts a legally cognizable privacy interest, according to Justice Chauhan, despite the lack of a property claim or an issue of sexuality, both of which were held at stake in the *Hatton* decision. Legally, it is the crowd that seizes the space for sleep, collectivizing Lévinas's image of the sleeper's task and politicizing it. Much like Honig's claim for a third body of the sovereign, these sleepers form a sanctuary, situated somewhere between the threat from legal coercion and the respect and vigilance due from law, which can be taken into the heart of the sleeper, promoting liberty and health.

This intermediate zone depends on and amplifies Justice Chauhan's terminology of the half-dead sleeper.[116] The zombie image of the half-dead conjures for me Colin Dayan's arguments about civil death, a denial of full legal personhood suffered by the prisoner and the enslaved (as well as the homeless, nocturnally fearful, and those denied sleep as torture), and raises questions regarding which half—living or dead—these rights to sleep adhere to, holding a mirror to the legal subject.[117] Perhaps we can see in the legal person, lacking culpability while asleep, its rationality always enslaved to sleep, a distortion of civil death. Imaginably this can best be denoted as a civil sleep, dependent on the vitality of a flesh only imperfectly captured by law but not without its capacity to be affirmed as a right that cannot be individually claimed but must be collectively extended.

The *Ramlila* case opens us to thinking Merleau-Ponty's phenomenology of sleep in a newly political sense. The person we mime in order to sleep is one place to reimagine and experience the sovereign's many bodies. The images of the sleeping homeless bodies in our streets (bodies that some cities, such as Portland and Boise, burdened by the increasing populations without shelter, have recently agreed to respect), or the native Hawaiian protesters of the giant telescope slated for the summit of sacred Mauna a Wakea (whose sleeping vigils the Hawai'i courts have ruled can no longer be legally banned at night), or those living in danger after dark in the inner city may give us a more democratic sense of the bodies we are as we prepare for sleep.[118]

CONCLUSION

Foucault hints at an affirmative biopolitics when he speculates not an end to the sovereign violence of juridical rule but a different rule of law: "We should be looking for a new right [*droit*] that is both antidisciplinary and emancipated from the principle of sovereignty."[119] The politics of sleep today is certainly a vestige of the sovereign politics of vigilance, but the sleeper as flesh extends underneath and beyond the juridical ideas of the person and the body and retains a history prior to Western sovereignty in its intrinsic sociality. Hortense Spillers has influentially argued that flesh preserves the hieroglyphics of violence and trauma of slavery hidden by the symbolic racialism of skin color.[120] Certainly, lacerations of the flesh continue after slavery and beyond the confines of race, sometimes with more silence and camouflage, often—as this chapter has tried to think through—taking place in the night as interruptions of sleep for some deemed expendable or in need of control.

The concept of a civil sleep brings back into legal thought an affirmative sociality of the flesh that mortality does not. Kamehameha showed one pathway to a civil sleep, and, more recently, the Supreme Court of India another. This idea of a civil sleep is in many ways uncontrollable. As one of Honig's "third bodies," the sleeping flesh is generative because it is social, even, at times, political. This politics is captured in the protests at the Maidan in India and on the summit of Mauna a Wakea, as well as in Tahrir Square in Cairo during the Arab Spring. Judith Butler notes in the Egyptian venue, "We are not just talking about heroic actions that took enormous physical strength and the exercise of compelling political rhetoric. Sometimes the simple act of sleeping there, in the square, was the most eloquent political statement—and even must count as an action."[121] The action of extending a right to sleep calls on and interpellates (calls to) inconceivable legal subjects that may unsettle legal persons and help us begin to rethink the possibilities inherent in other bodies, sleeping and awake.

_____

CHAPTER TWO

IT CAME UPON YOU IN THE NIGHT

The law was angry
The law was rabid
It came upon you in the night
The paterollers seeking you out . . .
Ghosts in the night
—**Colin Dayan**

Democracy bears the colony within it, just as colonialism bears democracy, often in the guise of a mask. As Frantz Fanon indicated, this nocturnal face in effect hides a primordial and founding void—the law that originates in nonlaw and that is instituted as law outside the law.
—**Achille Mbembe**

I do declare it, that one good black man, can put to death six white men.
—**David Walker**

In order to perform the political event, first light and dark must be torn asunder. —**Richard Sherwin**

Much has been written in the past decade about the now-familiar 2012 murder of a young, Black, unarmed Trayvon Martin walking in public with candy and a drink in his hand. Martin was shot by George Zimmerman, who was acting as a self-appointed "neighborhood watch captain" in a predominantly white, suburban South Florida neighborhood. This vigilante killing galvanized the Black Lives Matter movement and caused a national soul-searching about racial justice and racial profiling, as well as the thoroughly racialized politics of self-defense. I am interested in returning to this episode to think through an overlooked dimension of this killing. Zimmerman shot Martin in the rainy gloom of dusk, his strained vision of this encounter narrated clearly in his emergency call to 911, seconds before he pulled his trigger. Martin was "a real suspicious guy" who "looks like he's up to no good or he's on drugs or somethin' . . . he looks Black . . . he's got somethin' in his hands, I don't know what his deal is." Martin "looked Black" in a dangerous way, but the lack of certainty in Zimmerman's descriptions, indeed, the implicit case for his perceived danger, depends on the darkness of descending night, the only reason for Zimmerman's defensive patrol of his neighborhood perimeter in the first place.

Zimmerman's right to carry a gun in public and to use lethal violence against an unarmed individual posed little problem for the investigating officers, who invoked their discretion under Florida's Stand Your Ground law to excuse the killing and avoid making an arrest; Zimmerman was not charged until months later, after a public outcry. Four years later, suburban St. Paul police stopped Philando Castile, who was driving with his girlfriend and her daughter at 9 p.m. Castile, who was Black, immediately told the officers that he was carrying a licensed gun. Video taken by his girlfriend showed that the police shot him to death while he was reaching for his driver's license. The officer who shot Castile, Jeronimo Yanez, made repeated statements about darkness and danger that resemble those made by Zimmerman:

> I know he had an object and *it was dark*. And he was pulling it out with his right hand. And as he was pulling it out I, a million things started going through my head. And I thought I was gonna die. And, I was scared because, I didn't know if he was gonna, I didn't know what he was gonna do. He just had somethin' uh his hands and he, the first words that he said to me were, some of the first words he said is that he had a gun. . . . *I just knew it was dark and I could barely see* and I thought it was a firearm and I thought he was gonna shoot and kill me and I thought he was gonna shoot and kill my partner right after that.[1]

Yanez was acquitted of second-degree manslaughter by a jury.

Both nocturnal killings and their judicial aftermaths were met with widespread protest and outrage because they shared a similar racial dynamic. Shooters acting as guardians claiming to be fearful for their own safety shot Black men on the apparently justifiable suspicion that their victims carried and were reaching for a gun. Both by private vigilante and by public authority, these killings and the justifications claimed by the shooters echo a long tradition in the governance of private arms. As Jennifer Carlson has observed, whatever their public framing, gun laws most often regulate "*which* people can do *what* with their guns and *where.* Historically, race has been central to these delimitations."[2] I want to add another delimitation to Carlson's list, illustrated by these two prominent killings: *when*, because the night has had special—though frequently unacknowledged—significance in the racial governance of lethal violence. Fifty-four percent of police killings of unarmed civilians take place at night; more than 30 percent of those unarmed people killed are Black, over two times the percentage of the Black population in the United States.[3]

Certainly, not all interracial violence takes place at night or seeks darkness for cover. The indelible images of Michael Brown's body lying uncovered in a suburban St. Louis street for hours following his noon-time shooting by police in 2014, or the video of George Floyd's 2020 suffocation by Minneapolis police officer Derek Chauvin in front of a crowd of horrified onlookers, suggest that such violence is imagined by its perpetrators to be acceptable for public eyes. Night may also be said to obscure race in some encounters. For instance, numerous "veil of darkness" studies of police traffic stops find a statistically valid racial bias against minority drivers during daylight hours that is attenuated in darkness, when it is hypothesized that police have a harder time seeing the race of the driver.[4] In some cases, such as the 2019 St. Louis police killing of Cortez Bufford, a Black man, darkness may have been a genuine prov-ocation to killing when an officer appeared to panic, even though police later asserted they could see a weapon despite the gloom, perhaps to avoid running afoul of opaque administrative regulations governing lethal use of a service weapon.[5]

Yet even where darkness is not an immediate challenge to vision, even in the full light of day, the enduring American relationship of night to interracial violence and the possession of lethal weapons plays a subtle role in how interracial killing is justified. How does night contribute to the racial dynamics of violence, gun rights, and the malleable laws of self-defense? I am drawn to these three subjects—all relevant to the Martin and Castile killings along with numerous ongoing others by private citizens and police—because they help elucidate the shared yet intruding borders among ideas about sovereignty, republican notions of citizenship, and the imagination of government capacity, a *dispositif* contributing to racial violence. The possession of guns has often symbolized individual and collective sovereignty—a right to kill for self and loved ones, a right to participate in the nation's own sovereign violence, making some die to let others live.[6] Guns are agents themselves, their materiality "loaded with civic signs."[7] The political and affective significance of these signs, and the associated rights to private ownership and immunized use of guns against others, I demonstrate in this chapter, have a historical debt to night and its consequence for white supremacy.

Central to my argument about the historical role of firearms within American civic sensibility is the dependency of the individual right to possession on the concomitant though often hidden duty to dispossess others of this right. Just as a speculative right to sleep requires a collective subject (as I have argued in chapter 1), the individual right to own guns is predicated on a duty to the wider community. There is, in short, no gun possession without dispossession, and the long history of firearm governance—particularly and fundamentally racial restrictions that today leave whites 50 percent more likely to own a gun than Black people—directs us to the night, where governance is both exposed and hidden.[8] The originary duty of dispossession, I argue, is an integral dynamic to comprehend the meaning of the militia referenced in the Second Amendment.[9] The militia is not a vestigial remnant, nor a popular republican nostalgia for a time anterior to a standing army. Rather, the militia is a living idea anchored in the belief that not all deserve the sovereign privilege of lethal protection and that those who are entitled can "watch[] over the internal peace of the confederacy," as Alexander Hamilton framed it.[10] This idea is prominently displayed today in public, armed demonstrations that attack Black Lives Matter, a social movement formed in the aftermath of Trayvon Martin's murder. But the militia's central role is most often obscured by administrative rules obstructing Black individuals from owning guns, by institutions of the carceral state that punish Black people disproportionately for owning weapons and mark them as felons unable to legally own guns, and by police and vigilante killings, often in the night.[11] The *dispositif* of legal and extralegal force revealed through this gunplay exposes the essential divisions of sovereignty and freedom, light and dark, captured in Richard Sherwin's epigraph.

POSSESSION

Antebellum rural nights in the South were pitch-black, devoid of artificial light, and thus an obstruction to legal and planter efforts to maintain spatial control of the enslaved. Darkness limited the power of surveillance. To compel labor during the day, as one novelist and historian wrote in 1854, the enslaved person "must be constantly watched and pressed; and if the whip is not used upon his shoulders he must at least see it brandished in the air as a spur to his activity."[12] The coercion of labor didn't end at sunset but often colonized the night, even when strategic "watching" was less successful. Some enslaved people reported that work in the sugar fields began at six in the morning and lasted till ten at night, with a half hour for eating, unless it was harvesttime, when the only hours off work were from eleven at night until three in the morning.[13] Another common source of social control after dark came in the form of work incentives. Some plantation owners would provide little or no clothing and inadequate food to those they enslaved, which compelled night work for survival, "raising tobacco and food for hogs, which they were allowed to keep, and thus obtained clothes for themselves. These patches of ground were little spots, they were allowed to clear in the woods, or cultivate upon the barrens, and after they got them nicely cleared, and under good cultivation, the master took them away, and the next year they must take other uncultivated spots for themselves."[14] Others worked at night raising chickens and other livestock they could sell at a discount to their owners.[15] Rarely, some slaveholders allowed the enslaved to accumulate cash from this night work in order to purchase their own freedom.[16]

Despite these controls, some who were enslaved prized loose some limited freedom of movement at night, creating what one historian has called a "rival geography" characterized by their furtive motion: "the secret movement of bodies, objects, and information within and around plantation space."[17] The enslaved sometimes realized and expanded this geography by improvising on the slaveholders' travel permissions. On some plantations, slaveholders withdrew their labor demands from Saturday night until Monday morning, during which time the enslaved might visit loved ones or enjoy community when they weren't working on their own plots. One journalist and historian writing in 1854 observed that in the night enslaved people are transformed into a nocturnal animal. . . . [T]hey do not think of sleep. They meet for talk and dances. The more daring secretly mount their master's horses and ride to visit their cronies upon some neighboring plantation. One goes courting, another to see his wife; some with dogs and axes hunt the opossum, a night-walker like themselves; some meet to preach and pray; others prowl about to see what thing of value they can lay their hands upon. Others yet, with bags of stolen corn or cotton on their heads, secretly set off to visit some petty trader, who receives their stolen goods in exchange for whiskey. Some have a bottle on hand, and collecting their intimates about them, they drink, and emboldened by the liquor, they discuss the conduct of their masters, or the overseer, with a keen freedom, a critical observation, an irony as bitter as it is just.[18]

As this critic recognized, the enslaved could preserve an expansive freedom at night to socialize, hunt, and roam the areas near their plantations. Although some slave owners used the deprivation of sleep as a form of social control, mobility at night at the expense of rest was also understood as a theft of time, a means to resist the demands to labor energetically during the day.[19] Additionally, refusing sleep was corrosive to the paternalism some slaveholders used for social control; "the freedom bondpeople tasted at night compromised their willingness to be deferential and obedient during the day."[20] These nocturnal freedoms also encouraged and facilitated escape. Harriet Tubman, the "Moses" of the Underground Railroad, who was always armed with a pistol, reported that she preferred to conduct those fleeing slavery to the North in the wintertime, when the nights were longest, and to start on Saturday night so most in her party were not counted missing until Monday morning.[21]

Guns facilitated more militant forms of resistance than escape. Some slave owners allowed or expected the enslaved to hunt, which afforded them the opportunity to develop technical knowledge as well as to gain private possession of firearms and knives that could be used to assert their own power at night.[22] Sometimes enslaved people purchased older guns in clandestine markets or stole them.[23] The historian Joseph Tregle Jr. gathered from Louisiana newspapers that "It was not unusual for slaves to gather on street corners at night, for example, where they challenged whites to attempt to pass, hurled taunts at white women, and kept whole neighborhoods disturbed by shouts and curses. Nor was it safe to accost them, as many went armed with knives and pistols in flagrant defiance of all precautions of the Black Code."[24] Licit and illicit access to weapons also facilitated plantation-wide uprisings that, in the perception of many whites, grew to challenge the institution of slavery itself.

It became well known that the earth-shattering 1791–1804 revolution against France by the enslaved in Haiti was plotted and begun at night and successfully undertaken with older scavenged firearms and farming implements.[25] The Haitian fight for freedom inspired numerous protests by free Blacks against racism in the American northern states and stirred uprisings of the enslaved throughout the South from 1795 in Louisiana to Nat Turner's rebellion in 1831.[26] News of the Haitian Revolution traveled rapidly to enslaved communities, brought primarily by sailors. Thereafter, many uprisings "shifted decisively from attempts to secure freedom from slavery to attempts to overthrow slavery as a social system."[27] In Kellie Carter Jackson's words, "Haiti was more than a noun; it was a verb."[28]

The Southern uprisings generally began at night. Turner's in particular created the sense for many whites that they were losing control of the night and that their lives were increasingly in peril.[29] One white Virginia man wrote in 1831, the year of Turner's failed attack, of this fear: "These insurrections have alarmed my wife so as really to endanger her health, and I have not slept without anxiety in three months. Our nights are sometimes spent in listening to noises. A corn song, a hog call, has often been a subject of nervous terror, and a cat, in the dining room, will banish sleep for the night."[30] One historian recollected in 1854 that the fear spurred by these uprisings brought "nights of agony and sleeplessness to hundreds of thousands."[31] Many whites of means carried guns for protection from the enslaved and from poor whites, who were sometimes hanged on suspicion that they had joined or would aid the enslaved in insurrection.[32]

Whether by design or through the limitations of government capacity, the control of weapons and efforts to govern the night in response to growing fears mixed legal enforcement with planters' paternalist regulations, both infused with private terror.[33] Gun confiscation often occurred after slave uprisings, such as the great rebellion of 1811 in the Orleans Territory of present-day Louisiana. This uprising (which also began at night) conjured fears among many of the local French—some of whom had moved from San Domingue after the Haitian revolt—of another incipient revolution.[34] As Carol Anderson has pointed out, the violent Whiskey Rebellion of 1794, which involved white farmers angry over a new federal tax, was quickly quashed, yet never provoked a similar effort at disarming its proponents.[35]

Although gun control laws were common in the antebellum South and applicable to all races, governmental efforts to restrict private arms tended to target Black people, even in the colonial period.[36] Free Black men were excluded from the federal militia under the Uniform Militia Act of 1792, which called for the enrollment of all white male citizens between the ages of eighteen and forty-five and commanded each of them to "provide himself with a musket or firelock, a bayonet, and ammunition."[37] Free Blacks often maintained firearms for safety and for hunting, but after the wave of slave rebellions early in the nineteenth century, compounded by the suspicion that free Blacks were arming the enslaved, slave states began banning all Blacks from owning guns. One notorious 1833 Florida law authorized white citizen patrols to seize arms found in the homes of enslaved and free Blacks, and provided that Black persons lacking a proper explanation for the presence of firearms should be punished summarily without benefit of any legal hearing.[38] In other states, free Blacks required a firearms license, and the enslaved might use firearms only with the permission of their owners. It was not until 1842 that Texas prohibited enslaved people from using firearms altogether, indicating substantial fear that guns remained in circulation among the enslaved.

This broad pattern of legal regulations of gun possession reflects—but also challenges—a republican sensibility. Since the mid-1970s, American historiography has explored and often emphasized the influence of the political theory of civic republicanism that inspired Thomas Jefferson and other leaders of the American Revolution.[39] Drawn through the absorption of Aristotelian, Ciceronian, and Machiavellian notions of government into Enlightenment thought—particularly the works of Jean-Jacques Rousseau and Montesquieu—republicanism was transformed by American intellectuals who emphasized the political imperative of nondependence on others. As Jefferson famously observed in his *Notes on the State of Virginia*, "Dependence begets subservience and venality, suffocates the germ of virtue, and prepares fit tools for the designs of ambition."[40] Although republicanism was understood by some in the late eighteenth century to complement monarchy and aristocracy, republicanism in America emphasized related yet transformative values: morality, freedom, civic duty, friendship, and its social vision, in the historian Gordon Wood's tally.[41] J. G. A. Pocock perceived these political dimensions to cluster around two poles: "a civic and patriot ideal in which the personality was founded in property, perfected in citizenship but perpetually threatened by corruption; [and] government figuring as the principle source of corruption."[42] These values of civic virtue and anticorruption offered a distinctive notion of liberty from that which derived from a Lockean liberal tradition ascendant throughout the nineteenth century.[43] Rather than the liberal imperative of noninterference by government and neighbor, the republican principle of nondependency valued community more than it was suspicious of it.

One important means of preserving republican community against corruption was through perpetual vigilance against a standing army. In the formation of a state or federal militia, citizens were brought together when necessary for a common defense. Imaginatively, the communal commitment defended against dangers to settlers from Native resistance to land encroachment on the frontiers and slave uprisings near plantations. Despite the laws against free Blacks holding weapons, during times of white panic, free Blacks were sometimes cajoled into joining allied militia actions against the enslaved.[44] Once armed, free Blacks again were considered dangers to white safety because of their assumed alliances with enslaved people. Efforts such as those in Florida to disarm all Blacks people revealed the racialized horizon of republican citizenship. Racial restrictions on gun possession also demonstrated what some historians have called the American paradox: not only was republicanism compatible with slavery, it was—as in classical Athens and ancient Rome—absolutely dependent on it.[45] "Historically and conceptually, 'enslavement and subjection are great evils' not because the free citizen hates slavery but because he thinks he does not deserve the servitude that others *rightfully deserve*."[46] A white militia at least theoretically sustained a caste boundary that excluded enslaved and free Black people, a limit that made the legal possession of a weapon a primal sign of racial and national belonging.

In European republican thought, a second form of civic virtue depended on the survival of an aristocracy to guard its virtues, one that slavery in the American context was expected to guarantee. Yet Americans had repudiated the idea of a natural or inherited aristocracy, and they lacked a house of lords composed of men of leisure, learning, and experience that could serve as an intermediary between government with its inherent corruptions and the common man.[47] To replace this institution, according to Pocock, American intellectuals creatively developed the concept of "All power was entrusted to representatives, and every mode of exercising power was a mode of representing the people."[48] Nonetheless, however central this concept of the people was to American sensibility, poor whites who lacked the education and leisure of elites remained economically and socially marginal, making them susceptible to strategies of racialized governance.

What I wish to stress here—without being overly reductive—is the significance of visibility that is tightly bound to the notion of representation, which in turn serves the framework for the political community, and the entire theory of republicanism. American norms of deliberation that are key to self-direction, the appeal beyond liberal self-interest, and efforts to build a polity despite the centrifugal effects of pluralism and the fears of corruption all require transparency and rely on metaphors of visibility for their justification.[49] This has been observed, if not overly emphasized, by several students of republicanism. Alexis de Tocqueville, for example, claimed that American "love and habits of republican government" were "engendered in the townships and in the provincial assemblies," where locals could see and interact with each other.[50] The philosopher Hannah Arendt commented approvingly about Jefferson's republicanism by noting the value of transparency: "The only remedies against the misuse of public power by private individuals lie in the public realm itself, in the light which exhibits each deed enacted within its boundaries, in the very visibility to which it exposes all those who enter it."[51] For José Luis Martí and Philip Pettit, the republican ideal depends on "a culture of democratic transparency that exposes government to constant invigilation and routine contestation."[52] The sociologist Émile Durkheim claimed that republican public deliberation keeps minds "clear" and prevents "blind" actions; discussion in the public milieu "in the full light of day" infuses a nation's "psychic life [ensuring] all the scattered reflections . . . react on the governmental thought which was their source."[53] For contemporary republican theorist Ekow Yankah, transparency and publicity develop legal norms; even civil disobedience designed to make evident social and legal contradictions depends on a willingness to openly demonstrate that one will accept the consequences.[54]

Liberal theory, in contrast, has emphatically held onto a certain darkness: a sealed private realm where individual interests, necessarily opaque to government, coalesce into a guiding "invisible hand." Liberalism's moral center is dependent on a "veil of ignorance," as the philosopher John Rawls argued; its willingness to blind itself to the lingering significance of the violent origins of sovereignty remains cocooned within its dedication to "color-blind" abstraction.[55] Discussing liberalism's incorporation of invisible-hand imagery, Michel Foucault has argued for its metaphorical dependence on an inability to see: "For there to be certainty of collective benefit, for it to be certain that the greatest good is attained for the greatest number of people, not only is it possible, but it is absolutely necessary that each actor be blind with regard to this totality. Everyone must be uncertain with regard to the collective outcome if this positive collective outcome is really to be expected. Being in the dark and the blindness of all the economic agents are absolutely necessary."[56] General darkness obscuring collective steering, along with individual blindness to one's neighbor's direction, is integral to the liberal economy in Foucault's framing—and yet neither form of looking away is secret; both hold a sacred place in the liberal imagination. Liberalism can draw on this sacred darkness in its appeal to rights, as it recently has in the case for individual gun rights, as I show later in the chapter. The need to secure the hearth from civic and criminal threats—particularly at night—comfortably makes nocturnal danger an essential reason for (mostly property) rights. Some forms of liberalism even extolled the centrality of this function in the positive nocturnal image of the vigilant, yet minimalist, night-watch state.[57]

Darkness holds no similar sacred place in republicanism, as gun laws revealed. Under a republican light, for example, it is not surprising that antebellum laws were almost universally opposed to concealed carrying of weapons. Concealing firearms was seen as a sign of a growing individualism perverting republican sensibility.[58] By 1813 Kentucky and Louisiana had both passed laws against carrying concealed weapons, followed by Indiana, Georgia, Virginia, Alabama, and Ohio in the next decade.[59] Open carry of guns, by contrast, was soon enshrined under state constitutional authority in Alabama (1840), Tennessee (1840), North Carolina (1843), Georgia (1846), and Louisiana (1850).[60] For one midcentury commentator, "the dangerous and criminal practice of wearing concealed weapons" should be checked by law; "the only conceivable object of course, in thus carrying these instruments of death, is to kill" and to give "nocturnal rowdies . . . the means of committing wanton murder on unoffending passers along the highway."[61] Where early gun laws regulated time, place, and manner for carrying weapons in line with the common law proscription against riding "armed by night nor by day in Fairs, Markets, nor in the presence of the Justices or other Ministers," night was of particular interest; many states prohibited the firing of weapons after sunset and before sunrise, or any gunplay after darkness fell.[62]

It may be true that republicanism has no theory of the night.[63] Nonetheless, nocturnal strategies were consuming projects developed to contain threats to those "people" who visibly counted as citizens and to others whose social significance depended on nocturnal labor. As the antebellum laws against concealed carry of weapons reveal, it was not only free Blacks and the enslaved who posed particular threats to republican aspirations but also those poor whites who were potentially and by propensity criminal. The historian Alexander Gourevitch has demonstrated that some white and Black wage laborers were able together to mobilize a still-viable republican ideal of nondependency in the latter part of the nineteenth century in order to organize the Knights of Labor, redeeming wage labor from its association with slavery and subordination and thereby revealing that republicanism could transcend its racist origins.[64] But in the antebellum South, the republican status of poor whites was loosely sutured by participation in elite efforts to secure slave labor and to mitigate the danger of circulating lethal weapons, two of the vital republican projects necessary to achieve civic ideals that legal edicts could not secure. Many of these activities were relegated to the night. Night work lacked political sanction, yet was vital to the political and legal sensibilities of the day.

"Your broad republican domain is hunting ground for men. . . . Where go[es] the merciless slave-hunter . . . man is not sacred. He is a bird for the sportsman's gun. By that most foul and fiendish of all human decrees, the liberty and person of every man are put in peril."[65] This stinging critique of the 1850 Fugitive Slave Act that Frederick Douglass delivered in an 1852 address points to a limit of political sensibility. Hunting, once a privileged sign of British aristocracy and abandoned as such in American revolutionary culture, had gradually been rehabilitated in early nineteenth-century American folkways; it was also racialized. Daniel Boone and Davy Crockett were idolized by enfranchised white men and contrasted to "coons," or Black small-game hunters lacking the manly sensibilities required for self-government.[66] Douglass's argument about the corrosive universalization of the slave hunter identified what Achille Mbembe, in this chapter's epigraph, would call a primordial and founding void "instituted as law outside the law." Even when only partially revealed, this involution exposes the poverty of political theory capable of explaining and containing the anxiety that Douglass invokes. Universalized slave hunting violates liberal sensibilities of the sacred, private realm to which the slave hunter gains legal access, and it makes the violent defense of human property the primary nexus of the republican community.

Indeed, the hunting of people eludes political and legal imaginations. In implicit agreement with Douglass's critique of the slave hunter, the contemporary philosopher Grégoire Chamayou argues that the hunt "appears to be a technology of power, [but] it does not figure among the political arts in the full sense of the term. The cynegetic modality of power is exercised only as the condition for the master's economic domination. As such it is not an art of the polis. The first problem is that of its justification. What authorizes someone to engage in manhunting? The question of the legitimacy of capture resonates with a Greek fear: that of being hunted oneself."[67] Night was the time for acquiring slaves in Africa, Chamayou recounts, and the anxiety he associates with hunting for and policing slaves is magnified in the dark, where hunter and prey maneuver, haunted by this (more than Greek) fear of the "constant possibility of a reversal of the relationship: the prey might become a predator, the hunted a hunter."[68] The uncertain outcome of combat is rhetorically different from the adversarial yet regulated justification of law, as an abolitionist editor in 1851 noted: "It need surprise nobody that in the game of slave-hunting . . . it should sometimes happen that the hunting party and not the hunted become the mark for bullets, and the law of self-preservation, and not the Fugitive Slave Law, be obeyed and triumph."[69] This supplemental law of self-preservation, made necessary by the instability of the hunt, excuses the violence that otherwise has no justification. It echoes today in the excuses of Zimmerman and police officers who kill because they "feared for their lives."

The policing of nocturnal movement, infused with the cynegetic power of hunting human beings, began as early as 1704 in South Carolina, spreading to other colonies and states as the fears of slave insurrection grew.[70] Mississippi codified its policing after seismic fears rumbled from the failed Denmark Vesey insurrection in 1822 (modeled on its Haitian precursor), and again in 1830 and 1831 soon after the publication of David Walker's prophecy that whites "will yet curse the day you ever were born" and on the heels of Nat Turner's violent rebellion.[71] Yet the system in Mississippi (as elsewhere) was "extremely ineffective," operating one night out of fourteen, and thus was dependent more on terror and feint than the horrific certainty of punishment.[72] Some enslaved people monitored patrol activity, passing information to those meeting clandestinely, a form of "sousveillance" that exploited the dark; others simply outmaneuvered and outran the patrols.[73] Oral histories demonstrate that memories of this nocturnal terror endured far into the twentieth century.[74] *Night riders* was the term given to the patrollers (or *paterollers* and other like-sounding terms spoken by the enslaved to facilitate secretive communication), a militia almost entirely composed of poor whites either obligated to serve one night every two weeks or hired by planters who could send a substitute for their civic obligations. Despite some legal efforts to restrain what punitive force patrollers could exert on those they intercepted who lacked their owners' permission to travel, they often acted with impunity to confiscate weapons and create fear in a futile effort to control the darkness.[75] The 1842 testimony of Lewis Clarke, a fugitive from slavery, recalls the acts of these vigilantes that went far beyond their legal parameters:

> The worst thing in the whole lot [slavery, were] the *patter-rollers* (patrols.) [*sic*] I suppose you know that they have patter-rollers to go round o' nights, to see that the slaves are all in, and not planning any mischief? Now these are jest about the worst fellows that can be found; as bad as any you could pick up on the wharves. . . . Because they are so mortal sure the slaves don't want their freedom, they have to put all power into their hands to do with the niggers jest as they like. If a slave don't open his door to them at any time of night they break it down. They steal his money if they can find it, and act just as they please with his wives and daughters. If a husband dares to say a word, or even look as if he wasn't quite satisfied, they tie him up and give him thirty-nine lashes. If there's any likely young girls in a slave's hut, they're might apt to have business there.[76]

For some patrollers, the sadistic pleasures they derived from these hunts sustained their activities, making their service to the law—especially the confiscation of weapons—a mere alibi. The exclusion of the nocturnal militia from civic republican discourse made the obscene pleasures of the hunt a major compensatory mechanism; republican ideals were put to sleep after dark.

Policing the night met its limits in numerous ways but not more spectacularly than at Christiana, Pennsylvania, in 1851, an exceptional event that reveals the ways that night could be made to signify for political ends, despite the secrecy of action in the darkness. While the idea and the duty of the militia were owned by whites, who arrogated to themselves the regulation of lethal weaponry, vigilante groups of free Blacks also formed organizations and networks to establish nocturnal security against white raiding parties and mobs that assaulted relatively prosperous Black neighborhoods. The African Greys were established in Provincetown in 1821, and less formal groups followed in Boston, Philadelphia, and Pittsburgh during the later antebellum period.[77] A number of looser Black organizations formed in the aftermath of the Fugitive Slave Act of 1850, which had essentially conscripted white and free Black citizens into a federal militia, duty bound to seize and return escaped slaves. Frederick Douglass, as we have seen, denounced the law as a republican sham, bringing the hunting of people—long kept in the dark—into the full embrace of law.[78] All Black people were vulnerable to seizure, and many free Blacks, already facing Blackbirder kidnappings in the northern states that spirited them to the South and slavery at night, worked to resist their increased legal and extralegal vulnerability.[79] This vulnerability was especially felt in the border states, such as Pennsylvania, where escaped slaves had become a significant rural community, and it was magnified dramatically when several free Black men were kidnapped early in 1851.[80]

The Christiana event began in the dark on September 11, 1851, when a Maryland slaveholder, Edward Gorsuch, holding warrants from a Philadelphia judge and accompanied by a posse (including his son and nephew) and a marshal, sought to seize several men who had escaped from Gorsuch's plantation and were living near Christiana. William Parker, himself a fugitive from slavery who lived in Christiana, had formed a Black self-defense organization in 1841 to facilitate what he called the "almost sleepless vigilance" he was forced into as the cost of his "stolen liberty."[81] He had been informed of the warrants by Philadelphia vigilance committees who, he claimed, were always ready to "thwart the barbarous and inhuman monsters who crawled in the gloom of midnight" to seize men and women for slavery.[82] Believing that Parker was hiding the men they sought, Gorsuch and his monstrous retinue had approached Parker's house in the gloom, yet they lacked the surprise they expected. Gorsuch's party had been observed in the night by a member of the Christiana vigilance committee, who had alerted others. When Gorsuch demanded his property, Parker's wife sounded a tocsin, and the Black vigilance committee—perhaps twenty-five armed men—converged through the woods. Parker himself was armed and ready.

Gorsuch and the marshal then broke through the front door, and Parker confronted and threatened them both, telling the marshal that if he took another step, he would break his neck.[83] Parker also toyed with Gorsuch, who continued to demand his property. "Go in the room down there, and see if there is anything there belonging to you. There are beds and a bureau, chairs, and other things. Then go out to the barn; there you will find a cow and some hogs. See if any of them are yours."[84] Parker continued to taunt Gorsuch, who persistently demanded his "property" even while surrounded by armed Black vigilantes. After Parker demanded that Gorsuch leave, the whites began shooting, and several ran. Gorsuch was killed by the Black gunmen, and his son and nephew were badly wounded; the marshal bolted for his life.

Parker also fled, expecting reprisal for the killing. The night before he crossed the border into Canada, Parker stayed with Frederick Douglass in Rochester, who hid him and helped arrange northern passage on a boat that was leaving the next evening. As Parker boarded the boat, cloaked in the dark of night, he handed Gorsuch's pistol to Douglass as a souvenir. Douglass wrote in one of his autobiographies that he "could not look upon [Parker and his allies] as murderers, to me they were heroic defenders of the just rights of men against men-stealers and murderers."[85] If many people did not fully agree, they were at least torn: despite forty indictments and several trials, no jury ever convicted anyone associated with the Christiana killings.

Parker's written account of the incident is redolent with images of night and darkness. Night, for him, is not only the time for kidnapping and hunting people but also a time for freedom and (overtly) manly resistance. Parker wrote of the joys of liberty that he felt during his own nocturnal escape from slavery. He utilized a rhetorical inversion, analogizing freedom won at night as day, and slavery as perpetual night. "Day and night are not more unlike," he mused.[86] Even after his initial escape from slavery, Parker once again had to flee at night: in the daylight he was more susceptible to the law and the bounty hunters who sought him for a prize. Successful self-defense for Black people has often increased white rage, yet the Christiana incident managed to do something else.[87] The occurrence at Christiana resonated throughout the North, galvanizing opposition to the Fugitive Slave Act and to slavery generally.

Dwelling on the images of hunting at night and exposing them as the real source of the law, the abolitionist press emphasized activities that had no easy republican or liberal political reference. William Lloyd Garrison used images of darkness to disparage Gorsuch's otherwise-legal actions, thereby casting suspicion on the law: "A man-stealer named Gorsuch, accompanied by his son and sundry abettors . . . lawlessly [broke] into a private dwelling under the cover of darkness, [and] attempted by stealth and violence to seize and make slaves of some of the occupants."[88] By transforming the Declaration of Independence's words of indictment, shared by William Shakespeare's Richard III, who has abjured day and light, another abolitionist editor reviled the Fugitive Slave Law as "pregnant with death, desolation and anarchy" and hence unfit for enlightened liberty.[89] For many abolitionists, Christiana justified Douglass's call to arms against slavery, and a significant number split from the Garrisonian nonviolence camp.[90] Douglass's possession of Parker's gun was emblematic of the turn.

The antiabolitionist press, alarmed that the resisters were armed and Black, disparaged the Christiana event as a "servile insurrection—if not also one of treason."[91] On the first day of publication for the *New York Times*, the Christiana "riot" was featured on page 1. Night and darkness were not mentioned—nor was the smoke from black powder that apparently obscured much of the shooting.[92] This helped the anonymous author of the *Times* article to impute blame solely to the "sixty or eighty armed blacks" who opened fire without apparent restraint.[93] There was no acknowledgment of the fugitives' free status in Pennsylvania. The article ended as follows: "A mulatto man, supposed to be the slave Pinckney owned by Mr. Gorsuch was seen yesterday on the hills near Lancaster, and several citizens had gone in pursuit of him."[94] This final stress on the daytime visibility of Pinckney helped to legitimate his pursuit by true(r) citizens, while also imaginatively evoking the power of both racial color and surveillance, essential to the legal order of slavery.

Despite infatuation with law, visibility, and control by the antiabolitionist press, Christiana reveals the ways that night can, indeed, politically signify in a republican regime. Used thematically by the abolitionists, Gorsuch's nocturnal furtiveness in alleged pursuit of justice challenges the transparent character of law—its ideology extolling due process as well as its public performance in open courts—thus resisting the incorporation in practical terms of all citizens into a pro-slavery militia by the Fugitive Slave Act. The Christiana event emphasized Douglass's earlier announcement that he no longer rejected the American Constitution because slavery always had been "a system of lawless violence that *never was lawful and never can be made so.*"[95] At the same time, a number of abolitionists redrew the imagined boundaries of their community to include those people who had always before been denied a place in its constitutionally sanctioned community.

The Christiana event also was used to highlight the vulnerability of cynegetics (the technique of hunting human beings) to a reversal of power, an instability that was always at play at night in the control of the enslaved and that could be turned to advantage with bold and sometimes violent action. Christiana is mostly forgotten today, but the contest of meaning over what can happen in the dark that it epitomized is genealogically linked to an ongoing commitment to a racial militia. The twentieth-century Black commitments to self-defense were again on the increase during the civil rights movement of the 1950s and 1960s.[96] The rise of liberal coalitions—including many Black leaders seeking an end to urban violence—that supported gun control during this same period targeted familiar fears of urban (Black) crime.[97] Black militants with guns inspired white support for the regulation of "Saturday night specials," cheap foreign-made handguns tied nominally to nocturnal racial imaginations.[98] As one observer noted in the early 1990s:

> Today the thought remains: if you let the poor, and especially the Black poor, have guns, they will commit crimes with them. Even noted anti-gun activists have admitted this. In his book *The Saturday Night Special*, anti-gun journalist Robert Sherrill frankly admitted that the Gun Control Act of 1968 was "passed not to control guns but to control Blacks." Barry Bruce-Briggs, in *The Public Interest*, stated that "it is difficult to escape the conclusion that the 'Saturday Night Special' is emphasized because it is cheap and it is being sold to a particular class of people. The name is sufficient evidence. The reference is to 'Niggertown Saturday Night.'"[99]

The reference to the night in the political shorthand for these guns, I believe, adds significance to its demeaning racialization because it signifies a long tradition of misrecognition going back to slavery through which Black people (along with the poor and immigrants) are identified as dangers to white safety, even though it is at night that Black people (who statistically have been less likely to own or carry weapons) are most vulnerable to white terrorism.[100] It also illustrates the ways that rights to possess guns for some depend on the dispossession of others deemed dangerous.

Jennifer Carlson has recently demonstrated how the idea of the militia—as I have been using it here to indicate the duty and practice of disarming the popular enemy—has partially migrated into administrative rules for credentialing concealed carry permit holders.[101] This task of racial management holds true, she shows, even in "shall-issue" states, where opaque bureaucratic process preserves white advantage in carrying firearms. Through observation of Michigan gun permit hearings, she noted disparities in the ways Black applicants were questioned, admonished, and humiliated for minor past infractions by a mostly white hearing board in what was essentially a "degradation ceremony."[102] Many others are automatically denied permits due to criminal records, reflecting an already racially biased criminal system. Ultimately, the difficulties that Black applicants face in obtaining guns legally constitutes a deadly paradox: those who survive the process and are granted concealed carry permits are extraordinarily well vetted to be "safe" to white elites, but their disproportionately smaller number compared with whites makes them exceptional and tends to heighten the perception of their dangerousness. One perverse ideological consequence is that those Black people going out while legally armed at night can be assumed to understand the risk that whites must feel, and by embracing this risk to others and themselves, they must therefore be up to no good. Philando Castile's emblematic killing at night, only seconds after he announced to police officers making a traffic stop that he had permission to carry the gun on his person, is a tragic reminder that something less rationalized by bureaucratic process and less captured by political policy haunts and hunts those victimized by white fears.

WHITE MOBS AND LIBERAL GUN RIGHTS

I have argued that night was historically experienced as a politically indecisive time. Although it could, with great effort, be made representative of civic republican political projects such as abolition (as it was in Christiana), night was pervaded by hunting and other forms of tactical maneuvering—often over firearms—that made it strategically instable. Following the Civil War, Black soldiers returned from their Union muster with guns, and other freedpersons accumulated arms to hunt (and thereby lessen their dependency on whites), to affirm their dignity, and to taste constitutional and legal rights.[103] For white people, the imagined threats of armed Black men once more provoked the white nightmares triggered by Haiti, Nat Turner, and other violent social upheaval, prompting vigilante action against Black people and their allies, including the occupying Republican federal government during Reconstruction.[104] White mobs and clandestine actions against Black vigilante groups helped end Reconstruction, restore white supremacy, and establish unofficial limits to the possession and use of firearms. So did lynching.

In this section I turn to problems of political representation that emerged in these postbellum mobilizations of white and Black citizens, and the recursions to night that added to political and legal order. My interest is not only to understand how this period established the conditions for white gun ownership but, particularly, to see how this history is reflected and deflected in the more liberal frameworks for individual rights to possession that have attended and driven the contemporary constitutional interpretation of the Second Amendment.

Many historians have stressed the continuity of postbellum Southern racial violence with violence that predated and played out during the Civil War.[105] Pre-Reconstruction Southern state legislatures promulgated the Black Codes, major elements of a dual legal system designed to control Black labor by criminalizing vagrancy, limiting land use, and seizing indigent children for work. Black people were legally excluded from juries and barred from being witnesses against whites. They also were disarmed and afforded only very limited authority to engage in self-defense.[106] Many of the Codes also tried to banish Black men and women from the civic night. In Opelousas, Louisiana, for example, "every Negro freedman found on the streets of Opelousas after ten o'clock at night without a written pass or permit from his employer, shall be imprisoned and compelled to work five days on the public streets, or pay a fine of five dollars."[107] In Georgia theft, arson, and burglary in the night were made crimes punishable by death for Blacks.

Nonetheless, the control of the night was rarely relegated to the regular processes of law. The fresh experience of guerrilla warfare—much of it nocturnal, often between Union Black and Confederate soldiers—had made the experiences of war (confiscation, trespass, arson) appear to whites as a "series of criminal activities, approaching a war of all against all."[108] This carried over to social and political change after the war, when Black political activity was seen by whites as criminality demanding suppression.[109] Black political organizing through the Union Leagues often occurred at night, causing further white anxiety, and armed Black militias sometimes secured ballot access.[110] Given the fear of political upheaval, even Black ownership was enough to court a violent death where "the act of building a fence approximated a kind of defiance" of white order.[111] Whites had been inured to policing Black people, and as one historian noted, "Most . . . just could not imagine a future in which someone was not responsible for monitoring black behavior, and this enabled the resort to racial terrorism."[112]

Yet, unlike the experience of the war, in which Black soldiers maneuvered—oftentimes successfully—against whites, there was a keen political asymmetry that encouraged white violence. Black people, now citizens, were a majority in three Southern states and in many other counties across Dixie. Democratic norms responded violently to this rebalance of political power. As Eric Foner recounts:

It is indeed true that slavery, which gave rise to numerous forms of black resistance, did not produce a broad tradition of violent retaliation against abuse. But the failure of nerve, if such it was, extended up and down the Republican hierarchy and was not confined to one race. Perhaps the problem was that Republicans, black and white, took democratic processes more seriously than their opponents. No Republicans rode at night to murder their political foes, nor did armed bands seek to drive Democrats from the polls. "We could burn their churches and schoolhouses but we don't want to break the law or harm anybody," wrote one black from a violence-torn part of Georgia. "All we want is to live under the law."[113]

The commitment to law and democratic process was the prize of emancipation and victory, but it was not resilient in the face of those refusing defeat.

Ironically, as many historians have noted, the white vigilante groups that emerged at this time, often under the umbrella of the Ku Klux Klan (KKK), believed fiercely that their violence was law making and law sustaining.[114] Deploying imagery from the social control of the enslaved, they referred to Black people as "unwhipt of justice," according to one conservative Southern press.[115] Vigilante groups committed themselves to defending the Constitution and to affirming local sovereignty.[116] One secret Klan oath, taken under penalty of "Death! Death! Death!" for its divulgence, began, "We are on the side of justice, humanity, and constitutional liberty, as bequeathed to us in its purity by our forefathers."[117] As one historian studying Southern lynching concluded, "In lynching an enemy of society they do not mean to violate or despise the law, but rather to vindicate and enthrone it. They are acting simply in their sovereign capacity as lawmakers. Laws seems [sic] to them local in their origin, therefore local in their application and in their breach; law to them is no longer an institution dominating the community—the community is the law."[118]

Western legality, however, has mostly required a public form such as open courts expressing ideals of transparency and enabling mechanisms of visibility. Vigilante violence, particularly at night, signified legality in quite different ways. As Elaine Parsons has shown, despite volumes of testimony by victims and (admitted) KKK perpetrators collected by Congress in 1870 and 1871, newspapers of all political stripes questioned whether the KKK actually existed, instead projecting this violence into "a ghostly space in American political and popular culture."[119] The KKK's own rhetorical use of comedic forms, exaggerated discourse, and isolated nocturnal activities that eliminated witnesses to its pernicious violence allowed it to slip past political capture. The KKK's republican connection between its enforcement of "law" and the community constituted by that law was thereby journalistically mediated by a public faith or doubt in the existence of conspiratorial violence, displacing "the previous screening mechanism based on condition of servitude."[120] Nocturnal violence was thereby hidden and could be walked back as mere exaggeration when inconveniently exposed, yet it was able to cohere the white and terrorize the Black communities.[121]

This skeptical journalistic discourse amplified the victims' trauma that the KKK's violence created.[122] While Black people were racially targeted and their guns confiscated at night in an effort to assure white domination and to break their resistance to the labor conditions on the remaining plantations, particularly during the early years of postbellum white vigilantism,[123] white Republicans were also assaulted, raped, and killed in the name of law and political expediency, and their guns likewise seized.[124] Yet if these nocturnal vigilante actions were genuinely law making, they infused law with the special pleasures and dangers of the night, violating its ideological transparency. W. E. B. Du Bois noted:

> The method of force which hides itself in secrecy is a method as old as humanity. The kind of thing that men are afraid or ashamed to do openly, and by day, they accomplish secretly, masked, and at night. The method has certain advantages. It uses Fear to cast out Fear; it dares things at which open method hesitates; it may with a certain impunity attack the high and the low; it need hesitate at no outrage of maiming or murder; it shields itself in the mob mind and then throws over all a veil of darkness which becomes glamor. It attracts people who otherwise could not be reached. It harnesses the mob.[125]

Glamorous violence under a veil of darkness competes with the majesty of law, secreting its own pleasures in the competition for survival at night. Yet fear cannot cast away itself; this aspect of night remains tangible, volatile, uncertain, unlawlike. Fear to cast out fear creates false equivalences; it facilitates misrecognition and allows the victimizer self-assurance of true victimization, and that enforcement of the rule of force is true law, legitimating another's violation. The white vigilante imagines rape of vulnerable whites while raping Black women and sexually humiliating Black men.

Although "disguise upon the public highway or upon the premises of another" was eventually made a federal offense by the Enforcement Act of 1871, the threat of identification by Republican authorities only made vigilantes more invested in obscuring their identities.[126] Disguise not only hid the leadership of participating elites whose civic republican sensibilities matched the public character of law (and, indeed, many publicly discouraged disguises) but also provided the "glamor" to bridge class division (as did the goals of disarmament and political grievance, and the special sadistic pleasures of rape and violence).[127] Many early KKK uniforms were black in order to stealthily hide night riders; only later did the contrasting and ghostly white become widespread, and fire the herald of the KKK's nocturnal presence.[128] Local KKK dens often would coordinate with distant groups to cross state lines in terror campaigns to suppress the vote, lessening the possibility of recognition.[129] Black people were sometimes convicted of being masked and in disguise, while white vigilante disguise was overlooked.[130] Such perverse misrecognition was the common logic of nocturnally enforced legality. According to a New Orleans Republican newspaper, nocturnal parades were designed to "make night hideous by unearthly groans, yells, cat-calls, and whatever else their fancies suggest, to provoke some hostile demonstration which they can resent, of course in pure self-defense, by massacring the offending victim."[131] Self-defense was legitimated by the political language of the militia—officially disbanded by federal order in 1867—but it also captured a nonlaw within the law: the militia was as much an informal, ad hoc process of limiting Black and Republican reaction to its own violent excess as it was an institution.[132]

Always pregnant with reversible surprise, the night could not be fully dominated by whites. Black people sometimes used arson as a weapon of terror against white targets at night, and theft at night by poor Blacks for survival was common after the war.[133] Black militias also assembled at night, sometimes to protect from lynching those Black people who had been arrested.[134] As in times of slavery, the night also provided cover for movement and escape. Yet, unlike the patrollers, whose policing presence was sporadic, night riders attacked almost nightly, especially prior to elections, forcing many Black families to (fitfully) sleep in the woods or seek out white patrons to escape their vulnerabilities at home.[135] This violence often left deep trauma: "Being attacked, seeing their disposability in the eyes of the perpetrators exposed both the world's dangers and human malevolence in the age of freedom."[136] This was magnified by the failure of community help and the particular consequence of nocturnal action and disguise. One survivor testified to the pain of neglect: "There never were any meetings, or anything of the kind, held for the purpose of putting [nocturnal violence] down. . . . These men traveled in the night; they were unknown to us; we might be conversing with one of them in the street and not know it."[137]

The prominence of night-riding gave way by 1872 to more organized paramilitary white supremacist violence, although night still played a critical role in channeling and hiding violent excesses.[138] A pivotal spasm of paramilitary violence occurred at Colfax, Louisiana, in 1873 that exposed the federal limits to accounting for nocturnal outrage.[139] Colfax was the seat of Grant Parish, several hundred miles from New Orleans, one of several new parishes gerrymandered (and named) to give Republicans a political edge. As legal historian Avi Soifer observes, "The peculiarity of honoring Republican politicians in the middle of Reconstruction Louisiana only begins to suggest the level of discord within state and community politics."[140] This discord grew to a crisis when two men claimed the governorship after a disputed election in 1872, each supported by their own militia, the Republican one partly organized under Black command, and the Democratic one under former Confederate command.

As open warfare seemed likely, each claimant scrambled for advantage, and the Republican, William Pitt Kellogg, sent his militia to Grant Parish to take control of the courthouse. Grant Parish had only a slight Black, and thus Republican, majority, and many of the white families who remained there after the war, when the subsequent national economic tailspin severely weakened the plantations, were small-scale, poor farmers. Black families began moving to Colfax for safety, especially after a party of white men brazenly killed a Black man working outside his rural house seven miles from town. White vigilantes, reinforced by the KKK and the Knights of the White Camelia, amassed outside the town as the Black militia began to dig a defensive earthwork around three sides of the courthouse.[141] White militia members later reported that before the violence, they had spoken around their nightly campfires about how the armed Black men were assuredly planning a white genocide. "The Negroes at Colfax shouted daily across the river to our people that they intended killing every white man and boy, keeping only the young women to raise from them a new breed," one later testified; "Negro men making their brags that they would clean out the white men & then take their women folks for wifes."[142] Committed to ending this imagined plot, the white militias advanced on the courthouse on Easter Sunday armed with a cannon, modern repeating rifles, and horses; the Black defenders were outmanned and severely outgunned as they had only older and smaller weapons.

Before the violence, the whites ordered the Black defenders to leave the courthouse and its vicinity. Following some minor volleys, they turned loose their weapons at the earthworks, forcing the defenders back into the courthouse. At gunpoint, white militia men compelled one Black prisoner to torch the building. Many of the defending occupiers sought to surrender to avoid the flames (some committed themselves to a fiery death) and stacked their guns outside the building, but the whites continued to shoot, believing, erroneously, that the defenders had killed two of their own sent to negotiate a ceasefire.[143] By 3 p.m., the fighting was over. At least thirty-seven surrendered Black fighters were amassed under a tree, yet the victors, who began drinking heavily, were not finished. A survivor told of the individual "who gave the order to shoot us after dark. He said, 'Kill the d___d niggers.'"[144] Guns went off "like popcorn in a skillet," according to one white witness.[145] Most of the prisoners were killed at 9 p.m.; only a few managed to escape in the dark. A total of 165 Black defenders lost their lives in the siege and the nocturnal massacre that followed; four white militia men were killed.

The massacre's aftermath ended the Enforcement Acts of 1870 and 1871, which were designed to quell the KKK. Despite identifying numerous perpetrators, the Justice Department hesitated to bring indictments and tried only nine white men a year after the massacre for intimidation to deprive Black citizens of their rights to assembly, bearing of arms, liberty, and the equal benefit of the laws, as well as their right to vote. One was acquitted, and a mistrial called for the remaining eight.

Justice Joseph Bradley, a dissenter in the *Slaughterhouse Cases* that narrowed the Fourteenth Amendment (announced the day after the Colfax massacre), joined the bench while riding circuit for the second trial several months later.[146] He acquitted the remaining defendants but split his judgment with the trial judge, assuring that the Supreme Court would take the case. Bradley's widely read opinion in *United States v. Cruikshank*, however, was taken as a harbinger of what the full court would do when it heard the appeal, immediately upsetting the delicate political balance that had sustained Reconstruction. Bradley ruled that the Enforcement Acts could not be constitutionally sustained because they specified crimes that intruded into state authority. Bradley maintained that while Congress "has power to enforce, by appropriate legislation, every right and privilege given or guaranteed by the Constitution," it could only "guaranty against the exertion of arbitrary and tyrannical power on the part of the government and legislature of the state, not . . . against the commission of individual offences."[147] The rights protected by the Fourteenth Amendment, in short, were merely particularized enunciations of the constitutional guarantee of republican government.[148] Although the Thirteenth and the Fifteenth Amendments created rights enforceable by the federal government and explicitly for the first time afforded Congress authority to enforce these rights, Bradley asserted that the rights to assemble and to bear arms belong "to the state government alone." Only where injury to another or deprivation of another's rights were "by reason of his race, color, or previous condition of servitude"—that is, with discriminatory intent—could the federal government act.[149] In this case, he argued, this newly minted prerequisite had not been alleged, much less proven.

Despite "the bloody proof that there was no law and no lawful government with enforcement powers in Louisiana in 1873" to protect the rights of freedpersons, the legal fiction of exclusive state governmental responsibility decimated the will of many of Reconstruction's increasingly reluctant supporters, including President Ulysses Grant.[150] Historical debates continue as to why the Republican court betrayed Reconstruction, some arguing that there are legitimate doctrinal reasons that motivated Bradley, others that the enforcement of the Second Amendment against the states had genuinely worrisome consequences in the context of the apparent anarchy in Louisiana. Some maintain that Bradley had pointed to a way to save federal efforts to bring democracy to the South.[151] Regardless of the motivation, Bradley's decision did anything but inspire another effort at federal intervention. As Eric Foner observes, "In the name of federalism, the [Cruikshank] decision rendered national prosecution of crimes committed against blacks virtually impossible and gave a green light to acts of terror where local officials were unable or unwilling to enforce the law."[152] This green light also changed the nature of terror, bringing much of it out of the dark as the federal protections were withdrawn.

Interracial lynching—its predominant social form only after the Civil War—had many rationales, and it lasted well into the twentieth century.[153] Ida B. Wells-Barnett's scholarship at the height of Jim Crow revealed that only 30 percent of the lynchings of Black men at the end of the nineteenth century were for accusations of the rape of white women, despite the vituperative white supremacist ideology "shielding itself behind the plausible screen of defending the honor of its women."[154] Murder, "insubordination," being "too prosperous," and other affronts to the status of whites were the more common justifications.[155] The fear of Black men's propensity to rape was used to justify the possession of private arms for whites; one white man in 1908 was quoted as saying, "We never take our eyes off the gun. . . . I never leave my wife and daughter at home without a [white] man in the house after ten o'clock at night—because I am afraid."[156] The growth of what Carlson calls "gun populism," the idea that good guys have guns to compensate for state incapacity to restrain the (often racialized) bad Other, justified disarming Black people, especially because firearms were sometimes successfully brandished against nocturnal lynching parties.[157] Largely through Black community vigilance, fewer lynchings occurred in counties where Black citizens were a large majority.[158]

Lynching was not merely caste rule by violent coercion, nor can it be reduced to publicly ritualized scenes of subjection, however.[159] With sufficient (white) community participation, racial killing and torture became what Michael Gorup has called "scenes of constitution," establishing the boundaries of the people: "In spectacle lynching, the people—usually a theoretical abstraction—was imagined to appear as a concrete reality, manifesting their power through the exercise of extraordinary violence. The violence of spectacle lynchings should thus be understood as a performative violence that made manifest the very people in whose name it was said to be authorized."[160] Spectacle lynching, stressing the visible projection of sovereign power, often took place during daylight hours, although it was not necessarily inhibited by the night; many nocturnal public lynchings gathered numerous white citizens without disguise for sadistic pleasures and were covered, sometimes luridly, by the local newspapers.

True to republican ideology, this bloody manifestation of the people was also the ritualized repetition of legality, demonstrating the utility of sovereign violence, which continued to overshadow disciplinary and biopolitical forms of power.[161] Although now and then some state officials intervened to prevent lynching, they also have been shown to have regularly yielded to lynching parties and to have facilitated and participated in others.[162] Additionally, whites acted with solidarity on juries, while Black fear and Jim Crow barriers to participation greatly hindered the official machinery of justice.[163] Because of the power of white accusations of Black misconduct to summon violent reprisal, Jim Crow laws "put the authority of the state or city in the voice of the street-car conductor, the railway brakeman, the bus driver, the theater-usher, and also into the voice of the hoodlum of the public parks and playground."[164]

Law was not only state-centric. The spectacle took what appeared lawless and made it into a law outside the law.[165] At its most potent, this law bound elite whites (who participated in and directed many lynchings) with poor and relatively powerless whites. This cementing of caste through coordinated violence—particularly violence that followed a commonly understood idea of legal proportionality and justice amalgamated from common law, statutory authority, and unwritten sensibility—produced a "good lynching." "Good lynchings" re-created the dualism of the Black Codes, constituting what some called "Negro law," which for Black homicide suspects in Mississippi often looked somewhat like this:

> If [a Black man] kills a white man, and is caught, he suffers death in some form or another, the time, place and manner of his execution depending on who caught him, the sheriff's posse or the friends of the deceased. If the sheriff's posse are the first to get him, he is hanged the first Friday after court adjourns, but if the friends of the deceased are the first to get possession of him, he is executed at once, at or near the place where the homicide occurred; the matter of his death being always a matter of [the] individual taste of the parties conducting the ceremonies.[166]

"Good lynchings" in line with "Negro law" were administered openly, with a general invitation to the white community—and infrequently to the Black community—which made participants and observers into a collective jury, at times consisting of up to thousands of people.[167] "Spectacle lynchings sought to reshape national imaginings of the people through the public performance of racialized violence."[168] "Good lynchings" could be extremely violent; some involved the collection of the deceased's body parts as tangible souvenirs of justice. Like the official law that they paralleled, a "good lynching" often displayed a "highly ritualized choreography."[169]

Before 1930, when lynching mostly became rarer and sought the cover of dark, perhaps only one-third of lynchings had such a public character.[170] The alternative "bad lynching" often devolved into mayhem. This type of violent vigilantism "featured a surfeit of liquor and firearms and an unruly, indiscriminate mob that threatened the peace of an entire community."[171] Bad lynching "means a burning."[172] Although this violence was rarely punished through the legal system, it nearly always met with community reproach.[173] A bad lynching was often conducted without the direction or support of elites and was frequently decried by the local press. Bad lynching took place in the dark of night with small parties, eschewing witnesses but leaving charred and mutilated bodies as reminders in the morning light.[174]

The differences between these forms of vigilante horror point toward the republican strictures of permissible quasi-legal norms. The cultural distinctions drawn between good, orderly vigilante justice and unacceptable killing that collapsed rule into "the cruelties of the mob" could publicly represent the republican values of the white community while upholding its internal social structure.[175] Both types of lynching created fear and heavily suppressed Black peoples' freedom and ambitions. Yet one was seen to exhibit an excess unnecessary to, and perhaps corrosive to, the republican values of refinement and "civilization" associated with white supremacy.

The "good" and "bad" vigilantism that created a legal order disarmed and weakened those who were feared as enemies and thus fulfilled the objective of the militia, which was always a central concern of republican ideology and was inscribed in the Constitution. *Militia*, as I have been using the term, should connote not just the formal military organization of the people but the panoply of efforts—even at night—to disarm and disadvantage those whose rights would only detract from the civic peoples' ambitions. Unlike "good" vigilantism, "bad lynchings" had motives and means that would not conform to legality, to representation, or to political norms, even though they reinforced white identity and, by sowing fear, white superiority. Constituting the majority of incidents, "bad lynching" played a significant role in the balance of social forces, even where it could not directly represent political order. The consequence might have been functional to white supremacy, but the means relegated such actions to spaces and times, especially night and darkness, that would not interfere with the legitimate modes of civic republican self-recognition. Indirectly and rhetorically, however, "bad lynching" helped to define "good lynching," smuggling nighttime mayhem into the jurisgenesis that was the law outside the law.[176] A "bad lynching" showed the unspoken power of another form of militia.

Even in contemporary times, as institutions such as the police and mass incarceration have transformed the character of racial violence, they continue to exhibit the republican antagonism of the militia within. Rogue, racist vigilante police organizations persist in the darkness. Behind their nocturnal moniker, the all-white "Midnight Crew" operating within the Chicago Police Department from the 1970s through the 1990s under Commander Jon Burge used horrifying tortures (including electrocution, suffocation, beatings, and more) against more than a hundred Black "suspects," many dishonestly claimed to be illegally purchasing a gun, to coerce false confessions.[177] Squads such as the Midnight Crew were formalized to a larger degree than bad lynchers ever were, but their scandal is no different. Their dark presence suggests that the militia has long persisted beyond its historical demise and has performed more than state theory can account for. And, like earlier vigilantism, the chance discovery and subsequent repudiation of dark forces ultimately reinforces the legitimacy of "normal" police violence.

This republican history is relevant for liberal rights, particularly for the individual right to possess handguns. Turning the corner on nineteenth-century doctrine, articulated in *Cruikshank* and subsequent decisions that refused to read the Second Amendment as securing individual rights to arms, the Supreme Court applied new reasoning, first in a challenge to strict gun laws in Washington, DC, in 2008.[178] Two years later, in a similar case from Chicago, the court, again split five to four, incorporated the Second Amendment to the states and invalidated a local gun control ordinance.[179]

Because of its relevance, I focus on Justice Clarence Thomas's concurring opinion in this second case, *McDonald v. Chicago*, which provided the final vote for incorporation. Rather than accepting the plurality's reasoning that the right to own guns was fundamental and could be absorbed through the due process clause of the Fourteenth Amendment, Thomas argued for eviscerating *Cruikshank* and the *Slaughterhouse Cases*, which had relegated the privileges and immunities clause to irrelevance, making the wholesale incorporation of the Bill of Rights impossible during Reconstruction. Thomas is only the second justice, after Thurgood Marshall, to take aim at *Cruikshank*, which Thomas called "not a precedent entitled to any respect."[180] Returning "faithful[ly] to the Fourteenth Amendment's text and history," including its design to overturn *Dred Scott* and affirm the rights of citizens "to keep and carry arms" while fully incorporating the Bill of Rights, Thomas combed through the history of post–Civil War legislation and amendments and concluded that "the right to bear arms was understood to be a privilege of American citizenship guaranteed by the Privileges or Immunities Clause."[181]

Thomas's historical account emphasizes the renewed anxieties among Southern whites over uprisings by freed Blacks that accounted for the singular focus of the postbellum states on controlling Black citizens' guns and that encouraged abolitionists such as Frederick Douglass to push for protecting the right to bear arms. *Cruikshank*'s denial of this right abandoned Black citizens and inflamed the long campaign of white vigilante violence that lasted into the second half of the twentieth century. As Thomas concludes his fifty-three-page opinion, he deploys a series of images to link this history to a liberal right to guns:

> The use of firearms for self-defense was often the only way black citizens could protect themselves from mob violence. As Eli Cooper, one target of such violence, is said to have explained, "[t]he 'Negro has been run over for fifty years, but it must stop now, and pistols and shotguns are the only weapons to stop a mob.'" . . . Sometimes, as in Cooper's case, self-defense did not succeed. He was dragged from his home by a mob and killed as his wife looked on. . . . But at other times, the use of firearms allowed targets of mob violence to survive. One man recalled the night during his childhood when his father stood armed at a jail until morning to ward off lynchers. . . . The experience left him with a sense, "not 'of powerlessness, but of the "possibilities of salvation"'" that came from standing up to intimidation.[182]

Thomas's salvific picture of a night vigil by a Black gunman tragically calls to mind the nocturnal slaughter at Colfax that the *Cruikshank* opinion ignored. The potential of individual rights to protect a community that Thomas invoked belongs to this night that has been abandoned by republican thought and republican law.

Thomas emotionally anchors his opinion to a memory of night terror that is not his own but is drawn from long-ignored testimonies and privately shared memories. Kidada Williams's study of nineteenth-century congressional testimony given by victims of KKK violence reveals patterns that may not have changed much since: "Although congressmen questioning witnesses did not ask specific questions about the emotional and psychological wounds of racial violence, and testifiers did not name 'trauma' as a consequence of violence, their testimonies about nightriding violence allude to traumatic suffering. Indeed, from victims' and witnesses' testimonies we can see that blacks wanted members of Congress and the public to know that white men's arrival in the middle of the night—both with and without warning—engendered in black families raw feelings of fear, vulnerability, and loss of control. All of these feelings are indicators of the traumas that some families endured."[183] Williams points out that apart from granting a forum to publicize this terror, Congress never protected those who testified. The rare prosecutions of the KKK by a reluctant government were never sufficient to suppress the perpetrators of nocturnal terror. Rather than becoming part of national memory, this testimony mainly left witnesses who testified vulnerable to white reprisal. James Baldwin famously argued, "For the horrors of the American Negro's life there has been almost no language."[184] When there is no political language to mark and bind the memories of nocturnal terror, when memory becomes essentially segregated, its recollection cannot create the political commitment necessary for its control.[185]

Thomas does not comment on white indifference to Black trauma, nor does he address the problem that Black citizens' possession of firearms (and rights generally) continues to provoke anxiety in many whites. He avoids these cultural and political concerns by universalizing an appeal to patriarchal and masculine ideals of "standing up to intimidation" and protecting others, as his example, Eli Cooper, could not do. These two ways of understanding his nocturnal gunman promote both the liberal commitment to the sovereign individual and the republican ideal of the militia, that is, bearing arms for security and for justice. In this manner, night itself becomes culturally assimilable and universal: its meaning as a time of danger and a time for individual self-help is comprehensible to all who have felt fear at night as a dark place to end legal argument.

Yet what is also universal about action at night, as Thomas's language suggests, is that the play of fear on fear leads to uncertain outcomes: "Sometimes . . . self-defense [does] not succeed." This admission by Thomas of the dangers to sovereign individuals that all private guns carry quietly agrees with Justice John Paul Stevens's dissent in *McDonald*, maintaining that "firearms have a fundamentally ambivalent relationship to liberty. Just as they can help homeowners defend their families and property from intruders, they can help thugs and insurrectionists murder innocent victims."[186]

In the same way that Thomas acknowledges that arms may not always succeed, so standing up to intimidation does not distinguish among vigilantes, white or Black, who perpetuate violence to promote the security of their respective communities. This, of course, includes the police, whose killing of (disproportionately Black, and many times unarmed) civilians is almost always justified by the stated fear for their own lives, especially in the dark. This aspect of the militia, the disabling and disarming of identified Others as a corollary to rights to possess and use lethal weaponry, is left unaddressed in Thomas's argument. For Black people to have an equal right to possess and carry guns, they also would have to be free of the odium of dangerousness or, alternatively, to be perceived as powerful enough to be let alone. The ways that Thomas puts night to work pale in comparison to how night in combination with Black arms was made to signify after Christiana.

STANDING YOUR GROUND

Thomas's prominent conclusory icon of a man standing up to intimidation presages George Zimmerman's legally protected killing of Trayvon Martin under the doctrine of "stand your ground." Stand your ground laws have proliferated, most notably in states with a larger and longer history of lynching and extensive racial segregation.[187] Successful use of stand your ground doctrine as an affirmative defense is also racially biased: killings of whites by Blacks are ruled justifiable in about 1 percent of cases, but killings of Blacks by whites raise no legal issues in about 11 percent of cases, and in almost 17 percent of cases in states with stand your ground laws.[188] Designed to protect those who kill under the standard that the killer subjectively feared for their life or the lives of their families, these laws end the common law "duty to retreat"; some extend the right to stand one's ground "beyond the castle," as Zimmerman did on his patrol in public space. Many laws allow shooters even to escape arrest—as Zimmerman did for many months—making police and not prosecutors the main discretionary authorities. That some killing under stand your ground doctrine never makes it into the criminal system renders the full consequences of these laws somewhat difficult to measure. Nonetheless, stand your ground laws, especially where killers are given an affirmative defense outside their homes, have been shown to aggravate interracial violence and killing while actually making little difference in crime rates, which suggests that something beyond rational policymaking drives their popularity.[189]

Although these laws exacerbate racial bias, the terminology of "stand your ground" does not originate in white vigilantism or sovereignty. Frederick Douglass was perhaps the first to use the term *stand your ground*, while recounting the murder of a slave named Bill Denby by overseer Austin Gore, but Douglass's meaning was the reverse of its contemporary usage. Denby refused to abandon the refuge of a creek at Gore's insistence that he submit to a flogging. Douglass writes, "It is said that Gore gave Denby three calls to come out, telling him if he did not obey the last call he should shoot him. When the last call was given Denby still stood his ground, and Gore, without further parley, or without making any further effort to induce obedience, raised his gun deliberately to his face, took deadly aim at his standing victim, and with one click of the gun the mangled body sank out of sight, and only his warm red blood marked the place where he had stood." Although Gore was arraigned for his cruelty, "he, calm and collected, as though nothing unusual had happened, declared that Denby had become *unmanageable*," using a term that, similar to the justifications for invoking stand your ground laws today, is subjective and ultimately incontestable when uttered by those given the privilege of belief in their subjective veracity.[190]

The value of standing your ground for Douglass was its masculinist appeal, similar to what one can impute to Thomas's more recent invocation of nocturnally standing guard. Appeals to masculinity became increasingly unsuccessful for Black men in the second half of the nineteenth century, however. The common charge of rape behind vigilante violence made Black male sexuality appear dangerous to many whites, and the sexual humiliation of men and of families, as well as the confiscation of weapons by vigilantes, generally reinforced the perception that Blacks were not true men or fellow citizens. "True men" did not retreat, as American courts began to assert in the nineteenth century, transforming the British common law of self-defense to merge in the South and the West with a frontier conception of honor.[191] Such honor grew, in part, through white male domination of Black and Native men and women, augmented by a changing "castle doctrine" that made no retreat by the male protector necessary in the home.[192]

The British common law of violent self-defense originally eschewed subjective elements, relying on night as a key to distinguishing permissible actions. One was allowed to kill for self-defense in the night, as obscurity left one at vulnerable disadvantage to burglars.[193] If there were "light enough to discern a man's features, it was not burglary," but this norm was changed to avoid the problems of subjectivity: for the purposes of self-defense, night was defined to "commence at nine, P.M., and to conclude at six, A.M., on the next day."[194] American law made no direct exemption for nocturnal defense, but it did absorb an objectively reasonable "duty to retreat to the wall" before a killing was considered justifiable. Eliminating this duty probably was prompted by the prevalence of guns, which were rare when the British common law of defense was refined. Guns could make the duty to retreat a death sentence.[195] As one of the first American legal opinions to strike down the duty of retreat argued:

It would be good sense for the law to require, in many cases, an attempt to escape from a hand to hand encounter with fists, clubs, and even knives, as a condition of justification for killing in self-defense; while it would be rank folly to so require when experienced men, armed with repeating rifles, face each other in an open space, removed from shelter, with intent to kill or to do great bodily harm. What might be a reasonable chance for escape in the one situation might in the other be certain death. Self-defense has not, by statute nor by judicial opinion, been distorted, by an unreasonable requirement of the duty to retreat, into self-destruction.[196]

Guns create enhanced danger because they are lethal at a distance and also because they are very quickly discharged. These two qualities also matter for the subjectivity of self-defense. Distance overcomes the psychic repugnance at killing, as Chamayou argues, and the instantaneous danger of guns liberalizes the legitimacy of even poorly formed subjective fears.[197] As Justice Oliver Wendell Holmes once felicitously observed, "Detached reflection cannot be demanded in the presence of an uplifted knife."[198] This distortion of rationality is further enhanced when faced with a gun. Add to this equation the context of darkness that boosts uncertainty and danger, and the imperative of diminished hesitation time is melded with psychic disinhibition, lubricating killing. The mere existence of guns means that one need not see another's weapon held in an aggressive and threatening position; darkness means that not seeing becomes the same provocation and justification as seeing a weapon.

Perhaps because night makes the reasonable response to the armed intruder so acute, extension of stand your ground doctrine is sometimes promoted with citations of the perils of night. One Ohio legislator arguing for adoption of stand your ground policy painted this picture to his fellow legislators: "Imagine being in your own home, sound asleep in your own bed. Suddenly, you wake up to an unfamiliar noise. As you stumble to turn on the light, you find that a stranger has forcibly entered your home, potentially to harm you or your family. There is a natural instinct that when someone is jeopardizing the well-being of you and your family, you will take every measure available and necessary to protect your loved ones and your home, even if it results in serious physical harm or death to yourself or the intruder."[199] The author of Florida's Stand Your Ground law, Senator Durell Peaden, relied on an example of a nocturnal killing of a stranger in the yard of James and Kathryn Workman to argue for legislative enactment:

"They didn't know whether the guy was trying to burglarize or what he was doing. They shot him."[200] Obscurity, the violence of night, confusion, and speculation (or projection) of bad intentions: all justify the right to kill without examination or trial.

The logic of stand your ground plays into the instantaneous decision of those who feel a threat. Behavioral and cognitive research suggests that Charles Lawrence III's important and oft-cited claim for the violence of unconscious racism greatly matters in such instantaneous decisions.[201] While explicit racial stereotypes are publicly discouraged, the unconscious nature of racial prejudice is revealed in psychological studies that show "how human mental machinery can be skewed by lurking stereotypes, often bending to accommodate hidden biases reinforced by years of social learning."[202] This research demonstrates that judges and juries recall facts in ways that are racially biased (e.g., remembering aggressive facts about a Black story character but not about white characters), that people implicitly associate guilt with Black characters, and that people are quicker to identify what they believe to be weapons in the hands of Black people than whites.[203] In a review of this literature, Cynthia Lee has concluded that these and additional studies

> provide strong evidence that individuals are quicker to associate Black individuals with weapons and to perceive Blacks as armed and dangerous, regardless of whether they are actually armed and dangerous. Given this strong tendency to associate Blacks with weapons, it may have been more likely that Zimmerman jumped to the conclusion that Martin's movements were life-threatening when he might not have perceived those same movements as life-threatening if they had come from a White person. While punching Zimmerman, Martin's hands presumably came close to Zimmerman's stomach area. Zimmerman may have thought Martin was attempting to reach for Zimmerman's gun when perhaps Martin had no such intention.[204]

While these behavioral studies conclude that the perceived need for a quick judgment about the danger of a stranger produces more violent actions against Black suspects, these studies have yet to ask how darkness or nighttime affects this decision-making, though they suggest a likely correlation.

One way to investigate the significance of night and race in this instantaneous decision to kill is to analyze police killings. Research has shown that police killings of Black individuals increase as a function of the rate of Black-on-white homicide (but not the inverse) and that a diverse police force tends to reduce the number of killings by police.[205] Police, like civilians, are administratively excused or otherwise avoid prosecution for killing when they successfully claim to act under the fear of imminent death in their encounters with civilians.[206] About forty to fifty police officers are killed feloniously per year in the United States; in turn, police kill about 1,100 civilians per year. These numbers, per capita, are dramatically higher than in much of the rest of the world: over one hundred times the rate in England and Wales, for example.[207] As with "bad lynchings" that were rarely politically counted, the *Lancet* has estimated that more than half of all police killings are unreported to the National Vital Statistics System, and race data for those killed are further obscured in many states.[208] The greatest underreporting was for Black men and women, whose deaths at the hands of police were 59.6 percent underreported.[209] This recent study, like others, uses alternative methods and statistical techniques to recover killings left in the shadows.

The *Washington Post* has independently collected ongoing statistics on a shocking 6,509 individual police killings in the United States from 2015 to August 2021, data that will be valuable for further analysis. Although only 0.6 percent of police deaths are caused by civilians wielding knives (a total that is zero in many years), on average police killed more than 135 people so armed during these years. As many as 95 percent of felonious police deaths occur from guns (about 47 per year, or an estimated 329 during this period). Police, in turn, killed 3,746 civilians who held guns or where guns were recovered from the scene.

Despite these virtual and potential threats to the lives and safety of police, 416 of the civilians killed by police during this period were unarmed, and they provide a subset, summarized in table 2.1, to enable us to see the effects of police misimpressions of the danger they face, and when these killings occur.[210] Of those who are unarmed and killed by police, 33 percent are Black, which overrepresents by more than two times the percentage of the Black population at large, a number that is also one-third higher than the overall rate at which police kill Black suspects who have weapons. When I researched this subset for the time of killing, I found that unarmed Black victims suffer death at slightly greater rates at night (by about 2 percent).[211] But in the Southern states with a long history of violent interracial vigilantism, as explored earlier in this chapter, over 49 percent of those unarmed civilians who are killed by police at night are Black. In comparison, if one considers all police killings in the South (of those armed

TABLE 2.1 Police Killings by Race and Time

ALL KILLINGS

	US population (%)	Civilians killed (%)	Unarmed (%)	Delta, pop[1]
BLACK	13.4	23.79	33.27	(+) 2.48
HISPANIC	18.5	16.61	18.75	(+) 1.03
WHITE	60.1	45.51	42.18	(−) 0.70
OTHER	8.0	3.75	3,57	(−) 0.45
UNKNOWN		10.34	2.23	
N		6,509	414	

NIGHT KILLINGS

	Unarmed (%)	Unarmed, South (%)	Unarmed, non-South (%)
BLACK	35. 27	49.41	26.62
HISPANIC	18.75	9.41	24.46
WHITE	40.18	38.82	41.01
OTHER	3.57	1.18	5.04
UNKNOWN	2.23	1.18	2.88
N	224	85	139

Sources: Washington Post, 2015 to August 2021. U.S. Census Bureau.
Night coding by author.
[1] Factor of over- or under-representation of unarmed fatal victims of
police by national racial population (Column 3 divided by Column 1).

and unarmed, during the day and at night) around 29 percent of those killed are Black.[212] (Black people make up 19.6 percent of the population in these Southern states.) When one out of every two police executions of unarmed Black people takes place at night, what must it take to overlook the blatant racial dimension of this violence? Of course, anti-Black violence in the North persists disproportionately, too, at twice the rate of the Black population, suggesting this is a national tragedy.

What can these figures tell us? Police who think they see a gun when they see a cell phone ("he [Stephon Clark] had something in his hands, looked like a gun from our perspective") or when they see a movement in the dark ("[Frankie] Anchondo continued to move laterally by side stepping and facing the officer with the object [electronic cigarette] in his hand") imagine a danger that is disproportionately racialized.[213] In too many cases, that suspect is killed within mere seconds. Even when there is a permitted weapon, as in the case of Philando Castile discussed earlier, a lethal response can swiftly ensue. Night certainly has a psychoanalytic affinity for the unconscious, including for racism, as Thomas's nocturnal gunman represents.[214] Considering the South's long history of nocturnal vigilante violence directed against Black people, these data may suggest that more than generalized unconscious racism is at stake. In addition, long-institutionalized police practices may contribute, including the lingering civic republican "virtues" of disarming and killing Black men and sometimes women.

In his extensive empirical studies of contemporary police killings, Franklin Zimring notes that American police forces are somewhat impervious to scientific or legal efforts to hold themselves accountable for killing. Law enforcement has frequently generated its own loose guidance for the use of deadly force without any demonstration of the reality of the dangers police face. Policing, disconnected from science and rational policy, is inherently anarchic and archaic, according to Zimring.[215] It also relies on the immediacy of fear. "In the overwhelming majority of all circumstances that produce lethal force by the police (more than 95 percent), it is the police who are believed to be at risk," a reflexive situation conducive to violence, especially in a darkness historically charged as the time for disarming and disabling racialized threats.[216] In a night that has long been contested for racial advantage, the tactical power of the hunt may predominate over any legal restraint. As Chamayou argues, "The cynegetic power inherited by the modern police force developed largely outside the judicial framework that now justifies it. So although the police officially justifies its existence by constant reference to the legal system and to the law, in practice it remains largely blind. [Alphonse] Bertillon is very clear on this subject: the police make no use of the legal system; therefore it is pointless to inflict elaborate legal training on them."[217]

As in the recitation of nocturnal threats that justify stand your ground laws, night and darkness may be more nefariously deployed as a cover for violent police actions and as a veil for the hunt. Body cameras, when worn or activated at all, don't work well in the dark and so can't live up to their promise of optical restraint.[218] It is troubling to think that the images of night deployed by Justice Thomas to legitimate a constitutional right to possess a gun for self-defense are similarly used as cover by police who kill on the mere suspicion that racialized Others hold weapons in the dark and pose a deadly risk to those who enforce the law.

CONCLUSION

Because of a tortured, racist history of nocturnal violence over the right to possess and carry guns, it is not surprising that many political advertisements advocating private gun ownership and Second Amendment rights rely on images of guns displayed in the light of day. Daylight and its promise of visibility continue to have strong republican and liberal associations with the idea and the exercise of public rights. Nor may it be surprising that few advertising images can be found illustrating the use of firearms against a human target; like beer ads, which in the United States do not include potentially "immoral" depictions of people actually quaffing the brew, the portrayal of gun use against intruders is rarely put front and center for public consumption. Yet there are a few politicized depictions of gun use, and there it is possible to find the night. Consider figure 2.1, which is an ad from a right-wing website dedicated to advancing gun rights and white supremacy, among other American values. The gloom of night in this advertisement obscures the invader. It hides—we are told—either a police intrusion or an invasion by "gangbangers" (read dangerous Black men). "Decide Now!" it orders, telling the reader at the bottom, "Bang! He wasn't a cop . . ." This Bang might resound from a gun held by the gangbanging invader, or it could explode from the well-prepared defender's firearm. In either case, this Bang is the cracking sound that cleaves a space and a time between (untrustworthy and unverifiable) state authority and armed Black intruders: night.

FIGURE 2.1 *Source:* http://watchmen-news.com/wp-content/uploads/2014/03/nighttime-raid-610x400.jpg.

Georg Wilhelm Friedrich Hegel's owl of Minerva flew at dusk.[219] This image suggests that, at the end of the day, philosophical reason can only follow a real event. This chapter has argued, alternatively, that the experience of night may stage the event itself and should not be allegorized purely as a time for contemplation, unhinged from the legal event. Through efforts to control danger, the radically egalitarian experience of nocturnal insecurity has been transformed within a racialized time in which imagination of threats to security and sleep justifies the right to own guns and to kill, to maintain an imagined autonomy from law for some who seek domination, and to remember the long night of racial terror that the law has actively facilitated or passively ignored for those who are prey.

The short cycles of day and night can call to mind the divergent origins of legal meaning. For whites promoting gun ownership, it is the enlightened time of the founders, who understood the virtue of a check on overweening government authority. Yet for many Black people hunted and killed in the maintenance of white supremacy, it is the incompletion of these rights of citizenship promised during Reconstruction, linked to the insistent unwillingness of the state to diminish nocturnal terror, the enduring violence of slavery that long predated the Constitution. Ironically, the gloom of night actually may help us to see race in a "postracial" or "color-blind" society, a cruel perspective advanced by courts and their supporters to roll back affirmative action, ignore statistical measures of racial treatment, and put the legal significance of race to sleep.

CHAPTER THREE

CURFEW, LEGALITY, AND THE SOCIAL CONTROL OF THE NIGHT

Conditions went from bad to worse. No one could tell when he might be arrested for breaking the curfew. You could not even move across the courtyard at night. Fires were put out early for fear that any light would attract the attention of those who might be lurking outside. It was said that some European soldiers were catching people at night, and having taken them to the forest would release them and ask them to find their way back home. But when their backs were turned they would be shot dead in cold blood. The next day this would be announced as a victory over Mau Mau. **—Ngũgĩ wa Thiong'o**

So it is evening. Don't ask the exact time, only the Germans know that; we have no clocks or watches. . . . This happens right in the middle of the street, the Kurländischer Damm, close to the ghetto boundary where most of the tailors used to be located. There stands the sentry, fifteen feet above Jacob, on a wooden tower behind the barbed wire stretched clear across the street. . . . "Am I mistaken, or is it forbidden to be on the street after eight o'clock?" the soldier says at last. One of the easygoing kind, his voice doesn't even sound angry, quite mild in fact. One might feel like having a chat; a touch of humor might not be out of place. "It is forbidden," says Jacob. "And what time is it now?" "I don't know." "But you ought to know," the soldier says. **—Jurek Becker**

Two early governmental responses to the coronavirus pandemic in 2020 were quarantine and curfew. In Nairobi, Kenya, a thirteen-year-old was shot dead on his balcony by police on the fourth night of a curfew, the second police killing at a time when only one Kenyan had succumbed to the virus; at least ten more were killed, and more still injured, within the first two weeks.[1] Without enacting martial law or emergency legislation, Puerto Rico restricted citizens to their homes from 7 p.m. to 5 a.m.[2] Thailand imposed a 10 p.m. to 4 a.m. curfew restricting all but essential workers to their homes but, unlike many other global responses, did not impose daytime restrictions.[3] In Rio de Janeiro, drug gangs imposed their own nocturnal curfew in the favelas under their control.[4] Nightly curfews were imposed in prior epidemics in some localities, but with other public health measures promoting what has been called *social distancing*, what does curfew add to quarantine?[5] What might explain Thailand's commitment to curfew over quarantine, for example? Or Kenya's use of lethal measures to prevent the lethality of disease?

In short, what difference does a curfew make? Temporal legal pluralism—the oscillation of systems of governance between day with its regimes of visibility, open courtrooms, and legal busyness and night with its surveillance, heightened suspicions, and privatized vigilance—already drives nocturnal confinement. The etymology of the English word is received from the French *couvre-feu*, a nightly order to return to dwellings and extinguish hearth and candle fires in light of the diminishing capacity of the state to offer anything but symbolic protection from vagabonds, witches, and the lascivious temptations of dance and debauchery.[6] Curfew is thus recalled as a sign (manifest by the giant chains slung nightly across roads to block movement) that night was a material factor in self and public order.[7] Not only was the collective threat of conflagration diminished by this early command to submit to a darkened dwelling. Additionally, "curfew served both to pre-empt political conspiracies, which the authorities thought were most likely to be cooked up after dark, and, above all perhaps, to preserve regular hours, in order to promote industry and piety."[8] Similar curfews were common in ancient Japan, China, India, and other countries.[9] What elements of these continuing concerns for safety, morality, and stability made immanent by nightfall are transformed by the political imposition of contemporary curfew orders?

Judging from the remarkable paucity of sociolegal, epidemiological, and historical research into curfew, we have left this question hanging in the dark.[10] The modern form of curfew—its functions and its meanings for legal thought as well as its specific forms of violence—seems somewhat obscured under these same early beliefs that night and darkness naturally pose problems for governance, problems that can be managed best by shutting in. Our lack of attention and inquiry seems most surprising when we consider the wide resort to curfew orders in the past century and the biopolitical value of curfews for defining and disabling particular populations. Curfews—primarily but not only nocturnal orders—have been widely imposed on youth around the world; have become an integral and sometimes permanent aspect of social control in colonial and settler-colonial contexts (for example, over fifteen thousand curfews were imposed in Palestine in the six years following the first Intifada in 1987); form a policy response to resistance against excessive police violence against Blacks in the United States, as happened in many American locales in response to the public execution of George Floyd in 2020; are casually applied to women and girls in the name of personal safety and sexual control; and provide a paradoxical form of controlling the homeless, who have no dwellings to which to retreat.[11] If night already allows cover for the racialized violence that reorders the day, if night hides the ghosts and witches of disorder as well as the all-seeing and never-sleeping eye of the sovereign discussed in chapter 1, what difference might the formal embrace of nocturnal constraints, as well as spatial limits for some, make for what we can know about law and the night?

That curfew becomes a potent place to think through these questions is evident in even mundane cultural language about it. Following the assassination of Martin Luther King Jr. in 1968, many urban curfews were imposed in the United States, ostensibly to contain the dangers of violent protest. One teacher, realizing her young students feared curfew as a "ghost or witch of some sort—something that comes only at night and (in their fantasies) hides under beds and in closets and even under their pillows," created a lesson to teach an answer to "What is a curfew?" and shared it in an article entitled "Cities Aflame . . . Young Imaginations on Fire":

> Yes, that's right—it's a time when you stay inside; it's a rule that you have to stay in your house for a while. Yes, every night we had a curfew—a rule that we had to stay inside. The mayor told the radio and television people, and you heard them announce it, didn't you? "There will be a curfew tonight from 4:00 o'clock until 6:00 o'clock tomorrow morning." "Curfew will start tonight at 7:00 o'clock," and so on. And

grown-ups read it in the newspapers and you heard them say, "Hey, curfew's at 5:30 this evening. We have to get home before curfew; come on!" That was the mayor's rule—the curfew—to help control the rioters by keeping them in their houses. And we all stayed in, didn't we? We didn't like curfew, but it was a good rule to help the rioters control themselves, wasn't it?[12]

In transforming the childish yet historically resonant images of fearful ghosts and witches hiding under the bed into reasonable rules aiding "rioters" to self-manage their internal demons, the curfew emerges in this lesson as a benign effort to limit chaos and disorder through governmentality. Behind the dissimulating image of a painless antidote to fear and terror, the curfew's own ferocity, racism, and exceptionality remain unstated and unimagined.

In this chapter I aim to tease out how curfew governs. I argue that modern curfew, which is justified as a special exception to the law necessary to save sovereign power and social order, entangles vigilance and law in ways that confuse the roles of public spaces with those of private spaces, the norms of state procedures with those of vigilantes, the valence of legal benevolence with lethality, and the temporality of discipline with the daily cycles of night and day. This confusion makes the curfew difficult to control ideologically, rendering its political value uncertain. In efforts to stabilize what is muddled, struggles over curfew borrow from cultural meanings of the night as a time of danger (made more so by reminders of state incapacity), and of a sometimes-insurgent, sometimes-exhilarating equality, as well as drawing on some of the ideological political and social values of the premodern curfew.[13] The recovery of meanings associated with night and legality forms the inquiry of this chapter. To illuminate what has been too long left in shadow, I read across various literatures and contexts that have addressed specific curfews in order to understand the life of this extraordinary and ordinary measure.

THE EXCEPTIONAL AMBIGUITIES OF CURFEW

One of the paradoxes of the state of exception lies in the fact that in the state of exception, it is impossible to distinguish transgression of the law from execution of the law, such that what violates a rule and what conforms to it coincide without any remainder (a person who goes for a walk during the curfew is not transgressing the law any more than the soldier who kills him is executing it). —**Giorgio Agamben**

When the law is in force only in the form of its suspension, no matter what mode of behaviour appears to be in line with the law in a normal situation—like walking peacefully down the street—this behaviour might also imply a transgression—as, for example, in the case of a curfew. Vice versa, the transgression may even be conceived of as carrying out the law. In this sense, one could say that in the state of exception, the law, inasmuch as it simply coincides with reality, is absolutely unobservable [*ineseguibile*], and that unobservability [*ineseguibilità*] is the originary figure of the norm. —**Giorgio Agamben**

Giorgio Agamben's references above to the modern curfew, published originally in 1995 and 2000, suggest that curfew epitomizes a paradox at the heart of a persisting sovereign power, one that he elsewhere blames for the genocidal experiences with biopower since the beginning of the twentieth century.[14] Agamben's concept of "biopolitical sovereignty," which captures his political analysis of the lingering effects of the murder of European Jews in the Shoah, combines (uneasily for his critics) a transcendental and unitary Schmittian/Hobbesian notion of sovereignty with Michel Foucault's dispersed idea of biopower.[15] In short, Carl Schmitt derives power ontologically (it is always already sovereign) and as a "borderline concept" that takes the exceptional to define the general case, exemplified by an authoritative decision to suspend law in order to save it.[16] As one commentator frames it, "Sovereign power is for Schmitt the legal concept of a transcendental power that rests on an arbitrary decision whose legitimacy is sustained by its (symbolic) authority."[17] This symbolic legitimation is energized by the irruption and anomie of life that both disturb the conditions of the norm and ground the basis of a decision to preserve the life of the nation. As Schmitt argues, "The exception is more interesting than the rule. The rule proves nothing; the exception proves everything: It confirms not only the rule but also its existence, which derives only from the exception. In the exception the power of real life breaks through the crust of a mechanism that has become torpid by repetition."[18]

Foucault opposed the sovereign origin of biopolitics and its exclusive power of life and death, instead tying biopolitics to a historically emergent set of powers, including disciplinary powers focusing on the body and regulatory powers governing populations, all of which govern life and make it the highest political value.[19] Biopower is not centralized for him, nor is it transcendental; immanent and incomplete, it is always breeding resistance, and it incites normative behaviors while producing knowledge and truth. Noticeably, neither Schmitt nor Foucault discusses the curfew in their many texts. In what ways does the example of the curfew hold together these disparate ways of approaching power for Agamben?

The curfew names a state of exception for Agamben, which—following Schmitt—is the convoluted form of sovereign power:

> The exception that defines the structure of sovereignty is . . . complex. Here what is outside is included not simply by means of an interdiction or an internment, but rather by means of the suspension of the juridical order's validity—by letting the juridical order, that is, withdraw from the exception and abandon it. The exception does not subtract itself from the rule; rather, the rule, suspending itself, gives rise to the exception and, maintaining itself in relation to the exception, first constitutes itself as a rule. The particular "force" of law consists in this capacity of law to maintain itself in relation to an exteriority.[20]

Agamben argues here that the exception, as an exteriority to law, tends to increasingly dominate the rule. The premodern European curfew regularly suspends diurnal freedoms of motion as a collective prohibition establishing security and enforcing a moral way of life—often naturally timed with the daily cycles of light and dark that reinforce some norms of life even where night may suspend the regular use of law. In contrast, the modern curfew serves as one example of the violent character of the exception when it eclipses the rule, backed by a level of force inconceivable in premodern times.

As both Ngũgĩ wa Thiong'o and Jurek Becker observe in the epigraphs to this chapter, the curfew can be intentionally injected with uncertainty, establishing the parameters of a game without any clear rules. Agamben claims the "true horror" of Auschwitz to be condensed in the seeming normalcy of a soccer game between guards and inmates that interrupts the daily horror of death. The rules of the game are not suspended, but the context of everyday life is deferred. "That match is never over; it continues as if uninterrupted. It is the perfect and eternal cypher of the 'gray zone,' which knows no time and is in every place."[21] Curfew, in contrast, depends on the play of a certain time and a particular place. Becker's character Jacob is permitted no wristwatch or clock by decree but is toyed with by his guard, who tries to trick Jacob into violating the 8 p.m. curfew. Ngũgĩ writes of an order that is itself imbued with violation: obey and be shot for breaking the curfew, disobey and suffer a similar fate for disregarding the immediate order to disperse. Both of these vignettes suggest that what Agamben calls the essential unobservability of the norm is something machined and constructed, hidden in the dark.

Slavoj Žižek tells a macabre joke from Poland following Wojciech Jaruzelski's 1981 military coup that provides another illustration of this ludic violence: "At that time, military patrols had the right to shoot without warning at people walking on the streets after curfew (ten o'clock). One of . . . two soldiers on patrol sees somebody in a hurry at ten minutes to ten and immediately shoots him. When his colleague asks him why he shot when it was only ten to ten, he answers: 'I knew the fellow—he lived far from here and in any case would not be able to reach his home in ten minutes, so to simplify matters, I shot him now.'"[22] Although this joke releases the black humor of sovereign violence, the laughter it provokes depends on the absurdity of what is, usually, impossible: establishing the prior identity of those who are blithely shot in the gloom of night. It is this knowledge that the curfew denies or withholds, not simply because of the indeterminacy of the norm but because this indeterminacy is often staged in darkness. What it means to achieve certainty at night has always been a problem for and lubricant of nocturnal governance.

TO BE VIGILANT

The play with temporal modes shifted by the curfew order in Žižek's joke dredges to the surface a phenomenological problem of knowledge experienced by those under the command of the curfew to be vigilant of emergency orders governing time and space. Vigilance is integrated into many facets of modern life, where it helps orient us to appropriate forms of individualized caution and legitimates authorities tasked with looking out for our interests. "Don't be afraid. Be vigilant" was the advice of American vice president Mike Pence in response to the threat of the coronavirus pandemic in 2020.[23] The imperative of vigilance over the long term may be overt in a neoliberal or risk society, where it condenses a new form of politics around the figure of the responsible individual who must practice self-care, while also reinforcing the more limited responsibility of the state for national security or public health.[24]

However, the curfew may drive this demand for and expectation of alertness beyond such representational schemes of governance by interrupting future temporality. The phenomenologist Edmund Husserl argued that the temporal event draws evenly from nonrepresentational retentions of recent experience and from "protentions" of future experience: "The essence of perception . . . has a punctual now in view and has dismissed from view a just-having-been [and] it goes over from now to now and fore-seeing faces each one. The wakeful consciousness, the wakeful life, is a living-in-the-face-of, a living from one now toward the next."[25] In his own existential phenomenology, Martin Heidegger also emphasized the future, weighing its significance more than the just-having-been. The "existential project of existence revealed itself as an anticipatory resoluteness . . . the being toward one's ownmost, eminent potentiality of being. . . . *The primary phenomenon of primordial and authentic temporality is the future.*"[26] Future time, emphasized in these otherwise-disparate views as essential to consciousness, being, and potential, is violently jolted in the curfew. Seen from the perspective of the victim in Žižek's joke, his vigilance about time and place, heightened by the impending curfew, is surprised and defeated by the soldier's simultaneous suspension and enforcement of the temporal rule starting the curfew.

Vigilance struggles with a loss of protention and future orientation in the curfew, leaving it in ontological tension with modes of consciousness able to account for law. As the philosopher Raymond Duval explains:

> In the diversity of its modes, vigilance remains ready to react in the face of the unpredictable and ready against any failure. . . . Doubt does not weaken awareness; on the contrary, it increases vigilance. And this is why vigilance, the confrontation of time, is always seized by time. . . . To be vigilant is to be ready to react to an event about which we do not know when it will happen, in what form it will occur, or even if it will happen. To be vigilant is to be ready in the face of an uncertain contingency so as not to be surprised. . . . *Vigilance is not based on any anticipation precisely because it opens to the unpredictable where any anticipation risks leading to a decrease in vigilance, insofar as it makes believe that one has reduced the unknown of what remains in suspense.*[27]

The vigilance without anticipation that Duval emphasizes is pure potential: an openness to a world without prediction and control that renders one vulnerable. As the feminist philosopher Erinn Gilson writes, "Vulnerability is defined by openness and affectivity, and such openness entails the inability to predict, control, and fully know that to which we are open and how it will affect us. That kernel of the unpredictable, uncontrollable, and unknown can prompt in us alteration that is likewise unpredictable, uncontrollable, and unknown."[28] Vigilance, in Foucault's words, is "a place without space, where eyes remain open, ears cocked, the entire mind alert, and words mobilized for a movement that [one does] not yet know."[29] Defying anticipation where cause and consequence are no longer mappable and where we are altered by our vulnerability, the extreme vigilance that Duval describes appears to flout the juridical, every bit as much as does sleep.[30] Every attempt at reasoning or anticipating a particular danger diminishes the vigilance necessary for the dangers unseen and unimagined.[31]

The heightened vigilance demanded by the curfew is self-defeating where the exception overtakes the rule and future threats cannot be anticipated. Political and social contexts exacerbating vigilance are limit cases with disabling potential. As Jacques Roux notes, "To call for vigilance is to emphasize a priority a priori and make invisible other options, diverting the citizen from an active posture of precaution by enlarging a danger (for example, playing on the emotional) or by not giving the opportunity to adequately situate oneself."[32] Without reliable or possible "protentions," ontological difficulties abound. One set of possibilities is uncertainty and anxiety. Heidegger argued that anxiety is, like extreme vigilance, a temporal attunement that finds no hold on things encountered in the world, no means with which to feel at home. Anxiety is akin to darkness. "In the dark there is emphatically 'nothing' to see, although the world is *still* 'there' *more obtrusively*." Anxiety "only brings one into the mood for a possible resolution," which may lead to new forms of sociality, or it may resolve itself once the temporal conditions for normative life return or when a longing for normality short-circuits this anxiety.[33]

The lack of possible protention might also lead to violence and misery. Henrik Vigh's ethnographic study of Bissau and Belfast, two cities with a history of perpetual social conflict, discovers a "hyper-vigilance" toward what he calls the "negative potentialities of social figures and forces." These are "shadow worlds" in which unseen and dangerous others, like the witches who inspired the original European curfews, threaten mayhem. The violence that results from the perception of so many threats, he suggests, is usually interpreted by the perpetrators as defensive. Ultimately, these conditions become ontological; bodies are transformed into signs that reproduce the conditions for hypervigilance.[34] Vigh's study is instructive for the curfew. Where the demand for vigilance is amplified, a barely hospitable and violent society can result.

INCITING LAW

Because of the difficult demands or impossible expectations of heightened vigilance that I have just discussed, definite rules and norms—or even their mere promise—confer individual and social relief. A curfew temporarily requires a particular kind of vigilance or self-discipline: an effort to timely heed the boundaries between the sanctuary of the dwelling, or the designated space, and the zone of enhanced danger. How might the curfew's oscillation between nocturnal exception and diurnal rule re-create the basis for juridical authority?

Agamben argues that concentration camps as well as refugee camps, both contrived arrangements like the curfew that are increasingly visible since the beginning of the twentieth century, form spaces situated ambivalently beyond and within the juridical order: "Insofar as the state of exception is 'willed,' it inaugurates a new juridico-political paradigm in which the norm becomes indistinguishable from the exception. The camp is thus the structure in which the state of exception—the possibility of deciding on which founds sovereign power—is realized *normally. . . . The camp is a hybrid of law and fact in which the two terms have become indistinguishable.*"[35] Camps, like other institutions such as penitentiaries and systems of parole, create permanent or lingering conditions of civil and social death in which rules and law lose their meaning.[36] Yet while the curfew may similarly confound fact and law, definitionally it is not total like the camp, a condition without which Žižek's joke would have no bite. Agamben emphasizes the quality of permanence denoted by the camp: "*The camp is the space that opens up when the state of exception starts to become the rule.* In it, the state of exception, which was essentially a temporal suspension of the state of law, acquires a permanent spatial arrangement that, as such, remains constantly outside the normal state of law. . . . The camp is the structure in which the state of exception is permanently realized."[37] The long-term endurance of camps such as Auschwitz initiates in world history "the irrecoverable crisis of authentic temporality. . . . The camp, the absolute situation, is the end of every possibility of an originary temporality. . . . Waking is now forever drawn into the inside of the dream."[38] The camp has made day permanently subservient to the hallucinations of the night.

Although Agamben deploys the curfew as the paradigm of the exception, as discussed above, it seems in tension with this oneiric permanence of the camp. Nonetheless, the significance of the cyclical nature of the curfew is hinted at by Agamben in several texts. It is, I think, realized but not emphasized by Agamben (or his critics) when he claims that *homo sacer*— that being occupying an increasingly common position lacking political or legal status, who can be killed without the symbolic value of sacrifice—is the ancient werewolf that "remain[ed] in the collective unconscious as a monstrous hybrid of human and animal, divided between the forest and the city."[39] The werewolf's "banishment is meant to increase the image of his presumptive dangerousness," making it a fitting allegory for one banned by the law.[40] The European cultural memory of the emblematic werewolf, which Agamben intimates "goes all the way back to the period of pre-social life," is frequently told as a lunar and nocturnal curse.[41] In many ancient narratives and most Hollywood scripts, the werewolf reverts to a man (and, rarely, a woman) imbued with all the elements of legal personality on the rising of the sun.

With important exceptions that I address later, the modern curfew *is* like the werewolf, imagined and instituted to be temporary in two senses. Like the premodern curfew, it most often applies only at night, and unlike the older style, it is imagined as enforceable for a finite number of days. Curfew is a restraint on space and time that promises release: there will be daylight and public forms of knowledge.[42] With this return to a panoptic regime of visibility, legal norms will again predominate.[43] Waiting for (or enacting a vigil for) daylight expresses a desire for an external vantage point and an escape from the temporal paradox of hypervigilant waiting, an outside not incorporated as an included exclusion, a witness to the excesses of nocturnal power. It is, Foucault reminds us, "the excitement and stir of light's promise" that entwines itself with the anticipation of nocturnal danger.[44] Of course, yearning for the day is not the same as anticipating justice. Attending the daybreak may be another way of accepting one's fate under a law oriented against one's interests and even one's life, and this may be the most potent lesson taught by the curfew.

This does not mean that forms of life are fully disrupted by the curfew; disciplinary power may continue to reproduce individual or family security. And in its confusion of rule and exception, curfew may secrete (both exude and cache) opportunities for resistance, whether by the soldiers who imperfectly guard the time of the curfew or by individuals who in their interrupted anticipation of the future find themselves capable of creating political and social innovation.[45] Significantly, the curfew's requirement for vigilance is temporary and regular: in the (however false) promise of predictability, it remains tied to the relatively greater certainty of rule and law. In this manner, the curfew may be said to incite law. The temporal aspects of curfew align with Schmitt's argument that the sovereign suspends the law in order to save it in the long run. But this deferral sits uneasily with Foucault's ideas of biopower. The application of the curfew may make some populations, entrapped in the uncertainty of fact and norm, more vulnerable than others. Because curfews are often nocturnal, it is more difficult to sustain knowledge of individuals who may be particularly dangerous to social order; for this reason, all are treated as populations that require restraint.[46] Curfews also require and teach individual discipline, as the guard toying with Jacob makes clear. Disciplinary power is explicitly temporal for Foucault, and it also opens the field of power to new places where law persists and fills around individuals, not just populations.[47] Foucault writes:

> Whereas the juridical systems define juridical subjects according to universal norms, the disciplines characterize, classify, specialize; they distribute along a scale, around a norm, hierarchize individuals in relation to one another and, if necessary, disqualify and invalidate. In any case, in the space and during the time in which they exercise their control and bring into play the asymmetries of their power, they effect a suspension of the law that is never total, but is never annulled either. Regular and institutional as it may be, the discipline, in its mechanism, is a "counter-law." And, although the universal juridicism of modern society seems to fix limits on the exercise of power, its universally widespread panopticism enables it to operate, on the underside of the law, a machinery that is both immense and minute, which supports, reinforces, multiplies the asymmetry of power and undermines the limits that are traced around the law.[48]

To the extent that the curfew—which demands individual compliance with time, space, and sometimes noise and light limits—remains contestable, there counterlaw may develop, Foucault's arguments suggest. Counterlaw is a law taken into the body formed by disciplinary power, a body that somatically knows sleep and the night and its morning release.[49] Eric Santner captures this corporeal tension between denial and desire for law through an analysis of Sigmund Freud's understanding of projection: "What is abolished internally, the *shelter* of the rule of law, returns in the real of the exception as *exposure* to the pure force of law."[50]

In her postscript to *Eichmann in Jerusalem*, Hannah Arendt expresses the difficulty of knowing within a given legal system (authoritarian or not) which order is so "manifestly unlawful" that it must be disobeyed (a question that Adolf Eichmann would not ask himself).[51] One can, she argues, look to appeals to necessity under the doctrine of raison d'état to argue that state crimes are an exception to the rule, rather than its foundation, a determination that escapes juristic concepts. Or one could argue that one acted on superior orders except where those orders are criminal. In assessing this alternative, Arendt looks at the Israeli trial court's cited precedent in a 1957 case at the border village of Kfar Qasim. This case involved a massacre by Israeli military of Palestinian civilians who were outside their houses without knowledge they were violating a recently imposed curfew order. Despite having the exceptional authority to shoot violators of the curfew, the soldiers were convicted of murder. They were, however, sentenced lightly due to the accepted defense that they were following superior orders, suggesting to Arendt the inadequacy of juridical concepts in environments of exception and, ultimately, the supplemental needs for justice and the judgment its realization requires. Nonetheless, her example of the curfew violence and the (at least formal) conviction of the soldiers is a reminder of the easier traverse toward law that can be found in curfew than in the environment dominated by the Nazi-devised Shoah. Curfew can incite a movement toward a transcendent notion of legality beyond emergency.

This incitement, as I have been arguing, is conditioned by the kinds of ambiguities enhanced by an oscillating form of governance that curfew delimits. Home becomes both shelter and prison depending on the time of day or period of curfew enforcement.[52] The state occupies the social position of vigilante, simultaneously expressing its coercive power and acknowledging its weakness at night through emergency action. Drawing from premodern images of the curfew (which itself produced a proto–police force via the night watch who oversaw it), the modern curfew nostalgically legitimates itself as benevolent (it is "willful nostalgia," according to Jonathan Simon) at the same time that it permits and promotes lethality.[53] In some cases, the curfew manufactures violations and criminals (and not just dead bodies) in the name of stopping crime and lawlessness. In these contradictions and ambiguities and their phenomenological consequences, regular legal order is not just overturned but called on, incited, by both the enforcer and the victim of the curfew, neither of whom controls the regular meanings of law that the curfew ostensibly is designed to restore.

Foucault captures the nature of this incitement when he writes:

If punishment could be provoked merely by the arbitrary actions of those who violate the law, then the law would be in their control: they would be able to touch it and make it appear at will; they would be masters of its shadow and light. That is why transgression endeavors to overstep prohibition in an attempt to attract the law to itself; it always surrenders to the attraction of the essential withdrawal of the law; it obstinately advances into the opening of an invisibility over which it will never triumph; insanely, it endeavors to make the law appear in order to be able to venerate it and dazzle it with its own luminous face; all it ends up doing is reinforcing the law in its weakness—the lightness of the night that is its invincible, impalpable substance. The law is the shadow toward which every gesture necessarily advances; it is itself the shadow of the advancing gesture.[54]

Foucault's magnificent nocturnal metaphors can become actual in the curfew, particularly where the juridical moment in its lethality and its regularity ensconces itself in the ambiguities of shadow. Early European and American curfews often contained legal exceptions for those who held a lantern while they were about, an interconnection between light and law—as well as Enlightenment and law—that was as tangible as it was metaphorical.[55]

THE CROWD

If the law haunts these shadowy, liminal spaces manifest in the emergency measure of the curfew, so does the crowd. Premodern curfews were legitimated in part by a stated fear of crowds circulating for nefarious amusement and sexual encounter, a common theme today justifying curfews on youth or in times of violent political protest.[56] Like the night, whose obscurity creates the conditions for (and sometimes a threat of) an equality where signs of hierarchy, social conformity, and identity are less visible and certain, crowds inherently express a radical equality, an immanent bodily exception to disciplinary power.[57] In reaction to hierarchies that inhibit sociality and freedom and that nearly always make legitimate, nonintimate touch into a sign of supplication, Elias Canetti argues that crowds free themselves from this disciplinary social order: "Only together can men free themselves from their burdens of distance; and this, precisely, is what happens in a crowd. . . . Distinctions are thrown off and all feel equal. In that density, where there is scarcely any space between, and body presses against body, each man is as near the other as he is to himself; and an immense feeling of relief ensues. It is for the sake of this blessed moment, when no-one is greater or better than another, that people become a crowd."[58] Crowds also anaesthetize via an ecstatic equality what is otherwise a nocturnal, creaturely fear of touch, a primal worry, Canetti posits, about being seized and killed.[59] In this ontological perspective, the crowd stands outside the norms of law and the character of politically defined life in different ways than *homo sacer*.[60] However, it symbolically shares a nocturnal character with that werewolf as well as the witches who were once imagined to fly over and thus violate political and social boundaries as they congregated at night.[61]

The fears of being touched by evil and other bodies are intentionally enhanced by the modern curfew, which authorizes a "cynegetic" power devolving from the hunting of violators by state agents and vigilantes that was explored in the previous chapter.[62] This power, deriving from the relation of hunter and prey that Ngũgĩ frames in his epigraph, makes the nocturnal crowd that has overcome the fears of individual fate all the more politically dangerous and monstrous. Amassed together, the individual fears of arrest and death are transmuted into collective power and resistance. The crowd becomes an emergent political formation interrupting that of the official emergency justifying the curfew.[63]

The sovereign's fear of crowds is certainly a fear of the people, whose performative equality threatens imposed order. But this fear of disorder can also extend to the state's own agents. As much as darkness augments the violent control of the subjects of a curfew, who, when exposed and isolated, cannot count on witnesses to make excess accountable, it also makes it more difficult to guard the guardians for the same reason. In 1667 the French seized the town of Lille and imposed one of the first total dusk-to-dawn curfew orders restricting residents to their dwellings. According to historian Craig Koslofsky, nightly duels among French soldiers, attacks by French officers on city dwellers, and nocturnal robberies of civilians carried out by common soldiers all threatened to destroy the value of this seizure as a test case for other imperial ambitions. About the curfew, Koslofsky suggestively asks, "Whom were the authorities policing?"[64]

Today the guardians' lack of restraint frequently assumes a racialized character. As we have seen, lethal violence by police against Blacks and other people of color occurs at rates far above what whites experience in the United States. This discrepancy raises questions about the necessity of a formal declaration of curfew to perpetuate the same antithetical relation to law and legality. Pass systems in apartheid-era South Africa instituted a racialized curfew requiring police to ascertain the race of those out and about to preserve the norm of "white by night."[65] Elsewhere, enforcement of unofficial "crimes" such as driving while Black, police violence against Black people transiting white neighborhoods, and other forms of selective enforcement pose an informal yet powerful type of curfew, just as the enslaved once experienced from sanctioned vigilantes intending to disrupt their freedom of movement. Do these kinds of curfews that live on without clear parameters or conditions for termination incite legal norms that effectively check racial supremacy, or do they merely breed calls for less radical reform? David Correia suggests that police reform regularly skips over the reality of violence: "Police reform never ends police violence, because police reform has always and only sought to improve the image of police and to shore up police legitimacy more generally. It has never sought to confront police as the lethal force it is, one charged by the state with managing poverty, patrolling the color line, and ruthlessly protecting establishment and economic interests."[66] Can calling these inchoate tactics that preserve racial hierarchies a curfew make a progressive political difference? Because an official curfew names an emergency, it always points to a time of restoration of law and rights, and perhaps this temporality can be used to critique the discretionary violence of the police.

SUBJECTIVITY

What is the phenomenology of curfew, and what kinds of legal subjects are captured in its snares? Judging from Jurek Becker's fictional protagonist, Jacob, the enforcement of curfew creates a deep uncertainty and confusion about rules and norms. The night of the curfew upsets rules regarding movement and magnifies the significance of even marginal forms of political subjectivity. Jacob becomes divided between bodily and symbolic fragments of his being—between what Agamben would call *zoe* (life) and *bios* (politically qualified life)—that the curfew establishes in policing its own division of law and emergency.

Grégoire Chamayou has argued that the veneer of law at most obscures the real basis (and pleasure) of police power, the hunt, which privileges the body over the person:

The police, as a power of pursuit, does not deal with legal subjects but rather with bodies in movement, bodies that escape and that it must catch, bodies that pass by and that it must intercept. . . . To be an efficient hunter, one must pursue the prey despite the law, and even against it. . . . In passing from the law to the police, we pass from one sphere of sovereignty to another, from the theology of the state—the legal system—to its material form—the police. From its spiritual existence to its secular arm. Both deal with the same objects, but from different points of view: subjects without bodies/bodies without subjects.[67]

The curfew establishes a division between bodies that can be hunted and those (however abject) subjects, barely legible at night, that are to be left alone.

Becker explores this fine line in his historical novel. In one episode Jacob finds himself plunged into a Kafkaesque hall of mirrors after a guard tells him to (falsely) report himself to the military office as a curfew violator and ask for a "well-deserved punishment" several minutes prior to the actual start of the nightly curfew.[68] Unable to contest the validity of this police order in any case (and forbidden to carry a watch that could aid him in becoming a vigilant subject of the law), Jacob enters into the building symbolizing law at night, where he wanders, as if in the dark, without encountering anyone seeing him. He nearly abandons his coat when it becomes stuck in a doorway. He may not need the coat for bodily survival, but its loss threatens to erase the only vestige he has of an identity as a mere Jew, which may, ironically, keep him alive:

> He has already slipped out of one sleeve when he remembers that he does still need the jacket. Not for the approaching winter—when you're in the ghetto the oncoming cold doesn't scare you—but for the duty officer, if Jacob ever finds him. The duty officer doubtless could stand the sight of a Jew without a jacket—Jacob's shirt is clean and only slightly mended—but hardly the sight of a Jew without a yellow star on his chest and back. (Ordinance 1). Last summer the stars were on the shirt, you can still see the stitch marks, but not anymore; the stars are now on the jacket.[69]

Jacob recovers his coat and spies a clock that reveals he still has time before the start of the curfew, proof he was only being toyed with by the guard. Nonetheless, he is now trapped in this edifice of sovereign power, a Jewish body out of place. He eventually finds the sleeping duty officer, waits while the officer wakens, and explains his orders. The officer, aware of the time, tells him to beat it:

> Should he believe it? How many people had the duty officer said that to without their ever getting out of here? What will he do with his revolver when Jacob turns his back? What's out there in the corridor? How will the sentry react when he sees that Jacob has eluded his well-deserved punishment? Why should Jacob Heym of all people, that insignificant, trembling little Jacob Heym with the tears in his eyes, be the first Jew to describe what the inside of the military office looks like? It would take another six days of the Creation, as the saying goes; the world has grown even more chaotic than it was then.[70]

That Jacob has wandered and observed the corridors of power, thereby gaining the knowledge to explain to others what they look like, suggests that there is some reality and structure to this power, some bureaucratic or lawlike order that can be known. But this is something that Jacob understands is not of immediate relevance during the curfew. Nonetheless, it seems to rouse his imagination.

Sneaking quietly from the building, avoiding the searchlight that would expose him to his predator in the dark, Jacob slinks across the twenty yards of the square and on to his house when he hears the sentry on the telephone repeatedly saying "yessir." As Jacob pictures the conversation on the other end, perhaps with someone in the building he has just escaped unscathed, he fantasizes the possibility that a moral intervention awaits, that he can be seen (if at all) as a human being with some character of rights that the guard—the police—need respect:

> Maybe it's a call from another sentry who is also bored. But he wouldn't keep saying, "Yessir," to him, of course he wouldn't. So it's the sentry's superior giving him some sort of orders? Actually quite irrelevant, but, assuming the best, it's the duty officer on the line: What the hell are you thinking of? Have you gone crazy, giving poor innocent Jews a scare like that? ("Yessir.") Couldn't you see the man was half out of his mind—his legs were trembling with fear! Don't ever let me catch you at it again, is that clear? ("Yessir.") At the fourth "Yessir," Jacob has reached the opposite corner; let the fellow go on talking till he's blue in the face. Then, in less than ten minutes, Jacob is home.[71]

The juxtaposition in this vignette of an invisible authority imbued with some kind of law against the lawless night where Jacob becomes a hunted body reveals the mechanism by which the curfew still produces a legal subjectivity. Unlike the camp, which is Agamben's preferred example to explain the topology of the "zones of indistinction" between inside and outside of law, space in the curfew is more triangular: law designates the emergency and orders two other spaces: the temporal and spatial zone of the lawless hunt, and the (however flimsy) zone of protection. It is reaching that sanctuary that drives Jacob's fantasy as a quasi-subject of a law that protects from the hunt, even if it cannot give him access to rights.

The distortion of legal subjectivity and its attendant dehumanization, attributable to the curfew, that Becker explores is sometimes explicitly cultivated by political entities, as it was in Nazi Germany, and other times experienced despite a formally declared intent. Gordon Hirabayashi challenged the nocturnal military curfew on aliens and "non-aliens" of Japanese descent living on the West Coast of the United States in 1942. The curfew order was established three and a half months following the Japanese attack on Pearl Harbor, Hawai'i, in December of the previous year, and shortly before the evacuation order that would send Americans of Japanese ancestry to concentration camps for the remaining years of the war. Hirabayashi was convicted of being absent from his residence after 8 p.m. and of refusing to evacuate, the trial court rejecting his defense that compliance with these orders would indicate he voluntarily waived his rights as a US citizen. In his appeal Hirabayashi challenged the constitutionality of the curfew and the evacuation orders as discrimination prohibited by the Fifth Amendment's due process clause.

The Supreme Court, which took the appeal, considered only the constitutionality of the curfew, explaining that since Hirabayashi was sentenced to serve three months on each count concurrently and any decision about the evacuation order would not affect his prison time, it need not examine the totality of the claim. Chief Justice Harlan Stone's opinion examined congressional history, and asked whether there was sufficient evidence to conclude that the curfew, applicable only to people of Japanese ancestry, was established solely as an emergency response to legitimate worries about a Japanese invasion. His opinion ignored the fact that months had elapsed since the Pearl Harbor attack without incident, attenuating the emergency.[72] The curfew, he concluded, was only a "protective measure" designed to deter sabotage and espionage that could aid the enemy. And he could not see any violation of equal protection:

The [equal protection] alternative which appellant insists must be accepted is for the military authorities to impose the curfew on all citizens within the military area, or on none. In a case of threatened danger requiring prompt action, it is a choice between inflicting obviously needless hardship on the many, or sitting passive and unresisting in the presence of the threat. We think that constitutional government, in time of war, is not so powerless and does not compel so hard a choice if those charged with the responsibility of our national defense have reasonable ground for believing that the threat is real.[73]

In short, as an expedient measure, the "hardship" of the racialized curfew was an efficient security measure rather than legally discriminatory; Hirabayashi had no grounds to challenge the denial of his rights as a citizen.

As with Jacob, Hirabayashi's experience of the curfew provoked an affective attachment to law. In a memoir written in 2013, Hirabayashi explained how the curfew order pertaining to alien and "non-alien" Japanese expressed a kind of "inequity" that awakened a legal consciousness and his willingness to resist: "As I thought the situation over . . . I reasoned that a citizen is a member of a state: a person, native or naturalized, who owes allegiance to a state and is entitled to protection from it. An alien is someone who is not a citizen. What, then, is a 'non-alien'? I felt forsaken as a citizen to be included in this categorization. . . . How is it that I could raise a question about being a first-class citizen when every day I experience differences that restrict my rights because of my ancestry?"[74] Hirabayashi understood the order's failure—by not acknowledging his citizenship and his "negative rights" to be left alone—to fully name the emergency, which should have included the threat to him but was instead diminishing the capacity of one part of the citizenry for the sake of the rest in an immunitary fashion.

Hirabayashi wonders in one passage of his memoirs whether a different living context could have mollified his resistance: "My dorm mates never turned me in. They could have. I never was arrested for curfew violation or caught as I was roaming around the University District [in Seattle]. If I had been living a half a block away at the Japanese Students Club, I would have been one of the forty or so residents who would be returning at five to eight. If that had been the case, I wonder whether openly confronting the racist curfew order would have occurred to me?"[75] Choosing not to live among other ethnic Japanese perhaps meant that the curfew order offended a more symbolic form of liberty to live as an individual despite ethnicity, rather than with it. This was not something that Jacob could have experienced under the Nazis, who commanded that Jews live only in the ghetto. The biopolitical distinction between ethnic Japanese "non-aliens" and Americans competed with norms of inclusion enjoyed with his friends, who were indifferent to the curfew, making the value of individual liberty more apparent and more dear. The enforcement of the curfew would have made the club a likely target for surveillance of Japanese compliance. Having been able to elude the curfew on his own and not having to wish solely for the release that would come with the day, Hirabayashi was more able to experience the spatial freedom enjoyed by most citizens at night.

CONTROLLING THE NIGHT CHILDREN

Youth curfews raise questions about the rationales for their promotion and the basis of their popularity because their extensive use since the mid-twentieth century has never been shown to be effective at achieving their stated ends.[76] Youth curfews "reflect widespread societal concerns about youth crime, the breakdown of the nuclear family, and the erosion of 'natural' adult authority," social ills that they claim to solve by banning youth from public and quasi-public spaces such as malls, encouraging youth to stay home, and enlisting parents as agents of governance.[77] Early youth curfews were seen as necessary reforms to address changing nocturnal sensibilities exemplified by the "night child," whose undesired presence complicated the changing "moral uncertainty of modern urban night, at a time when the increase in nocturnal work and leisure activities brought more people into contact with the dubious activities that had long characterized hours of darkness."[78] As the night economy was becoming an opportunity for new experiences of sexuality, the inadvertent lessons for observant children, who had neither full political and legal subjectivity nor acknowledged sexuality, were of broad moral concern. *Street-Land: Its Little People and Big Problems*, published in 1915, observed, "Night life is eventful. It brings to youth strange experiences which are out of keeping with its daily life in home and school. It whets new appetites which cannot be satisfied legitimately. The greatest dangers of night life are its excesses."[79]

Many children are still imagined to be vulnerable to nocturnal excess, although they are given more liberties. Brian Amsden has characterized the modern youth curfew as a compromise between biopolitical desires for governance and juridical ideals of liberty that were not as evident in the early twentieth century. Children are often constructed in law or culture as only potentially capable of fulfilling liberal ends: ideally, they are neither rational nor autonomous but legitimately dependent. They are, at best, sympathetic, romantic characters: innocent, noble savages. But if not yet political subjects, (at least white) children should also not be treated as unmediated objects of biopolitical governance. Mall curfews that ban unchaperoned children under sixteen—day or night—gain public support or indifference "because they effectively manage competing demands for liberty and normalcy, figuring bio-political administration as a force that manages space rather than bodies, and as a force that emanates from the private domain of nuclear family relations."[80] The conscription of parents as agents of governance reinforces earlier ideals of the curfew where private dwellings were seen as proper refuges from the dangers of the night. While in office, President Bill Clinton advocated youth curfews for fulfilling this nostalgic role. Curfews were "just like the old-fashioned rules most of us had as kids—'When the lights come on, be home, Bill.' . . . They help keep our kids out of harm's way. . . . They give parents a tool to impart discipline, respect and rules at an awkward and difficult time in children's lives."[81] Clinton's curfew is imagined as a benign and universally efficacious policy for family and political governance.

However, attentive parents able to provide secure supervision at home are not sociologically distributed in an even manner. Nor is recognition of childhood innocence comparably spread across social class, race, or gender. Particularly, boys of color have a difficult time being seen as innocent children.[82] In some cases, cultural presumptions of innocence may work against the liberty of some youth. Despite a curfew for girls being championed as a responsible and civic-minded measure for their care at the turn of the century, recent research into girls' delinquency shows that curfew violations, among other status offenses such as running away, are two times more frequently charged against girls than boys.[83]

Youth curfews do little to curb the perceived dangers of youth crime, and they often exacerbate racial and class hierarchies because only certain urban areas are targeted by police for enforcement. Social scientific studies have repeatedly found no correlations between a curfew and a reduction in street or juvenile crime rates. "What is certain," according to Loïc Wacquant, who has summed up these studies, is the inverse:

> These curfews significantly increase chances of incarceration for the young residents of poor urban areas. According to FBI data, some 751,000 youths were arrested on this basis in 1992, twice as many as for theft (excluding car theft) that year. And the rate of juvenile arrests for loitering and curfew violations more than doubled between 1992 and 1997, when it peaked at 700 per 100,000 juveniles. The ability to modulate their implementation at ground level according to the geographic, class, and ethnic origins of those caught by them gives curfews a privileged place in the panoply of new techniques for the punitive containment of young men from the neighborhoods of relegation gutted by the neoliberal restructuring of market and state.[84]

The idea that juvenile curfew laws *produce* the crime they claim to control has parallels in medieval witch trials, which tortured women until they confessed to magical transportation in aid of nocturnal conspiracies, testimony that further reinforced justifications for curfews.[85] It also resembles some forms of colonial curfew. As one critic of South African apartheid enforcement noted, "The curfew tries to suppress crime by creating crime. It turns otherwise innocent people into criminals and makes them liable to arrest, prosecution and imprisonment."[86] While juvenile curfews are enforced with less lethality and torture than colonial or premodern curfews, they similarly operate to bring populations lacking full legal personality into unwanted contact with law (a notable contrast to Jacob's and Hirabayashi's desire to be within law's protective embrace). This productive character of the youth curfew raises significant questions about law's relationship to the exception. Rather than permitting "the juridical order . . . [to] withdraw from the exception and abandon it," as Agamben argues, the curfew binds itself tightly to criminal law.[87]

The glue for this binding takes the form of the increasingly racialized construction of the abnormal. Foucault has argued that the genealogy of the abnormal can be found in three figures: the monster, the "individual to be corrected," and the masturbating child. The monster appears in the seventeenth and eighteenth centuries within a persisting "juridico-biological" field, violating human and natural laws (as did the nocturnal werewolf and witch before) while leaving law "with nothing to say. It traps the law while breaching it. When the monster violates the law by its very existence, it triggers the response of something quite different from the law itself. It provokes either violence, the will for pure and simple suppression, or medical care or pity."[88] The "individual to be corrected" appears slightly later within the field of disciplinary power, making its frame of reference the family—what Foucault calls a "background body"—in relation to the "school, workshop, street, quarter, parish, church, police."[89] The third form of the abnormal, the masturbating child, is discovered in the nineteenth century in a "field of appearance" narrower than the family: "The bedroom, the bed, the body; it is the parents, immediate supervisors, brothers and sisters; it is the doctor: it is a kind of microcell around the individual and his body."[90] While remaining distinct until the early nineteenth century, all three are superimposed when "a technology of abnormal individuals appears precisely when a regular network of knowledge and power has been established that brings the three figures together or, at any rate, invests them with the same system of regularities."[91] I suggest that the youth curfew serves as one of these technologies, where fear of the monstrous sexual predator, concern for the proper role of the supervising family, and anxiety over childhood sexuality are all mobilized into a mechanism for control of children's presence in the night.

Because the monster and the "individual to be corrected" express humanness as a matter of body over mind instead of the usual emphasis on mind more than body, as Andrew Sharpe has argued, they are amenable to racialization and gendering.[92] In the dark, curfew enforcement sees and only needs to know bodies rather than minds, making race and gender significant proxies for danger and for control. In this manner, the youth curfew disperses legal responsibility to the family as it criminalizes some, particularly Black children.

In studies of the uprising in mostly Black neighborhoods in Los Angeles during the summers from 1964 to 1967, which often took place in violation of curfew, researchers found that whites commonly explained Black participation as a matter of criminal conspiracy or irrational whimsy rather than the sympathetic action of politically aggrieved citizens who were inappropriately sanctioned by harsh policing.[93] To the extent that these racial attitudes continue to diverge in the case of urban youth, the curfew, often enforced in minority rather than white and middle-class neighborhoods, reifies predetermined sentiments of abnormal criminality and criminal vulnerability, both of which the curfew seeks to contain by forcing youth off the streets and into their homes, or alternatively into prison. Young Black men report police harassment at all times of the day—suggesting that despite the law of the curfew, harassment is practiced for them territorially but not temporally—but young Black women report unwarranted police attention mostly at night for curfew violations. Rather than intervening in (anticipated) drug crimes or preventing teenage sexuality, enforcement of curfew enhances opportunities for sexual predation and harassment by police; indeed, police appear generally unresponsive to reported sexual crimes among youth.[94] Even when women are not arrested as criminals, crime is nonetheless produced at the hands of police who operate with the curfew as their justification and as their cover, as witnesses are rare and unreliable in the night of the curfew.

The lack of witnesses created by enforcement may be one of the paradoxical advantages of the curfew for some youth, allowing them to take illicit pleasure in the night. While the youth curfew increases the relative presence of supervising adults, its successes simultaneously lessen peer pressure on some youth, allowing new social experiences and forms of life to proliferate. "Once on the street, particularly late at night, youth are exposed to further social influence pressure to participate in gang criminality, not to mention risks of criminal victimization. Curfews help extricate juveniles from these pressures. Against the background of such laws, being out at night becomes a less potent means of displaying toughness because fewer of one's peers are around to witness such behavior. Likewise, staying off the street loses much of its reputational sting once the street loses its vitality as a center of nighttime social life."[95] Diminishing peer-to-peer coercion by targeted youth means others can more easily seize fleeting opportunities to experience the night. But even where youth obey the orders to abandon the night, many young people still overwhelmingly support curfews for reducing the coercive governance of their own peers.[96]

COLONIAL CURFEW

The genealogy of the youth curfew can be found in colonial efforts to control populations considered excitable, quasi-civilized, both innocent and dangerous, and therefore unable to properly manage time. The colonized were frequently imagined by the colonizers to live within distinctive temporalities, which aided the justification of ownership and governance of their lands. As Achille Mbembe caricatures the colonial image of the "native," "The native was a great child crushed by long atavism. . . . Quick to slip back into the most brutal excesses of the animal world, he/she was incapable of resisting violence and could not, alone, succeed in the long and difficult ascent toward the good and the beautiful."[97] The belief that the colonized had only a limited ability to account for time or to live in anything but the present moment—a permanent and inured form of vigilance—implied that for the colonizer time was spatialized, necessitating distinctive rules and legal norms.[98] The imposition of progressive time—productive, history-making, civilizational—was a benefit brought by the colonial project and ideologically necessary to counter the temporal meaning of Indigenous priority that could be deployed to question colonial authority.[99] Imputed temporal differences justified distinctive, plural legal orders for colonized and colonizer. Efforts to regulate the social rhythms of night and day were also aspects of governing space and instructing the colonized in the proper use of time. The night held the threats of cultural reversion, political resistance, and revolution for the colonizer and became a focus for control, bringing colonizer and colonized into a common temporal cycle defined and enforced by curfews.

What was prominent in colonial enterprises in Africa and Asia in the nineteenth and twentieth centuries had antecedents in earlier settler-colonial states. Many American and Australian cities had "sundown" laws restricting the movements of Indigenous and racially subordinated peoples after dark.[100] In colonial New England and Pennsylvania, concern over the interactions of urban enslaved and free Blacks (who could not be simply told apart by white authorities) focused on the hours after work, when supervision was minimal. Special ordinances such as curfews limited the number of Black and Native people who were legally able to congregate, restricted their access to taverns, proscribed gambling on the Sabbath, and forced subaltern individuals to carry lanterns or candles after dark.[101] As these elite concerns also ranged to many working populations, curfew restrictions were extended to everyone in Philadelphia, but following the alleged Conspiracy of 1741, in which Blacks were suspected of plotting to burn New York, the curfew was explicitly targeted to stop Black persons' movement "half an hour after sunset."[102] Daytime punishments for nocturnal curfew violations involved public whippings and lynchings, which Black people were forced to watch in efforts to spectacularly inculcate respect for law.[103] As bodies were left rotting in chains for days, the nocturnal curfew anchored legality through terror.

Colonial control of autochthonous populations in nineteenth-century sub-Saharan Africa also terrorized and humiliated the colonized through racialized curfews that rigidified architectures of spatial closure. Despite divergent theories of difference (the British and Germans held to a biological notion of racial hierarchy, the French and Portuguese to cultural difference between colonizer and colonized), strict segregation of housing became one of the "arts of colonizing."[104] Curfews were designed to aid this separation. In 1904 the French imposed a 9 p.m. curfew in Brazzaville, the newly named capital of the French Congo, to prevent drumming and dancing, which ostensibly interfered with the peaceful sleep of the colonial community. The curfew law minutely organized time and space:

> Tams-tams and other noisy dances are formally forbidden within the urban perimeter of Brazzaville except in an area from the Felix Faure bridge to the Dutch House and from the so-called Glacière River to the Djoue river on the other side, where tams-tams and other noisy dances will be authorized in exceptional cases on advance demand, and all natives who want to obtain such permission must pay a fee of five francs. . . . These dances can only be authorized once a week from 6 P.M. on Saturday until Sunday morning and any contravening of this decree will be punished by a fine and 1–5 days in prison or either of these.[105]

The enforcement of this and similar statutes interrupted vital ceremonial and social life among colonized peoples. By 1926 these earlier efforts at humiliation and moral instruction led to a curfew on all African movement after 9 p.m. in Brazzaville.

In many British colonial enclaves, curfews were justified on the basis that the witchlike anopheles mosquito carrying malaria flew only at night; the curfew protected the nocturnal cordon sanitaire separating African from English habitations by a distance of 440 yards. This was considered the maximum distance a mosquito could fly in a night, although this science of malaria meant that the populations could sanitarily mix during the day when labor was required.[106] Frantz Fanon's famous observation—expressing something likely experienced first at night in colonial Africa—became manifestly resonant: "The colonial subject is a man penned in."[107]

Of course, no pen is inescapable, and spatial segregation aided by curfews made the night a particularly charged time for subversion. Fears of crime and concerns for the safety of colonizers intensified the impossible desire for "facilities in to which Africans could check-in and be locked up every evening and then released every morning."[108] The power of observation that spatial segregation enabled, particularly the heightened elevation of colonial areas, which assisted visual surveillance of the colonized populations, meant that darkness sharply diminished the effectiveness of panopticism while offering opportunities for resistance to curfew orders.[109] As Tirop Simatei has argued:

> The spatial stratification of physical space in conquered territory is the means by which colonialism annexes and marks exclusive ownership of the land, and yet, ironically, the privileged enclosures, the no-go zones that this demarcation creates, invite the violation it intends to forestall. In other words, the violent transgression of the bounded space with all the hegemonic subjectivities it encodes is adopted by the "native" as a form of resistance to colonial presence. The hit-and-run guerrilla tactics adopted by the Mau Mau fighters would later constitute the main form of transgressing the space of the colonizer who, in turn, reacts by creating more barriers aimed at isolating Mau Mau in the forests but which in reality are markers of the increasing instability of the colonial world. The curfew that followed the State of Emergency declared in October 1952 may be seen in this respect as the ultimate attempt to control violation of the privileged colonial space.[110]

Perhaps because visual forms of power neither comprehend nor attempt to "know" the night, curfew became—and remains—a trial of administration, while entire populations became tests of and targets for sovereignty.[111] That the colonial and modern curfew more generally carry the sign of emergency, implying that control is not assured and in question, makes the curfew's gambled success so necessary.[112]

Curfew enhances some strategies for state or elite success. Colonial restrictions on movement were designated for some, but rarely all, populations. This facilitated vigilantism to aid state control, sometimes by dividing colonial (and, later, postcolonial) populations, permitting some to control others. Paul Brass's study of postcolonial India showed that curfews in the wake of riots in the twentieth century restricted Muslim populations while freeing roaming Hindu crowds to loot, kill Muslims, burn Muslim houses and businesses, and in some cases destroy entire communities, the land under which was quickly purchased by Hindu real estate speculators.[113] Curfews that are not total prolong the violence they are said to assuage, sometimes by allowing the circulation of rumors among those who effectively experience and assert mobility.[114] States also use deception to justify harsh responses to curfew violators. In Senegal the 1988 electoral challenge by Abdoulaye Wade, thwarted (probably illegally) by the incumbent president, Abdou Diouf, led to the imposition of the nation's first postcolonial curfew the day following the election. The announcement of a *couvre-feu* was made only in French (and even then never explained to an unaccustomed public), justifying arrests among Wade's Wolof-speaking followers.[115] The killings at Kfar Qasim in 1957, discussed earlier in this chapter, were the result of Israel's declaration but (intentionally?) unsuccessful dissemination of curfew orders, producing the violations it sought in order to sow terror, a technique that subsequently became more common in that settler state.[116]

What is the relationship of curfew orders to the internalization and incitement of the law when curfew is used in such a clandestine fashion? Palestine is, perhaps, the limit case not only because the curfew has been used so extensively by Israeli forces since occupation but also because the curfew has increasingly become detached from natural rhythms of night and day. Israel borrowed the technology of the curfew from the British deployments against Mau Mau in Kenya, in an effort to augment Palestinian dispossession.[117] Both militarized responses to the defiance of colonial authority developed architectures of closure designed to contain populations and facilitate the taking of land, the resistance to which mandated ever more sophisticated tactics, some of which used and then abandoned the cover of night. In Palestine, surveillance tactics included a typical colonial, biopolitical mania for population counting, for which the curfew became instrumental.[118] Anat Liebler recounts how, after the declaration of statehood in 1948, a curfew was imposed in order to count Arabs and Jews in situ; Arabs (but not Jews) unable to reach their homes during this census were declared "present-absentee" and are still prevented from returning to their lands.[119]

As curfew in Palestine has become increasingly separated from circadian rhythms—an Israeli innovation—it has become a mechanism to manipulate and weaponize time with the expectation that it will dispirit and disable Palestinians in order to make them decide to leave and thus forfeit their land claims.[120] Curfews are imposed for indefinite periods of night and day. As Sam Bahour writes:

> When Israel applies a curfew upon Palestinians it is total, comprehensive, and unannounced: businesses close, schools are dismissed, government offices lock their doors, pharmacies shut down, and medical services are, for all intents and purposes, inaccessible to the public. This total lockdown is accomplished by Israeli jeeps, tanks, and armored personnel carriers roaming the narrow Palestinian streets with loud speakers notifying all, in an awful Arabic accent, to go home or risk

being arrested or shot. This announcement is regularly accompanied by rapid machine gun fire in the air and the detonation of tear gas canisters and stun grenades in the open markets—to make sure people get the message. If the closure takes place in midday, within a maximum of sixty minutes the city becomes a ghost town. If the closure is announced during early morning hours (5–7 A.M.), as has increasingly been the case, the city never wakes up.[121]

Spontaneous closures create psychological stress, destroy businesses, deny health care, and close schools.[122] Rather than a technique to inculcate discipline through the regulation of time for work, sleep, and worship, as many colonial projects embraced, "immobilizing the Palestinian in a web of physical and bureaucratic restrictions that are arbitrary, inconsistent, capriciously applied, and not legally legible or coherent imposes chaos and disorder rather than . . . rationality."[123] Spur-of-the-moment curfews help make "occupation time," which depends on keeping Palestinians ignorant of how long they will have to wait to cross checkpoints, and uncertain whether or how they will be able to control their day, a timescape that contrasts with the rapid mobility visibly enjoyed by Israelis.[124] Pass laws, like those that once constituted nocturnal curfews for those designated Native in South Africa, provide Palestinians one of the few experiences of movement tied to the clock, but they are infantilizing and humiliating reminders of how little control one actually has.[125]

Resistance to this imposed timescape imbricated in policies of closure takes numerous forms, such as leisure activities, including parkour and bicycling, that "give embodied expression to an imagined world of porous borders."[126] But resistance is rarely given expression, as it once was for Gordon Hirabayashi in the United States, through a turn to law. Without a regular pattern, the temporal disruptions of the curfew in Palestine lose their exceptional character. No longer a tactic, they have become a vital part of a strategy of spatial and psychological disruption. "The exception of the curfews and daily invasions has been slowly normalized through lengthy experience and frequent reoccurrence. Thus, when these conditions disappear from the city the inhabitants perceive it as an exception to the normal."[127] When normal is the exception, Agamben's argument that the curfew exemplifies the conditions where the law is unobservable seems to have the most resonance. Rather than being couched in darkness, however, the curfew aids a situation where the law cannot be experienced as anything other than force in the light of day.

Some forms of resistance to colonial curfews try to assert older meanings of the night, sometimes even reenacting medieval curfews. Gustavo Esteva recounts how for several months in 2006, the Indigenous Popular Assembly of the Peoples of Oaxaca faced off against the governor of that Mexican state, who had been sending armed men in the night to attack the assembly's guards who were maintaining security at public buildings and radio stations. "The people responded by putting up barricades. More than a thousand barricades were put up every night at 11 p.m., around the encampments or at critical intersections. They would be taken down every morning at 6 a.m. to restore normal traffic. Despite the attacks, there was less violence in those months (fewer assaults, deaths and injuries or traffic accidents) than in any similar period in the previous 10 years."[128] The building of nocturnal barricades reconstructs European town walls of old but inverts the nature of the threat from outlaws to the state. This form of curfew is not unlike a nocturnal general strike protecting assembly and valued forms of labor. These efforts to maintain an Indigenous curfew were eventually crushed by a tremendous show of state force. They nonetheless demonstrate the ways in which organized control of the night by a curfew temporally, and temporarily, upholds law, not just disorder and exception, in colonial contexts.[129]

CURFEW AND DISEASE

Colonial administrators believed anopheles mosquitoes bit at night, justifying curfews and racial segregation with pseudoscientific rationales. But what makes a curfew seem appropriate during the Great Plague of London in 1665 or during the coronavirus pandemic in 2020, with a general demand for "social distancing," orders to close restaurants and bars, and commands to stay in one's home except for necessary shopping or health care?[130] Let me return to a question posed at the outset of this chapter: What does curfew add to quarantine?

In a series of studies about epidemic disease and biopolitics, Foucault examined the different *dispositifs* that formed government efforts at control. Distinguishing the "purifying" distancing commanded for leprosy from the efforts to produce a healthy population via quarantine of plague victims, and later refining his ideas to discern an emergent *dispositif* of security in responses to smallpox, Foucault suggested an analytic grid or "historical schema" that could facilitate the study of biopower. The division in the Middle Ages between who was a "leper" and who was not was a binary distinction and exclusion (often by exile) based on juridical laws and regulations and religious concepts that together constituted sovereign power. In the sixteenth and seventeenth centuries, this model of culling the sick from the healthy was modified during the epidemics of plague through the disciplinary spatial and temporal grid of quarantine that was enforced through surveillance. Security, emergent in eighteenth-century reactions to smallpox, relies less on exclusion or surveillance and more heavily on concepts of probability, normativity, uncertainty, and population. Foucault is at pains to caution that these *dispositifs* of power are not historical successions from law to discipline to security; rather, "security is a way of making the old armatures of law and discipline function in addition to the specific mechanisms of security." All three *dispositifs* are "concerned with multiplicities"; security helps to reveal the dynamics of all three.[131]

Foucault's emphasis on the governance of disease is not, for some, ancillary to thought about biopolitics. Roberto Esposito argues that "the figure of the immune system rises out of the heart of biopolitics" because it serves as a hub to link and distinguish the body and those other things or machines on which it is dependent, as well as "the individual and collective, the male and female, human and machine."[132] Immunitary politics, mixing legal and biological notions of immunity, secures life through the death and social marginalization of some.[133] Eugene Thacker argues that the governance of disease is one manner to study the unhuman qualities of life— circulation, flux, and flow—that contemporary politics engages with.[134] In short, from the standpoint of the survival—life—of a dangerous-to-humans virus, bacterium, or parasite, the issue is less one of biology and more one of human sociology and political governance.

Neither Foucault, Esposito, nor Thacker addresses the curfew, yet we can glean from their work some notion of its utility in an epidemic. The deployment of a curfew is not intrinsically related to a pathogen; it is at most a tool to protect a community, to obstruct the circulation, flux, and flow that are conducive to a pathogen's success. The curfew straddles Foucault's three *dispositifs*, raising issues of sovereign power to control the night with a ban and the deployment of violence, of disciplinary power that concerns itself with the problems of surveillance challenged by darkness, and in small part of security, which calculates the efficacy of these measures. In contemporary governance of epidemics, however, the disciplinary and sovereign characters of the curfew seem to predominate. With security-oriented efforts to "flatten the curve" of infection that shift to a temporality of prediction that Thacker has called "epidemic time," and with quarantine orders in place as I write this, why have some governments called for a nightly curfew, or substituted curfew entirely for quarantine, as in Thailand?[135]

One reason that may be evident in the American response to the first year of the COVID-19 pandemic may be the underlying structure of sovereignty that this disease has made evident. Viruses know no territorial boundaries, and global flows of businesspeople and tourists, as well as disrupted ecologies, mix and spread pathogens without regard to jurisdiction, quickly ballooning from epidemic to pandemic. Despite the historical rarity of hate and scapegoating during epidemics, the renaming of the coronavirus as the Chinese virus by President Donald Trump and the anti-Asian violence that resulted injected a form of racist and nationalist immunitary discourse into a global challenge.[136] Other challenges to sovereignty are, perhaps, intrinsic to epidemics. Thucydides observed that in Athens in 430 BCE, "plague was the beginning of increased lawlessness in the city. . . . No one was prepared to persevere in what had once been thought the path of honour, as they could well be dead before that destination was reached. Immediate pleasure, and any means profitable to that end, became the new honour and the new value. No fear of god or human law was any constraint."[137] Today hope for personal safety may restrain such hedonism, but lawlessness still abounds because of the limits of health care facilities and real shortages of personal protective equipment.[138] Thefts of medical masks and fraudulent schemes to protect investments and entitlements were reported around the United States. And police were calling in sick from the virus, limiting surveillance and response.[139] Finally, the curfew itself, as we have seen in other contexts, helps to create the lawlessness it purports to restrict by increasing the opportunities for arrest.

Sovereignty is also challenged and made manifest in ways other than lawbreaking. Trump became president by smashing many of the emblematic forms of past leadership. His brashness on social media, disdain for constitutional structure, and refusal to secure leadership and legitimacy beyond his minoritarian "base" made him the first American president to act without a symbolic second body. As we have explored elsewhere in this book, medieval kingship in western Europe ritualized a fictionalized second body to secure the continuity of sovereignty when kings' mortal bodies expired.

Disdaining a second body, Trump distinguished his own mortal body as a singular source of knowledge and authority in the face of an epidemic threatening the bodies of the political community. Rather than acknowledge a common vulnerability felt by the public, told by other authorities to distance themselves and quarantine, Trump publicly refused to wear a protective mask (while instituting a medical protocol in the White House isolating him from the virus), and he publicly feuded with scientists institutionally responsible for public health. Perhaps this was no better symbolized than by his insistence that an unproven pharmaceutical—hydroxychloroquine—would be effective against the virus, a drug he later claimed to be taking as a prophylactic. In a press conference with the government's leading epidemiologists, who insisted the science hadn't shown the protocol to be effective, Trump said about the drug, "May work, may not. I feel good about it. That's all it is, just a feeling, you know, smart guy."[140] A former dean of the Harvard Medical School starkly captured the tension between science and the executive that such comments created: "The president is short-circuiting the process with his gut feelings. We are in an emergency and we need to rely on our government to ensure that all these potential therapies are tested in the most effective and objective way."[141] Trump's mercurial gut feelings can be seen to privilege his body as the site of state security, rather than the traditional organs of public health securitizing the body public. Even after contracting COVID-19 and being hospitalized, Trump continued to demonstrate his physical invincibility by eschewing masks. Constitutionally, states are the jurisdictions with "police powers" responsible for public health, and the intrusion of Trump's innards, which popularized and made scarce a valuable drug while delegitimating the scientific institutes run by the federal government, lessened the authority states had to control the epidemic.

Governors' and mayors' responses across the United States frequently reverted to emergency sovereign actions in light of the weakness of a legitimate national directive and the local lack of resources, such as sufficient testing, to pursue more securitized strategies of containment. Curfews, and in some cases unprecedented (and likely unconstitutional) checkpoints to deter or deny travel from people beyond state or local jurisdictions, built authority by reinforcing territorial integrity and controlling the night, traditionally sovereign powers. In Honolulu a three-night curfew over the Easter weekend was imposed; the mayor later explained that it had "a minimal impact but also sends a strong message, and part of that is no one should be out between 11 and 5 unless you really are an essential worker doing essential business."[142] Whatever message this was meant to send was enhanced by the novelty of a general curfew, last imposed in Hawai'i during

World War II, but also by the implicit meanings of curfew. As people are made more vulnerable in the night, the order to stay home or confront the police reinforces the idea of home as sanctuary. Orders such as these also are directed toward night's other dimensions of equality and conviviality, values and venues such as bars that the virus could be expected to exploit. In addition, the time of the curfew, tied to arbitrary hours associated with night, interrupts (and perhaps lengthens) the longer temporality of epidemic time. These ideas of sanctuary and an arbitrary start to nightly confinement that bolster the curfew are sovereign as well as disciplinary. To the extent that they are mostly inconvenient or symbolic in the United States, or, in the case of Kenya's response, deadly, curfews also create the conditions to appreciate and long for the "normal" time of quarantine.

CONCLUSION

As we read across these philosophical, cultural, and historical experiences of a distinct form of state violence, the curfew reveals the ways in which subjection to temporal legal pluralism creates unique biopolitical disadvantages for some. Most often tied to the cycles of night and day, and the ideological beliefs clinging to each context of governance, the curfew is a mechanism and opportunity for creating and challenging hierarchy, sometimes through an incitement to law as an alternative to the disorder of the night, sometimes through the escape that darkness can facilitate.

What might be the consequence of naming as "curfew" those social and political tactics that restrict some people's access to night under other guises? The houseless people who call urban streets their home are often banned from sleeping or even from stopping at night and are restricted from business zones, parks, and toney residential areas.[143] Women are told to watch themselves at night, to take personal responsibility for sexual violence and harassment that may await by restricting their movements, behaviors, and self-presentation. The Israeli Knesset once considered a nocturnal curfew on women to protect them from sexual violence, in response to which Prime Minister Golda Meir suggested the curfew be, instead, for men, because they were the ones doing the raping.[144] While states have the option to enforce and name such restrictions as curfew, social pressures on women to avoid the night, just like efforts to punish the houseless, have rarely been given that label.

The curfew expresses certain ideological notions about home and the night that confound public and social policy. Social restrictions on women's nocturnal freedom in the name of self-protection overstate the dangers of public spaces for sexual violence, which is most likely to occur in the home. Houseless people are frequently seen as threats both to others, especially at night, and also to each other when congregated, even though their proximity to each other in some urban areas at night most likely creates safer conditions through mutual care and the availability of witnesses.[145] Women and the houseless are vulnerable populations particularly burdened by the night. Calling these restrictions a curfew would reinforce a well-worn idea that night is a time of disorder and diminished state capacity that a curfew appropriately contains, especially for precarious populations.

The curfew also expresses the idea that dwellings are private places of reasonable security beyond the spaces appropriated by the hunt for those who would violate the curfew. However, patriarchal norms and violence against women and children challenge the simple idea that the walls of the dwelling adequately demarcate state action from private authority. The need to be left alone from domestic violence within the home makes law important, especially at night. For the houseless, who definitionally lack such a dwelling, the establishment of common shelters works against autonomy and the safety of collective sleeping in public spaces. However inadequate, dangerous, and unappealing they may be, evening shelters for those on the streets are an alibi for the inability to make a meaningful choice about security, erasing the paradox of nocturnal curfew-like policies that forbid the houseless to sleep on the streets.

Modern curfews bring assumptions about night, time, and safety that often reach back to older times and that incite law that awaits the dawn.

CHAPTER FOUR

TAKE BACK THE NIGHT

Reclaim the night and win the day
We want the right that should be our own
A freedom women have seldom known
The right to live, the right to walk alone without fear
—**Peggy Seeger**

How can one reclaim, repossess, and take back the night? Did women once have an originary ownership in night? How can night help win the day? These philosophical enigmas haunt the imperative to take back the night under which marches and vigils protesting violence against women have been organized since at least 1973.[1] Marching in the darkness toward "a freedom women have seldom known" enacts an ambivalent commitment to Enlightenment ideals. It shares with Immanuel Kant an emancipatory march toward freedom and right, dissipating what he called, in his celebrated essay "What Is Enlightenment?," the "danger which threatens [those trying] to walk unaided," while acknowledging that centuries of Enlightenment freedoms have produced little liberty for women.[2]

Indeed, women have long been heavily policed at night, whether by state authorities organizing prostitution in set-aside districts, male vigilantes or intimate partners, or women themselves, who practice safety in numbers. Matthew Beaumont observes, "Solitary women, because of a long history of discrimination and patriarchal oppression, have been especially susceptible to . . . suspicion. If women appear on the streets of the city at night alone they are commonly portrayed in terms of two roles, both defined in relation to men: they are either predators, in the form of prostitutes; or the predated, the potential victims of sexual assault.

In both cases, they are denied a right to the city at night."[3] Using night spaces for feminist political activism challenges these and other *dispositifs* of power governing the night, but it does not necessarily call on rights to the nocturnal city, as Beaumont does, nor the right to live without fear, as Peggy Seeger sings. In fact, it demonstrates the limits of legal forms of governance for women.

Looking back to the Enlightenment, Michel Foucault saw in the commonplace metaphor of darkness the recognition of a danger to ideals of progress and self-development: "A fear haunted the latter half of the eighteenth century: the fear of darkened spaces, of the pall of gloom which prevents the full visibility of things, men and truths. It sought to break up the patches of darkness that blocked the light, eliminate the shadowy areas of society, demolish the unlit chambers where arbitrary political acts, monarchical caprice, religious superstitions, tyrannical and priestly plots, epidemics and the illusions of ignorance were fomented."[4] Jeremy Bentham's nineteenth-century project, which Foucault called *panopticism*, established "the formula of 'power through transparency,' subjection by 'illumination.'"[5] This was augmented by various technologies of order to replace the vision that darkness diminished; to accommodate new temporal forms of capital, work, and leisure; and to respond to the transgressions that multiplied in response. Take Back the Night demonstrates the historical inability of these technologies to fully accommodate women's desires and needs for freedom and security without subjecting them to men. Taking back security for women against rape and assault and breaking what Adrienne Rich plainly called "the fear of walking out at night" encompasses an effort to rethink governance in a more fundamental manner, represented by a return to and control over the dark medium of night.[6]

This chapter explores the meanings and the politics of seizing the night in the interest of women's power and freedom from violence. I take two novel directions in this endeavor. The first is to pursue the feminist question of property and its transposition to night, encapsulated in the phrasing of "taking back" the night. I seek in this effort to theorize the potentials and limits in treating the night as a possession. The second is to explore the feminist philosophy of Andrea Dworkin, who was prominent in early Take Back the Night activism and who wrote explicitly about the significance of night for women's freedom. In both pursuits I am interested in following and further developing the critique of Enlightenment reason that this feminist mobilization poses for our understanding of law's nocturnal power.

OWNING THE NIGHT

Robert Williams has identified three post-Enlightenment modalities of governance oriented against the fears about undetected and unregulated flows of bodies in the night. These include channeling, in which lights, messages, and affects make some spaces more inviting; marginalization, by which informal codes and official zoning impress social hierarchies on space; and exclusion, which relies on walls, prices, and the dispersion of fear to control access.[7] For some, such as homeless women faced with hostile police and regularly threatened by rampant crime and sexual assault, these modes of governing nocturnal space create nothing less than a "war zone."[8] Whereas war is fluid and fragmenting, political reassertions of movement in nocturnal spaces hold the potential to reterritorialize space, disrupting the modalities of order at night. In the European protests in 2016 that came to be known as Nuit Debout (roughly, Rise Up at Night), activists angrily opposing neoliberal austerity and associated emergency orders used nocturnal gatherings to "stretch and frustrate attempts to constrain protest by pushing at rhythms of governance [such as police wishing to end their shifts] . . . disrupting the routines and patterns of . . . big business . . . or a middle class perceived to be associated with state interests."[9] For several months, Nuit Debout established a new counterpublic in these nocturnal public spaces, modeling bourgeois norms at a novel time of day.[10]

Take Back the Night marches, like manifestations such as Nuit Debout, interrupt the forces constitutive of nocturnal public space, but do they accomplish more than temporarily transgressing norms where women do not belong? What kinds of freedom do they demand and perform, and how different is this from a politics of visibility, of strategies emphasizing "coming out," pride, and recognition? Women's marches assemble bodies in manners and times often denied to women, challenging the gendered effects of channeling, marginalization, and exclusion, as many feminist forebears have done. The temperance movement of the nineteenth century, which held public protests, also decried violence against women, linking its domestic diminishment to (husbands') abstention from alcohol and women's enfranchisement, which would augment their political power to close drinking establishments.[11] Protests for suffrage, held from the mid-nineteenth until the early twentieth century, likewise encouraged women, in Elizabeth Cady Stanton's words, to "step outside the prescribed limits."[12] Yet Take Back the Night does not link women's power to inclusion in an array of democratic institutions or to coalitions with other social movements as these earlier struggles did. Nor does it turn metaphorically from the dark "long night of sorrow" toward the light of "Crusade fires," as the temperance activist Eliza Daniel Stewart ("Mother Stewart") depicted her mission, nor accept the strategic value of "a politics of 'seeing as believing' . . . attuned to the sensibilities of the watching crowds," as was true of suffrage's spectacular and representational efforts.[13] Instead, it declares the need, in Andrea Dworkin's words—reinforced by the cadence of the marchers' footsteps—to "conquer the dark" anew.[14]

If Take Back the Night affirms the importance of controlling the night, it does so in the assertive idiom of property: of possessing, taking, or reclaiming night. While the meaning of possessing night is itself a cipher, property of other kinds is an originary issue for feminist argument and organizing, and this permits some speculation about what night as property could mean. To frame this hermeneutical task, it is helpful to recount the Enlightenment ideals of property theorized by John Locke. Locke was the first philosopher to integrate consciousness and the possession of things in the forms of property. Consciousness persists "in the memory of one's past self and actions continued on under the consciousness of being the same person, whereby every man owns himself," Locke wrote.[15] This property in oneself, as Étienne Balibar argues, is the condition of possibility for the ownership of alienable things, thematically linking "own," "owning," and "ownership."[16] For those capable of asserting this ownership—and Locke made exceptions for Native peoples, who lived without history, law, and private property, but not for women, who were free to struggle against patriarchy—the continuity of oneself through appropriation of memory made possible the possession of things, which are likewise incorporated into the self.[17] This "candle, that is set up in us," wrote Locke, "shines bright enough for all our purposes."[18]

Western women's struggles have often symbolized the difficulties of lighting this candle, or using this shining light to appropriate the self in relation to men, and to own property exclusively; there has been too little experience of the liberty that Locke linked to ownership, too little education, too few rooms of one's own. Despite Locke's unwillingness to explicitly denigrate women's autonomy and potential for selfhood, he wrote against prior forms of property that were more collective and much more conducive to women's self-rule. As Rosalind Petchesky has shown, many women activists identified with the Levellers and the Diggers mobilized in the seventeenth century against the privatizing enclosures Locke championed.[19] These women demanded respect for established collective property norms and were the first to argue for self-ownership as key to autonomy. Locke later famously individualized and masculinized their political discourse as "every Man has a *Property* in his own *Person*."[20] Since women (like slaves and children) were not legally considered "persons," property in a philosophical sense was narrowed and politicized.

Women's property interests were not simply excluded from Enlightenment political and legal philosophy. Contemporaneous witch hunts by ecclesiastical and governmental authorities forcefully targeted women's sexual autonomy and knowledge about contraception by eliminating midwives and community healers.[21] Also in their repressive crosshairs were poorer women, especially widows, who lost customary rights to bodily sustenance in older property regimes—access to food, wood, and other feudal estovers—at the same time as the emerging culture of commerce discouraged and punished begging. Hunting witches, Silvia Federici has argued, was an ancillary process of primitive accumulation that aided the destruction of women's property claims, which were essential to their autonomy and survival, riving class solidarity along gender lines among enemies of the privatization that Locke advocated.[22] Alternative collectivist ideas about property and self-possession, particularly its significance for women's autonomy, have persisted among some Indigenous and Black activists and scholars, whose claims for self-possession aim to recover what colonialism and slavery violently took—and continue to take—from them.[23] In light of this history, numerous feminists have debated whether Locke's individualized notions of property and its ancillary notions of contract and ownership of the body are useful or politically dangerous institutions today.[24]

The mid-twentieth-century American and predominantly white feminist movement recovered some pre-Lockean collectivism. Consciousness-raising as a method for social change traced women's individualized experiences of subordination to men in order to affirm collective memories as the conditions of possibility for owning history and asserting women's distinctive realities. bell hooks remarked that consciousness-raising "was just another indication of the privileged living conditions of middle- and upper-class white women that they would need a theory to inform them that they were 'oppressed.'"[25] Without addressing the relation of privilege and knowledge, Dworkin embraced consciousness-raising in quasi-Enlightenment terms: it allows women to see but also to see differently than men:

Sometimes we dissent. We see the violence done to us as violence, not love, not romance, not inevitable and natural, not our fate, not to be endured and suffered through, not what we are for because of what we are. . . . Feminists call this often painful process of learning to see with our own eyes *consciousness-raising*. We discard the eyes of men, which had become our eyes. We break the isolation that violence creates; we find out from each other how much we are treated the same, how much we have in common in how we are used, the acts of insult and injury committed against us because we are women.[26]

Learning to see afresh as women and to recognize the injustice of being used by men depends on looking into and through the darkness left to women by the Enlightenment, what Trinh T. Minh-Ha called *endarkenment*, the radical questioning of authority now abandoned by Western knowledge.[27] Such a task is a form of post-dispossession reasoning essential to self-ownership, an idea, Locke stressed, that is never far astray from property. The repossession of night might indicate, then, a turning away from the masculinist forms of reason (including the legal institutions of property) or an insurgent recovery of institutions collectively protecting women's bodily integrity and social value. Or perhaps both. As Petchesky has argued, "For . . . early-modern European radicals, the claim to self-ownership was not a formal abstraction, an economic demand, or an instrument of personal striving. Rather, it was an oppositional stance against interference by public authorities in one's sexual and bodily life."[28]

The political struggle over private property reemerged distinctly in the nineteenth-century feminist concerns over the legal framework of marriage. Coverture subsumed married women's property under a corporate personality controlled by the husband; on death or divorce, a woman's full legal subjectivity and the right to contract in her own name were repossessed. Coverture was challenged implicitly, and later explicitly, by assertions of women's citizenship and rights to vote independently of their husbands. As the historian Mary Shanley argues in the case of Great Britain, "Coverture was . . . used as a reason to deny women the vote and public office because of the assumption that a married woman would be represented by her husband. The end of coverture certainly ranks along with suffrage as the sine qua non of public recognition of women's autonomy and personhood."[29] Although married women of the middle and ruling classes often controlled real property to a greater extent than the doctrine declared, coverture nonetheless was used to justify incidents and threats of domestic and sexual violence by husbands and was legally suspended in the case of women's violent resistance to this abuse (called *petty treason*), when criminal subjectivity overcame women's presumed lack of agency in private law.[30] According to the historian Isabel Marcus, "Coverture cannot be said to have disappeared when its essential enforcement mechanism [i.e., violence] is available and widely used to maintain power and control in marriage."[31]

The contemporary feminist legal philosopher Catharine MacKinnon makes a compatible theoretical link between property and sexual violence. She famously wrote, "Sexuality is to feminism what work is to Marxism: that which is most one's own, yet most taken away."[32] In this manner, she argued, sexuality is primarily experienced as theft, with rape the vehicle. Echoing and excoriating the rule of legal coverture as well as the legal concept that rape is larceny of another man's property, MacKinnon added, "To the extent possession is the point of sex, rape is sex with a woman who is not yours, unless the act is so as to make her yours."[33] In these pithy and oft-quoted critiques, property emerges as a social relation, and as a patriarchal form, it is patently false for MacKinnon. She later argued, "Analysis of rape in terms of concepts of property . . . fail[s] to encompass the realities of rape. Women's sexuality is, socially, a thing to be stolen, sold, bought, bartered, or exchanged by others. But women never own or possess it, and men never treat it, in law or in life, with the solicitude with which they treat property. To be property would be an improvement."[34] MacKinnon's arguments about the status of property reveal a convergence of women's experience with other forms of dispossession. Locke's universal ideal of "property in one's person" is limited, as Carole Pateman has shown, to those who count as a person, which is itself a legal fiction and not an ontological term.[35]

What, then, might MacKinnon and others point toward to support the claim that women "own" their sexuality in the first place? On first reflection, the idea that one owns one's sexuality is perhaps no stranger a notion than owning one's ideas as intellectual property, which extends the legal person to one's imaginative creations.[36] Property, as Locke, Karl Marx, and those who predated the liberal and radical traditions realized, is a broad and expansive way of thinking and talking. In Enlightenment legal theory, property is evidently plastic, manipulated by and through ancillary discourses. For Peter Fitzpatrick, property becomes "the foundation of civilization, the very motor-force of the origin and development of society, the provocation to self-consciousness and the modality of appropriating nature."[37] According to Margaret Davies, "Property-thought, or thought of the proper, regulates not only the distribution of resources in society, it regulates our conceptions of self, knowledge, group identity, sexual identity, law, and language."[38] For Carol Rose, "acts of possession," or property discourses, are background narratives with a particular social and political form in which all must cooperate to uphold the regime of property, even where philosophical theories about property argue that property in oneself is intrinsically prenarrative, natural, or given a priori.[39] Despite the lack of immediate political "purchase" of self, body, or sexuality, which lack legal concepts, the assertion of their ownership that can be imperiled by sexual violence nonetheless serves as a foundation for sexual critique.[40] Traditionally, it is the male who has been assumed to be the autonomous owner of objects and self. What might it mean that men now own the night, which women, in the name of an intrinsic ownership of sexuality, wish to repossess?

Taking back the night, I think, can serve to undergird a different story about property, the tale hidden in the dark. Like Rose's notion of a fundamental narrative, the rhetorical need to dispossess men of the night undermines the intrinsic ownership of male sexuality, alongside the exaltation of violence and individualism propounded by male culture. It does this by revealing that these patriarchal ideas, despite individualism and naturalism as their ideological form, constitute a common regime of property: an agreement to uphold the legal and social rules of who can demand what and when. Exhortations to repossess the night uncover the unusual form this temporal property now takes. The value of night does not depend on the right to exclude, which common property regimes designed for grazing, or fishing in open waters, or conserving the status of whiteness share with other kinds of property.[41] Rather, it stems from what Dworkin suggests to be a policed inclusion: the license to hunt and prowl for women, whose presence in nocturnal life guarantees an abundance of prey and sexual satisfaction. Night may be a common property of men, but it has worth only at the expense of women and because of a tacit agreement among men that night is their time for control. Control of and property in night is managed primarily by extralegal forms of power that make and keep women available.

One implication of the argument that night may be a form of common property that can now be reclaimed by women is that women have a sexuality that is "most their own," in MacKinnon's terminology, only because they can ultimately make it such. As Petchesky puts this in broader terms, "The language of owning—which, after all, means being the author of, the authority over, the caretaker of—seems an appropriate one for signifying women's collective need to reconstitute ourselves as political actors."[42] Collective efforts to make and enforce new forms of property are acts of *jurisgenesis*, in Robert Cover's terminology. Jurisgenesis "never exists in isolation from violence," but it also "requires no state. . . . The creation of legal meaning . . . takes place always through an essentially cultural medium. Although the state is not necessarily the creator of legal meaning, the creative process is collective and social."[43] The role of judges who act for the state, for Cover, is not to let a thousand legal flowers bloom but contrarily to "suppress new law, to choose between two or more laws, to impose upon laws a hierarchy."[44] To the extent that this diurnal *jurispathic* action by official legal agents guards androcentric legal norms—for example, narrow definitions for rape and high hurdles for proving harassment— the male property in night is made to appear vulnerable to (a quasi-legal) "taking" by assertions of different norms, particularly once the courthouse has closed. Seeking to understand the "taking" in Take Back the Night may therefore attune us to ways that women develop and defend new bases for rules, new definitions of violation, and new frameworks for asserting control in spaces and times when formal law, already winnowed by jurispathic processes, appears flimsiest.

Property also operates within feminist theory on another, ontological level by contrasting Enlightenment ideas of liberty not only against tolerated domestic violence and legal rules such as the marriage contract but dialectically against those who *are* property. The early feminist Mary Wollstonecraft, writing in 1792, for example, frequently analogized the darkened state of (white) women's sexual subservience to men to the experience of slaves and the state of slavery: "Strengthen the female mind by enlarging it, and there will be an end to blind obedience; but, as blind obedience is ever fought for by power, tyrants and sensualists are in the right when they endeavour to keep women in the dark, because the former only want slaves, and the latter a plaything."[45] Adopting this rhetoric, temperance activist Elizabeth Cady Stanton in 1854 argued, "The wife who inherits no property holds about the same legal position as does the slave of the Southern plantation. She can own nothing, sell nothing. She has no right even to the wages she earns; her person, her time, her services are the property of another."[46]

As the feminist philosopher Sabine Bröck-Sallah points out, recourse to the trope of slavery to describe women's condition "anchors the white

Western women's movement within the emerging discourse on humanity and rights by way of separating 'woman' from 'slave' in the very move of analogizing their situation."[47] Wollstonecraft's rhetorical "darkness" that women are forced to endure skims above its purported target; the abolition of actual slavery is not essential to women's full humanity in her account. Although slavery is not a contemporary legal institution as it was in Wollstonecraft's time and during early temperance movements, its lingering significance—what Bröck-Sallah names the persistent ideology of *enslavism* and what Frank Wilderson calls the enduring "grammar and ghosts of . . . the trade in human cargo"—continues to inflect the meaning of dispossession and emancipation for much feminist theory, as it does for other liberation movements.[48] As Hortense Spillers argues, "The black person mirrored for the society around her and him what a human being was not," a contrastive void precluding laws against sexual violence, caging Black women particularly "in the center of . . . Manichean darkness."[49]

In this darkest of night, slavery and Blackness retain their rhetorical availability for the making of white gendered subjects, a parasitism that for Spillers and others moves Black life to a place untouched by Enlightenment symbolism, and even beyond dominant notions of gender difference.[50] Slavery involved both hard work and massive sexual violation, making "the quintessential 'slave' . . . a female" but not the female a slave.[51] Without a legal right to her children, which deprived her of kin (and rendered her children orphans at birth), or control of her body, by which she could claim assault, for Spillers "sexuality as a term of power belongs [only] to the empowered."[52] Those who remain outside power's interpellations in this view fall into an ontological darkness, a place of nonbeing; "Black women are the beached whales of the sexual universe, unvoiced, misseen, not doing, awaiting *their* verb."[53] Without an active grammar, this ontological void is nonetheless activated within feminist thought. For Saidiya Hartman, "the figurative capacities of blackness enable white flights of fancy while increasing the likelihood of the captive's disappearance."[54] The metaphorical relationship of women to slavery "dress[es] up as a kind of being" this ontological otherness.[55]

The ontological denial of Black being (and its attendant—if not essential—sexual violence) suggests that possession of night and its relation to freedom must be considered from discordant positions. What Frederick Douglass called "the dark night of slavery" and Simone de Beauvoir "the sleep of slavery" against which liberation and Enlightenment have asserted themselves may not coincide as the same night.[56]

As Wilderson has argued, slavery is vital to humanism because it allows "freedom" to appear as an infinite category, while always remaining within the realm of political experience (e.g., freedom from patriarchy or from exploitation), where it "immediately loses its ontological foundations."[57] Ontological darkness diverges from experiential darkness by its infelicity to rhetorical manipulation. For this reason, self-possession holds uncertain value for Black feminists and others in the Black radical tradition who reconcile the experience of being property with humanist being more generally. As Robert Nichols has emphasized, postemancipatory rights to property are granted in the nineteenth century in forms shown by Friedrich Nietzsche, Karl Marx, and Michel Foucault to be infused with social domination and punishment: "The whole historical period appears as a battlefield in which the scope of rights and personhood is being expanded even as it is being reformulated in a new, punishing idiom. . . . Each of these thinkers (in their own distinctive ways) reveals that the nominal expansion of formal, juridical right may not only coincide with but can also facilitate the expansion of new forms of subjection and domination."[58] Contemporary efforts to achieve proprietorship are frequently caught up with the desire for punitive recognition, to bring the power of the state onto those who transgress one's property rights. In this manner, Enlightenment humanism backs up against property and is also riven by the experiences of racial subjugation.

I have argued that night and property are historically and theoretically imbricated in a complex manner. The enduring Lockean idea that ownership of property is qualified by the uneven capacity to have historical memory intrinsic to Enlightenment and civilizational norms—ideas that left some *as* property and others dispossessed of land in what Brenna Bhandar has called racial regimes of ownership—conditions the meanings of darkness and law along experiential and ontological dimensions.[59] At a basic rhetorical level, Take Back the Night appears to reverse the usual humanistic effort to enlighten darkness by prioritizing possession antecedent to the light of legal norms, as it also turns away from the modern disciplinary ideas of punishment. In this manner, it subtly shares with some Black feminist thought an anti-Enlightenment position at odds with state institutions and progressive history.

To further explore the value of this teleological inversion infusing this feminist mobilization, I treat possession broadly in this chapter. In what follows, I trace Andrea Dworkin's complex reflections on power and the night, drawing from and amplifying a nearly forgotten piece delivered as a speech at a Take Back the Night march in 1979 and published first in 1993, "The Night and Danger," as well as a speech from 1978, "Pornography and Grief," added to the antipornography collection entitled *Take Back the Night*. I look to themes she used regarding self-possession, demonic possession, the possession of territory, and the racialization of night. Each contributes a perspective on the significance of night and law—Enlightenment's handmaiden—to Take Back the Night's efforts at lessening violence against women and advancing women's freedom.

NIGHT BEFORE DAY

> Every woman walking alone is hunted, harassed, time after time harmed by psychic or physical violence. Only by walking together can we walk at all with any sense of safety, dignity, or freedom. Tonight, walking together, we will proclaim to the rapists and pornographers and woman-batterers that their days are numbered and our time has come. And tomorrow, what will we do tomorrow? Because, sisters, the truth is that we have to take back the night every night, or the night will never be ours. And once we have conquered the dark, we have to reach for the light, to take the day and make it ours. This is our choice, and this is our necessity. It is a revolutionary choice, and it is a revolutionary necessity. For us, the two are indivisible, as we must be indivisible in our fight for freedom. Many of us have walked many miles already— brave, hard miles but we have not gone far enough. Tonight, with every breath and every step, we must commit ourselves to going the distance: to transforming this earth on which we walk from prison and tomb into our rightful and joyous home. **—Andrea Dworkin**

Dworkin's exhortations to conquer the dark and reach for the light invert the usual story of civilization's day breaking through the savage darkness of night.[60] While she draws inspiration from the genealogy of light as the Enlightenment triumph of knowledge, wisdom, and reason—the desire to "reach for the light"—she asks women to conquer darkness first, to transform the cave of confinement and entombment without commitment or access to the Enlightenment liberties that have firmly entrenched the male privilege to oppress and hunt women.

Dworkin's words predate the political debacle of the antipornography civil law ordinances propounded and defended by Dworkin and

MacKinnon in the early 1980s in Canada and several US cities, which ignited the intrafeminist "sex wars." Although much has been written about these struggles, the sudden turn to law and policy as a solution to representational harm has not always been noted, nor the politics prior to this shift fully examined.[61] Although Dworkin and the radical feminists among whom she wrote are mostly passé, rejected in part for their gender essentialism and for what appeared to be a joyless rejection of sexual pleasure in their amplification of the dangers of heterosexuality, returning to Dworkin's work today is not entirely novel. Jessica Joy Cameron, among others, has looked back at Dworkin through lenses developed in more contemporary, postmodern feminism, restoring the vitality of radical feminist strategic thought.[62] Both adherents of radical feminism, including Dworkin, who centralize a critique of the ideology of heterosexuality and recognize a commonality among women and also those who invest in poststructuralist analyses refusing the universality of gender experience are engaged, for Cameron, in "passionate attachments" to theory, performative processes that draw sustenance from each other.

Also bridging theoretical and political differences among various feminisms across time is the significance of violence against women and the failures of governance to restrain it. American surveys by the Federal Bureau of Investigation (FBI) reveal that sexual assault—whether by better reporting or growing prevalence of crimes—has been steadily on the rise for decades, more than doubling from 2001 to 2017.[63] As many as 75 percent of sexual assaults in the United States take place in the home or among intimates, and as the global explosion of domestic violence in the COVID-19 pandemic and quarantine of 2020–21 revealed, there is no sanctuary from male violence at home that women can count on.[64] Feminist frustrations about the continuity of violence against women have raised acute questions about governance and the value of women's entanglement with state power.

Although Take Back the Night marches highlighting violence against women continue across the world, sometimes in conjunction with International Women's Day and often at dusk, they are frequently understood by scholars in resurgent liberal or neoliberal terms today: articulating the problems of unequal access to urban public spaces, problematizing the roles and contributions of men to feminist organizing, or advocating increased incarceration for sexual predators.[65] The radical feminist theory and politics propounded by Dworkin and her many allies in the 1980s is today largely supplanted by scholarly theory more attendant to intersectionalities of race and class with gender; sex-positive, postmodern, Black and Indigenous feminisms; queer activism and theory; affect theory; and other frameworks.[66] However, the Enlightenment attachment to law and legality that has some relevance for these alternative theories, as I hope to show, has perhaps never been articulated in such a radical manner as Dworkin provided by her attention to night. What does the continuity of night as a focus of activism tell us about the changing imaginations of feminist politics and about the changing forms of governance since Dworkin's exhortation? How does the binary of night and day pose a challenge to liberal and neoliberal concepts of property, and to legality?

The link between night and pornographic as well as physical violence against women that Dworkin posits in the epigraph to this section is presented as self-evident. It is "our necessity" to "take back the night every night" and "proclaim to the rapists and pornographers and woman-batterers that their days are numbered and our time has come."[67] This causal linkage is remembered and recited in the marches ever since, but nowhere clearly explained. The challenge of understanding this connection is made acute when we recognize that the embrace of darkness and night troubles even a form of tacit knowledge. Contemporary feminist theorists inspired by Ludwig Wittgenstein utilize his concept of language games to comprehend women's practical knowledge.[68] Yet the practical sense of taking back the night and darkness poses problems of its own. "Don't think, but look" at how language is deployed, Wittgenstein famously declared, a method made at least metaphorically inoperative by political manifestations at night, when vision and looking succumb to darkness.[69] Feeling and "reaching for the light," in Dworkin's words, rather than looking for this interconnection between night and liberation, take her stumbling along a winding path.

DEMON TIME

Dworkin's depiction of night as a distinctive timescape—a temporal mode of psychic and propertied alienation—is analogized to a notion of demonic possession, impugning male "reason" and denaturalizing whatever claims men hold. "Night is the time of romance. Men, like their adored vampires, go a-courting. Men, like vampires, hunt."[70] The accusation of vampirism evokes and plays in a complex historical terrain. Magic and the supernatural have often been associated with extreme forms of social control during periods of political upheaval.[71] The freedom that many women could experience at night, including the freedom to pursue romance, was partly curtailed through accusations of demonism as well as threats by magical and malevolent forces.

The supernatural was not always seen to be malevolent, however. Prior to the sixteenth century, ancient European beliefs in the "wild hunt," constituted by "the ranks of those who had died prematurely and passed through village streets at night, unrelenting and terrible, while the inhabitants barricaded their doors for protection," were one form of nocturnal governance, marking the night as a creepy if not thoroughly dangerous time for city and town dwellers.[72] Nonetheless, women and men who were out were not automatically associated with evil, even when they were involved in what could be construed as supernatural escapades. Women who professed or were said to gather at night and who transgressed diurnal corporeal limits by flying in spirit or in body (sometimes in the shape of small animals such as mice) were not, for all these powers, essentially diabolical. For many peasants, they were understood as the retinue of the deity Diana, feasting and drinking together after dark, visiting the houses of the well-to-do and bestowing blessings when they found the domicile "well-swept and orderly."[73] Some men, calling themselves the "good walkers" (*Benandanti*), fought malevolent male witches in the dark to secure the fertility of the crops and perform cures, supporting the activities of these women.

These benevolent invasions and other mild transgressions of social norms became increasingly labeled as demonic as the church and its Inquisition began to crush folk beliefs in the guise of rooting out the devil starting in the thirteenth century around what is now northern Italy.[74] The anathema of the evil witches' sabbath (or *synagogue*) that emerged by the fifteenth century in these alpine lands followed the increasing persecution of "lepers," Jews, and witches.[75] Not until accusations of witchcraft moved from ecclesiastical to legal courts in the middle of the sixteenth century, as they did in England and the American colonies at that time, was witchcraft seen as a particularly feminine and often sexual crime involving the (now male) devil, denying women's legitimate legal and religious access to the night.[76] The benevolence of nocturnal magic has never been completely extinguished, ritualized by queer feminists in modern times and retained in the terminology for effeminate queer men, called *fairies*, who gathered in the twentieth-century urban night.[77]

This contrasting background places Dworkin's accusations of heterosexual men's nocturnal demonism and women's subordination in historical tension. Women bore the brunt of ecclesiastical and legal witch trials (though some men who strayed at night were accused by church and state authorities of being werewolves in league with the devil).[78] In Dworkin's rhetoric, the supernatural and the legal are once again arranged in a *dispositif* but this time clearly within the framework of vampiric (and normative) masculinity. Similar to the Sabbath of old but differently gendered, "night is magical for men," the darkness offering "cover . . . solace, sanction, and sanctuary."[79] Whatever "evil" is attributed to women originates with men's vampiric metamorphosis: "The woman who transgresses the boundaries of night is an outlaw who breaks an elementary rule of civilized behavior: a decent woman does not go out—certainly not alone, certainly not *only* with other women—at night."[80] Fleeing from law and malignant demons, transgressing norms, outlawry holds the potential for liberation. "Banditry is freedom," Eric Hobsbawm wrote about peasants fortunate enough to gain an illicit mobility; fugitive movement—"stolen life"—is escape, "its relation to law . . . reducible neither to simple interdiction nor bare transgression . . . that makes black social life ungovernable," according to Fred Moten.[81] The outlaw's straddling of the legal and illegal was key to lesbian survival in the late twentieth century, according to Ruthann Robson.[82]

Women's condition is temporally bounded in Dworkin's account: women become outlaws by remaining "out" at night. This is not just an allusion to public space, where suspicions of danger are high at night but where sexual violence is relatively rare. More expansively, women possess no nocturnal sanctuary to call on for redemption, no place to remain "inside" the law. Night, as an evenly textured, hostile space that men colonize to legitimate their sexual domination, becomes an actor and alibi, adhering to no visible, diurnal boundaries. Like the imagination that witches once left their beds, altered shape, and flew through space, night, too, overflows every container of security and agency: "Night licenses so-called romance and romance boils down to rape: forced entry into the domicile which is sometimes the home, always the body and what some call the soul. The female is solitary and/or sleeping. The male drinks from her until he is sated or until she is dead."[83] In its invasive and deadly formlessness, night also provides men legal cover for what would otherwise be a crime: "All distinctions of will and personality are obliterated and we are supposed to believe that the night, not the rapist, does the obliterating."[84]

Dworkin's rhetoric positioning night as an actant parallels more contemporary posthuman feminism attending to what Donna Haraway has called "material-semiotic nodes or knots in which diverse bodies and meanings coshape one another," confounding modernist assumptions about autonomous subjects and objects.[85] Posthumanist feminism has focused on assemblages (sometimes of humans with nonhuman animals or machines) in an effort to decenter the subject and explore the production and control of bodies that matter, to "highlight the forces that make subject formation tenuous, if not impossible or even undesirable."[86] Night has rarely been brought into analysis since Dworkin's discussion. Because Dworkin's men hide within—but more problematically behind—the night by making night their (unbelievable) excuse, they appear to demonstrate the poverty of institutions (such as law) that ideologically depend on rational and individually culpable actors. Stripped of the anonymity of night that has coshaped their aggression, men are revealed to stand beyond law.

Women, too, have a tenuous relationship to legality. Dworkin's observation of women's essential outlawry at night conflates the constraints of "rules of civilized behavior" with the reach of criminal law in a particular manner. Rape is a crime only where the perpetrator cannot hide under the obliteration of night, nor blame women for being (ir)responsible for entering this sphere of men. And men act as the night watch responsible for, yet uninterested in, prosecution: "The policemen of the night—rapists and other prowling men—have the right to enforce the laws of the night: to stalk the female and to punish her."[87] Dworkin's claim of men's sovereignty over night—the essential right to enforce law and to punish—brings sanctuary and sovereignty together in a terrifying imagination. Without mercy or other limit, the policemen of the night enjoy both sanctuary and sovereignty exclusively. Giorgio Agamben, commenting on Walter Benjamin's claim that the police mark the limit of what the state can legitimately attain, similarly observes, "If the sovereign, in fact, is the one who marks the point of indistinction between violence and right by proclaiming the state of exception and suspending the validity of the law, the police are always operating within a similar state of exception. The rationales of 'public order' and 'security' on which the police have to decide on a case-by-case basis define an area of indistinction between violence and right that is exactly symmetrical to that of sovereignty."[88] In the case of violence against women, this indistinction between violence and right is most gallingly visible in the sexual predation of police officers on the women and public they swear to defend.[89]

Although there is some historical evidence of women using medieval sanctuary to escape the harshest strictures of law, for Dworkin, the nocturnal policing of norms by men occludes any visible alternative to women's outlawry today where men decide the exception (in Agamben's terminology).[90] And in the same manner as the contemporary Black Lives Matter movement has highlighted the particular police-enforced rules that Black people alone must live by and that whites tacitly authorize, male violence for Dworkin makes concrete rules in the night that are obscure or absent in the written law, yet maintain the full force of the state.

Dworkin's claim of women's elemental exposure—stripped of sanctuary and lacking the retreat of private property—is not necessarily totalizing. Women as outlaws, like wolves and witches of old, can be hunted by all. Yet this vulnerability is evidence, as Eric Hobsbawm and Grégoire Chamayou have argued, that the sovereign has renounced (or never held) the monopoly on legitimate violence.[91] Where all men have become police, licensed for the hunt, sovereignty is weakened: "The political secret that was betrayed by hunts for wolf-men is that, historically, sovereign power was relatively powerless."[92] Thus, the Take Back the Night march is not a mimetic enactment of women's nocturnal vulnerability; it is an effort to gain control of this precarious structure of sovereignty.[93]

Dworkin's structural analysis of policing serves as a caution to a feminism increasingly devoted to the criminalization of male excess. "Carceral feminism" was named by Elizabeth Bernstein in 2010 to identify feminist policies and activism (such as antitrafficking) "fueled by a shared commitment to carceral paradigms of social, and in particular gender, justice . . . and to militarized humanitarianism as the preeminent mode of engagement by the state."[94] Anti–domestic violence activists slowly turned to the criminal law (e.g., by championing "must arrest" and "no-drop prosecution" statutes and "victimization" frameworks, while abandoning demands for social support for those most vulnerable), due in part, as Mimi Kim has recently argued, to a loss of financial resources for independent women's shelters and other sanctuary institutions as a consequence of neoliberal retrenchment.[95] Kim also explains this "carceral creep" by the suppression of race and class concerns "under a gender essentialist framework" that has enabled carceral strategies with a more severe impact on people (including women) of color and the poor.[96] Certainly, the valuation of gender over other structural dynamics is substantiated throughout much radical feminist analysis and has been subjected to an intensive critique.[97] While

Dworkin rejects the premises on which carcerality is based, is race completely lost in her night?

RACE AND NIGHT

In "Night and Danger," Dworkin acknowledges some dynamics of race that complicate the primary significance or essentialism of gender, especially at night. Racism is one appearance of nocturnal power. She writes, "In the United States, with its distinctly racist character, the very fear of the dark is manipulated, often subliminally, into fear of black men in particular. . . . The imagery of black night suggests that black is inherently dangerous. In this context, the association of night, black men, and rape becomes an article of faith. Night, the time of sex, becomes also the time of race—racial fear and racial hatred."[98] While Black men have long been suspected of—and murdered for—perpetrating real or imagined sexual violence, particularly against white women, Dworkin's identification of an ideology linking night, Black men, and rape not only critiques but subtly reproduces its structure. It fails to explain the ways in which the fear of Black men—and, separately and together, the historical meanings of rape—has been manipulated, even by women, for economic and political ends.[99] For instance, the fear of rapacious Black men was cited in support of white women's domesticity in the early twentieth-century resurgence of the Ku Klux Klan and its women's auxiliary, and it permeated white women's arguments for suffrage.[100] Some of Dworkin's Black feminist contemporaries, such as Angela Davis, denied racist environmental explanations "that Black men are motivated in especially powerful ways to commit sexual violence against women," a naturalization in danger of seeping back into Dworkin's argument when she ahistorically posits "the very fear of the dark."[101]

Dworkin is right, however, to implicate the powerful ways darkness is subject to manipulation for racist ends. Raising the fear of Black men lurking in the dark has been a means to limit white women's access to public spaces. Yet depictions of Black culture, commodified for the excitement of white audiences in the latter half of the twentieth century, extolled danger and packaged fear, making this play with affect an attraction for women and men. "Black hip-hop culture, with its images of urban neighborhoods as wild, out-of-control, criminal havens, its rap artists as self-proclaimed gangstas, and its rejection of conservative family values via young mothers with babies and no husbands also entered American homes. Invoking historical stories of Black promiscuity, depictions of Black women's sexuality were central to this sense of excitement and danger."[102] These arguments of Patricia Hill Collins about the libidinal investments of whites in Black culture are useful for considering the asymmetry at play in Dworkin's arguments about race. The stereotypical fear of Black men and exoticization of Black sexuality that she declares is not shared by those who are objectified in a racist society. That Dworkin is mostly talking to white women seems apparent when considering the experience of many Black people who would disagree with her characterization of the black of night as naturally fearful and inherently dangerous. Looking back at her life in a segregated community, bell hooks recalls deeply contrasting imagery: "Returning to memories of growing up in the social circumstances created by racial apartheid, to all black spaces on the edges of town, I reinhabit a location where black folks associated whiteness with the terrible, the terri- fying, the terrorizing. White people were regarded as terrorists."[103] hooks's emphasis on the trauma of racism, which reverses the valence of whiteness and blackness, disrupts Dworkin's natural and cultural associations of dark with danger. White terrorists, not darkness, make the night a dangerous time for Black people.

While culture and commodification certainly contribute to the ra- cialization of the night, what better coheres an assemblage of Blackness, danger, and night is the lingering institutions of slavery. As discussed in chapter 2, the night was understood by many slave owners to offer a cloak for resistance to their control. As early as 1657, a Barbadian slave owner opined, "Runaway Negroes . . . feast all day, upon what they stole the night before; and the nights being dark, and their bodies black, they scape un- discern'd."[104] For the enslaved, night held the possibility of liberty and the special dangers of the nocturnal patrols. The constrained freedom of night has been a long theme in Black cultural life. As Robin D.G. Kelley writes, "For black folk . . . the night represents pleasure *and* danger, beauty *and* ugliness. Besides its blackness, with all its mystery and elegance, richness and brilliance, the night is associated with hooded Klansmen and burn- ing crosses, the long night of slavery, the oppression of dark skin. Yes, 'it's always night,' which is why we absolutely need light: the light of social movements ('I've got the light of freedom'), the light of hope ('facing a rising sun / of a new day begun'), the light of spirit ('this little light of mine / I'm gonna let it shine')."[105] Night's dangers do not extinguish liberty in Kelley's imagery, which, it is worth observing, is still expressed in shared Enlightenment idioms.

Nocturnal liberties and pleasures were frequently racialized by whites and fused with long-standing concerns over Black sexual violence. Fears about Black rapists had been magnified by stories circulated by French colonists fleeing the Haitian Revolution, which was completed in 1804. According to Robin Mitchell, "Lost in these rape narratives by returning refugees was any discussion about what had been the systematic rape of black women at the hands of white French men in the centuries preceding the Haitian Revolution."[106] Rather than acknowledging that systematic rape was an integral part of New World slavery, conditions that could have been used to interpret these later rapes as acts of comprehensible (though reprehensible) revenge, Black men were culturally objectified. This was reinforced even in the American North through crime literature that slowly eroded a more sentimental and evangelical tradition of explaining interracial sexual violence through the lenses of reform and redemption, reinforcing "protoracist depictions of Black men as violent sexual predators."[107] Thousands of American "sundown towns" that forbade the presence of Blacks after dark perpetuated the association of Blacks with nocturnal dangers. Many of these nocturnal ordinances were established after accusations of interracial rape and the lynchings that sometimes followed. The vast majority of sundown towns were located outside the South, and many enforced their nocturnal bans as late as the 1970s.[108] These institutions and beliefs were certainly at play in the twilight killing of Trayvon Martin and the exoneration of his killer on the basis of Martin's potential dangerousness. Thinking of night historically and experientially rather than naturally reveals a more complex view of race than Dworkin's thoughts on darkness provide.

Dworkin similarly simplifies Black women's historical legacies. What links the vulnerability of Black men and women to subordinating stereotypes is slavery, where the sexuality of both women and men was controlled by owners. The reaction to Black women's freedom of sexual expression after emancipation fortified stereotypes about Black women but was also a consequence of women's agency. As Davis explains elsewhere, the forward sexuality of women blues singers was a sign "that slavery no longer existed . . . especially since the economic and political components of freedom were largely denied to black people in the aftermath of slavery. . . . For recently emancipated slaves, freely chosen sexual love became a mediator between historical disappointment and the new social realities of an evolving African-American community."[109] Dworkin's representations of Black women reduce these historical struggles and their symbolic connection with sexuality to the consequences of their current economic marginalization and objectification under capitalism: "The prostitute problem is disproportionately made up of black women, streetwalkers who inhabit the night, prototypical female figures, again scapegoats, symbols carrying the burden of male-defined female sexuality, of woman as commodity. And so, among the women, night is the time of sex and also of race: racial exploitation and sexual exploitation are fused, indivisible."[110] The commodified experiences of Black women carry the universal burden of women's sexual dispossession for Dworkin. While night is imagined as the anomalous "time of sex and also of race," melding racial and sexual exploitation, night's metaphorical darkness theoretically obscures the nature of this temporal *dispositif.*

In several senses, gender, generally, and women, in particular, begin to disappear in night's shadowy obscurity in Dworkin's account. For one, the privileges that Black men qua men receive and the particular harms that Black women endure are left in the shadows. If, indeed, there are no privileges for Black men worth considering, the structural primacy of gender begins to dissolve: not all men hold advantage over women. This erasure of gender relations also recapitulates what Spillers calls an enduring American grammar of slavery in which Black women are imagined outside "the traditional symbolics of female gender," and the relationships among Black men and women are rendered insignificant and indecipherable.[111] The nocturnal fusion of racial and gender exploitation that Dworkin cites does not allow racial oppression its own history and logic, the distinctive forms of power that make Black women and men face distinctive forms of oppression. Nor does it pose as a problematic the understanding of white gender imaginaries, assuming away white women's complicity in racial oppression.

Dworkin's failure to emphasize the epistemological limits of white women's understanding of race had more than theoretical significance to the Take Back the Night marches. Racial conflict was prominent from the origin of the Reclaim the Night marches in the United Kingdom, for example. In 1978 a socialist women's group accused the Leeds organizers of the protest of "unthinkingly" marching through a Black neighborhood to reclaim an area they considered dangerous for women.[112] Although the organizers countered that they had thoroughly considered the route and had many allies and members in the neighborhood who felt the need to protest women's perceived endangerment, the claims of racism lingered over the marches for many years.

Dworkin's analysis of racial and gender oppression elides the role of the state in perpetuating slavery and condoning sexual and racial violence, which would have told a more nuanced story about racial oppression. In contrast, she does address the state with her references to the Nazi Holocaust, which illustrates for her the totality of the state's nocturnal moral perversity:

> The pogrom of Crystal Night, 9–10 November, 1938, when German Nazis firebombed and vandalized and broke the windows of Jewish shops and homes throughout Germany—the Crystal Night, named after the broken glass that covered Germany when the night had ended—the Crystal Night, when the Nazis beat up or killed all the Jews they could find, all the Jews who had not locked themselves in securely enough—the Crystal Night that foreshadowed the slaughter to come—is the emblematic night. The values of the day become the obsessions of the night. Any hated group fears the night because in the night all the despised are treated as women are treated: as prey, targeted to be beaten or murdered or sexually violated. We fear the night because men become more dangerous in the night.[113]

The "values of the day" are perceptible after this emblematic night in the shards of glass—normally transparent but now visible objects—that reveal the threatening destruction of property and violations of sanctuary. The Night of Broken Glass is exemplary for Dworkin, not because it reveals the logic of racial hate that can be analogically transposed to women—a hate that is public in its practice, as are the littered shards—but rather because it exposes the hidden logic of gender violence where there is no place, public or private, left to hide.[114] In this symbolic night, both humanistic recognition and property are revealed as meaningless shields for Jews and for women when states abandon both. This night also drives home that the democratic state cannot be distinguished from the totalitarian: the risible rights of Jews are the same as those "enjoyed" by women, where neither home, body, nor soul gives security. Whether by omission of historical projects such as slavery or the totalization of state power as expressed in Nazi Germany that gives women no rights to work with, augmenting women's control of the night is shown ultimately to be dependent on their own hands.

Dworkin's illustrations of structural violence that substituted the nocturnal experiences of Jews or Black women for women's experience in general served as an implicit argument for recognizing forms of power that cannot be readily seen and easily named. This facilitated her implicit call for coalitions among women despite divergent racial and ethnic histories, fused in a common night. Dworkin's ideas were written shortly after the Combahee River Collective of Black feminists issued its statement on the "interlocking" nature of systemic racial, sexual, heterosexual, and class oppressions and their collective disillusionment with white feminism. "In our consciousness-raising sessions . . . we have in many ways gone beyond white women's revelations because we are dealing with the implications of race and class as well as sex."[115] The collective's efforts to disentangle these structures of oppression led them to refine their analysis of Black women's oppression and refigure their political solidarities (including with progressive Black men), influencing intersectional feminism for many years.[116] Intersectionality has subsequently been criticized for itself simplifying the historical and avoiding the theoretical processes of subject formation and the various forms that power takes.[117] Dworkin was not anticipating intersectionality, of course, and her framework of night as a time and place where differences among women's oppression are obscured by the equalizing and commensurate experiences of darkness may seem inadequate for contemporary feminism committed to understanding and addressing the particularities of all women's experiences.

Nonetheless, her account of night as a fusion of various kinds of power—while metaphorically hidden in the dark—is not without potential today. Dworkin's temporal pluralism does highlight the importance of some of the particular histories, dangers, and freedoms that account for sexual culture and violence. For instance, urban queer cultures have often sustained themselves at night, concentrated (often by antagonistic police vice squads) in secluded parks and public areas, and more commonly in commercial establishments that provide temporal "spaces of care and community against wider contexts of oppression and violence."[118] As Roderick Ferguson observes, urban nocturnal venues of sexual "transgression" also provided opportunities for (inter)racial formation while simultaneously provoking state oppression, "thereby establish[ing] a formal relationship between racial exclusion and sexual regulation."[119] Racialized prostitution also has mattered for the dominant meaning of womanhood but not as Dworkin's synecdoche. Rather, "the meaning of womanhood was dialectically related to the changing meaning of black womanhood."[120] What is interrelated at night, as Dworkin argues, is significant for understanding dominant relations in the day. The night is a time of becoming advancing over being, even if there are no institutions promising sanctuary.

Dworkin's lamentation of the loss of sanctuary for women particularly emphasizes the limits of private property as a source of protection. Whereas medieval and early modern ideas about the dangers of night were met with the symbolic and often the material security of "shutting in" to private dwellings, Dworkin's insistence on the vulnerability of women to the night of the hunt—to rape and domestic violence, to the culture of sexual exploitation that she understood to fuel both—is significant for grasping the particular vulnerabilities that women may face when there is no place of retreat. "Even when the woman, like a good girl, locks herself up and in, night threatens to intrude. Outside are the predators who will crawl in the windows, climb down drainpipes, pick the locks, descend from skylights, to bring the night with them."[121] Dworkin's night flows across borders and through bodies like a ghostly ether, bringing with it a gendered vulnerability to stranger and familiar alike.

This depiction of an overflowing night has a particularly phenomenological feel that Dworkin used to diminish the identity politics that some of her examples seemed to acknowledge. Her images of night echo the thoughts of Eugène Minkowski, written in 1933. Minkowski argued that we commonly use the frames of "lived distance" and "visual space," dependent on visual clarity, but, he emphasized, "we also live in the night. Isn't it necessary, perchance to turn our eyes toward it? But I no longer have the black night, complete obscurity, *before me*; instead it covers me completely, it penetrates my whole being, it touches me in a much more intimate way than the clarity of visual space."[122] Maurice Merleau-Ponty, who took up Minkowski's invitation to turn toward night, argued that our intimacy with night is temporally as well as spatially indistinct: "When . . . the world of clear and articulate objects is abolished, our perceptual being, cut off from its world, evolves a spatiality without things. This is what happens in the night. . . . Night has no outlines; it is itself in contact with me and its unity is the mystical unity of the mana. Even shouts or a distant light people it only vaguely, and then it comes to life in its entirety; it is pure depth without foreground or background, without surfaces and without any distance separating it from me."[123] For the feminist phenomenologist Cressida Heyes, even common experiences of "anaesthetic time" brought about by a glass of wine, or drugs to alleviate anxiety, depression, and the like, create the pleasurable experience of timelessness. "Anaesthetic time loves the night and doesn't care about the future," she writes.[124] Heyes's recent scholarship has concerned itself with the consequences of denials and violations of women's unconscious life—while sleeping, drugged or anaesthetized, or comatose—suffered at the hands of men. In arguments challenging the primacy of Enlightenment rationality for subjectivity, Heyes argues that sexual assault on women while unconscious "exploits and reinforces a victim's lack of agency and exposes her body in ways that make it especially difficult for her to reconstitute herself as a subject. . . . Deviations and interruptions in the stream of sensory perception, and the anonymity unconsciousness (usually experienced as sleep) provides are just as important to subjectivity and to feminism as discussions of waking agency and the cultivation of individuality. Sexual assault while unconscious can make the restful anonymity of sleep impossible, leaving only the violent exposure of a two-dimensional life."[125] Heyes's emphasis on the importance of anonymity, the value and pleasure of allowing sleep or our tools of anesthesia to disembody our existence in order to recover the ability to inhabit ourselves as subject, acknowledges the uneven sociological terrain on which this takes place.[126] The horror with which phenomenological feminists approach violence against incapacitated women also acknowledges the difficulty experienced by some, such as prisoners, queers, and racial minorities, in achieving and enjoying anonymity, in retaining a vital "zone of nonbeing," in Frantz Fanon's enduring words.[127] For some, even the night does not adequately hide difference.

The need for nonbeing (sleep, intoxication, anonymity) that Fanon, Merleau-Ponty, and Heyes emphasize suggests that the dismembering and border-dissolving violations of night are dangerous in their denial, not only in their experience.[128] If one reads Dworkin from this ambivalent perspective, it is the ideology of romance, the cultural justification for the hunt, that dismembers while taking away the pleasures and necessities of an autonomy it denies. Rather than seeking recognition, women can take back the night by owning the experience of melting away, of moving autonomously, of embracing the darkness—and, as the march enacts, also by experiencing some of this while remaining steadfastly among other women, offering powerful opportunities to remake themselves as subjects.

FEAR AND PUBLIC SPACE

A Take Back the Night March goes right to our emotional core. We women are especially supposed to be afraid of the night. The night promises harm to women. For a woman to walk on the street at night is not only to risk abuse, but also—according to the values of male domination—to ask for it. . . . Night means, for all women, a choice: danger or confinement. Confinement is most often dangerous too— battered women are confined, a woman raped in marriage is likely to be raped in her own home. . . . We must use our bodies to say "Enough"— we must form a barricade with our bodies . . . to take back this night and every night so that life will be worth living and so that human dignity will be a reality. —**Andrea Dworkin**

Dworkin's identification of an emotional core to the night suggests an additional avenue of nocturnal transformation: rather than succumbing to the affect of fear, women must use their bodies collectively to make life worth living again.[129] Night has long had an association with fear that in some accounts is primal, or at least prior to consciousness.[130] Brian Massumi, for instance, identifies a "visceral sensibility" quickening fear even before the rational recognition of nocturnal danger: "Walking down a dark street at night in a dangerous part of town, your lungs throw a spasm before you consciously see and can recognize as human the shadow thrown across your path."[131] Certainly, Massumi's unremarked coding of a "dangerous part of town" is neither a priori nor ahistorical; dangerous spaces and dangerous times are overdetermined by changing cultural ideas of dangerous people, by memories, and even by the absence of shadowy threats.[132] While Massumi argues that the affect of fear, and visceral perception generally, "registers intensity" immediately, for feminists like Sara Ahmed, fear is more than visceral sensibility.[133] Not all bodies fear all bodies, even when there is statistical reason to do so. Rather than a response to an objective threat or a primal reaction to darkness, fear is structurally mediated by the threat of violence "shaped by the authorization of narratives about what is and is not threatening, and about who are and are not the appropriate 'objects' of fear."[134] Apart from registering an intensity, fear works on the body to mark and maintain space: "The openness of the body to the world involves a sense of danger, which is *anticipated as a future pain or injury*. In fear, the world presses against the body; the body shrinks back from the world in the desire to avoid the object of fear. Fear involves shrinking the body; *it restricts the body's mobility precisely insofar as it seems to prepare the body for flight*."[135] In Ahmed's theory, the shrinking body marks a topology similar to that marked by private property: the external space of danger opposed to the internal space of security, love, and sanctuary. "The turning away from the object of fear also involves *turning towards* the object of love, who becomes the defence against the death that is apparently threatened by the object of fear."[136] This "contradictory space," in Henri Lefebvre's terminology, is made manifest where bodies most matter: at night. Lefebvre writes, "The body, sex and pleasure are often accorded no existence, either mental or social, until after dark, when the prohibitions that obtain during the day, during 'normal' activity, are lifted."[137]

Nonetheless, the spaces of safety are not always apparent for women, who experience domestic as well as public dangers, especially at night. The field of public geography has explored the significance of affect by mapping the spaces women themselves assign as dangerous. Women's perceptions of their environments diverge from those of men (even though both men and women report some degree of fear in public spaces), in part, as Dworkin stressed, because of the resonant and amplifying experiences across private and public sexual safety.[138] For Rachel Pain, one of the first scholars to explore the geography of fear, spatialized affects intertwine: "While many people strongly associate fear with specific places, reflecting wider ideologies of public space as dangerous and private space as safe, fear and safety in different spaces are interconnected—for example, experiences of danger in private space affect feelings of security in public at an individual and societal level."[139] The attribution of women's fear to public space in Pain's analysis depends on independent ideologies and discourses that suppress the statistical fact that women are more endangered at home, while men's risk rises in public spaces.[140] These include, as Dworkin notes, ideologies that brand women in public space, especially at night, as asking for, and thus deserving of, trouble. Feminist geography reveals complex linkages between affect and space, showing the significance of the social, economic, and political subordination that women, the poor, and social minorities face, including crimes of hate, elder abuse, and the like in both private and public spaces. Political identification of fearful and feared groups, especially in the context of heightened policing during the war on drugs, discounts the experiences of some—such as men of color—who are seen as perpetrators rather than more likely victims of public violence.[141] But it is also the not-seen threat—an impossible vigilance—that magnifies the fearful imaginations of those who are too afraid to go out or who fail to encounter the object of fear. "The structural possibility that the object of fear may pass us by . . . makes everything possibly fearsome. This is an important dimension in the spatial politics of fear: the loss of the object of fear renders the world itself a space of potential danger, a space that is anticipated as pain or injury on the surface of the body that fears."[142]

Much of the geography of fear has suggested policy to design fear out of public spaces, including architectural rules, public lighting, and increased police presence, interventions that promise to make lurking dangers visible and manageable—in short, a return to Robert Williams's modalities of nocturnal urban governance, discussed earlier in the chapter. This perspective has inflected the meaning of nocturnal feminist activism for some. Nancy Duncan, for example, has written that "the feminist slogan 'Take Back the Night' should be seen as a suggestion not for women to disregard personal safety, but for all those who can (not just women) to organize and ask for public funds to transform public spaces to make them safe and accessible to everyone at night as well as during the day."[143] However, a focus on public policy doesn't sufficiently attend to the lack of private sanctuary from domestic dangers, ultimately ignoring the spatial dynamics of gender, as Dworkin has made clear.[144] Nor does it adequately account for neoliberal economic projects such as efforts by some cities to develop a "night economy" energized by the willingness of middle-class patrons to pay to brave "dangerous" urban spaces unhindered by police and other signs of security.[145] This commodification of fear is also writ large in Mike Davis's arguments about late-capitalist Los Angeles developers who intentionally stoke white fears that people of color devalue white neighborhoods through participation in crime and social "encroachment" in order to sell security, "which generates its own paranoid demand."[146] Today even women's safety is commodified where women's fear of sexual violence sustains urban-renewal development.[147]

The augmentation of fear for economic ends reinforces the rationality of neoliberal, privatized responses to nocturnal danger. Many women report resorting to self-control, risk avoidance, and risk management, often using male escorts to lessen the perception of nocturnal risks.[148] Such privatized responses have been criticized as reinforcing the image of women's weakness.[149] The geography of fear also tends to reify the distinction between public and private spaces, mapping them to a sedimented heteronormative ideal.

Take Back the Night marches have engaged fear not only through critique but also, fundamentally, by "form[ing] a barricade with our bodies," in Dworkin's exhortation. For Ahmed, threats align bodies, but realigning bodies may work against fear. One Swedish participant in a 2001 march reported, "I was there, on Götagan in Stockholm on March 8 and together with hundreds of women we chanted that we will take back the night. During the demonstration, in the protection of the group, I felt strong and for once courageous. But just half an hour later, fear had overtaken me again. On the subway train home, I sat just as tensely as always."[150] Another recounted, "It's a very powerful feeling, I remember in one of my first Take back the night; it was a really annoying guy who came after us, he was drunk and shouted. The whole demonstration stopped and shouted at him. I stopped and I saw this host of people. It was such an incredible powerful feeling to be a part of a crowd in which we back each other up. If someone would say something rude to me, I have all those people behind me."[151] The proximity of like-minded bodies builds affective solidarity, yielding strength and courage in these accounts. "Only by walking together," Dworkin exhorted the assembled marchers, "can we walk at all with any sense of safety, dignity, or freedom."[152] Fear, she writes elsewhere, is confusing and debilitating, but it is, foremost, isolating.[153] Fear has no particular object here; "it is this lack of residence," for Ahmed, "that allows fear to slide across signs and between bodies."[154] In Kathleen Stewart's words, affect is "transpersonal or prepersonal—not about one person's feelings becoming another's but about bodies literally affecting one another and generating intensities."[155] For Elias Canetti, the jostling, surging, and rubbing bodies that form a crowd overcome primal nocturnal fears of being touched in the dark. Freed of this individuation, the crowd forms a boundary, "a space for itself which it will fill."[156] For Ahmed, this boundary can also be seen in the "mobility of some bodies; their freedom to move shapes the surface of spaces, whilst spaces surface as spaces through the mobility of such bodies. It is the regulation of bodies in space through the uneven distribution of fear which allows spaces to become territories, claimed as rights by some bodies and not others."[157] The uneven distribution of fear is manufactured by the crowd, in the march. But it can also collapse when the crowd disperses, as happened in Mälmo, Sweden, when six feminists were beaten after a march, prompting one marcher to observe, "After a 'take the night back' march comes the darkness and extinguishes the light."[158]

The quenching of activist illumination by the dark reality of violence in this marcher's metaphorical phrasing raises the question of what it might take and what it might mean to finally own the night. Dworkin remarks, "The truth is that we have to take back the night every night, or the night will never be ours."[159] Other crowds mark property in a cyclically temporal manner. Eve Darian-Smith writes about an old Roman tradition of annually "beating the bounds," still observed in parts of England, when church and lay people ritually walk the perimeter of the parish boundary stones. Beating the bounds sustains a "mental boundary" around the parish, demarcating property rights, responsibilities, and social roles. The contemporary ceremony is a "public declaration of concern for the local common, which in turn helps to reinstate an informal property regime that puts value in 'public' land."[160] Take Back the Night engages different issues, especially individual and collective fear and gender violence, yet it, too, ritually claims to effect a possession of space during a time of perceived augmented violence.

Taking back the night, in Dworkin's texts, is necessary but not sufficient for women, who must also retake the day once the night is theirs. Unlike beating the bounds, which depends on affirming visual markers of law and authority such as boundary stones, the ceremony of taking back the night at least rhetorically challenges the idea of representational authority, which is hard to see during the dark hours of the march. "Taking back the night means making visible the limits that patriarchal norms have built," according to one media report, yet visibility—except as a sign of self-knowledge—is metaphorically antecedent to night and dependent on day.[161] Nor do the circuits of public space that the English ritual traces correspond to Dworkin's aims. While it is not uncommon to hear that Take Back the Night is about the freedom for women to equally occupy public space without fear, the restriction to public space is not Dworkin's stated ambition. Night, as a smoky mist, metaphorically interferes with legal demarcations of public from private. The emphasis on darkness turns away from representation, explaining why pornography and free speech were early and convenient targets of the marches. That women experience less fear in the solidarity of the marches suggests that owning the night may require norms of cooperation—a new regime of common property—that can survive into daylight.

SLUTWALK

The complexity of Dworkin's strategy is rendered starker when comparing Take Back the Night to the experiences and rhetoric of SlutWalks, which are more common feminist manifestations today. Although Take Back the Night marches still occur, they have assumed different forms. No longer do they commonly target pornography and the commercial sex industry, as did the earliest US marches. A few take place in daylight to allow women participants to feel safer, thereby acknowledging the symbolic or felt danger of night without the experience of overcoming fear.[162] Many marches have engaged with the troubling issue of male and transgender allies and the related concerns over the kind of structural analyses propounded by Dworkin and many radical feminists.[163] These conflicts have been exacerbated by a politics of gender fluidity that challenges the binary topology projected onto night and day in the original marches. Others have confronted concerns over the usefulness of a politics of victimization as well as the mismatch between public marches and the experiences of intimate sexual assault in private venues. Many of these unresolved tensions provoked new forms of protesting sexual violence that would account for a sex positivity that had replaced radical feminism.

SlutWalk has challenged the centrality of Take Back the Night on the basis of these political issues. The original march, held in Toronto in 2011 with more than three thousand participants, took its name from a remark by a Toronto police officer at a public safety forum who advised that women should avoid dressing like sluts in order to elude rape.[164] Outrage at this victim blaming led to the organization of a protest in Toronto. The aim of the march was to avoid "slut-shaming" and "sexual profiling," while bringing attention to the persistent problem of sexual violence in a form consciously distinctive from the legacy of Take Back the Night.[165] The Toronto website for the march made clear its focus on institutional reform more than men's power generally: "Our plan was to call foul on the comment made by a representative of our Toronto Police and speak to the bigger picture of common, persistent and documented victim-blaming within Police Services, the justice system and social spheres around us."[166] Within a year of the first march, autonomous local groups, influenced by social media, organized SlutWalks in over two hundred cities in at least forty countries, across nearly every continent.[167] Some Slut-Walk participants parody the cultural image of the slut by wearing skimpy clothing while protesting that their dress does not justify rape. SlutWalk contests law-enforcement attitudes toward victims of sexual violence and promotes the freedom and enjoyment of women's sexual agency without the sexist cultural binary of good girl/bad girl.

SlutWalk participants have celebrated their diversity from the outset. Judith Butler recounted participating in an early Turkish march

> with a group of transgender women, queer activists, human rights workers and feminists, people who were both Muslim and secular, [where] everyone objected to the fact that transgender women were being killed regularly on the streets of Ankara. So, what's the alliance

that emerged? Feminists who had also been dealing with sexual violence on the street. Gay, lesbian, queer people, who are not transgender, but are allied because they experience a similar sense of vulnerability or injurability on the streets. SlutWalk is another way of doing this by working together in modes of solidarity that insist upon walking freely without violence and harassment.[168]

In contrast to Butler's praise for their diversity, SlutWalks have nonetheless been criticized by Black women as insensitive to the historical meanings of the term *slut*, which have been integral to the sexual dynamics of white supremacy: "In the United States, where slavery constructed Black female sexualities, Jim Crow kidnappings, rape and lynchings, gender misrepresentations and more recently, where the Black female immigrant struggle combine, 'slut' has different associations for Black Women. We do not recognize ourselves nor do we see our lived experiences reflected within SlutWalk and especially not in its brand and label."[169] This criticism of elitism has been levied in international contexts as well. In India, for example, the marches have met resistance because the protest is seen as overtly middle class and too individualistic.[170]

Although SlutWalks identify the dangers of rape culture in a parallel manner to Dworkin, the marches take place in the day, signaling the centrality of visual representation to women's subordination. Manner of dress is often used to blame women for their own experiences of sexual violence. Visual representation also underscores the significance of performative politics designed to queer or reclaim the *slut* epithet. As Annie Hill explains this logic:

> SlutWalk protesters contest the discursive and visual ideology of sexual violence when they speak back to rape logic and enact an oppositional gaze. . . . Feminist resistance must oppose dominant ways of looking because rape logic operates by exteriorizing sexuality and distributing women's desire across the bodily surface. Rape logic depicts the female body as a surface of sexual signifiers and male attention is directed by the body that stimulates it: citing a woman's unspoken yet visible consent locates responsibility for sex on her body, in her choice of clothes, and in her desire to appear as an object of desire for men.[171]

Hill's account of the oppositional gaze renders bodies as a surface of signifiers, in a similar way to radical feminists' critique of pornography. For Dworkin, "the most insidious thing about pornography is that it tells male truth as if it were universal truth. Those depictions of women in chains being tortured are supposed to represent our deepest erotic aspirations. And some of us believe it, don't we? The most important thing about pornography is that the values in it are the common values of men."[172] Dworkin's theory that women's imputed sexuality is not easily severable from oppression, that insufficient daylight for rhetorical challenge can be found between sexual representation and desire, is denigrated and deflected by darkness in Take Back the Night marches. The male gaze, as a form of truth opposed by SlutWalk activism, is, in contrast, metaphorically dependent on vision and light. It is resisted by resignification in marches that take place in the daylight.

This resignification takes many forms. Affectively, SlutWalk shifts Dworkin's concern for women's *fear*, resulting from men's sexual terrorism, to *shame*, which originates in the internalization of the gaze of the other. For Sonya Barnett, who first named the march SlutWalk, overcoming shame involves a public embracing of sexual pleasure and freedom: "I would label myself a 'slut' before a 'feminist.' . . . I've always enjoyed sex, hot sex, consensual sex. . . . I got the reputation of 'slut,' and was pretty pissed that I got stuck with that label when the guys I slept with got high fives. . . . In the last few years, I've come to embrace my sluthood, especially after honing a certain code. Sex should always be between consenting adults and all parties involved (because sometimes there are more than two) need to know and be fine with such an intimate exchange."[173] Owning and affirming one's own sexuality without shame and demanding the respect and protection the police would deny on account of women's "slutty" appearance disentangles the body from the marks of others' sexual property. No longer burdened by the sartorial signs of the respectable woman or the propertized body of the prostitute, women are free to embrace what Jo Reger calls a personalized "ethical code as a sexual person."[174] Individualizing this code also opens a space for a diversity of sexual identities and experiences to emerge. If shame can be "experienced as the affective cost of not following the scripts of normative existence," according to Sara Ahmed, dispelling shame lessens the grip of a dominant sexual code, replacing collective judgment with individual choice and contractual logic.[175] Overcoming shame is, as Martha Nussbaum argues, a fundamentally liberal goal.[176]

Based in liberal rights to sartorially represent oneself as one chooses without judgment or punishment, SlutWalk imputes the Enlightenment contractual value of consent to sexual agency. One Tasmanian organizer of a local march explained, "We are walking to spread the word that our clothes are not our consent and that sexual assault is never justified and victims are never at fault."[177] This counterclaim to the argument that women ask for and acquiesce to sexual violence by their self-representation undergirds the framework of consent under which SlutWalks operate. This is most often tacit, but SlutWalks have sometimes been rebranded as "ConsentFest" to make this clear.[178] Consent is, in legal theorist Deborah Tuerkheimer's condensation, SlutWalk's touchstone.[179]

The liberal argument for consent is not derived from women's pleasure; consent is not essentially sexy.[180] Rather, consent stems from the always already existing potential of self-ownership, with several consequences. For one, this ontological foundation creates racial tensions within the movement not dissimilar to those experienced by Take Back the Night. In a 2011 statement from the Black women's Crunk Feminist Collective, SlutWalk was criticized for its unacknowledged privileging of whiteness that presumed the freedom of consent:

> To organize a movement around the reclamation of a term is in and of itself an act of white privilege. To not make explicit and clear the privilege and power inherent in such an act is to invite less-informed folks with privilege (in other words, folks who know just enough to be dangerous) to assume that reclamation can be applied universally.... For Black women, our struggles with sexuality are to find the space of recognition that exists between the hypervisibility of our social construction as hoes, jezebels, hoochies, and skanks, and the invisibility proffered by a respectability politics that tells us it's always safer to dissemble. To reclaim slut as an empowered experience of sexuality does not move Black women out of these binaries. We are always already sexually free, insatiable, ready to go, freaky, dirty, and by consequence, unrapable. When it comes to reclamations of sexuality, in some senses, Black women are always already fucked.[181]

Powerful critiques such as this have sometimes been read as invitations for renewed liberal dialogue and inclusion by SlutWalk's sympathizers, such as Tuerkheimer: "It may be that inclusion of the perspectives of Black women will result in a far more critical stance toward using sexuality to end rape."[182] In non-Western venues, this white bias has not automatically been problematic. For Ratna Kapur, the freedom to bring sexuality out of the dark resists the ideology of the passive Indian woman, in whose name many repressive Hindu nationalist policies have been enacted: "[Slut-Walks] challenge fossilized accounts of cultural belonging as well as the idea that body exposure is an invitation to rape. That is a good thing. Sex is out of the closet and it is no longer a dirty depraved, disgusting thing that only 'bad' or 'loose' women flaunt or engage in."[183] For Kapur, SlutWalk is "feminism lite": it lacks a big revolutionary punch and provides little theory of social transformation, but it does offer a potential for critiquing liberal reformism and governance.

However, the critical potential of SlutWalk to develop new ideas of governance marches in tension with its reliance on (often heterosexual) representational politics and the ideology of consent. The representation of the slut that visually dominates the parodic march orients critique to heterosexual assumptions of women's availability to men. As Lorna Bracewell has argued, this narrows the focus on choice and freedom in a manner that was foreign to the original impetus behind Take Back the Night:

> [The] emphasis on self-expression and personal choice, especially as it pertains to the conventionally feminine and heterosexual women who bear the brunt of the "slut" stigma, distinguishes SlutWalk rather starkly from the sexual politics of sex-radical feminism. . . . Sex-radical feminists vindicated a vision of sexual freedom so expansive that it seems scandalous and utopian even today. They demanded not merely more space for individual women to enact fairly conventional forms of feminine heterosexuality, but an end to all legal and extra-legal methods of enforcing erotic conformity including statutory rape laws, child pornography laws, laws prohibiting public sex, family violence, employment and housing discrimination; and psychiatric diagnoses and hegemonic norms that punish the "perverse" and reward the "normal." In stark contrast, the SlutWalk movement shows little interest in addressing these multifarious forms of sexual oppression.[184]

This disinterest in the *dispositifs* of oppression constrains SlutWalk's diversity, but, more important, the various criminal laws and social norms regulating sexual choice that go unmentioned in SlutWalk protests bracket from critique some of the institutions and agencies that ultimately facilitate sexual violence.[185]

Apart from its narrowing of the problem of rape and assault (and the range of those who suffer from it), SlutWalk's emphasis on consent and the celebration of sexual agency slyly but surely allies the movement with the state's carceral impulses. The original criticism of advice by police to assume responsibility for one's personal safety by limiting what one wears ironically has come to embrace police responses to keep women safe. As

Bracewell remarks, "[SlutWalk's] macro level demand that police respect and protect 'sluts' just as they would any other citizens bolsters the carceral state's image as masculine protector and aggrandizes its power. . . . The goal of . . . North American SlutWalks was not to highlight police and law enforcement complicity in sexual violence and rape culture but to figure the 'slut' as a supplicant before the law deserving of its benevolent protection as any other citizen."[186] If SlutWalk is distractedly charmed by the ideal of legal protection, it fails to address the institutional power facilitating rape and sexual assault in another manner. The liberal emphasis on consent and the cultural value of representational freedom avoids an analysis of rape law for which consent is irrelevant.[187] Despite its own disinterest in legal critique, Take Back the Night's identification of night with danger inadvertently engages rape law's concern about the use of force in the definition of sexual assault. But consent itself has become an issue within rape law in only a handful of jurisdictions, and even if it *should* be more widespread, it is embedded in cultural contexts that SlutWalk doesn't acknowledge or analyze.

One problem is that women agree to sex for reasons other than pleasure, making consent too broad a category for sex-affirmative arguments voiced in SlutWalk. Criminal law overlooks discursive consent entirely, or in the few jurisdictions where consent has legal relevance, the significance of force and resistance is still smuggled into trials through prosecutorial and defense narratives.[188] As Tuerkheimer points out, the criminal law constructs female sexuality as nonagentic: force is so fundamental to the crime of rape that even where some jurisdictions criminalize anaesthetic sex (sexual touching during incapacitation), it is the incapacitation and not the lack of consent that makes the crime. Women who are assaulted still can be interrogated for historical patterns of sexual activity that are deemed culturally deviant or "distinctive," including prostitution, group sex, or even a one-night stand, which build a "presumption of unrapability."[189] "Women who transgress sexual boundaries are suspected of proclivities toward perpetual consent."[190]

Bringing to light the problems of consent may be a reasoned addition to rape law to advance women's interests. Nonetheless, legal reform has rarely if ever been the focus of SlutWalk protests. Take Back the Night is not reformist, either, but for reasons that seem much more critical. The police that Dworkin accuses of facilitating the nocturnal hunt of women by men are emblematic of a state that perversely violates its own liberal categories, particularly those maintained by property relations. Rather than protecting all its citizens' autonomy, the state shields men whose pleasure in violence makes no distinction between public and private, pretends no room for individual consent, and pays no attention to women's self-representation or shame; owning one's consent is an insufficient foundation for political action. Dworkin thinks from the dark, but as the Take Back the Night march is designed to reveal to its participants, the dark spaces of the night are not all colonized by danger. Night holds a liberatory potential that we can only feel our way toward: an individual and collective overcoming of fear, an opportunity for sexual minorities to build community, a dark consciousness-raising that metaphorically and ironically denies the "point of view" or standpoint that has been the hallmark of so much feminist thought. As MacKinnon rhetorically captures this argument, "Women's situation offers no outside to stand on or gaze at, no inside to escape to, too much urgency to wait, no place else to go, and nothing to use but the twisted tools that have been shoved down our throats. If feminism is revolutionary, this is why."[191] For MacKinnon, the impossibility of facile escape into representation was what made "unmodified" feminism so radical.

WINNING THE DAY

> When we women struggle for freedom, we must begin at the beginning and fight for freedom of movement, which we have not had and do not now have. In reality, we are not allowed out after dark. In some parts of the world, women are not allowed out at all but we, in this exemplary democracy, are permitted to totter around, half crippled, during the day, and for this, of course, we must be grateful. —**Andrea Dworkin**

> We are forced to play Russian roulette; each night, a gun is placed against our temples. Each day, we are strangely grateful to be alive.
> —**Andrea Dworkin**

Dworkin's radical rethinking of Enlightenment values, read into the nocturnal march against violence, is worth a second look.[192] Reports of violence against women have grown apace, marked by women's continued feelings of being excluded from the freedom of movement at night. Imaginatively putting the night before the day dims the light of feminism's various turns toward state power, policy, and representational politics as forms in which to secure equality, security, and justice. Returning to the dark and reappropriating idioms of common property, Dworkin's politics suggest that only where social norms among women allow them to break through fear and establish new forms of power without mediation is there a way to win the day. This is a sexual politics rather than a legal politics, but it need not be seen as a complete turn away from law. Dworkin's arguments raise the question how law may still codify the tortious injuries suffered and defined by women, how it may remove the gun from too many women's heads.

Dworkin's commitment in the early 1980s to the antipornography ordinances, along with MacKinnon and others, not long after she wrote the text on night, is not easily squared with the potential of her theoretical directions. The ordinances would allow civil suits for pornographic harm, expressing hope and faith that law, policy, and willing juries would facilitate seizing the day for women. Putting all her chips on the elimination of pornographic representation met furious resistance, alienated women of color, courted antifeminist allies, and hastened the move toward new ideas of feminism less focused on the dangers of heterosexuality.

Dworkin's early insistence on controlling and owning the night is, I think, a reminder to rethink law from its roots, returning to a time before the earliest Enlightenment commitment to an individualistic law of property that reduced women's autonomy and indeed left too many women and men as property, and others dispossessed of land and chosen ways of life. Judith van Allen illustrates this historical problem in her discussion of the impact of British colonialism on Igbo women in early twentieth-century Nigeria.[193] At first culturally unable to recognize Igbo women's parallel political authority to men, the British efforts to co-opt male authorities to facilitate colonial control upended women's cooperative institutions that shared information and organized women's interests in village decision-making. These women's institutions also demanded men's responsibility to limit sexual violence and took matters into their own hands when men failed to do so. Through a mechanism translated as "sitting on a man," women collectively surrounded the compound of a violent man or one who disrespected women's property. Sitting on a man involved "dancing, singing scurrilous songs which detailed the women's grievances against him and often called his manhood into question, banging on his hut with the pestles women used for pounding yams, and perhaps demolishing his hut or plastering it with mud and roughing him up a bit. A man might be sanctioned in this way for mistreating his wife, for violating the women's market rules, or for letting his cows eat the women's crops. The women would stay at his hut throughout the day, and late into the night, if necessary, until he repented and promised to mend his ways."[194] These sometimes-nocturnal efforts to enforce women's individual and collective authority escalated into a monthlong women's war on colonial authorities in 1929 in which women "'sat on' Warrant Chiefs and burned Native Court buildings, and, in some cases, released prisoners from jail."[195] The British called the uprising "irrational" and exonerated the soldiers who fired on the women, unable, according to Van Allen, to see women's traditional and ongoing political roles. Van Allen calls this a blindness to women's power that emerged unexpectedly from the dark.

There are contemporary parallels. The Reclaim These Streets vigil held at Clapham Common in London in early 2021 to protest the nocturnal killing of Sarah Everard, allegedly by a police officer, occurred spontaneously after authorities banned the protest due to pandemic regulations, explicitly telling women to stay home for their own security. Violent efforts by police to arrest and subdue women protesters were met with shouts of "Hey, mister, get your hands off my sister!," "Arrest your own," "Shame on you," and "Who do you protect?" Shared videos of police violence created a political firestorm and energized continued protest across the United Kingdom on behalf of Everard and others, targeting the lack of police attention to crimes against women in private and public spaces.[196] These spontaneous efforts to act beyond the law and challenge legal authorities echo the history of British Reclaim the Night activism: they are collective efforts by women to take back and rhetorically own again the mechanisms of collective power that were never willingly ceded. They also are powerful echoes of the history of struggles to preserve Clapham Common as shared, common property, finally secured against vigorous efforts at enclosure in 1877.[197]

Dworkin never directly argued that women's power to suppress male violence (in the ways the Igbo had) had a historical antecedent in the West, but the rhetoric of nocturnal feminist marches and protests implies this historical potential, hearkening back to the early struggles against enclosure, and the witch trials that men rarely protested. Taking *back* the night or *reclaiming* the streets implies that there once was a time of women's countervailing power that was lost, perhaps before the demonization of women, the Enlightenment norms of property ownership, and the advent of laws regulating violence and rape. In an institutional spirit like sitting on a man, marching to own the night returns political and legal thought to a framework for women's power ripe for rediscovery.

CHAPTER FIVE

TRANSLATION IN THE DARK

The hallucinations of the night, be they of the flesh or of the spirit, always dissolve into air with the first light of morning, the light that reorders the world and restores it to its usual orbit, once more rewriting the books of the law. —**José Saramago**

Just as a tangent touches a circle lightly and at but one point—establishing, with this touch rather than with the point, the law according to which it is to continue on its straight path to infinity—a translation touches the original lightly and only at the infinitely small point of the sense, thereupon pursuing its own course according to the laws of fidelity in the freedom of linguistic flux. —**Walter Benjamin**

The violence of an injustice has begun when all the members of a community do not share the same idiom throughout. —**Jacques Derrida**

Can we, should we, bring legal thought to the night? Law has long been seen to move and grow along various paths and lines of flight, assimilating its immunities and its penalties to new contexts, at its best arcing toward justice.[1] For example, civil rights and antidiscrimination law have often expanded protections to new social identities such as disability and sexual orientation through comparison to established ideals and characteristics of race and gender equality (such as immutability, discreteness, and liberty of choice).[2] Does this extension of protected categories on the basis of being "like race" or "like gender" serve as a model (an analogy, a metaphor) for fully subsuming nocturnal life to legal norms?[3] In previous chapters I have examined how night has hidden the violence that legal order demands to control and how it has cloaked new social formations that make demands for different legal orders. I have argued that the rhythmic daily movement of day to night is critical for understanding how curfew governs, and that sleep embeds in physiological need new kernels of legality. What might it take to think of law more completely from its dark, nocturnal corners to its radiant power without presuming or reconstituting its mythical continuity? Is there a master metaphor or analogy that can account for the oscillation between nocturnal and diurnal *dispositifs* and forms of life? Can we adequately think about the night without obliterating it, without disrupting or displacing communities and tactics of resistance, without shining a light into its dark places and rendering it daylike? In short, what might it mean to translate between law's relevance to night and its more common enlightened categories, terms, and meanings?

The general question of legal translation has often devolved to a concern over movement. Does legal translation preserve and conserve community and legal ordering, or does law travel badly between orders, failing to touch lightly (as Walter Benjamin suggests in the epigraph with his metaphor of the tangent) and stumbling over the idiomatic meanings that yield only with a certain violence of injustice?[4] Metaphors, as Jacques Derrida reminds us, are also matters of (and certainly for) translation: they are already movement. "*Metaphora* circulates in the city, it conveys us like its inhabitants, along all sorts of routes, with intersections, red lights, one-way streets, no-exits, crossroads or crossings, and speed limits. . . . We are already circulating in translation."[5] Derrida's metaphorical language suggests that this space of translation is always already legal, moving within the syntagmatic rules of the road. Certainly, much contemporary legal scholarship has considered the travel of metaphor and the philosophical grounds for measuring this traffic and gauging these rules.[6] Many agree with Derrida on this point: "Metaphor is never innocent. It orients research and fixes results."[7]

How is this different for the novelist José Saramago's image above of the orbital daily movement of hallucination into dawn's wakeful legal order? The waking duty of rewriting the books of the law suggests that law is perpetually being reconstituted as a foundation for its authority and that it also remains evanescent, dissolving into the madness of night, obscured by the delusional mists of the unconscious, where it rarely orients our research or fixes results. In this project to think about the law at night, I have explored the genealogy of legality after the sun sets in several different venues, touching lightly on various historical periods, philosophy, sociology, political theology and theory, as well as legal doctrine, in ways that challenge part of Saramago's image. The idea that legality reassembles itself in daylight, implying its necessary absence at night or when unconscious, is certainly wrong. Yet the insight that modern legality projects itself in metaphorical light is mostly true, ill fitting an analysis of the law in the dark.

I noted in the introduction to this book that night was once more prominently written into the Western premodern law. Although modern law has formally left the night behind, cultural ideas of night's distinctiveness endure, as Saramago makes clear: night is a time of different reason, of the loss of subjectivity in sleep, of potentially violent, chaotic, and fearful encounter. Night is also a time of greater social freedom as signs of status are more easily confounded and legal and social norms evaded and reconstructed. While social control differs at night, most modern law, in contrast, has metaphorically forgotten night, imagining law as a constant radiation.[8] Law circulates with its dominant metaphors of enlightenment that render darkness, blackness, and night as frontiers to which law will naturally propagate in order to illuminate and reorder, maintaining law's unitary image of a book.

What do we gain from this quest to translate legal ideas between day and night? Law today resists night's particularity, overlooking its significance for achieving justice. Seeking to translate enlightenment metaphors to nocturnal experience holds the potential to grant us a greater appreciation for the violence that suffuses law—sometimes or often unseen—as well as the limits to state authority, which are most pronounced at night. The homeless, the racialized minority out of place after dark, the abused woman, the youth or the Palestinian controlled by the curfew, the prisoner denied sleep: these characters who find a sympathetic place in this book suffer a violence often facilitated by the daily rhythms of law, particularly once the courthouse has closed its doors and turned off the lights. I don't suggest that such an act of translation to dignify the night and the violence some experience after dark is itself an act of justice: bringing legal grammar into consonance with the experiences of night may or may not promote equality, fairness, or integrity. These Enlightenment values need to respect the potentially dangerous ideological power of light to colonize opposing ideals and diminish dreams of different futures. As Hans Blumenberg writes, light can be a "dazzling superabundance," an "illumination capable of conquering without force."[9] If we acknowledge that justice is greater than the decisions and policies of the state and that power is now located beyond the juridical and theological realms that once sought to contain it, then politics and sociality that take place shadowed from the bedazzlement of light must be accounted for. In this regard, translation may offer to some the opportunity to bring to light from their dark origins new legal and political ideas.

The translation that I therefore seek is not a simple search for nocturnal metaphor. Too much that happens at night is beyond language even though we may assume it lies potentially within the ambit of law. Sleep, as Saramago suggests and as I have argued in this book, is one such nocturnal nonlinguistic experience. This does not mean that the study of metaphor is meaningless for our quest to translate between day and night, for I agree with Derrida that there is no linguistic outside to metaphor. I argue, however, that to formally comprehend the relationships of law to the night explored in this book, a supplement to metaphor is essential. Night holds aspects of social life that are, at best, quasi-events lacking conscious presence and lived within distinct social ontologies held fast in the dark, which must infuse our search for the social justice of translation.[10] I will look for these supplements in ideas of sleep, vigilantism, the curfew, and nocturnal politics that I have discussed in the previous chapters. Let me first address the general problem of metaphor for law and the night.

LIGHT ON METAPHOR

The day is for honest men, the night for thieves. —**Euripides**

Paul Ricoeur has argued that metaphor enlarges meanings by inviting secondary meanings, but only in some contexts—such as the genre of tragedy—does it open us fully, ontologically, to other worlds.[11] Interpretation, he writes, is "a process in which the disclosure of *new modes of being*—or, if you prefer [Ludwig] Wittgenstein to [Martin] Heidegger, of new *forms of life* gives to the subject a new capacity of knowing himself."[12] If metaphor expands meaning without fully revealing other worlds, it is, perhaps, unable to competently map the social problems, much less the "truth" law ideologically claims to engage with.

With less philosophical rigor, jurisprudence has also been cautious with metaphor. Before sitting on the Supreme Court, Judge Benjamin Cardozo famously and ironically quipped in dicta, "Metaphors in law are to be narrowly watched, for starting as devices to liberate thought, they end often by enslaving it."[13] The concern that semantic freedom is paradoxical—that it ends in (a metaphorical) mental enslavement—has a long history. Peter Goodrich notes that "even the greatest practitioners of rhetoric admitted that it was dangerous, that probability was not truth, that persuasion was not conviction and that analogy (metaphor) was not essence (necessity/ uniqueness)."[14] Language, and rhetoric more generally for Aristotle, Cicero, and other classical thinkers, "*was* power for those who had access to the realm of public discourse."[15] The centrifugal aspects of rhetoric and metaphor reinforce, for jurisprudence, the (desperate?) hold of syntactic rule and code. Thus, despite scholarship exploring the rich and diverse metaphors of law, it is common to hear admonitions to get law back on its road to social betterment. On battle, sports, and sex: "Metaphors lie behind substantive, procedural, and ethical rules that reward competition and discourage greater cooperation; they keep us from seeing the extent of problems within the adversary system and possible solutions to those problems."[16] On slime and darkness: "Metaphors can hamper understanding when we lose sight of their status as tropes and take them for reality."[17] On walls of separation and penumbrae: "Metaphors . . . have their drawbacks. They do not yield precise legal tests."[18]

Despite revealing the rhetorical worlds of the law, many works on legal metaphor have (rhetorically!) dodged the horror that perhaps language is, as legal theorist Jack Balkin writes, "inescapably metaphorical and figural; that a logically pure language, divorced from metaphor, has never existed."[19] As if never wanting to drop the preordained map of their legal landscape while traveling with metaphor, legal scholars often cozy up unannounced to the side of metaphysics. For Martin Heidegger this is not surprising since, he writes, "the metaphorical exists only within metaphysics."[20] Friedrich Nietzsche similarly indicts the ways that metaphor is manipulated to create metaphysical hierarchy from the plurality it could otherwise expose: "the construction of a pyramidal order according to castes and degrees, the creation of a new world of laws, privileges, subordinations, and clearly marked boundaries—a new world, one which now confronts that other vivid world of first impressions as more solid, more universal, better known, and more human than the immediately perceived world, and thus as the regulative and imperative world. . . . Only by forgetting this primitive world of metaphor can one live with any repose, security, and consistency."[21] What this repose, security, and consistency based on the neglecting of metaphor produces for Nietzsche, along with a "world of laws," is a (for him, disturbing and repressive) sense of "social justice" and the suspicious residue of "truth": "illusions that are no longer remembered as being illusions, metaphors that have become worn and stripped of their sensuous force, coins that have lost their design and are now considered only as metal and no longer as coins."[22] Nietzsche's *longue durée* of active forgetting suggests to many of his interlocutors that (especially tired) metaphor signals our numbness to the possibilities of being. Rarely, however, has this span of forgetful time been imagined on the quotidian nightly scale that Saramago's image measures, a timescale I reconsider in more depth later in this chapter.[23]

Beforehand, I want to traverse the images of light and dark that rhetorically enliven law in order to discover a possible place for night. This voyage involves, I show below, travel through the heliotropic metaphors that illuminate modern law while navigating the two aspects of night that have structured this project and that will provide some critical signposts of our journey: night as a time of heightened danger and the imagination of lesser state capacity, and night as a time of relative equality where some signs of status are diminished and possibilities for resistance to diurnal order increase.

That dawn light holds the capacity to "rewrit[e] the books of the law" suggests that the mystical foundation of legal authority is likely as much a product of its historical relationship to an originary—and likely revolutionary—event, as Benjamin claims it to be, as of the daily event of night and the nocturnal orders that law must displace.[24] Understanding the generative nature of nocturnal forms of life animates metaphor in a different manner, exposing the ways that meaning assembles alongside forms of violence and through affect, translating us to new destinations we might provisionally designate a "dark law."[25] The paradoxical tension in this journey is palpable; how we see the dark without being able to see in the dark is a conundrum and a spur to new destinations, to new scholarship. The onerous translation of one set of metaphors to another, of moving between realms of light and dark, must therefore resist what Robert Cover has called a jurispathic desire in law that seeks to eliminate the plurality of meanings that rhetoric actively, passionately promotes.[26] Legal metaphor must ultimately disrupt the metaphysical.

The aspiration to make this move through the escape of "metaphorics" is an impossible one, as Derrida has famously argued, as is the ancillary authoritarian hope for a "metaphorology" that could neutralize or at least hold meaning fast. Such dreams nonetheless undergird a myth that produces Western culture as well as the subjectivity and supremacy of a racialized whiteness. "What is metaphysics? A white mythology which assembles and reflects Western culture: the white man takes his own mythology (that is, Indo-European mythology), his *logos*—that is, the *mythos* of his idiom for the universal form of that which it is still his inescapable desire to call Reason. . . . What is white mythology? It is metaphysics which has effaced in itself that fabulous scene which brought it into being, and which yet remains, active and stirring, inscribed in white ink, an invisible drawing covered over in the palimpsest."[27] If the escape is impossible, must it also be so for those who do not share a berth in, or are subordinated by, Western metaphorics? Derrida emphasizes a whiteness to which he does not necessarily claim to belong. He is an Algerian Jew victimized by Vichy, an outsider whose philosophy never gained the influence or respect in France that it did elsewhere.[28] Although, as Pal Ahluwalia has argued, Derrida's own philosophical deconstruction of white mythology and the primacy of Western thought has itself paradoxically become "a pre-eminent sign of Western intellectual domination," the possibilities of an outside to the limitations of Western metaphysics and Enlightenment have nonetheless tantalized numerous philosophical projects, sometimes under the sign of night.[29]

One reason is the recognition that travel within metaphor risks those who are committed to its road maps getting lost because, as Derrida argues, metaphoricity precedes metaphor and concept, making for too many street signs, a "bottomless overdeterminability."[30] He writes:

> I cannot produce a *treatise* on metaphor that is not *treated with* metaphor, which suddenly appears intractable. . . . I can brake only by letting skid, in other words, letting my control as driver slip away up to a certain point.[31]

> If we wanted to conceive and classify all the metaphorical possibilities of philosophy, there would always be at least one metaphor which would be excluded and remain outside the system: that one, at least, which was needed to construct the concept of metaphor, or to cut the argument short, the metaphor of metaphor.[32]

As soon as translation and motion become chaotic, at the "moment of its most invasive extension," metaphor—as Nietzsche saw—withdraws, repetitively leaving a trace in what Derrida expansively calls the text.[33]

This withdrawal is most evident in darkness and night. Beginning with Aristotle in the Western tradition, Derrida points out, the metaphor of metaphor invokes the sun and light, the possibility of sight.[34] Heliotropic metaphors are bad metaphors (a tautological necessity of *any* metaphor, which has no proper orientation to a truth) because, Aristotle suggests, it is difficult to know what is proper to the sun.[35] Derrida writes:

> The sun, from this [Aristotelian] point of view, is a sensible object par excellence. It is the paradigm of what is sensible *and* of what is metaphorical: it regularly turns (itself) and hides (itself). The trope of metaphor always implies a sensible kernel, or rather something which, like what is sensible, may always fail to be present actually and in person.[36]

> Any metaphor may always be read at once as a particular figure and as a paradigm of the very process of metaphorization: *idealization* and *appropriation*. Everything in talk about metaphor . . . is articulated on the analogy between *our* looking and sensible looking, between the intelligible and the visible sun.[37]

The ambiguity created by appearing and disappearing—including the oppositions of day/night, visible/invisible, present/absent: "all this is possible only under the sun."[38] In addition, this metaphor cannibalizes itself. Derrida explains, "The sun is never properly present in discourse. With every metaphor, there is no doubt somewhere a sun; but each time that there is the sun, metaphor has begun. If the sun is already and always metaphorical, it is not completely natural. It is already and always a lustre: one might call it an *artificial* construction if this could have any meaning in the absence of nature. For if the sun is not entirely natural, what can remain in nature that is natural?"[39] What the heliotrope does is set up its own conditions for its disappearance, "its own death within it."[40] The sun is both blinding and luminous.[41] It returns to itself, rising in the (Oriental) east but traveling toward the (European) West.

Rather than behold a singular source of radiation, when we stare into the metaphorical sun, using such tools as deconstruction that trace the pathways of metaphorology, we comprehend multiple emanations. "As soon as we admit that in an analogical relation all the terms are already individually set in a metaphorical relation, the whole begins to function, no longer as a sun but as a star, the pinpoint source of truth, of what is proper, remaining invisible, or nocturnal."[42] The pathway to these stars—for they are ultimately manifold—is what Rodolphe Gasché has called a quasi-transcendental movement intimating a plurality that cannot be rendered fully visible. Nor, as Martin Jay has emphasized, is it amenable to any singular sense such as vision.[43] Nor, I would add, does this plurality imply the same kinds of vulnerabilities that in the case of the sun are metaphorized as "blindness," nor the same kinds of power that organize themselves around vision (e.g., surveillance, panopticism, cynegetic relations, which I have explored in earlier chapters). Knowledge in and of the night may remain metaphorical, but the forms that knowledge must take are distinct from the model of the heliotrope. Indeed, it is here that an outside to metaphor and to its juridical expression might tentatively be located. The struggles of the enslaved to escape into a starry night their captors could not control, the possibilities of sleep as a politics beyond or tangential to law, marching in solidarity through the night: all push against or add to Enlightenment forms of knowledge, and all have potentially adverse relationships to law.

Much legal writing on metaphor captures some plurality, but the heliotrope in its modeling of knowledge and its centripetal motion toward (and constitution of) a center remains of overriding significance. Bernard Hibbitts, for example, catalogs and explores both common visual and aural metaphors that herald a "reconfiguration of American legal discourse":

> We frequently consider law as a matter of looking: we "observe" it; we evaluate claims "in the eye of the law"; our high courts "review" the decisions of inferior tribunals. Alternatively, we speak of law as something one would usually look at: it is a "body," a "text," a "structure," a "bulwark of freedom," a "seamless web," and even a "magic mirror." . . . We associate legal reasoning with the manipulation of visible geometric forms: we try to "square" precedents with one another; we repeatedly agonize over "where the line [between different doctrines and situations] can be drawn." We discuss legality in terms of light and darkness: we search for "bright-line" tests, we consider an area of concurrent jurisdiction to be a "zone of twilight"; we seek to extend constitutional protections by probing the shadowy "penumbras" of well-known guarantees.[44]

For Hibbitts (as with Derrida), these metaphors organize the power of elites (men, whites, "Anglos," Protestants) over subordinates. "By making special use of the written word to secure or extend their cultural authority, members of the former groups have gained a special respect for vision and the visual that they have unilaterally made the standard for 'American' culture as a whole."[45] Legal professionals have respectively developed a phenomenology of sight that organizes thinking about law as ideally "abstract, disengaging, objective, determinate, timeless, systematic and differentiatory."[46]

Aural metaphors have become more common among disadvantaged groups, where "voice," "speaking," having a "hearing," "listening," breaking "silence," and the like organize progressive legal mobilization and infuse much critical American jurisprudence. Hibbitts emphasizes a phenomenology of sound that projects law as "concrete, relational, subjective, multivariate, dynamic, process-oriented, and transcendent."[47] In contrast to law's abstraction perpetuated by visual metaphor, sound is *im*-mediate; "sound waves literally reach out from their source to touch us; in certain circumstances . . . we can actually feel sound as physical vibration."[48]

Nonetheless, I argue, the rhetorical use of aural metaphor does not escape the sun's orbit nor the power of the heliotrope in this account. The critical belief that law should attend to diversity through listening and hearing still proposes an image of law's ear as centralized and—as anyone in a cacophonous, trendy restaurant can attest it must be—as centrally ordered to make sense from noise. Additionally, sound, like darkness, does not only organize voice. Nietzsche, who argued that sound in the form of music had the capacity to oppose the Apollonian demand for order, understood that it was the stirring of emotion able to "discharge . . . all its powers of representation, imitation, transfiguration, transmutation, every kind of mimicry and play-acting" that drowned out abstract reason.[49] Especially at night in those places where legal order is more uncertain—its symbols absent, its terror less constrained—sound commonly provokes fear and dread. The nocturnal evolutionary impetus perfecting the ear depends on the fearful experiences of night, according to Nietzsche. "In bright daylight the ear is less necessary," he wrote.[50] If sound can "touch" us directly (a nocturnal dread), there is no reason to discount fear and panic as characteristics every bit as significant as "having voice" or "demanding a hearing."[51] The radical plurality imagined as stars in the night that Derrida finds in the deconstructed heliotrope emerges not intrinsically in aural metaphors of legality but in the nonlinguistic emotions and affects of the night.

Similar problems arise in some scholarly work on the penumbra and its vexing meaning stemming from its liminal relation to light and night. The philosopher Gérard Genette has argued that there is a semantic dissymmetry between night and day whereby night is marked (representing accident, alteration, distance), while day remains unmarked and normal. This dissymmetry causes discrete problems of meaning for intermediate times as well as for shadow. He writes, "Nature, at least at our latitudes, moves imperceptibly from day to night; language itself cannot so pass from one word to the other: between day and night, language can use several intermediate terms such as dawn and dusk, etc., but it cannot speak of night and day at the same time, a little bit of day and a little bit of night."[52] The metaphorical penumbra, which famously guides the reasoning of Justice William O. Douglas in *Griswold v. Connecticut* but has a long tradition of use in legal doctrine before, has been used in different ways to indicate uncertainty and indeterminacy, an extension of legal limits, and a periphery or fringe.[53] Yet much as Genette's argument that day remains grammatically unmarked, the penumbra reproduces the central metaphor of light and sun from its marginal imagery.

Consider Justice Douglas's arguments in *Griswold* for a right to privacy, which relied on the following language of precedent: "The foregoing cases suggest that specific guarantees in the Bill of Rights have penumbras, formed by emanations from those guarantees that help give them life and substance."[54] Douglas cited many such emanations, including the First, Third, Fourth, Fifth, and Ninth Amendments. One emanation, the Fourth and Fifth Amendment protections of "the sanctity of a man's home and the privacies of life," could have called to the nocturnal medieval and early modern practice of shutting in that I have explored in earlier chapters and that historians have regarded as one source of the Fourth Amendment.[55] Yet is a penumbral emanation originating in or moving toward darkness or light?

Christopher Rideout understands the penumbral metaphor to be spatial, a specific form of a general metaphor of the container often used in formal legal reasoning. According to him, Douglas violates the logic of this metaphor in two ways. First, "if the specific guarantees in the Bill of Rights have penumbras (a peripheral region), then those specific guarantees should lie in the umbra, or shaded portion (the core region next to which the penumbra is peripheral). But the shaded portion could not at the same time have emanations."[56] Penumbras are the product not only of light but also of shadow. Second, the idea of "emanations" can only stem from light sources that stand as metaphors for ideas. "Light is good, and darkness and shadow are not. In addition, we 'find' things in the light, but we do not find things in darkness. So, if in Douglas's telling, the right to privacy lies in the penumbral shading, this location violates the entailment of his second metaphorical schema. We would expect to find the object of his inquiry, the right to privacy, in the light, not in the shade."[57] Whether a more successful deployment of the metaphor would make better law, a question that has occupied many legal analysts, is not my interest here. Rather, I wish to point out that even where there has been an opportunity to draw inspiration from the night or from shade, and to make meaning from the multiple and fragmented sources of "emanations" (like stars), it has been forsaken for the heliotrope.

Darkness is included in numerous legal metaphors, but as Martha Grace Duncan has extensively demonstrated, nearly all connote negative, outlaw sentiments. Criminals are associated with filth, excrement, and slime, attributions that are linked together through their affinities to darkness.[58] "The association with profound darkness suffices to render an act more suspect than it would have been if done in the light."[59] Darkness feeds further metaphorical ideas about the criminal subject (evil, racialized, reptilian), progress (decay), and health (disgust, odor, death, disease). Duncan argues that the fascination with and unconscious allure of filth and sometimes the criminal keeps darkness close at hand. And yet, as William Shakespeare's Macbeth notes with his observation that "light thickens," darkness is often "portrayed not as the absence of light, or as a void, but rather as a denser, more solid form of light."[60] These associations suggest night and dark must wait for law and light to fill in shadow rather than to reach (and perhaps stumble) in the "other night" incapable of capture in the heliotrope.[61]

STUMBLING IN THE DARK

[Lady] Justice only writes law through winding paths. . . . *For her to speak justly, she must have hesitated.* —**Bruno Latour**

There is no metaphor between the visible and the invisible.
—**Maurice Merleau-Ponty**

That night may lie beyond the searchlights of the heliotrope suggests that translation might not complete the journey I have sought.[62] If law is a metaphorical language, according to Derrida, then it must be dominated by the violence of light. What conditions of possibility are necessary to fully represent law beyond illumination at night? And what legal ideas and fragments reveal night's legal force? In this section I return to several themes I developed earlier in this book to understand law at night and in the dark on its own social and historical terms. I consider Ricoeur's argument, addressed earlier, that forms of life cannot be adequately expressed metaphorically. I agree that metaphor is insufficient to transit from day to night, but I nonetheless argue that ontologies are critical to rethinking the night and thus understanding where law holds its darkened place. I consciously use the plural *ontologies*, because night, beyond the heliotrope, is pointillist, plural like Derrida's image of the stars dispersed without orbit. Night can, I argue, supplement the heliotropic metaphor but not with legal rhetoric as we commonly understand it.

VIGILANTISM

If night sanctions public and private actions securing social domination, it may do so in part because night is the time that social hierarchies are most threatened. As I have explored earlier, vigilantism has a historical American role of maintaining white supremacy, from the patrolling of slave-holding plantations by white civilians to the vastly disproportionate police killing of unarmed Black civilians. Unlike the law-conserving violence of the heliotrope that projects reason, truth, and legal justice as conditioned by and transparent within light, nocturnal violence may have no discernible metaphorical form. This is especially true when such violence escapes frameworks of political theory, such as civic republicanism, that are deployed to distinguish "necessary" from "unnecessary" violence. Derrida claims that this uncertainty may be true of much violence regardless: "All the exemplary figures of the violence of law are singular metonymies, namely, figures without limit, unfettered possibilities of transposition and figures without figures. Let us take the example of the police, this index of a phantom-like violence because it mixes foundation with conservation and becomes all the more violent for this. . . . By definition, the police are present or represented everywhere that there is force of law. They are present, sometimes invisible but always effective, wherever there is preservation of the social order."[63] Derrida argues, following Benjamin, that police confuse law-founding and law-preserving violence: they don't just "enforce the law, and thus . . . conserve it; they invent it, they publish ordinances, they intervene whenever the legal situation isn't clear to guarantee security."[64] By inventing law on the fly, police and vigilantes risk preserving social order in ways that defy public justification, truth, and reason, the *dispositif* that forms a central radiating point that violence is ideologically required to respect.

One implication is that there is no monopoly on violence that isn't purely rhetorical, that doesn't somehow depend on some mystical and metaphorical foundation. Robert Cover seems to argue as much in his *dispositif* of word, deed, and role: the integuments of violence and legality that must be respected even by dissenters to the law:

> The citizen or dissenter's constitutional interpretation cannot be *less* the deed than that of the state's officials. If the officials of the state realize their vision in blood, the dissenter must also either suffer or impose a parallel form of violence. [Chief Justice] Warren Burger and his group may or may not be ready to kill with their own hands. But they are ready to kill. . . . If a movement such as the right-to-life movement is to make law, it too must be ready, as it is, to suffer or impose violence for the constitutional vision it develops.[65]

It is this conversion to law—to a constitutional *vision*, in Cover's words—that conscripts or contorts violence into justice, so that the claim to monopoly can be preserved.

Of course, violence need not be oriented toward constitutional ends, as the right-to-life movement's efforts to repeal *Roe v. Wade* must in Cover's example.[66] And some violence oriented toward constitutional interpretation, such as that which establishes gun rights, as I have explored earlier, occurs in nocturnal obscurity and in violation of other constitutional and political frameworks. In this case, deed and role lose their distinct contours. While actions may be referred back to old ideas roughly captured by terms such as *the militia*, the role of who enforces these principles is no longer formalized. How the deed will be done can't be effectively constrained by symbol.

Why have I chosen in this book to call such vigilantism by hallowed and seemingly outdated terms such as *militia*? Why give so many despicable acts constitutional terminology or an organizing metaphor to which such violence does not fully conform? My deployment of the term is a means to validate others' reality that has escaped but simultaneously supplements and sustains the formal metaphor. What has been forgotten in the white mythology includes several historical and ongoing experiences: endangerment when some are targeted by proponents of the Second Amendment who have never universalized their constitutional claims, objectification as enemy by police sworn to uphold everyone's safety, and dismissal of memories of hidden and unauthorized violence. Living through these experiences of dispossession exposes an alternative meaning of a right (for some) to keep and bear arms conditioned by an informally expressed duty to ensure that others are actively stripped of this right. Thus, while my use of a term such as *militia* may appear fuzzy or ill defined to scholars or lawyers committed to theoretical precision or conceptual formalism, *militia* as I have reclaimed the term includes those social relations that have been experienced by many in the dark of night.

Darkness does not require nor does it at times permit a legitimating vision, thus confounding any myth of the progressive path of the law. Significantly, it cloaks temporal experiences where many people realize their sense of the law. George Zimmerman does not announce his legal vision that dark-skinned people remain hidden at night; he announces only his fear and his own confusion: Is Trayvon Martin friend or foe? It is this undecidability along with the self-made decision that the uniformed police are inadequate to respond to a potential threat at night that exonerates murder. Not unlike in the nocturnal abduction of Emmett Till or many other "threats" to white supremacy, by daylight the social order appears as an unmodified rewriting of Saramago's "books of the law." Where expanded forms of equality thrive at night, an excessive vigilante power that exceeds the mystical foundation of the law reinforces order. This is an unwritten supplement to the law, what Slavoj Žižek has called "an obscene 'nightly' law that necessarily accompanies, as its shadow, the 'public' law."[67] The obscenity he names may be that Medusa in the dark that we can't and must look at, knowing that once we see it, it is too late for us to give it a name.

This pattern of obscenely denying some their rights so that others may enjoy their legal entitlements all the better is certainly repeated in other contexts, even where the cover of night is not as explicit. The opposition to lesbian and gay rights was sometimes waged with the justification that there were insufficient resources to expand civil rights protections for all and that prior commitments to some (such as Black people and women) were endangered by these newer demands for protection.[68] Recent constitutional law extends antidiscrimination protection to transgender and gay individuals in the workplace under the expansive terms of long-standing federal employment antidiscrimination law, which bars unfair treatment on account of sex. Justice Neil Gorsuch's majority opinion in *Bostock v. Clayton County* (2020) argued that *sex* was a word that could constitutionally radiate into new contexts unimagined by the drafters of the 1964 Civil Rights Act: "The limits of the drafters' imagination supply no reason to ignore the law's demands. When the express terms of a statute give us one answer and extratextual considerations suggest another, it's no contest. Only the written word is the law, and all persons are entitled to its benefit."[69] Despite the Supreme Court's decision to extend the path of the law, efforts continue in many states to ban transgender students from competing in athletics, to prohibit medical treatments for young transgender children, and to prevent any discussion of nonnormative sexuality in schools. These laws tend to punish transgender people by denying them safe access to bathroom facilities, leading them to face humiliation and abuse when forced to use amenities corresponding to the sex listed on their birth certificates, effectively denying them access to public space. The reactionary anti-transgender movement uses legislation to refute the idea that sex has an expansive metaphorical or a plastic grammatical meaning; sex is nature determined at birth.

Some of this legislation is justified as necessary to shield sex-normative citizens from possible endangerment in sex-segregated public bathrooms and to protect this vulnerable majority from the "sexual aggression" imputed to evolving forms of public sexual expression.[70] These legislative efforts tend to subtly reproduce what Elizabeth Freeman calls *chronobiopolitics*, as the night once again becomes the sole option for safe movement (as well as intensified experiences of private danger) for transgender individuals.[71] Freeman argues, "In a chronobiological society, the state and other institutions, including representational apparatuses, link properly temporalized bodies to narratives of movement and change."[72] These efforts to dismiss transgender identity from the legal narratives embracing progressively expansive meanings of *sex, gender*, and *sex discrimination* reimpose sovereign and patriarchal control through the denial of rights beyond the play of metaphor and meaning. The targets of their ire will increasingly be forced to live outside the radiance of the law. As with guns, dispossession and nocturnal silence are an essential reactionary *dispositif* of sexual rights.

SLEEP

Sleep, in its craving for darkness, unconsciousness, and inertness, interrupts the heliotropic metaphors of the law. The light by which the legal subject performs its vigilant duties and gains recognition for its rights is confounded by the sleeper into whom we all transform ourselves quotidianly. I have argued that Emmanuel Lévinas's and Maurice Merleau-Ponty's phenomenological studies expose a parallel, fleshy world in which we remain paradoxically vigilant for—if not *in*—sleep, pulling us beyond the juris*diction* of the law, whose central voice we can no longer hear in our slumber. Nonetheless, we sleep within governing social networks—what I have called a *civil sleep* when they are activated and respected—that provide the security we require without our conscious command. If we are to translate from the waking to the sleeping world, and expect the law to apply to both, we must find a way to incorporate an unconsciousness into our jurisprudence.

Derrida has argued that the problem of general metaphoricity is that "since everything becomes metaphorical, there is no longer any literal meaning, and, hence, no longer any metaphor either."[73] This condition of language sets up what Gasché has called a logic of contamination, in which we lose the "reassuring opposition of the metaphoric and the proper, the opposition in which the one and the other have never done anything but reflect and refer to each other in their radiance."[74] To gain reassurance and immunize against contamination, it is essential to create the initial distinction between the proper and the metaphorical, to impose a sort of catachrestic violence through "irruptive tropes," which, Derrida suggests, have often relied on the body.[75] "The living body provides the 'vehicle' for all these nominal examples in the order of nature: *light* is the first—and the only—example chosen when we turn to the moral sphere: [quoting Pierre Fontanier:] '*light* for clarity of mind, for intelligence, or for insight; *blindness*, for disorder or dimness of reason.'"[76] In what way does sleep provide a similar catachrestic irruption? Sleep is not equivalent to blindness but is sometimes metaphorized with death (a truly dead metaphor), perhaps its most frequent bodily catachresis, but one that is hardly useful.

To the extent that we all sleep only because another symbolically or tangibly watches over us, building the security in which we can both "let ourselves go" and, as Lévinas argues, create our conditions for consciousness, we move within the nonrhetorical relationship that Derrida has called the gift. Arthur Cools has argued that Derrida's concern to explain subjectivity within metaphorical language, which continuously erodes and eventually erases the possibility to determine meaning, is made comprehensible by this concept. For Cools, "the gift is an event *par excellence*: it exists because of the act of giving. It implies a displacement from the giver to the receiver. As such it opens an economic logic because it raises the question of the proper use and meaning of the gift and it partakes in a process of transfer. However, unlike the notion of use, the gift implies an address. . . . The gift allows the relationship between giver and receiver to appear in the economic semantic field."[77] Derrida's conceptual use of the gift is not without its ambiguity. Naming the gift as such establishes obligation. And in his example of the Torah story of Isaac, the gift that God gave Abraham and Sarah is the same child who must be sacrificed to an unnamable and unrepresentable deity, suggesting that obligation escapes normal economic and legal logic.[78] Nonetheless, it is this mode of fixing interpersonal meaning that holds a different ethical—and perhaps legal—sense from the moral language of the body that the trope of catechresis can offer. As Cools notes, "The gift . . . bridges the gap between the undefinable metaphoricity of language and a language that is able to distinguish between the meaningful and the meaningless. While the gift is not sufficient to stabilize this relationship or to replace the former by the latter, subjectivity is the name of this substitution."[79]

The sleeper may hold a similar place of subjectivity through an idea of a collective vigilance as a gift we give others, a gift perhaps even affirmed speculatively as a right to sleep without ever becoming a debt. Just as sleep is beyond our will to command, so is a gift of sleep to another difficult if not impossible to recognize. We cannot assure ourselves that we have, in fact, allowed another to enjoy a good sleep, nor identify others who have guaranteed our own. Therefore, when we do cooperate to give each other the gift of sleep via our care for others' vulnerability, this becomes a hidden circulation we cannot map without risk of the gift fully entering a commoditized logic of economy. Derrida has argued that "as soon as a gift is identified as a gift, with the meaning of a gift, then it is canceled as a gift. . . . The event called gift is totally heterogeneous to theoretical identification, to phenomenological identification."[80] As pure event, a civil sleep depending on the collective flesh nurtured by all is physiologically and metaphorically disabled by illumination. It has no metaphorical quality. Such a right to sleep may not easily translate itself to legal governance as we know it today, but it might make us think differently about human vulnerability and our social dependencies, to help remake a law to come.

Thinking through this vulnerability into new ideas of legality is critical as women lose their constitutional rights to abortion in the United States. The unprecedented event of a constitutional right stripped away by a handful of judges following half a century of recognition and jurisprudence raises questions about how ways of life that have been built around this freedom to determine for oneself whether and when to become a mother can be abandoned. The right to abortion has its American genealogy in privacy law (also the grounding for the first *Hatton* right-to-sleep case, discussed in chapter 1), which stems from reasoning couched in *Griswold*'s penumbral metaphors of light and dark and now threatened by right-wing judges. These metaphors can only increasingly resonate as women who lack the means to travel to states guaranteeing abortion rights again seek clandestine ways to terminate their pregnancies. Luc Boltanski has argued that abortion in the West has a history of concealment that has long been its condition of possibility. Abortion, he writes,

> remains most often *in the dark*. Morever [*sic*], it is probably the fact of being left in the dark that allows the practice to be perpetuated in an ambiguous position of moderate tension between what is acceptable and what is prohibited. As a possibility, it can be left unmentioned. As a practice, it is most often concealed, but in a way that oscillates between actual clandestinity (especially during the period stretching from the mid-nineteenth century to the second half of the twentieth, when it became illegal and subject to penalties in Western countries) and the discreet practice that allows people who prefer to know nothing about it to behave as if it were not happening (as was the case in Western societies until the nineteenth century).[81]

Following many decades of legal abortion in the twentieth and twenty-first centuries, returning to the dark necessitates—indeed, depends on—(re)activating networks of activists who anonymously provide access to medical care, much as the Underground Railroad anonymously rescued many from enslavement in the dead of night. In the case of abortion, this clandestine mobilization will be for a declared nonright, a law made dark by the courts but, as a gift, never fully extinguished.

CURFEW

The need for vigilance as we sleep—vigilance over ourselves and the gift of vigilance from others—gives us one trope for linking law to night beyond the heliotrope, for this vigilance need not rely on sight to produce its distinctive collective subjectivity that could be made legal. Curfew, I have argued, is a technique of power that cyclically manipulates orders of law over space and time and also requires a form of heightened vigilance at night. Curfew creates the conditions for the subject's desire for law; curfew is, I have argued, an incitement for order temporarily denied. Although the contrast of dark and light does not fully capture night in modern times, it comes close in the curfew with its tactical oscillation of diverging nocturnal and diurnal orders. I suggest that this oscillation animating curfew can be seen as a form of translation unconstrained by legal metaphor and symbolization. From the deliberately enhanced feeling of vulnerability and consequent affect of fear in the dark of night, curfew ontologically incites a movement toward a transcendent notion of legality beyond emergency.

Robert Cover provides a perspective useful to understand the distinctive ontological value of the curfew for the law. Legal and normative orders are composed of private and public interpretive commitments, he argues. They differ in meaning depending on the regard their subjects hold for their precepts. Even when they appear similar, legal principles may be venerated or thought unjust. These distinctions are often confused, he argues, by a tendency to project a chronological distinction onto what is primarily an ontological one. "We speak of one legal order as 'decadent' or 'crumbling' and often think that this quality will *make a difference*—will cause a change over time. This projection onto chronology may entail a serious prediction, of course, but I would suggest that it is as frequently [an untestable] metaphor . . . for a deficiency we believe to inhere in a state of affairs."[82] The metaphor Cover identifies is in service to a jurispathic commitment to a unitary system; it is in this manner heliotropic.

The curfew is not a metaphor in this manner because it works not by manipulating ideologies of decadence but rather by fusing the chronological to the ontological in a complex manner. The curfew makes an exception to the law in ways that conflate public and private spaces, actors, and temporalities that make night the time of discipline. I have argued that this *dispositif* makes the curfew difficult to control ideologically, rendering its political value uncertain. In the demand for self-discipline, especially at night, the curfew increases the opportunities and possibilities for resistance. But this demand for vigilance is temporary and regular: in the promise of predictability, as in nature's promise of the rising sun, it remains tied to the rule and the law even as it suspends legal norms. Waiting for daylight expresses an anxious desire for an external moral and legal perspective, a witness to the excesses of nocturnal power.

The witness, Giorgio Agamben argues, is the ethical subject, and for him the ultimate witness is the being who witnesses the still-living but thoroughly hollowed-out man of the extermination camp—whom Primo Levi witnessed in Auschwitz being called the *Muselmann*—whose degradation destroys language, metaphor, and identity. Agamben writes, "The subject of testimony is constitutively fractured; it has no other consistency than disjunction and dislocation—and yet it is nevertheless irreducible to them. This is what it means 'to be subject to desubjectification' and this is why the witness, the ethical subject, is the subject who bears witness to desubjectification. And the unassignability of testimony is nothing other than the price of this fracture, of the inseparable intimacy of the Muselmann and the witness, of an impotentiality and potentiality of speaking."[83] Nocturnal violence, as I have endeavored to show, has its own forms of unspeakability and, certainly, its own forms of witnessing. I have tried in this book to bear witness to some of the invisible, secretive, and ignored violence hidden in the dark of night. "Eye" witnesses who share place and time with those subjected to nocturnal vigilantism, police killings, and the violence of the curfew are often discredited in the courtroom. Neither able to see clearly enough at night for a legal system committed to vision as a means to truth, nor possessed of sufficient probative character because immorally out at night (such as sex workers), witnessing at night often lives purely as unshared private or "segregated" collective memory, lacking universal credibility.[84] Derrida has associated this form of witnessing not with the violence of the camp, as does Agamben, but with the Marrano, the Sephardic Jew whose ancestors have hidden their origin as a response to the fifteenth-century Inquisition. For Derrida, the Marrano is "anyone who remains faithful to a secret that he has not chosen, in the very place where he lives, in the home of the inhabitant or of the occupant, in the home of the first or the second arrivant, in the very place where he stays without saying no but without identifying himself as belonging to. Well then, in the *unchallenged night* where the radical absence of any historical witness keeps him or her, in the dominant culture that by definition has control over the calendar, this secret keeps the Marrano even before the Marrano keeps it."[85] The Marrano, like Agamben's *Muselmann*, betrays language and knowledge but must be intellectually apprehended on the scale of a single life, or in a span of generations, making the "unchallenged night" figurative.[86] While this perspective creates the conditions for (and limitations of) memory, solidarity, and knowledge, the witness of state violence and horror at night—the individual harmed in the curfew, the community destroyed as the authorities look the other way—may still desire (more than mere survival itself) a return of subjectivity, comprehension, recognition, and relationality that can come with daylight, and the restored possibilities of a legitimate and constraining form of witnessing.[87]

The desires for light, law, and witness—the components of a normative universe in Cover's terminology—that the curfew creates maintain a connection to the heliotrope. Derrida's comment on Plato's cave and its metaphor of the sun—"The sun is there, but as the invisible source of light, in a kind of insistent eclipse"—seems apt for the ways in which the insistent desires for legal order produced by the curfew may never fully eclipse the sun.[88] Nonetheless, the interruptions and oscillations of ontological frameworks make the curfew more than just shadow or eclipse. The violence of the state working in the interstices of the triangle made by law, the rules of suspension, and the promise of temporal restoration is an ontological supplement that, as Ricoeur reminds us, is unlikely to be captured in metaphor.

NOCTURNAL PROTEST

The loss of some social hierarchy at night means that night more easily than day can be seized as a time for the invention or modification of social and legal ideas, for the becoming of new ways of life. This seizure is sometimes literary, as it was in the violence at Christiana, as I have explored in an earlier chapter. This antebellum night raid designed to abduct freely living Black men and drag them back to bondage, witnessed and made an event in the press, created a powerful allegory for what was unjust about the legal buttresses for slavery, consolidating abolitionist commitments. In Ben Gallan's terminology, this ability to bring what happens in the dark to light can be seen as a historical and ontological project of *becoming crepuscular*: "the process of attempting to recover and honour our relationship to day and night, and to make this task central to the dreams of our cities and everyday life."[89]

The honoring of night takes seriously the ways that night can enliven new philosophies, extending concepts beyond Enlightenment norms that tend to shunt nocturnal thought into anxieties over chaos and unreason. Opposed to "a certain stability of Being (desire for groundedness)," Jason Mohaghegh identifies an alternative strain of thought in which "night provides gateways and trajectories of becoming (desire for flight or freefall). In this way, it is a war between the throne and the open sea, a war between significance and the ingenious manipulation of meaning within the folds of pure meaninglessness. The conceptual schism between day and night therefore marks the existential border between those with a pathological need to rule and those with a *diabolical impulse* to abandon, subvert, and reinvent the game of mortal experience."[90] Mohaghegh's diabolical impulse resists the heliotrope in its foregrounding of ontological change. Deleuze argues something similar in his praise for Franz Kafka's stories "The Metamorphosis" and "The Judgment," in which familial characters rapidly change form and temperament during the night, or while lying in bed. "Kafka deliberately kills all metaphor, all symbolism, all signification, no less than all designation. Metamorphosis is the contrary of metaphor."[91]

Feminist nocturnal protest, as I suggested in the previous chapter, is not itself driven by diabolical impulse, in Mohaghegh's terminology, nor by inexplicable metamorphosis, as in Kafka's transmutation of man to bug. Nonetheless, Andrea Dworkin uses—while distorting—the theological and legal meanings of the diabolic to invert the gender order that accusations of magic have historically upheld. As the distinction between reason and the diabolic collapses in the dark, Dworkin attaches magic to law and patriarchy where all three can be confronted bodily. The phenomenology of nocturnal marching among women supplements and supplants the translation associated with metaphor as it enacts a fleshy solidarity that is a lost practice of guarding women's means to keep each other safe and thriving, what is understood as taking property in and possession of the night. The night march is an event that provides its participants renewed sensations of power without needing to rely on symbolism, institutions, and legal frameworks of the state.

Night marches build new legal ideas from social *movement* rather than representation, which darkness inhibits. While the slogan of the night to be taken or reclaimed is certainly metaphorical, as is the property one gains by taking back the night, the nocturnal march and assembly of protesting women makes knowledge and extends meaning in a different manner. Marching in the dark acknowledges some women's fear while it provokes the sensation of individual and collective strength. It creates memories of occupying space through the rhythm of marching feet. These interruptions of normal nocturnal practice reveal the fragility of legality: its dependence on recognition that darkness hides, its use of police who often operate beyond the law to uphold privilege, its truths enforcing hierarchical gender and racial norms. In movement alone the night becomes the inspired property of women to do with as they can, and to bring this to a new day that justly rewrites the books of the law.

Women's nocturnal activism shares some elements of the efforts to secure the night against postbellum lynching that I explored in chapter 2. Antilynching struggles were most often successful in Southern counties that were majority Black and that developed extralegal institutions of self-help. What differentiates nocturnal mobilizations for survival and safety from those vigilante actions seeking a (contestable) ideal of hierarchical racial or patriarchal "justice"? Women's marches and collective efforts at self-help against vigilantes dreaming of racial and gender supremacy do not require the generation of legal metaphor, nor do they advance their aims through secrecy. They do not necessarily wait for an external legal order that may not come; they show little obeisance to law or order that they do not make themselves. They seek to control the night. Vigilantes, in contrast, do await the daylight order that privileges some aspects of their social positions, even when their unofficial and uncelebrated contributions to that order are not symbolically counted and extolled. Their night violence has its own rewards and pleasures that remain unlinked to the schemes of "justice" that they nonetheless work to uphold and by which they live the day. The heliotrope they sustain ignores their multiple, nefarious, starlike actions by night.

* * *

Translation from day to night, I have argued in this final chapter, is not equivalent to the movement effected by metaphor. To the extent that legal knowledge and reason *are* expressed in metaphor, they are beholden to the heliotrope with its twinned images of radiation and illumination. Yet night is more than a metaphorical darkness. It is, in its excesses of violence and its facilitation of political and ontological opportunities, a time for experiences that outstrip the meanings of a setting sun. Yet, if night is event, is it the origin of law and legal meaning? Has our journey of translation ended here?

Perhaps, as Derrida argues, there are no origins to which we have access. Metaphor is a reminder that we have forgotten that we have forgotten the name; all origins, in other words, are textual and textually irrecoverable. What constitutes (re)presentation—or translation—is, for Derrida, a "generative act of repetition":[92] "The presence-of-the-present is derived from repetition and not the reverse."[93] Nocturnal ways of life are likewise lived in repetition. They rehearse memories (e.g., of night riders and other vigilante violence, of the confusion and destruction of the curfew, of the making evil and condemnation of night "magic") as well as the nightly problems and necessity—made worse for some such as the homeless and abused—of sleeping life without consciousness and self-protection. Simultaneously accessible and inaccessible to us in language (and thus in law), night is perhaps better understood as a quasi-event partially without presence, only quasi-deconstructable because not fully metaphorical. If we have no access to origin, we likewise have limited access to our destination. Some experiences of night repeat that which works invisibly behind the "white mythology" of the law without creating another myth. The nocturnal experience of racial violence and other attempts to order the social hierarchies that law will at daybreak illuminate "on the books"—these experiences of night—can help us explain what we mean and what we lose by our overbearing metaphors of light within the law.

These illustrations of night as quasi-event reveal the potential significance of temporal legal pluralism, the divergence of regimes of nocturnal and diurnal governance. Temporal legal pluralism, in turn, helps to provide a provisional resolution to Michel Foucault's quizzical statement, presented as an epigraph in the introduction of this book, that the law's ultimate power and presence is its concealment. Legal order that pictures and translates itself moving through chains of metaphorical, analogical reason—the belief that law could be adequately deciphered "between the lines of a book," in Foucault's imagery—in some cases thrives on furtive, affective, tactical, or even sleepy activities obscured in the dark. Sometimes, law effectively exiles people to the night. Other times, private and public night agents—progressive and reactionary—confound political and legal norms to reinstate public orders. Law's power in these many examples secures itself before and after the courts are closed. The *dispositifs* of diurnal and nocturnal orders, the visible and the invisible, the rhetorical and the ontological that we can find today, are not just vestigial pre-Enlightenment artifacts from times when night explicitly marked law's acknowledged limited capacity to provide security. These *dispositifs* are an essential supplement to legal order, the stars that continue to shine brightly in the day.

If we are to seek a law more closely bound to justice, we must anticipate and account for night. If legal order is partially built on power that seeks its secret cover in shadow and darkness and not in text, that abandons the most vulnerable as its premise for security and rights for the rest, that affords little embrace to the sleeper who lives within us all, then it is to the night we must turn for revival, even when we stand in the light. If law has held tightly to that which is relegated by its champions as nonlaw, then must we not appraise law's potential for justice equally with its cultivation of injustice in the night? Can we avoid any longer the power of night that is hidden in the day?

_____

INTRODUCTION: INTERRUPTIONS

Epigraph 1: Carbonnier, *Flexible droit*, 61 (translation mine).

Epigraph 2: Foucault and Blanchot, *Maurice Blanchot*, 33.

Epigraph 3: Dworkin, "Night and Danger," 15

1   D. Shapiro, "Case of the Speluncean Explorers." The article has been cited hundreds of times in the secondary legal literature and been the object of several symposia. It has also attracted a number of updates and "further proceedings." See, for example, Kozinski et al., "Case of the Speluncean Explorers"; Eskridge, "Case of the Speluncean Explorers"; and D'Amato, "Speluncean Explorers."

2   Plato, *Republic*, bk 7. Pound sometimes used Plato as a device for explicating his legal theory. See Pound, "American Law School."

3   Fuller, "Case of the Speluncean Explorers," 642.

4   Fuller, "Case of the Speluncean Explorers," 624, 628, 637–38, 644.

5   Hibbitts, "Making Sense of Metaphors," 230–32; and Mnookin and Kornhauser, "Bargaining." In an interesting article on how the blind "see" race, Osagie Obasogie has argued that visuality is socially constructed, pointing toward the significance of such metaphors. Obasogie, "Do Blind People See Race?" Penumbras of constitutional amendments (Griswold v. Connecticut, 381 U.S. 479 [1965]) draw from this daylight metaphor, as do references to legal "twilights" such as this: "The law that governs between states, has at times, like the common law within states, a twilight existence during which it is hardly distinguishable from morality or justice, till at length the imprimatur of a court attests its jural quality." New Jersey v. Delaware, 291 U.S. 361, 383 (1934), Justice Benjamin Cardozo. See also Youngstown Sheet and Tube v. Sawyer, 343 U.S. 579, 637 (1952), Justice Robert Jackson, concurring: "zone of [Constitutional] twilight."

6   Freud, *Totem and Taboo*, 164–67. See also Schroeder, "Totem"; and Fitzpatrick, *Modernism*, 11–36. Jacques Derrida, particularly, casts the story in a different light, suggesting it is a nonevent that reveals an "impossible story of the impossible." Derrida, "Before the Law," 198–200.

7   Foucault, *History of Madness*, xxxiii. Foucault argues that madness will always persist as a "carcass of night," as a "relationship of a culture to the very thing that it excludes" (542, app. 1), a parallel to my arguments about law.

8   E. Mensch, "Mainstream Legal Thought." Although Carl Schmitt's European theory of the sovereign and legal exception played little role in American jurisprudence during Fuller's time, his work now anchors this thought in Anglo-American and Continental legal theory. See Schmitt, *Political Theology*; and Agamben, *Omnibus Homo Sacer*. See also Fuller's subsequent debate with H. L. R. Hart on the moral nature of law. Hart, "Positivism"; and Fuller, "Positivism."

9   Fuller, *Morality of Law*; Derrida, "Force of Law"; Žižek, *Plague of Fantasies*, 93; Benjamin, "Critique of Violence"; Cover, "Violence and the Word"; Agamben, *State of Exception*; Schmitt, *Political Theology II*; and Badiou, *Theory of the Subject*, 159–75. See also Bosteels, "Force of Nonlaw."

10 I borrow the terminology of *excessive absence* from Davina Cooper, private communication.

11 "If a thief be found breaking up, and be smitten that he die, [there shall] no blood [be shed] for him. If the sun be risen upon him, [there shall be] blood [shed] for him; [for] he should make full restitution; if he have nothing, then he shall be sold for his theft." Exodus 22:2–3 (King James version). For an extended discussion of this limit, see Kopel, "Torah and Self-Defense," 26–27.

12 Blackstone, *Commentaries*, 2:222; and Ekirch, *At Day's Close*, 40.

13 Shoemaker, *Sanctuary and Crime*, 158.

14 Title 13, Art. 63, in L'Ouverture, *Haitian Revolution* (translation modified).

15 Goodrich, *Oedipus Lex*, 3, quoting Marsilio Ficino (1480).

16 Ekirch, *At Day's Close*, 84; Carbonnier, *Flexible droit*, 63; and Koslofsky, *Evening's Empire*, 199. One antecedent barring nocturnal legal practice can be seen in the debates over the legitimacy of the trial of Jesus. "The Mosaic code was the law applicable in the Jewish court, to the trial of Jesus. Under this law a trial could not be held in the nighttime and sentence of guilty could not lawfully be pronounced until the third day after the finding and after a second vote of the court. It was an axiom of this law that the function of the court was to protect human life." White, *Law in the Scriptures*, 312n10.

17 Beaumont, *Nightwalking*, 124.

18 Kantorowicz, *King's Two Bodies*, 142n167. Similar problems were grappled with in ancient Chinese political theory, where sleep and drunkenness were mutual threats to leadership. See Richter, "Sleeping Time," 31. The Japanese emperor had institutionalized watches representing his rule while he slept. Steger and Brunt, "Introduction," 14.

19 Loewen, *Sundown Towns*.

20 See Matricciani, Olds, and Petkov, "In Search of Lost Sleep"; Dement, *Promise of Sleep*; and Barnes, Ghumman, and Scott, "Sleep."

21 Deleuze, "Postscript on Control Societies"; see also Crary, *24/7*.

22 Ekirch, *At Day's Close*, 339; see also Crary, *24/7*.

23 Santner, *Weight of All Flesh*, 33.

24 Melbin, *Night as Frontier*.

25 R. Williams, "Night Spaces," 525.

26 "Where relations between right and power are concerned, the general principle is, it seems to me, that one fact must never be forgotten: In Western societies, the elaboration of juridical thought has essentially centered around royal power ever since the Middle Ages." Foucault, *Society Must Be Defended*, 25.

27 Heidegger, *On Time and Being*, 67.

28 Agamben, *What Is an Apparatus?*; Foucault, "Confession of the Flesh"; Deleuze, "What Is a Dispositif?"; Esposito, "*Dispositif* of the Person"; and Panagia, "On the Political Ontology."

29 Agamben, *What Is an Apparatus?*, 12.

30 Deleuze, "What Is a Dispositif?," 162.

31 Deleuze, "What Is a Dispositif?," 163.

32 McCann, *Rights at Work*, 9–10; see also Scheingold, *Politics of Rights*, preface.

33 Ewick and Silbey, *Common Place of Law*. See also Nielsen, "Situating Legal Consciousness"; Engel and Munger, *Rights of Inclusion*; and Engel and Engel, *Tort, Custom, and Karma*.

34 Calavita, *Law and Society*, 44.

35 Engel and Munger, *Rights of Inclusion*, 242.

36 Deleuze writes, "In each [dispositif] we have to untangle the lines of the recent past and those of the near future: that which belongs to the archive and that which belongs to the present; that which belongs to history and that which belongs to the process of becoming; *that which belongs to the analytic and that which belongs to the diagnostic.*" Deleuze, "What Is a Dispositif?," 164.

37 Auden, "Law like Love."

38 Goodrich, *Languages of Law*, 51; Holmes, "Path of the Law"; and Cardozo, *Judicial Process*, 53. On belief in the constitutional framers' historically fixed thought-worlds, see Scalia, "Originalism." Henry Maine could see one path through both law and society as a movement from familial status to individual contract. Maine, *Ancient Law*.

39 On colonialism and law, see K. Davis, *Periodization and Sovereignty*; see also Greenhouse, "Just in Time"; McClintock, *Imperial Leather*; Fitzpatrick, *Mythology of Modern Law*; Bhandar, *Colonial Lives of Property*; Mills, *Racial Contract*; Grovogui, *Sovereigns*; and Anghie, *Imperialism*. On the imperial "politics of time, see Fabian, *Time and the Other*, x.

40 Engel, "Law, Time and Community"; and Kunal Parker, *Common Law*.

41 Kantorowicz, *King's Two Bodies*. See also Santner, *Royal Remains*.

42 Kunal Parker, *Common Law*. See also Mawani, "Times of Law," 262.

43 Wells, *Island of Doctor Moreau*, 149.

44 Melville, *Billy Budd*, 57.

45 Marcel Mauss described a parallel type of pluralism among northern peoples who oscillated between winter and summer forms of family and property law. Mauss, *Seasonal Variations*, 62–75.

46 The argument that there is a measurable quantity of law is one of the premises of Donald Black's work, for example, Black, *Behavior of Law*. Black does address the night in his book in several places in order to bolster his claim that "the quantity of social control varies across settings" (110), though his attention to night is not sustained.

47 Scott, *Seeing like a State*. James Scott's metaphor of the state's active vision does not account for the metaphor or social facts of night.

48 Latour, *Making of Law*, 151–52. Marc Galanter has noted the significance of delay in Indian civil litigation, as well as in the tactics of litigation that advantage parties with sufficient resources to wait. Galanter, "Why the 'Haves'"; and Galanter, "Legal Torpor."

49 William James understands this ontologically: "Pluralism stands for the distributive, monism for the collective form of being." W. James, "One and the Many," 114.

50 Davies, "Pluralism and Legal Philosophy," 587. See also H. L. A. Hart's "internal aspect of rules," Hart, *Concept of Law*, 56; and Oliver Wendell Holmes's "bad man." Holmes wrote, "If you want to know the law and nothing else, you must look at it as a bad man, who cares only for the material consequences which such knowledge enables him to predict, not as a good one, who finds his reasons for conduct, whether inside the law or outside of it, in the vaguer sanctions of conscience." Holmes, "Path of the Law," 459.

51 Merry, "Legal Pluralism."

52 Griffiths, "What Is Legal Pluralism?," 5.

53 Manderson, *Songs without Music*, 169–70.

54 Davies, "Pluralism and Legal Philosophy," 586 (echoing Jean-Luc Nancy).

55 See Davison, "Some Observations."

56 Philosophically, this position is perhaps best enacted by Friedrich Nietzsche's Zarathustra's ten years of solitude, patiently waiting every morning for the sun to rise. This is what Deleuzian thought might call a *becoming-same*. Nietzsche, *Thus Spoke Zarathustra*, 3; and Zourabichvili, *Deleuze*, 174.

57 Foucault reviews a novel, *La Veille* (1963), by Roger Laporte in these terms. "To keep vigil for Laporte, means to be not after evening but before morning, without any other 'before' this lead that I myself am on all possible days. And in this night, or rather (because the night is thick, closed opaque; the night partakes of two days, draws limits, lends drama

to the sun that it restores, prepares the light that it restrains for a moment) in this 'not yet' of morning, which is gray rather than black and as though diaphanous to its own transparency, the neutral word vigil gently glistens." Foucault, "Standing Vigil," 218.

58   Levos and Zacchilli, "Nyctophobia"; Edensor, "Gloomy City"; and Dunn, *Dark Matters*. In contrast, Polynesian cosmologies understand night (pō) as female, generative, and productive of sovereignty. Pualani Warren, "Theorizing Pō"; and Silva, *Aloha Betrayed*, 100.

59   Galinier et al., "Anthropology of the Night," 820.

60   On witches and werewolves as benevolent, see Ginzburg, *Night Battles*; Ginzburg and Lincoln, *Old Thiess*; and Federici, *Caliban and the Witch*. On the church's attitude toward them, see Levack, *Witch-Hunt*, 46–50; and Verdon, *Night*, 57. Brian Levack suggests that belief in flying witches was not common in England compared with the Continent. Levack, "Possession, Witchcraft, and the Law," 1614. Night flight was also noted as a belief about witches in the area of early twentieth-century Ghana. See John Parker, "Northern Gothic," 359. Werewolves were men thought to prowl at night and throw themselves onto the backs of other men, an image of homosexual practice. See Bernhardt-House, "Werewolf as Queer"; and Spadoni, "Strange Botany." For Derrida, the werewolf shares with the sovereign a position outside or beyond the law. Derrida, *Beast and the Sovereign*, 1:64.

61   Noel Johnson and Koyama, "Decline of Witch Trials"; and E. Peters, *Magician*. Accusations of witchcraft continue to be a prod to legal development in Africa, Oceania, and Islamic countries, among others. Forsyth, "Regulation of Witchcraft."

62   Thomas Dekker, quoted in Ménager, *La renaissance et la nuit*, 10 (translation mine).

63   Beaumont, *Nightwalking*, 27.

64   O. Williams, "Regimentation of Blacks," 333. See also Schivelbusch, *Disenchanted Night*, 82.

65   On light pollution, see Meier et al., *Urban Lighting*; Edensor, "Reconnecting with Darkness"; and Stone, "Value of Darkness." Taylor Stone notes nine values behind the desire to preserve darkness: efficiency, sustainability, ecology, healthiness, happiness, connection to nature, stellar visibility, heritage and tradition, wonder and beauty. On illumination as protective, see Katyal, "Architecture as Crime Control." Although Neal Kumar Katyal husbands the traditionally accepted evidence for a positive association of lighting and crime reduction, recent studies have been less certain about this relationship. See Brands, Schwanen, and van Aalst, "Fear of Crime"; and Perkins et al., "Effect of Reduced Street Lighting."

66   Ekirch, *At Day's Close*, 85.

67   See, for example, Ahmed, *Cultural Politics of Emotion*, 69.

68 Edensor, "Gloomy City," 423.

69 Koslofsky, *Evening's Empire*, 200.

70 Koslofsky observes, "The night significantly facilitated all aspects of the passage from single youth to husband or wife. From meeting a group of potential spouses at a spinning bee or village dance, to getting to know a specific individual in the dim intimacy of a chamber during a Heimgarten visit or while bundling, to the physical consummation of the relationship (ending, it was hoped, in marriage), the night was a constant companion to the couple. Church and state gave their sanction to the marriage during the day, but husbands and wives were made at night." Koslofsky, *Evening's Empire*, 209.

71 Ekirch, "Sleep We Have Lost."

72 Ekirch, "Sleep We Have Lost," 370; and Koslofsky, *Evening's Empire*, 214.

73 Cabantous, *Histoire de la nuit*, 165.

74 Koslofsky, *Evening's Empire*, 219.

75 Schlumbohm, "Gesetze," discussed in Koslofsky, *Evening's Empire*, 222.

76 Simon, *Governing through Crime*; Simon, "Fear and Loathing"; Murakawa, *First Civil Right*; and Garland, *Culture of Control*.

77 *New York Times*, "Protest Groups Defy Curfew."

78 On how enslaved people made use of the night, see Reiss, *Wild Nights*, ch. 4; and Palmer, *Cultures of Darkness*. See extensive discussion in chapter 3 of this book. On vigilantes, see Fry, *Night Riders*.

79 Somerville, *Queering the Color Line*, 45.

80 Pain, "Gender, Race, Age and Fear."

81 Snedker, "Explaining the Gender Gap"; G. Valentine, "Women's Fear"; and G. Valentine, "Geography of Women's Fear."

82 R. Shaw, "Pushed to the Margins," 118.

83 Dunn, *Dark Matters*.

84 Shakespeare, "Rape of Lucrece," in *Complete Works*, 1088, line 107.

85 *Midsummer Night's Dream*, act 5, scene 1, lines 21–22.

86 Kipling, *Second Jungle Book,* 191.

87 Poe, "Man of the Crowd," 181.

88 Lévi-Strauss, *Elementary Structures of Kinship*, 495. On Freud's intimation that the fear of darkness is commonly experienced by children, see *Three Essays on Sexuality*, 90. Freud commonly used metaphors of darkness to discuss women's psyches. See Khanna, *Dark Continents*; and Macey, *Lacan in Contexts*, ch. 6. See also Lucretius, who acknowledges the childhood fear of the dark. Lucretius, *Nature of Things*, 46.

89 Nietzsche, *Daybreak*, 250.

90 Consider the ways in which civil rights activism was transmuted into criminality, and the ways that immigrants are blamed for violent crime today, for example. See Beckett, *Making Crime Pay*; and Murakawa, *First Civil Right*. Simone de Beauvoir writes, "Fear is always mixed with the

blame attached to woman's licentious conduct." Beauvoir, *Second Sex*, 204.

91   Haygood, "Police No Longer Need." Wil Haygood argues, in light of the well-publicized killings of George Floyd and Ahmaud Arbery that provoked national and global responses, that police no longer feel bound to the night: "American society has landed on the other side of its nocturnal nightmares."

92   Naudé, *Political Considerations*, 59–60, also quoted in Foucault, *Security, Territory, Population*, 266 (with a different translation).

93   Epigraph: Excerpt from Hughes, "As I Grew Older," in *The Collected Poems of Langston Hughes*, 93–94, 1926.

94   Canetti, *Crowds and Power*, 15.

95   Melbin, "Night as Frontier," 13.

96   Certeau, *Practice of Everyday Life*, 18.

97   Woodward, *Strange Career of Jim Crow*, 15, quoting from Richard C. Wade, *Slavery in the Cities*, 259. Wade argued that "slaveowners considered these rendezvous extremely dangerous; the public consistently attacked them; the police tried every expedient to suppress them. Yet they multiplied and apparently prospered." Wade, *Slavery in the Cities*, 85.

98   Mohaghegh, *Night*, 1. See also Dunn and Edensor, *Rethinking Darkness*; Palmer, *Cultures of Darkness*; and Ekirch, *At Day's Close*.

99   Nancy, *Fall of Sleep*, 39.

100   Nancy, *Fall of Sleep*, 21.

101   Ekirch, *At Day's Close*, 287. This sentiment may have classical roots as well. Sophocles's Antigone does the moral deed of burying her brother against the directive of Creon, the sovereign, under cover of night.

102   Ekirch, *At Day's Close*, 88.

103   Jay, *Downcast Eyes*, 95–97. On David's painting, see Santner, *Royal Remains*, 89–94.

104   Ekirch, *At Day's Close*, 135.

105   Ekirch, *At Day's Close*, 227.

106   Rancière, *Proletarian Nights*, 20. See also Palmer, *Cultures of Darkness*, 104–5.

107   Blanchot, "Sleep, Night," 264; and Rancière, *Proletarian Nights*, 20.

108   Rancière, "Thinking of Dissensus."

109   Cixous, *Stigmata*, 60.

110   H. Lefebvre, *Production of Space*, 319–20.

111   Beauvoir, *Second Sex*, 204.

112   Gallan, "Night Lives"; Roberts, "'Big Night Out'"; Thomas and Bromley, "City-Centre Revitalisation"; Van Liempt, "Safe Nightlife Collaborations"; and Van Liempt, van Aalst, and Schwanen, "Introduction."

113   Anker, *Ugly Freedoms*. Anker argues that the concept of ugly freedom captures not only the freedom to exploit and subjugate others (as have

gun rights, opposition to vaccines, and slavery at various times) but also those excoriated freedoms that emerge below dominant social and political judgments. In this regard, night freedoms may be one form of ugly freedoms.

114　Ekirch, *At Day's Close*, 230. For contemporary discussions of nocturnal queer life, see Campkin and Marshall, "London's Nocturnal Queer Geographies."

115　Busby, "London's Night Czar Criticised"; and Campkin and Marshall, "London's Nocturnal Queer Geographies," 83. Other night officials such as Washington, DC's "night mayor" are appointed to address problems interfering with the night economy. Codrea-Rado, "Europe's 'Night Mayors'"; Delgadillo, "Rise of the 'Night Mayor'"; and Zaveri, "Washington Wants to Hire."

116　The term is from Nancy Gonlin and April Nowell, "Introduction to the Archaeology of Night," in Gonlin and Nowell, eds. *Archaeology of the Night*, 11–12. See also Galinier et al., "Anthropology of the Night"; and Dowd and Hensey, *Archaeology of Darkness*.

117　"Night means the time between the end of evening civil twilight and the beginning of morning civil twilight, as published in the Air Almanac, converted to local time." Title 64, Code of Federal Regulations, ch. 1, "Federal Aviation Administration," § 1.1, 2022. Night's definition was changed in 2012 in reaction to several air accidents. See Tipton, "FAA Measures."

118　Medellin v. Texas, 552 U.S. 491, 566 (2007), Justice Breyer, dissenting.

119　Kierkegaard, *Gospel of Sufferings*, 36. This phrase has been made more prominent by President Joseph Biden's repetition.

120　Laruelle, "On the Black Universe," 106; originally published as Laruelle, "Du noir univers."

121　Masciandaro, "Secret," 50.

122　Masciandaro, "Secret," 56.

123　Masciandaro, "Secret," 58.

124　Badiou, *Black*, 34.

125　Consider the extralegal "dark zones" of the repressive state, or the black bars used to redact a document. Here, "black exists in these states simultaneously—a color, a non-color, a practice, a presence, an absence, and a *void*. Therefore, as with the illegible spaces of black sites and black ops, in its most critical application we take black as the singular warning—'there is nothing to see' (and you're seeing it)." Linnemann and Medley, "Black Sites, 'Dark Sides,'" 345, quoting Thacker, *Starry Speculative Corpse*, n. 79.

126　Badiou, *Black*, 48–50.

127　Badiou, *Black*, 10.

128　Blanchot writes, "But when everything has disappeared in the night, 'everything has disappeared' appears. This is the *other* night. Night is this apparition: 'everything has disappeared.' It is what we sense when dreams replace sleep, when the dead pass into the deep of the night, when night's deep appears in those who have disappeared. Apparitions, phantoms, and dreams are an allusion to this empty night." Blanchot, "The Outside, the Night," 162. See also the beautiful interpretations of Blanchot in Farbman, *Other Night*.

129 Lévinas, *Proper Names*, 137, quoting Laporte and Noël, *Deux lectures de Maurice Blanchot*.

130 Luhmann, *Law as a Social System*, 75 (see also the following pages).

131 Mbembe, *Critique of Black Reason*, 72, 152.

132 K. Hall, *Things of Darkness*. This construction of light/dark, civilized/barbarian, as an essential cultural expression is not unique to the West. See James Scott's arguments on Southeast Asia: Scott, *Art of Not Being Governed*, 116–19.

133 Fanon, *Black Skin, White Masks*, 146.

134 Morrison, *Playing in the Dark*, x.

135 P. Williams, *Alchemy of Race*, 117.

136 McKittrick, "On Plantations," 953.

137 Schivelbusch, *Disenchanted Night*; and C. Harrison, "Extending the 'White Way.'"

138 I am indebted to Sankaran Krishna for this imagery. Private communication with the author.

139 Serres, *Five Senses*, 70. See also Helms, "Before the Dawn," 179.

140 Blackstone, *Commentaries*, 2:187.

141 Cover, "Bonds of Constitutional Interpretation."

142 Gallan and Gibson, "New Dawn or New Dusk?," 2511.

CHAPTER 1. IS THERE A RIGHT TO SLEEP?

Epigraph 1: Aristotle, *Politics of Aristotle*, bk. 5, 1314a24–25.

Epigraph 2: Hart, *The Concept of Law*, 195.

1 Karandinos et al., "Moral Economy of Violence," 20.

2 Dayna Johnson et al., "Association of Neighborhood Characteristics"; S. Johnson et al., "Neighborhood Violence"; Simonelli, "Perceived Neighborhood Safety"; Chen-Edinboro et al., "Neighborhood Physical Disorder"; Umlauf, Bolland, and Lian, "Sleep Disturbance"; and R. Gruber, "Short Sleep Duration." For a sociohistorical analysis of the linkages between the institution of slavery and contemporary sleep disparities, see Reiss, *Wild Nights*, ch. 4.

3 On abuse and sleep, see Lowe, Humphreys, and Williams, "Night Terrors"; and Simonelli et al., "Impact of Home Safety." On homelessness and sleep, see Beckett and Herbert, *Banished*; Hayes-Jonkers et al., "Hidden

Racism"; and Menih, "'Come Night-Time.'" Katherine Beckett and Steve Herbert write, "For some [homeless], the sense of insecurity stemming from an exclusion order was so powerful that they had difficulty sleeping at all. Jose describes how he got through the previous night after being kicked out of the park [by police] in which he feels comfortable: 'I just walked all night long. My eyes hurt right now. I'm not gonna lie down and have some crackhead think that maybe I got three dollars. No, I'll walk all night. Sometimes I'll walk over to that park called Freeway Park and I'll sleep over there, but that's not very safe. Mostly I walk.'"*Banished,* 122. Contrast this coercive form of nightwalking with its history as an aristocratic privilege and bourgeois transgression with romantic connotations. There are shared meanings as well: "Nightwalking seems to have functioned as a sort of floating signifier used by the authorities to criminalize or ostracize any errant, irritating or undesirable activity after dark." Beaumont, *Nightwalking,* 27.

4   Flynn, "'I Accept It.'"

5   Kamakau writes, "This became the law over the whole Hawaiian group in the time when Kamehameha ruled over the kingdom." Kamakau, *Ka Po'e Kahiko,* 15. This alternative translation is from Silva, "Mana Hawai'i," 48.

6   Kamakau, *Ruling Chiefs,* 232.

7   Kamakau, *Ruling Chiefs,* 157. Kamakau writes about the Māmalahoa, "Its great characteristic (*'ano*) was as an edict that determined life or death. If a chief was about to die, and Kamehameha placed the *kanawai* Mamalahoa on him, he would live. If, on the other hand, the chiefs and the *kuhina nui* (chief counselor) wanted the man to live, but Kamehameha did not agree and pronounced the Mamalahoa, then nothing could release it; it was absolute (*pa'a loa*) and the man died." Kamakau, *Ka Po'e Kahiko,* 15. See also MacKenzie, "Ka Lama Ku O Ka No'eau," 14–15.

8   MacKenzie, "Ka Lama Ku O Ka No'eau," 15; and Silva, "Mana Hawai'i," 49. It is perhaps significant that the Hawaiian juxtaposition of sleep, night, and law did not share with Western ideas any contrast to enlightenment or reason. Night was the origin of the main gods: "Ku, Kane, Kanaloa, Lono and perhaps some of the other deities are said to be *no ka po mai,* to date back to the night, a time far antecedent to history and tradition." Malo, *Hawaiian Antiquities,* 316. "The female night, is ancestor of all Akua; she is the source of life, of divinity, and of ancestral wisdom. Akua communicate with humans by dreams in the night. One says, 'Mai ka pō mai' (from the night, or the beginning of time) to connote wisdom and customs that come from antiquity. . . . *Ua hānau ka pō*: the night gives birth." Kame'eleihiwa, "Nā Wāhine Kapu," 72. Contrast this with the first passages of Genesis in the Semitic traditions. Elisabeth Bronfen notes, "By calling darkness 'night,' God distinguishes a terrestrial event from its original chaotic formlessness and includes it as one of two temporal

cycles in the newly created world order. The separation between daytime and nighttime occurs once God further declares the light to be 'good.' His command is thus performatively brought into being. Although darkness is not explicitly declared as belonging to the realm of evil, God's privileging of light becomes unequivocally clear." Bronfen, *Night Passages*, 45.

9   Much of the speculation involves problems of translation from the vast Hawaiian-language archive that I cannot evaluate.

10   *Pu'uhonua* were personalized in rare cases. Kamehameha granted to Ka'ahumanu, his favored wife and regent, the power of *pu'uhonua*, perhaps in an effort to gain her loyalty. Lilikalā Kame'eleihiwa, a historian, explains that "in traditional times, the principle of Pu'uhonua allowed relief from the strict kapu system. For should anyone transgress a kapu, fleeing to the sanctuary of the Pu'uhonua allowed one to escape from the required death penalty." Kame'eleihiwa, *Native Land*, 72. Kamakau writes, "Among those laws that helped to sustain life (*kalana ola*), laws for the fisherman, the tapa maker, the dyer, the house builder, the provider of those things which benefit the body and bring about the general peace and welfare of the race, may be classed those laws which provided for the pardon by the ruling chief of transgressors of the law. This word itself, 'life sustaining,' is an excellent word and occurs in the prayer chants and chants of praise to the god and the chiefs." Kamakau, *Ruling Chiefs*, 369.

11   The definition of *kāhuna* is taken from M. Brown, *Facing the Spears*, 33. To "make live" refers to to Michel Foucault's insight into the nature of biopower, which has a different basis than the sovereign power to take life. "The right of sovereignty was the right to take life or let live. And then this new right is established: the right to make live and to let die." Foucault, *Society Must Be Defended*, 241. The Hawaiian practice of sanctuary may share some elements of pastoral power applicable to people on the move, while also being beneficent. See Foucault, *Security, Territory, Population*, 125–30. For a discussion of sovereignty and its integral relationship to pastoral power that upholds sanctuary in Western thought and practice, see Lippert, "Sanctuary Practices." For a discussion that links pastoral power to colonial contexts, see Pandian, "Pastoral Power."

12   On the imputation of European governing beliefs to Hawaiians, see Merry, *Colonizing Hawai'i*, 56; and Hay, "Property." Douglas Hay calls mercy an ideology for the ways in which acts of grace pardoning the convicted were the "tissue" of paternalism and ruling-class power. On law as upholding life, see Archer, "He Pou He'e i Ka Wawā." On *ali'i* governance as protective, see Silva, *Aloha Betrayed*, 25–26; Kauanui, *Hawaiian Blood*, 13; and Lindsey, "Native Hawaiians," 243. On the significance of disease, see Kamakau, *Ruling Chiefs*, 236.

13   Article 9, Section 10 of the Hawai'i State Constitution. This section reads: "PUBLIC SAFETY Section 10. The law of the splintered paddle, mamala-hoe

kanawai, decreed by Kamehameha I—Let every elderly person, woman and child lie by the roadside in safety—shall be a unique and living symbol of the State's concern for public safety. The State shall have the power to provide for the safety of the people from crimes against persons and property." A proposed constitution for a new Hawaiian nation also includes this language.

14   Pukui, *Hawaiian Dictionary*, 249.

15   Yuhas, "Honolulu Upholds Ban." In Hawai'i jurisprudence, see De-Occupy Honolulu v. City and County of Honolulu, 2013 U.S. Dist. LEXIS 71969 (D. Haw. May 21, 2013), which called on the Law of the Splintered Paddle to protect the rights of protestors to security of property and person while protesting in a public park. See also State v. Sturch, 921 P.2d 1170, 82 Haw. 269, 1996 Haw. App. LEXIS 62 (Haw. Ct. App. 1996) (denying a right to sleep in a vehicle on the road). Beyond Hawai'i, see Joel v. City of Orlando, 232 F.3d 1353, 2000 U.S. App. LEXIS 28523, 14 Fla. L. Weekly Fed. C 153 (11th Cir. Fla. 2000) (denying a "homeless" person the right to "camp" on public property). Obviously, there is no right to "lie about" public property, either.

16   Musharbash, "Night, Sight."

17   Foucault, *Power*, 302, 303. Friedrich Nietzsche also notes the relationship between this pastoral activity and sleep: "He shall always be the best shepherd in my view who leads his sheep to the greenest pasture; this is compatible with good sleep." Nietzsche, *Thus Spoke Zarathustra*, 18.

18   Schivelbusch, *Disenchanted Night*, 89.

19   P. Baldwin, *In the Watches*, 24.

20   P. Baldwin, *In the Watches*, 15; Denys, "Development of Police Forces"; Cabantous, *Histoire de la nuit*, 235–37; and Ekirch, *At Day's Close*, 75–84.

21   Chamayou, *Manhunts*. Black and Indigenous people were ordered off the streets of Boston, Newport, New York, and other American cities in the early eighteenth century. I discuss the nocturnal control of enslaved people in the next chapter.

22   Hawkins and Thomas, "White Policing"; Browne, *Dark Matters*; Campbell, *Crime and Punishment*; and Chamayou, *Manhunts*, ch. 5. I discuss this issue at greater depth in the next chapter.

23   Gérard Genette has noted the grammar of night and day, demonstrating the linguistic asymmetries that subordinate night to the imperatives of day. Genette, "Le jour, la nuit." This passivity associated with night can be read in the neoliberal concept of the well-slept citizen. S. Williams, *Sleep and Society*, 44.

24   Nietzsche, *On the Genealogy of Morals*, 57. On the responsible legal subject, see Derrida, "Force of Law," 931; Lacey, "Responsible Subject"; and Naffine, "Who Are Law's Persons?"

25 Teacher, "Sleepwalking." On sexsomnia, see Xu, "Sexsomnia"; D. Peters and Rubin, "Sexsomnia Case"; and Weiss et al., "Parasomnias."

26 S. Hartman, "Seduction," esp. 540–44; and Dayan, *Law Is a White Dog*.

27 See Derickson, *Dangerously Sleepy*.

28 C. Jones, Dorrian, and Rajaratnam, "Fatigue"; and Radun et al., "Driver Fatigue."

29 Locke, *Essay Concerning Human Understanding*, 312.

30 Locke, *Essay Concerning Human Understanding*, 310.

31 Rights, in this perspective, are empowering not solely through a claim against state violence but in the yet unforeseen subjectivities and "jurisgenetic" possibilities articulated around rights. Cover, *"Nomos* and Narrative," 11; P. Williams, "Alchemical Notes"; and McCann, "Unbearable Lightness of Rights."

32 Nancy, *Fall of Sleep*, 13.

33 Kantorowicz, *King's Two Bodies*, 423, 420–31.

34 Kantorowicz, *King's Two Bodies*, 133. See also Santner, *Royal Remains*, 36.

35 Gaines Post writes that *lex animata* meant that the king "was everywhere; and if he was everywhere, he was pantheistically, so to speak, the State itself. The head was tending to absorb the corporate body." G. Post, *Medieval Legal Thought*, 303. See also Mayali, "Lex animata"; and Goodrich, *Languages of Law*, 271–72. For *rex exsomnis*, see Santner, *Weight of All Flesh*, 36.

36 Baldus de Ubaldis quoted in Kantorowicz, *King's Two Bodies*, 142n167.

37 Similar problems were grappled with in ancient Chinese political theory, where sleep and drunkenness were mutual threats to leadership. See Richter, "Sleeping Time," 31. The Japanese emperor had institutionalized watches representing his rule while he slept. Steger and Brunt, "Introduction: Into the Night and the World of Sleep," in *Night-Time and Sleep*, 14.

38 See R. Jackson, "Sleeping King"; and Kantorowicz, "Oriens Augusti."

39 R. Jackson, "Sleeping King," 541, 543 (translations in brackets mine).

40 Derrida, *Beast and the Sovereign*, 1:286–87.

41 One can also wonder if it is possible to sleep with too much vigilance: anything but unobtrusive watching may impede sleep. Indeed, even early protolegal authorities, the night watch, may have ironically impeded sleep with their own form of vigilance. As A. Roger Ekirch argues (with not a little humor), "Slumber in towns and cities was light and fitful, due, at least in part, to loudmouthed watchmen. The irony of this was not lost upon contemporaries, accustomed to being awakened by paeans to sound slumber. 'For though you lay you downe to sleepe,' fumed an early seventeenth-century poet, 'The Belman wakes your peace to keepe.'" Ekirch, *At Day's Close*, 79.

42 Santner, *Royal Remains*, 33. Santner suggests that political theology be understood as a main "operator of secularization" (xii). See also Esposito,

Bios, 51; Schmitt, *Political Theology*, ch. 3; Frank, "Living Image"; and Herzogenrath, *American Body-Politic*. Consider also Foucault's insistence that "the king was [and is] the central character in the entire Western juridical edifice." Foucault, *Society Must Be Defended*, 26.

43 On the early and medieval Christian observance of vigils, see Helms, "Before the Dawn."

44 David A. Johnson, "Vigilance and the Law," 575, 583.

45 Browne, *Dark Matters*, 16. See also Chamayou, "Fichte's Passport."

46 Certeau, *Practice of Everyday Life*, 37, 41. Tactically exploring the night expresses the value of time over evanescent space; "tactics [depend] on a clever *utilization of time*, of the opportunities it presents, and also of the play it introduces into the foundations of power" (38–39).

47 "Hillary Clinton Ad"; and Alexovich, "Clinton's National Security Ad." That advertisement, over images of sleeping children, asked, "It's 3 a.m., and your children are safe and asleep. Who do you want answering the phone?" A bespectacled Hillary Clinton is then shown answering a telephone in a semidarkened room. Clear evidence of concerns about presidential succession can be found in the debates over the Twenty-Fifth Amendment to the US Constitution, which addresses the problem of continuity in the case of a disabled president. See Feerick, "Problem of Presidential Inability."

48 Crary, *24/7*, 5; and Dayan, *Law Is a White Dog*, 29.

49 Guenther, *Solitary Confinement*, 21.

50 Wortham, *Poetics of Sleep*, 84. Simon Williams writes that "sleep . . . doubles as both a *problem* and *prism*, a *site* and *source*, of political power relations and investments in the late modern age." S. Williams, *Politics of Sleep*, xi–xii. See also Wolf-Meyer, "Modern American Sleep"; and Moore, "Nature of Sleep."

51 Blanchot, "Sleep, Night," 264.

52 See Parris, "'Body,'" 129–32; and Freud, "Some Character-Types," 165–66.

53 Lévinas, *Existence and Existents*, 53. Lévinas writes elsewhere, "There is a non-coinciding of the ego with itself, restlessness, insomnia, beyond what is found again in the present." Lévinas, *Otherwise Than Being*, 64.

54 Freud famously writes, "All dreams are in a sense dreams of convenience: they serve the purpose of prolonging sleep instead of waking up. Dreams are the guardians of sleep and not its disturbers." Freud, *Interpretation of Dreams*, 253.

55 Lévinas, *Existence and Existents*, 63. Benjamin Parris argues that insomnia is a threat to kingly authority in Shakespeare's *Macbeth* by "imping[ing] upon the monarch's ability to maintain watchful rule," which, I argue, could also be seen as the failure to rule the kingly self. Parris, "'Body,'" 102.

56 Lévinas, *Existence and Existents*, 62.

57 Lévinas, *Existence and Existents*, 66–67 (emphasis mine).

58   Trigg, *Thing*, 50; and Wortham, *Poetics of Sleep*, 102.

59   Wortham, *Poetics of Sleep*, 142. Jon Elster writes sympathetically, "One cannot will sleep, but one can will taking a sleeping pill and hence sleep, at one remove." Elster, *Sour Grapes*, 53.

60   Esposito, "*Dispositif* of the Person."

61   Goodrich, "Theatre of Emblems," 49–51.

62   Esposito, "*Dispositif* of the Person," 19.

63   On the legal person as the full subject of rights, see, for instance, Wolff, "Nature of Legal Persons."

64   Balibar, "Citizen Subject," 34. Warren Montag has called these divided parts of the subject "the subjected subject, the subject of a sovereign, the sovereign's subject as opposed to the sovereign subject." Montag, "Between Interpellation and Immunization," n.p.

65   Balibar, "Citizen Subject," 45.

66   Esposito, *Immunitas*, 70. Esposito calls this a *dispositif* in later work to reflect its irresolvable contradictory nature. See Esposito, *Bios*; and Esposito, *Two*, ch. 2.

67   Esposito, *Immunitas*, 71; and Esposito, "*Dispositif* of the Person," 22; see also Esposito, *Two*, 100–101.

68   Esposito, "Community, Immunity, Biopolitics," 85.

69   See Barkan, "Roberto Esposito's Political Biology." This globalization of lethality has increasingly made immunity a vital concept within contemporary social philosophy, also engaging such thinkers as Niklas Luhmann, Donna Haraway, Emily Martin, and Derrida. These philosophers have tracked the discourse of immunity to show the mutual imbrication of actor and knowledge, rendering bodies as always "material-semiotic generative nodes [whose] boundaries materialize in social interaction," in Haraway's words. Haraway, "Biopolitics of Postmodern Bodies," 208. With a genealogy in law, and later developments in theology, anthropology, and politics, these generative nodes today often are found at the intersection of law and medicine, protecting individuals from the demands of or—as Esposito emphasizes—the debt held to community. See Luhmann, *Social Systems*; Haraway, "Biopolitics of Postmodern Bodies"; Haraway and Wolfe, *Manifestly Haraway*, 249; Martin, *Flexible Bodies*; Derrida, "Autoimmunity"; Derrida, *Rogues*; Derrida, *Beast and the Sovereign*, vols. 1 and 2; Esposito, *Immunitas*; Esposito, "*Dispositif* of the Person"; and Esposito, *Communitas*.

70   Bodei, *Life of Things*, 4.

71   Crary, *24/7*; National Commission on Sleep Disorders Research, United States, and Department of Health and Human Services, *Wake Up America*; S. Williams, *Politics of Sleep*; and Santner, *Weight of All Flesh*. On antisleep norms, see Derickson, *Dangerously Sleepy*. These masculinist norms were evident in the famous Brandeis Brief in which the dangers of

overwork and lack of sleep were uniquely identified for women in *Muller v. Oregon* (1908); however, the court's opinion does not mention sleep at all., Muller v. Oregon, 208 U.S. 412 (1908).

72   Esposito, "Interview," 54–55.

73   Esposito, *Persons and Things*, 41; on father and son, see Esposito, *Two*, 6, 84.

74   Esposito, *Persons and Things*, 41.

75   Other claims included the denial of a legitimate domestic remedy (under Article 13) and damages (under Article 41). I do not discuss these arguments here. For further discussion, see H. Post, "Judgment of the Grand Chamber."

76   Hatton v. UK 2001, at para. 97.

77   Hatton v. UK 2001, at page 29 (Separate Opinion of Judge Costa).

78   Hatton v. UK 2003, ECHR (36022/97), at paras. 123, 128.

79   Hatton v. UK 2003, Joint dissenting opinion, at para. 11. It is interesting, in contrast, to note that in the long line of US privacy cases from *Griswold* onward that protect private and intimate life, sleep is never mentioned.

80   Hatton v. UK 2003, Joint dissenting opinion, at para. 17.

81   See Khanna, "Right to Sleep," 353.

82   Benveniste, *Problems in General Linguistics*, 224–25.

83   Esposito, *Third Person*, 15.

84   Hobbes, *Leviathan*, 18.

85   Hobbes, *Leviathan*, 17. See the discussion in K. Shaw, *Indigeneity and Political Theory*.

86   Merleau-Ponty, *Phenomenology of Perception* (1995), 189–90. I have changed the phrase "anonymous alertness" in the English to "anonymous vigilance," which is my translation of "la vigilance anonyme" in the original French in an effort to think a more complex idea of vigilance. See also Merleau-Ponty, *Phénoménologie de la perception*, 191.

87   See K. Shaw, *Indigeneity and Political Theory*, 20–22.

88   Freud, *Totem and Taboo*, 164–67.

89   Merleau-Ponty, *Visible and the Invisible*, 252.

90   Merleau-Ponty, *Visible and the Invisible*, 253–54.

91   Esposito, *Bios*, 164; Esposito, *Immunitas*, 119; and Esposito and Nancy, "Dialogue," 71, 86. The flesh is "desubjectified" in Bonnie Honig's useful terminology. Honig, "Charged," 151.

92   Esposito and Nancy, "Dialogue," 85–86.

93   See also Hardt and Negri, *Multitude*, 192. Flesh, associated with the multitude, is "pure potential, an unformed life force, and in this sense an element of social being, aimed constantly at the fullness of life."

94   Santner, *Royal Remains*, 4. Human life is intertwined with symbolic entitlements and investitures because "biological life is amplified and perturbed by the symbolic dimension of relationality at the very heart of

which lie problems of authority and authorization." Santner, *Psychotheology of Everyday Life*, 30, quoted in Goodman, "Introduction," 5.

95   Melzer and Norberg, "Introduction," *From the Royal*, 10–11, quoted in Santner, *Royal Remains*, 31, (emphasis Santner's).

96   Moten, "Touring Machine," 283.

97   Goodrich, "Judge's Two Bodies," 129; and Sherwin, "Law in the Flesh," 40.

98   Thacker, "Necrologies."

99   Santner, *Royal Remains*, 28, in reference to Esposito.

100   Santner, *Weight of All Flesh*, 23. On libido, Santner writes, "We are libidinal beings, that is, we desire in a human rather than an animal sense, because our enjoyment is entwined with the signifier, with titles and entitlements, with the various 'offices' with which we come to be invested in the world. The strange surplus flesh that Freud called libido and that constitutes the stuff of our erotic attachments in the world is 'born' from the fact that our being is compelled to unfold within a matrix of signifying representations, a field never quite made to the measure of the animal that we also are." Santner, *Royal Remains*, 68.

101   Crary, *24/7*.

102   Santner, *Weight of All Flesh*, 34.

103   Honig, "Charged," 155.

104   Honig, "Charged," 155–56.

105   Honig, "Charged," 161. On the history of refuge and asylum, see Carro, "Sanctuary." It is interesting in this regard to consider that political refuge was long a part of ancient Hawaiian governance and reemerges even today in some prison policy. See Goldberg-Hiller, "Prison and Place."

106   Honig, "Charged," 156. Honig builds this argument in her book *Emergency Politics*. Her analysis of the discretionary decision-making of US assistant secretary of labor Louis Post during the red scare post World War I—who expanded rights for aliens—suggests that fretting over the Schmittian suspension of the law should be tempered with recognition of the discretionary decision of the administrative state to advance democratic ends. This is, I suggest, another way to think the problem of affirmative biopolitics that Esposito advances.

107   Sherwin, "Law in the Flesh," 56.

108   One of the first nocturnal protests, the long-lived Greenham Common Women's Peace Camp, which began in 1981 to protest the emplacement of cruise missiles nearby, also experienced nocturnal raids by police and bulldozers taking advantage of the sleeping protesters. R. Shaw, "Pushed to the Margins," 119; and Harford and Hopkins, "Introduction," in *Greenham Common*, 27.

109   Ramlila Maidan Incident v. Home Secretary, [2012] 4 S.C.R. 971, 1136F, 1138B Chauhan, J.

110   *Ramlila*, [2012] 4 S.C.R. at 1138F Chauhan, J.

111   *Ramlila*, [2012] 4 S.C.R. at 1139G Chauhan, J.

112   *Ramlila*, [2012] 4 S.C.R. at 1141C Chauhan, J. This is a probable allusion
      to the *Nicomachean Ethics*, where Aristotle writes, "Of the element with-
      out reason, one part seems to be common: the vegetative, the cause of
      nutrition and growth. . . . The virtue of this element is clearly something
      shared and not specific to human beings. For this part and its capacity
      are thought more than others to be active during sleep, and the good
      and bad person to be hardest to distinguish when they are asleep (hence
      the saying that the happy are no different from the wretched for half of
      their lives which makes sense, since sleep is a time when the soul is not
      engaged in the things that lead to its being called good or bad), except
      that in some way certain movements on a small scale reach the soul, and
      make the dreams of good people better than those of ordinary people."
      Aristotle, *Nicomachean Ethics*, 21 (1102a 23–1102b 14). See also the second
      epigraph to this chapter by Hart.

113   *Ramlila*, [2012] 4 S.C.R. at 1140A Chauhan, J.

114   *Ramlila*, [2012] 4 S.C.R. at 1140C, 1141A Chauhan, J.

115   Perhaps the better source is Anatole France, whose perverse and ironic
      notion of equality is found in the denial of the right of all, poor and rich,
      to sleep under the bridges of the Seine. France, *Le lys rouge*, 118.

116   Justice Chauhan cites Homer's reference to Hypnos, the god of sleep, as
      the twin of Thanatos, death. *Ramlila*, [2012] 4 S.C.R. at 1141B.

117   Dayan, *Law Is a White Dog*.

118   Bernton, "Portland Allows Homeless"; *Martin v. City of Boise*, (9th Cir.)
      902 F.3d 1031 (2018); *Hawaii Tribune-Herald*, "Mauna Kea Rules Nulli-
      fied"; and *Mauna Kea Anaina Hou v. BLNR*, 136 Hawai'i 376, 363 P.3D 224
      (2015).

119   Foucault, *Society Must Be Defended*, 40. Ben Golder has called Foucault's
      vision for law a "critical counter-conduct of rights." Golder, *Foucault*, 20.

120   Spillers, "Mama's Baby, Papa's Maybe," 67. See also Weheliye, *Habeas
      Viscus*, 33–45; and Moten, "Touring Machine."

121   J. Butler, *Performative Theory of Assembly*, 89–90.

CHAPTER 2. IT CAME UPON YOU IN THE NIGHT

Epigraph 1: Dayan, *Law Is a White Dog*, 252.

Epigraph 2: Mbembe, *Necropolitics*, 27.

Epigraph 3: Walker, *Appeal*, 27.

Epigraph 4: Sherwin, "Law in the Flesh," 44.

1   Quoted in Berman, "What the Police Officer" (emphasis mine).

2   Carlson, *Policing the Second Amendment*, 61.

3   Statistics compiled by author using the *Washington Post* database of police killings, 2015 to present (August 2021). This racial disparity is not matched by any other. I return to these statistics later in this chapter.

4   Grogger and Ridgeway, "Testing for Racial Profiling"; and Vito et al., "'Does Daylight Matter'?" These studies have generated many methodological debates, and not all studies have found racial disparities. See Stacey and Bonner, "Veil of Darkness."

5   Buford's parents claimed, "They got him in the darkness." This interview transcript of police conversations and journalists' interrogations with the shooter, Lucas Roethlisberger, who killed Buford reveals the legal implications of the dark:

> INVESTIGATOR: How far could you see?
>
> SECOND OFFICER: I could not see in the gangway. It was very dark. I can't recall. I remember dropping my flashlight as I got out of the car, to go run to Officer #1. I don't remember how far I could see down. I can definitely tell it was somebody laying down, though.
>
> ALISON FLOWERS (REPORTER): And, to an extent with what [Lucas] Roethlisberger [the police shooter] says before force investigators kind of circle back, point out that he said it was really dark and that he didn't have a flashlight.
>
> LT. JOHN GREEN (OF THE INTERNAL FORCE INVESTIGATION UNIT): It was dark back there. Did you have any light or anything?
>
> LUCAS ROETHLISBERGER: No, I did not have a chance to retrieve my flashlight from my pants.
>
> JG: OK.
>
> LR: Because the fact that he had a firearm was more important for me, that I had control with both my hands free.
>
> AF: And then they say, "Well, how was your vision in that?" And now he seems to register that point of emphasis in the interview. His lawyer certainly did. His eyes kind of dart up to see what Roethlisberger was going to say and do. And Roethlisberger says, "I could see, I could see."
>
> JG: I know it was pretty dark. How was your vision in that?
>
> LR: I could see. I could see.
>
> JG: OK. You sure?
>
> LR: I'm sure.

Scahill, "Killed in the Darkness."

6   Kautzer, "Self-Defeating Notion"; Harvey Shapiro, "When the Exception"; and Carlson, "States."

7   Luke, "Counting Up AR-15s," 74; see also the other essays in Obert, Poe, and Sarat, *Lives of Guns*.

8   The Pew Research Center's best measurements from 2017 show that 24 percent of Black citizens own guns, and another 8 percent report living in a household with guns. Thirty-six percent of white citizens own guns, and another 13 percent live in a house with guns. Fifteen percent of Latinos own guns, and 6 percent more live in a household with guns. Kim Parker et al., "Demographics of Gun Ownership."

9   The Second Amendment reads, "A well regulated Militia, being necessary to the security of a free State, the right of the people to keep and bear Arms, shall not be infringed."

10   Hamilton et al., *The Federalist*, 140 (no. 29).

11   As many as one-third of Black males have a felony conviction, while only 8 percent of all American adults do. Shannon et al., "Growth." In 2016, 51 percent of federal convictions for gun violations were of Black people. Carlson, *Policing the Second Amendment*, 59.

12   Hildreth, *Despotism in America*, 52.

13   Testimony of John Homrn, 1847, in Blassingame, *Slave Testimony*, 256.

14   Narrative of James Curry, 1840, in Blassingame, *Slave Testimony*, 130. See also Stampp, *Peculiar Institution*, 80.

15   Testimony of Alexander Kenner, 1863, in Blassingame, *Slave Testimony*, 393. See also Ball, *Slavery in the United States*, 43.

16   Testimony of Tabb Gross and Lewis Smith, in Blassingame, *Slave Testimony*, 346.

17   Camp, "Pleasures of Resistance," 535.

18   Hildreth, *Despotism in America*, 53.

19   The Savannah River Anti-Slave Traffick Association of South Carolina slaveholders expressed outrage about "night meetings." In 1846 they wrote regulations to restrain the "'hundreds of negroes it may be said without exaggeration are every night, and at all hours of the night, prowling about the country," for likely purposes of "stealing, trading, drinking, and meeting, almost certainly for secular affairs, " according to Stephanie Camp. Included in the association's concerns was recognition that enslaved people were using the night to harm slaveholders' pocketbooks and also to resist their authority. "The negroes themselves are seriously impaired in physical qualities. . . . Their nightly expeditions are followed by days of languor." Quoted in and summarized by Camp, "Pleasures of Resistance," 569. On the use of sleep deprivation by owners for the purposes of social control, see Reiss, *Wild Nights*, ch. 4.

20   Camp, "Pleasures of Resistance," 570.

21   Interview of Harriet Tubman, 1859, in Blassingame, *Slave Testimony*, 460. See also interview with John Moore, who convinced his wife's owner in a nearby plantation that he was no longer interested in his wife. His wife's owner thereafter allowed her some liberty at night, giving her the opportunity to flee with her husband to Canada. Blassingame, *Slave Testimony*, 275.

22   Nicholas Johnson, *Negroes and the Gun*, 41; and Ball, *Slavery*, 352.

23   Nicholas Johnson, *Negroes and the Gun*, 41.

24   Joseph Tregle Jr., "Early New Orleans Society," 33, quoted in Eugene Genovese, *Roll Jordan Roll,* 413. See also Turner and Gray, *Confessions of Nat Turner*; and S. Hartman, *Scenes of Subjection*, 67.

25   C. James, *Black Jacobins*, 82, 86.

26   As early as 1804 in Philadelphia, free Blacks staged a counterdemonstration for July 4, Haitian independence day, which became a violent confrontation with whites celebrating US independence. Fanning, "Early Black Nationalism," 42. On the importance of the Haitian Revolution, see also C. Anderson, *Second*, 50; and Aptheker, *Nat Turner's Slave Rebellion*. Numerous communities of free Blacks in the early nineteenth century were named for the revolution and its leader, Toussaint Louverture. See Clavin, "American Toussaints," 116.

27   Genovese, *From Rebellion to Revolution*, 3. See also M. Jackson and Bacon, *African Americans*.

28   Carter Jackson, *Force and Freedom*, 5.

29   Benjamin Reiss argues that Turner's careful nocturnal planning demonstrated the inability of slave owners to control the sleep of the enslaved. Reiss, *Wild Nights*, 128. On the details of Turner's nocturnal strategy, see Tomlins, *Matter of Nat Turner.*

30   Unidentified author ca. 1832 quoted in Aptheker, *Nat Turner's Slave Rebellion*, 64.

31   Hildreth, *Despotism in America*, 89.

32   Cornell, "Early American Origins," 582.

33   Stephanie Camp has argued that "black mobility appears to have been the target of more official and planter regulations than other aspects of slave behavior." Camp, "Pleasures of Resistance," 534.

34   See Paquette, "'Horde of Brigands?'"

35   C. Anderson, *Second*, 54, 65.

36   Nicholas Johnson et al., *Firearms Law*; and C. Anderson, *Second*, 82. In 1680 a colonial Virginia law "Act for Preventing Negroes Insurrections" proscribed "any negroe or other slave to carry or arme himselfe with any club, staffe, gunn, sword or any other weapon of defence or offence." Hening, *Hening's Statutes at Large*, 2:481–82. Virginia and South Carolina banned guns for enslaved and free Blacks prior to the Articles of Confederation. See 7 Statutes at Large of South Carolina 353, 1836.

37   Militia Act of 1792, Ch. 33, 1 Stat. 271 (1792) (repealed 1903).

38   Act of Feb. 17, 1833, Ch. 671, §. 15, 17, 1833 Fla. Laws 26, 29.

39   Pocock, *Machiavellian Moment*; Wood, *Creation*; Skinner, *Liberty before Liberalism*; Bailyn, *Ideological Origins*; Appleby, "Republicanism and Ideology"; Shalhope, "Toward a Republican Synthesis"; and Horwitz, "Republicanism and Liberalism."

40   Jefferson, *State of Virginia*, 172.

41   Wood, *Creation*, vii.

42   Pocock, *Machiavellian Moment*, 507.

43   Cornell, "Early American Origins," 572.

44   This was the case in the 1811 slave insurrection in Louisiana. Buman, "To Kill Whites," 33; and C. Anderson, *Second*, 63–66.

45   Morgan, "Slavery and Freedom"; and Gourevitch, *From Slavery*.

46   Gourevitch, *From Slavery*, 14. See also Patterson, *Slavery and Social Death*, 99.

47   Pocock, *Machiavellian Moment*, 514.

48   Pocock, *Machiavellian Moment*, 517.

49   It is important to note that American republicanism, rather uniquely, emphasized the centrality of deliberation. Rousseau, for example, refused to concede that the general will was manifest in deliberation. "It follows . . . that the general will is always right and tends to the public advantage; but it does not follow that the deliberations of the people are always equally correct." Rousseau, *Social Contract*, 25.

50   Tocqueville, *Democracy in America*, 302 (see also 125–27).

51   Arendt, *On Revolution*, 253.

52   Martí and Pettit, *Political Philosophy*, 156–57.

53   Durkheim, *Professional Ethics*, 80–81.

54   Yankah, "Republican Responsibility," 465. "Law abidingness on such a view is not slavish and unthinking devotion to legal norms no matter how immoral. This is true for two reasons. The first is that breaking the law is not always a sign of a lack of civic virtue. Those who engage in open civil disobedience in order to draw attention to legal injustice with a willingness to accept the legal consequences of punishment are often displaying the highest levels of civic virtue. Those engaged in civic disobedience in the Jim Crow South, for example, illustrate beautifully that one can disobey particular laws without disrespecting law generally."

55   Rawls, *Theory of Justice*, 118–23; A. Smith, *Theory of Moral Sentiments*; and Sherwin, "Law in the Flesh."

56   Foucault, *Birth of Biopolitics*, 279.

57   Horwitz, "Republicanism and Liberalism"; and Nozick, *Anarchy*, ch. 3.

58   Cornell, "Early American Origins," 583.

59   Cornell, "Early American Origins," 584–85.

60   Enright, "Constitutional 'Terra Incognita,'" 926; and Meltzer, "Open Carry for All," 1513–16.

61   Joseph Gales, in O. Smith, *Early Indiana Trials*, 465–66.

62   Statute of Northampton, 1328, 2 Edw. 3, c. 3 (Eng.). It is important to recall Gordon Wood's important insight that "the colonists stood to the very end of their debate with England and even after on [the] natural and

scientific principles of the English constitution. And ultimately such a stand was what made their Revolution seem so unusual, for they revolted not against the English constitution but on behalf of it." Wood, *Creation*, 10. On prohibitions on using guns at night, see Meltzer, "Open Carry for All," 1508–9.

63   I do not argue that republicanism has no theory of terror; I show later that it can accommodate fear and violence. Yet republicanism cannot account for what this means when the people is not signified as it rarely is at night.

64   Gourevitch, *From Slavery*.

65   Douglass, "Meaning of July Fourth," 199.

66   Herman, "Hunting and American Identity," 61.

67   Chamayou, *Manhunts*, 6.

68   Chamayou, *Manhunts*, 74.

69   Sidney Howard Gay, quoted in Nash, *Christiana Riot*, n. 29 (no page number discernible).

70   "The police is a hunting institution," argues Chamayou. Chamayou, *Manhunts*, 89; see also Fassin, *Enforcing Order*; and du Plessis, "Hunting."

71   Walker, *Appeal*, 71; see also Crane, "Controlling the Night," 122.

72   Crane, "Controlling the Night," 120. "The system's purpose . . . was less to monitor slaves' movements than to increase slaves' fear. The system also served to assuage white fears of nocturnal crimes committed by the population they held in bondage" (128).

73   Camp, "Pleasures of Resistance," 553. Sarah Fitzpatrick, enslaved in Alabama and interviewed in 1938, explained, "De Pattero's . . . wuz white folks whut went round at night an' caught 'Niggers' when dey went off de place an' ef dey didn't have no pass dey'd beat'em and run'em back home. Dats whar dat song come f'om 'bout 'Run Nigger Run, de Pattero's ketch'ya.' . . . Lots o' 'Niggers' nuver would git a pass to go out at night. Dey jes' pend on outrunning' de white folks. . . . Some 'Niggers' so mean dat white fo'ks didn't bodder'em much." Blassingame, *Slave Testimony*, 641–42.

74   Fry, *Night Riders*. See also the epigraph and account of slave regulation within Dayan, *Law Is a White Dog*.

75   A Florida law of 1846 "was typical. Patrollers were permitted to inflict a 'moderate whipping' of up to twenty lashes on slaves outside plantations without a ticket or without a white person present. All of these laws expressly authorizing third parties to whip a slave included limits." Morris, *Southern Slavery*, 197. Mississippi law limited punishment to fifteen lashes. See Crane, "Controlling the Night," 123.

76   Blassingame, *Slave Testimony*, 156–57.

77   Cottrol and Diamond, "Second Amendment," 341–42.

78   Douglass, "Meaning of July Fourth," 196–200.

79   Ignatiev, *How the Irish*, 140. The genealogy of these kinds of nocturnal kidnappings includes early abductions of Native peoples in North America for work on plantations in the seventeenth century. See Lepore, *Name of War*, 155. Harriet Tubman ceased bringing freed slaves to the northern United States in 1850, believing that only Canada could create a safe haven for free Blacks. Forbes, "'By My Own Right Arm,'" 161. See also J. Katz, *Resistance at Christiana*, 26.

80   W. Parker, "Freedman's Story," 279. Although there is some scholarly question as to the extent of William Parker's contribution to his story, written fifteen years after the event—though not its accuracy—it is not directly relevant for my use of this text.

81   W. Parker, "Freedman's Story," 160.

82   W. Parker, "Freedman's Story," 281.

83   W. Parker, "Freedman's Story," 283.

84   W. Parker, "Freedman's Story," 283.

85   Douglass, *Life and Times*, 349.

86   W. Parker, "Freedman's Story," 158.

87   C. Anderson, *Second*, 123.

88   Garrison, quoted in Nash, *Christiana Riot*, at n. 32 (no page number discernible.)

89   Worcestor Spy, quoted in Nash, *Christiana Riot*, at n. 34 (no page number discernible). In Shakespeare's play Richard speaks an oath to Queen Elizabeth, "Day, yield me not thy light; nor, night, thy rest!" and says several lines later that without his daughter's love he expects "Death, desolation, ruin, and decay." *King Richard III*, act 4, scene 4, line 410. In the Declaration of Independence, King George is accused of deploying his armies for "death, desolation, and tyranny."

90   Carter Jackson, *Force and Freedom*, 57–61; and Rice, "Legacy Transformed," 102.

91   A Philadelphia newspaper, unnamed, quoted in Still, *Underground Railroad*, 353.

92   Nicholas Johnson, *Negroes and the Gun*, 64.

93   W. Johnston, "Fugitive Slave Riot."

94   W. Johnston, "Fugitive Slave Riot."

95   Douglass, "Change of Opinion Announced," 174.

96   Nicholas Johnson, "Firearms Policy," 1556.

97   Forman, *Locking Up Our Own*, esp. ch. 2.

98   Bruce-Briggs, "Great American Gun War," 37.

99   Tahmassebi, "Gun Control and Racism," 80.

100 Robert Cottrol and Raymond Diamond argue that the concern over the Saturday night special can be traced to the Sullivan Law, passed in New York City in 1911 to regulate firearms. This law targeted Italian immigrants. They note, "If the story of New York's Sullivan Law suggests

that a fear of and a desire to control suspect classes of undesirables bears likeness to the story of the white South's ventures into gun control in the Reconstruction and post-Reconstruction periods, it is true as well that the Sullivan Law, like the Southern statutory and constitutional provisions inaugurated in those periods spoke to what on its surface was a legitimate society goal in advancement of the case of public safety." Cottrol and Diamond, "Never Intended," 1334. See also Gulasekaram, "'The People,'" 1562.

101   Carlson, *Policing the Second Amendment*.

102   Carlson, *Policing the Second Amendment*, 160.

103   "Left to their own resources, the freedpeople were 'not going to starve,' and everyone knew it." Fitzgerald, "Ku Klux Klan," 190. See Dickerson, *Reconstruction Era*, 44. For similar reasons, Southern Blacks also planted sweet potatoes, which gave them more food security and less dependency on laboring for whites. See Keith, *Colfax Massacre*, 48.

104   Fitzgerald, "Ex-Slaveholders," 156; and Fellman, *In the Name of God*, 112. Michael Fellman notes, "It must be emphasized that in the 1870s fears of an imminent and well organized armed black revolution were only panic-inducing fantasies, but they galvanized white counterrevolutionaries. To prepare for this nightmarish black uprising, white leaders began to use the telegraph and the railroads to concentrate a considerable, well-armed private militia that could be called upon whenever the need might come. Along the borders of Alabama and Louisiana, Mississippians also could depend on white fighters to cross the state line rapidly when summoned."

105   Byman, "White Supremacy"; Fellman, *In the Name of God*, 74–76; Cardyn, "Sexualized Racism/Gendered Violence," 685–86; and J. Goldstein, "Klan's Constitution," 293.

106   Du Bois, *Black Reconstruction*, 166–80; Richardson, "Florida Black Codes"; Foner, *Short History*; and Dickerson, *Reconstruction Era*.

107   Du Bois, *Black Reconstruction*, 177.

108   Fellman, *In the Name of God*, 74.

109   K. Williams, *They Left Great Marks*, 38.

110   "Report of the Joint Select Committee," 273, 277. "[The Ku Klux Klan (KKK) or Pale Faces] organization arose [in 1868] about the time the militia were called out, and Governor Brownlow issued his proclamation stating that the troops would not be injured for what they should do to rebels; such a proclamation was issued. There was a great deal of insecurity felt by the southern people. There were a great many northern men coming down there, forming Leagues all over the country. The negroes were holding night meetings; were going about; were becoming very insolent; and the southern people all over the State were very much alarmed." Generals N. B. Forest (Tennessee) and John B. Gordon (Georgia), testimony incorporated into "Report of the Joint Select Committee," 449.

111   Keith, *Colfax Massacre*, 88. LeeAnna Keith points to Jesse McKinney, who was shot dead by whites while at home, with his family looking on, a precursor to the Colfax massacre of 1873. See also K. Williams, "Never Get over It," 67–68.

112   Fitzgerald, "Ex-Slaveholders," 155. General John B. Gordon of Georgia testified in Congress to his knowledge of the origins of the KKK in his home state. "The first and main reason was the organization of the Union League, as they called it, about which we knew nothing more than this: that the negroes would desert the plantations, and go off at night in large numbers; and on being asked where they had been, would reply, sometimes, 'We have been to the muster;' sometimes, 'We have been to the lodge;' sometimes, 'We have been to the meeting.'" "Report of the Joint Select Committee," 431.

113   Foner, *Short History*, 188.

114   For the origins of the KKK and other groups, see Cardyn, "Sexualized Racism/Gendered Violence"; J. Goldstein, "Klan's Constitution"; Byman, "White Supremacy"; Trelease, *White Terror*; and Olsen, "Ku Klux Klan." Other significant groups include the Knights of the White Camellia, Southern Cross; the Innocents; the Brotherhood; the Pale Faces; and others.

115   Olsen, "Ku Klux Klan," 343.

116   J. Goldstein, "Klan's Constitution," 296.

117   "Report of the Joint Select Committee," 48.

118   Hershey, "Lynch Law," 467; see also Olsen, "Ku Klux Klan," 342–44. W. E. B. Du Bois and Allen Trelease disagree, calling the postbellum South essentially "lawless." Du Bois, *Black Reconstruction*, 670; and Trelease, *White Terror*, 9.

119   Parsons, *Ku-Klux*, 206.

120   Parsons, *Ku-Klux*, 212.

121   This process has modern analogues in the ironic imagery of the new right. Pepe the Frog, for instance, is used to signify anti-Semitic commitments, while remaining "just a frog" when accusations are leveled. See Wilson, "Hiding in Plain Sight"; Wendling, *Alt-Right*; and Askanius, "On Frogs."

122   K. Williams, "Never Get over It."

123   Trelease, *White Terror*, 8. "It seems, in certain neighborhoods a company of men, on the night before Christmas, under alleged orders from the colonel of the county militia, went from place to place, broke open negro houses, and searched their trunks, boxes, &c., under pretense of taking away fire-arms, fearing, as they said, an insurrection. Strange to say, that these so-called militiamen took the darkest nights for their purpose; often demanded money of the negroes, and took not only fire-arms, but whatever their fancy or avarice desired. In two instances negroes were

taken as guides from one plantation to another, and when the party reached the woods the guides were most cruelly beaten. I really believe the true object of these nightly raids was not the fear of an insurrection, but to intimidate and compel the blacks to enter into contract." Testimony from Alabama, "Report of the Joint Select Committee," 267–68.

124 "The Klan sought to make certain that it would be the only armed organization in the up-country." Herbert Shapiro, "Ku Klux Klan," 44. See also Olsen, "Ku Klux Klan," 353; and Trelease, *White Terror*, 176.

125 Du Bois, *Black Reconstruction*, 677–78.

126 18 U.S.C. § 241, 1871, also known as the Third KKK Act.

127 On the discouraging of disguises, see Trelease, *White Terror*, 33. Trelease notes that the conservative *Pulaski Citizen* newspaper called for a trial of all Klansmen guilty of wearing disguises. On bridging of class divisions, see Fitzgerald, "Ex-Slaveholders," 151, 153–54. On rape and sexually sadistic pleasures against freedpeople, see Cardyn, "Sexualized Racism/Gendered Violence." Trelease writes that "in general, the more politically motivated Klan operations were at any time and place, the more upper-class elements were apt to be involved." Trelease, *White Terror*, 307.

128 Trelease, *White Terror*, 53.

129 Byman, "White Supremacy," 80.

130 Olsen, "Ku Klux Klan," 349.

131 Quoted in Trelease, *White Terror*, 129.

132 Army Appropriation Act, 14 Stat. 485 (1867).

133 Trelease, *White Terror*, xix.

134 K. Williams, *They Left Great Marks*, 127.

135 K. Williams, *They Left Great Marks*, 40; and Trelease, *White Terror*, 30. Even some white Republicans testified that they slept in the woods to avoid the KKK. See "Report of the Joint Select Committee," 38.

136 K. Williams, "Never Get over It," 71.

137 "Report of the Joint Select Committee," 67.

138 Frederick Douglass observed that year that the "scourging and slaughter of our people have so far ceased." Quoted in Pope, "Snubbed Landmark," 405.

139 Hogue, "1873 Battle of Colfax," 7. James Hogue argues that there were three phases of counterrevolution following the Civil War. Vigilante action by the KKK in the early years gave way to paramilitary action (1873 to 1877) and, finally, quasi-legal coups d'état that succeeded in Louisiana and Arkansas. There is, of course, strong evidence of the persistence of nocturnal violence throughout and after these phases were complete.

140 Soifer, *Law*, 120. See also Hogue, "1873 Battle of Colfax," 9; Keith, *Colfax Massacre*, 46–49; Pope, "Snubbed Landmark," 387–88; M. Johnson, "Colfax Riot of April, 1873"; and Lane, *Day Freedom Died*.

141 "Condition of the South," 13.

142 Quoted in Keith, *Colfax Massacre*, 90.

143 Hogue, "1873 Battle of Colfax," 18.

144 Keith, *Colfax Massacre*, 105.

145 W. Lod Tanner, quoted in M. Johnson, "Colfax Riot," 417.

146 Slaughterhouse Cases, 83 U.S. 36 (1873).

147 United States v. Cruikshank, 92 U.S. 542, 710 (1876).

148 Art. IV, § 4, United States Constitution.

149 *Cruikshank*, 92 U.S. at 709.

150 Soifer, *Law*, 123. Using more contemporary terms, Daniel Byman calls this anarchy a "failed state." Byman, "White Supremacy," 56.

151 See, for example, Brandwein, *Rethinking the Judicial Settlement*; Pope, "Snubbed Landmark"; and L. Goldstein, "Second Amendment."

152 Foner, *Short History*, 531.

153 McMillen, *Dark Journey*, 228.

154 "The new cry," in Wells-Barnett, *Southern Horrors*, 14. See also Hill Collins, *Black Sexual Politics*, 221; and Patterson, *Rituals of Blood*, 174. Orlando Patterson suggests 25 percent of lynchings were for rape allegations. On the raping of Black people by white vigilantes, see Cardyn, "Sexualized Racism/Gendered Violence," 719.

155 Neil McMillen's list of accusations justifying lynching in the Southern newspapers includes "talking disrespectfully," slapping a white boy, writing an "insulting letter," owing ten dollars for an unpaid funeral bill, organizing sharecroppers, being "suspected [of] lawlessness," killing a horse, conjuring, and being mistaken for someone else. McMillen, *Dark Journey*, 236.

156 White "Deltan," quoted in McMillen, *Dark Journey*, 236.

157 Carlson, *Policing the Second Amendment*, 13. See also Cottrol and Diamond, "Second Amendment," 354.

158 McMillen, *Dark Journey*, 230.

159 S. Hartman, *Scenes of Subjection*.

160 Gorup, "Strange Fruit," 820. Christopher Waldrep argues similarly regarding vigilante lynchings in San Francisco, California, in the mid-nineteenth century, quoting three nineteenth-century historians of this violence who noted, "This was not a mob, but the *people*, in the highest sense of the term." Waldrep, *Many Faces*, 56.

161 Brendese, "Worlds Neither New nor Brave," 26.

162 See Wells-Barnett, *Red Record*, especially "Awful Barbarism Ignored."

163 McMillen, *Dark Journey*, 249.

164 Woodward, *Strange Career of Jim Crow*, 107.

165 Gorup argues that "lynching represented a species of lawlessness internal to American racial democracy, not an exception at its limits." Gorup, "Strange Fruit," 824. I argue here that this violence did not make an exception but revealed what Mbembe has called the "law outside the law"

(see epigraph). Regina Bateson argues that the extralegal character of vigilantism implies that it can only occur against the backdrop of the law, that it occurs in realms where the state monitors behavior, and that state agents are not precluded from acting as vigilantes. I contest her fourth point, that vigilantism "entails contestation with the law and the state. Because their actions go 'beyond the law' citizens engaging in vigilantism necessarily challenge, usurp, supplant, or displace the state's authority." In the republican context of the antebellum South, vigilantism did necessary work for the state. Bateson, "Politics of Vigilantism," 927–28. On vigilantism and its complex relationship with law, see also L. Johnston, "What Is Vigilantism?"

166 Judge Sidney Fant Davis, quoted in Moye, *Let the People Decide*, 7.

167 McMillen, *Dark Journey*, 242. Invitations to the Black community, one can surmise, were coercive and not easy to refuse.

168 Gorup, "Strange Fruit," 828.

169 W. Fitzhugh Brundage, quoted in Patterson, *Rituals of Blood,* 179.

170 Gorup, "Strange Fruit," 829; and Patterson, *Rituals of Blood*, 179. Gorup cites the increase in capital executions by the state, the solidification of police departments, and the success of Jim Crow laws as causes for the decline of (private) lynching by this date.

171 McMillen, *Dark Journey*, 241.

172 James Howell Street (1934), quoted in John Howard Parker, "Life and Works," 68.

173 Even for a bad lynching, "an indictment proved rare, a conviction practically impossible, and an appropriate sentence never." Boyett, *Right to Revolt*, 17.

174 These bodies, sometimes photographed, became a contested site over their racial meaning. See Raiford, "Lynching."

175 James Howell Street, quoted in John Howard Parker, "Life and Works," 68.

176 I am indebted to Charles Lawrence III for this insight. Private communication with the author.

177 The Midnight Crew "used electric shock, simulated suffocation, and mock executions, often accompanied with virulent racial epithets and attacks to the genitals, to coerce false confessions that formed the basis for wrongful convictions and Draconian prison terms including death sentences in at least ten instances." G. Taylor, "Long Path to Reparations," 330; see also Linnemann and Medley, "Black Sites, 'Dark Sides,'" 351; and Muhammad, *Condemnation of Blackness*, xxi. For original documents from the investigation of the Midnight Crew, see Chicago Police Torture Archive.

178 Decisions that did not support an individual right to bear arms were *Cruikshank*, 92 U.S. 542 (1876); Presser v. Illinois, 116 U.S. 252 (1886); and Miller v. Texas, 153 U.S. 535 (1894). The 2008 case that reversed this was District of Columbia v. Heller, 554 U.S. 570 (2008).

179   McDonald v. City of Chicago, 561 U.S. 742 (2010). Justice Clarence Thomas filed a concurring opinion and concurred in the result.

180   *McDonald*, 561 U.S. at 855. Marshall addressed *Cruikshank* in Regents of the University of California v. Bakke, 438 U.S. 265, 391 (1978).

181   *McDonald*, 561 U.S. at 806, 823, 838. Chief Justice Roger B. Taney denied rights to Black people because, in part, "it would give to persons of the negro race, who were recognised as citizens in any one State of the Union, the right to enter every other State whenever they pleased, singly or in companies, without pass or passport, and without obstruction, to sojourn there as long as they pleased, to go where they pleased at every hour of the day or night without molestation, unless they committed some violation of law for which a white man would be punished; and it would give them the full liberty of speech in public and in private upon all subjects upon which its own citizens might speak; to hold public meetings upon political affairs, and to *keep and carry arms* wherever they went. And all of this would be done in the face of the subject race of the same color, both free and slaves, and inevitably producing discontent and insubordination among them, and endangering the peace and safety of the State." *Dred Scott v. Sandford*, 60 U.S. 393, 417 (1857). Thomas cites the italicized part of this section in *McDonald*, 561 U.S. at 823.

182   *McDonald*, 561 U.S. at 857–58.

183   K. Williams, *They Left Great Marks*, 49.

184   J. Baldwin, *Fire Next Time*, 69. Saidiya Hartman suggests that there is also frequently no will to make memory and language about traumatic racialized abuse. "Alongside the terrible things one had survived was also the shame of having survived it. Remembering warred with the will to forget." S. Hartman, *Lose Your Mother*, 16.

185   Brendese, *Power of Memory*; see also Fentress and Wickham, *Social Memory*.

186   *McDonald*, 561 U.S. at 891. Stevens uses this observation to argue that states have an interest in mitigating this danger as an exercise of their police powers.

187   Dirlam, Steidley, and Jacobs, "Link to the Past."

188   Roman, "Race, Justifiable Homicide," 7; see also Rolnick, "Defending White Space," 1654–55.

189   Wagner, Kim, and Hagler, "Stand Your Ground," 8; and Cheng and Hoekstra, "Does Strengthening Self-Defense Law."

190   Douglass, *Life and Times*, 39–40 (emphasis mine). I am indebted to Prof. Samson Opondo for this historical insight (private communication with the author.) David Walker earlier (1824) used phraseology similar to Douglass's, arguing, "Let no man of us budge one step, and let slave-holders come to beat us from our country. America is more our country, than it is the whites—we have enriched it with our *blood and tears*." Walker, *Appeal*, 64.

191   See Erwin v. State, 29 Ohio St. 186, 195 (1876); and Levin, "Defensible Defense," 529. On frontier honor, see Kamir, "Honor and Dignity."

192   On masculinism and the castle doctrine, see Suk, *At Home*; and Messerschmidt, "Victim of Abuse." It is worth recalling that the common law barred a dweller of a house from the crime of burglary; thus, men committing violence within the home could not easily be held criminally responsible.

193   "If any person attempt to rob or murder another in or near the highway, or in a dwellinghouse, or attempt to break any dwelling-house in the night-time, and be killed in the attempt, the slayer shall be acquitted and discharged." 24 Hen. VIII. C. 5 (1532). On the English common law of self-defense, see Malcolm, "Right of the People." On the growth of American self-defense law, see Light, *Stand Your Ground*.

194   R. v. Polly and Bowell, 1 Car. & K. 76 [English Reports], 720 (1843).

195   R. Brown, *No Duty to Retreat*, 19.

196   State v. Gardner, 104 N.W. 971, 975 (1905); see also Kopel, "Self-Defense Cases."

197   Chamayou, *Theory of the Drone*, 114–17.

198   Brown v. United States, 256 U.S. 335, 343 (1921).

199   Quoted in Suk, *At Home*, 76.

200   Quoted in M. Lee, "Originating Stand Your Ground," 114.

201   Lawrence, "Id"; Lawrence, "Unconscious Racism Revisited"; and Lawrence, "Implicit Bias." See also Levinson and Smith, *Implicit Racial Bias*; Krieger, "Content of Our Categories"; and C. Lee, "Making Race Salient."

202   Levinson and Smith, *Implicit Racial Bias*, 2.

203   Levinson, "Forgotten Racial Equality"; Levinson, Cai, and Young, "Guilty by Implicit Racial Bias"; Payne, "Prejudice and Perception"; and Amodio et al., "Neural Signals."

204   C. Lee, "Making Race Salient," 1585–86.

205   Legewie and Fagan, "Group Threat"; and Nicholson-Crotty, Nicholson-Crotty, and Fernandez, "Will More Black Cops Matter?"

206   Under a standard announced by the Supreme Court in 1985, police can legitimately kill only to prevent death or serious injury, including to themselves. Tennessee v. Garner, 471 U.S. 1 (1985).

207   For comparison, police in the United States kill at a rate 125 times that in England and Wales, and by similar margin more than that in Germany and India. South Africa and Brazil have higher rates of police killing. Per 10 million people, police in the United States kill 33.5; the equivalent number is 9.8 in Canada, 8.5 in Australia, 2.0 in New Zealand, 1.3 in Germany, 0.2 in Japan, and 0 in Iceland and Norway. Zimring, *When Police Kill*, 77, 82; Osse and Cano, "Police Deadly Use"; and Prison Policy Initiative, "Not Just 'a Few Bad Apples.'"

208   The article found that "the NVSS did not report 17 100 deaths (95% UI 16 600–17 600) out of 30 800 deaths (30 300–31 300) that we estimated, accounting for 55.5% (54.8–56.2) of all police violence deaths from 1980 to 2018." "Fatal Police Violence," P1243; see also Zimring, *When Police Kill*.

209   From 1980 to 2018, 5,670 deaths of Black people were missing out of 9,540 estimated. Underreporting for other races was also high, including for white people, Hispanics, and Indigenous peoples, though not as high as for Blacks. "Fatal Police Violence," P1243.

210   Frank Zimring has shown how police facing a civilian armed with a knife are statistically in very little danger of being harmed. Nonetheless, police regularly kill those brandishing a knife (949 times between 2015 and August 2021, according to the *Washington Post* database), despite studies showing there is no support for the subjective judgments of police. Zimring, *When Police Kill*, 101.

211   If a killing by police took place during the hours of darkness, seasonally adjusted to the location, I coded it as night. In eight cases out of the 414 unarmed killings information on the time of the killing could not be ascertained.

212   I coded South for the following states: Alabama, Arkansas, Florida, Georgia, Kentucky, Louisiana, Mississippi, North Carolina, South Carolina, Tennessee, Texas, Virginia, and West Virginia.

213   D. Brown, "Sacramento Police"; and Kellogg, "Shooting of Frankie Anchondo." Stephon Clark was killed in Sacramento, California, in 2018. Clark was holding out a cell phone when confronted by police in a dark backyard. Clark was shot eight times, six times in the back. Frankie Anchondo was killed in Farmington, New Mexico, in 2019.

214   Charles Lawrence III describes the mechanisms of unconscious racism as both psychoanalytic and cultural/historical. Lawrence, "Id," 322–23. Elizabeth Bronfen, examining Sigmund Freud's idea of the unconscious, stresses the nocturnal dimension: "Functioning along the lines of a primordial night, primal repression produces the unconscious as the nocturnal side of the psychic apparatus. . . . It is in this dark place that desires and affects can develop in absolute freedom, because the unconscious contains everything forbidden by everyday consciousness." Bronfen, *Night Passages*, 92. Alain Badiou points out that the moniker Black Panther Party, a Black resistance group of the 1960s and 1970s that advocated arms, played to the white unconscious: "The black panther is the epitome of animal beauty, but it is also the fiercest, most graceful of felines, the one that prowls by night as a terrifying, unconscious menace in white people's dull dreams." Badiou, *Black*, 98.

215   Zimring, *When Police Kill*, 100. Zimring quotes a police use-of-force instructor who observes, "Law enforcement is more inclined to be archaic

and married to non-forensic speculative dogma that often goes unchallenged and becomes widely accepted as fact" (101). See also Zimring and Arsiniega, "Trends in Killing."

216 Zimring, *When Police Kill*, 63.

217 Chamayou, *Manhunts*, 90.

218 Some police have argued that some body cameras work too well, especially those with night vision features. Police "were worried that the night vision would provide superiors and the courts with a much clearer picture than what they were able to actually see at the scene of the incident [adding] personal risk to the officers in terms of how their conduct might be judged." C. Katz et al., "Officer Worn Body Cameras," 16; see also Glasbeek, Alam, and Roots, "Seeing and Not-Seeing"; St. Louis, Saulnier, and Walby, "Police Use"; and Gonzales and Cochran, "Police-Worn Body Cameras."

219 Hegel, *Philosophy of Right*, 23.

CHAPTER 3. CURFEW, LEGALITY, AND THE SOCIAL CONTROL OF THE NIGHT

Epigraph 1: Ngũgĩ wa Thiong'o, *Weep Not, Child*, 93.

Epigraph 2: Becker, *Jacob the Liar*, 3.

1 Bearak and Ombuor, "Kenyan Police Shot Dead"; Ombuor and Bearak, "'Killing'"; and Kiplagat, "Court Declines."

2 Coto, "1st Coronavirus Curfew Lawsuit."

3 *Washington Post*, "Thailand Imposes 6-Hour Nightly Curfew."

4 Londoño, Andreoni, and Casado, "Bolsonaro, Isolated and Defiant."

5 On measures, including curfew, in the 1918 influenza epidemic in one county in Wisconsin in the United States, see Shors and McFadden, "1918 Influenza."

6 William the Conqueror instituted a national curfew for England in 1068 with exceptions for doctors, midwives, priests, and veterinarians—the agents of life and death dear to the heart of sovereign power—as well as collectors of night soil. Ekirch, *At Day's Close*, 64. This early curfew was established nightly at 8 p.m.; only at the close of the Middle Ages was this time relaxed until 9 or 10 p.m. for the general population. In eighteenth-century Paris, the curfew was sounded at 8 p.m. in summer, 7 p.m. in winter. Delattre, *Les douzes heures noires*, 31. On witchcraft and its relationship to European sovereignty and law, see Koslofsky, *Evening's Empire*, ch. 2; and Murray, "Medieval Origins." See also references in the next chapter. Early European policing took the form of the night watch (there was no day watch), but this was often ineffective, as I have explored in other chapters.

7   Ekirch, *At Day's Close*, 63–64; and Cabantous, *Histoire de la nuit*, 231.

8   Beaumont, *Nightwalking*, 2. See also 295. On Jacobin conspiracies indeed
        hatched after dark, see Palmer, *Cultures of Darkness*, 95–99. See also the
        vital work of Rancière, *Proletarian Nights*. On the politics and aesthetics
        of contemporary nightwalking, see Dunn, *Dark Matters*. On African
        insurgency in the night, see Mbembe, "Domaines de la nuit," esp. 101–3.
        Perhaps the greatest of the political conspiracies to succeed at night,
        according to Jürgen Habermas, is the construction of civil society in
        the coffee houses and salons of northern Europe. Habermas, *Structural
        Transformation*, 30.

9   Henshall, *History of Japan*, 57; Wang, "Communication Regulations";
        Cao, "Relaxation of the Curfew Rule"; and Kirk, "Town and Country
        Planning."

10   Exceptions include Brass, "Collective Violence," 323–28; and Correia,
        Police, 43–47. While there is little more written on the curfew as a general
        form of governance, there are numerous studies of particular curfews,
        and it is from these that many of the ideas in this chapter are developed.
        Compare the lack of studies of the curfew with the numerous studies of
        the death penalty, another state form of punishment and control, which
        has been thought within and beyond particular contexts while generating
        empirical, historical, and philosophical treatments. See Hay, "Property";
        David T. Johnson and Zimring, *Next Frontier*; Sarat, *Pain, Death*; and
        Derrida, *Death Penalty*.

11   On youth curfews, see Sukarieh and Tannock, "Global Securitisation of
        Youth." On Palestine, see Hanieh, "Politics of Curfew," 327.

12   Ellison, "Cities Aflame," 264.

13   Matthew Beaumont has argued that the early curfew was predominantly
        ideological rather than legal. Beaumont, *Nightwalking*, 294.

14   Epigraphs: Agamben, *Homo Sacer*, 37–38; and Agamben, *Time That
        Remains*, 105.

15   Agamben, *Homo Sacer*, 68. For his critics, see Deleixhe, "Biopolitical
        Sovereignty and Borderlands"; and Fitzpatrick, "Bare Sovereignty."

16   Schmitt adds, "A borderline concept is not a vague concept, but one
        pertaining to the outermost sphere. This definition of sovereignty must
        therefore be associated with a borderline case and not with routine. It
        will soon become clear that the exception is to be understood to refer to
        a general concept in the theory of the state, and not merely to a construct
        applied to any emergency decree or state of siege." Schmitt, *Political The-
        ology*, 5. See also Schmitt, *Concept of the Political*, 35.

17   Deleixhe, "Biopolitical Sovereignty and Borderlands," 654–55.

18   Schmitt, *Political Theology*, 15.

19   Foucault, *History of Sexuality*, 139–45; Foucault, *Society Must Be Defended*,
        244–54; and Foucault, *Birth of Biopolitics*, 21.

20   Agamben, *Homo Sacer*, 18.

21   Agamben, *Remnants of Auschwitz*, 26.

22   Žižek, *Sublime Object of Ideology*, xxx.

23   Quoted in Blake, "Trump's Eruption."

24   Roux, *Être vigilant*; and Beck, *Risk Society*.

25   Husserl, *Phenomenology of Internal Time-Consciousness*, 141.

26   Heidegger, *Being and Time*, 310, 314.

27   Duval, *Temps et vigilance*, 123–24 (translation and emphasis mine).

28   Gilson, *Ethics of Vulnerability*, 127.

29   Foucault, "Standing Vigil," 218.

30   Jean-Luc Nancy observes in this regard, "Whoever relinquishes vigilance relinquishes attention and intention, every kind of tension and anticipation; he enters into the unraveling of plans and aims, of expectations and calculations. It is this loosening that gathers together—actually or symbolically—the fall into sleep." Nancy, *Fall of Sleep*, 2–3. See also extended discussion in chapter 1.

31   Heidegger uses a similar idea to define Dasein's openness to the world, making this form of vigilance a portal to the ontologically human. In his *Heraclitus*, he asks, "But how can anything at all approach us within an obedient relation to what is to be encountered, without what is approaching us already having us, insofar as we somehow already belong to it? Would then a listening (i.e., a hearkening) be an obedience to something to which we already belong by virtue of our listening to it, an obedience that has nothing in common with subjugation, since this originary listening is nothing other than the being open to the open—in other words, freedom itself? But, if this is the case, who *are* we? Who is the human? The human is the essence that is alone open to the open, and only because of this openness can the human also close himself off from the open in a certain way: namely, by allowing what is to be encountered in it only to be an object, an objectified thing, and thereby through his calculating and planning lie in wait to ambush it. Who is the human if an originary obedience belonging to his essence determines him as vigilant, and if all discord stems from a lack of such vigilance? This question besets us here." Heidegger, *Heraclitus*, 187. See also Ulrich Beck's notion of the irony of risk, where "past experience . . . misleads us into measuring risks against completely inappropriate standards and into treating them as calculable and controllable, whereas catastrophes always occur in situations of which we know nothing and which as a result we cannot anticipate." Beck, *World at Risk*, 48.

32   Roux, *Être vigilant*, 17 (translation mine). For Jacques Derrida, this contextual problem is, perhaps, no more than an exaggeration of a problem of vigilance already baked into Husserl's phenomenology of the temporal event. The uncertainty of the adequate temporal retention—the discrim-

ination between an "absolute past" that is never present and that which is retained in the "now"—marks a trace that is pre-originary: a vigil over a current vigilance, here expanded by a context that makes a protention into a choice. See Cross, "*Vigil* of Philosophy."

33 Heidegger, *Being and Time*, 183 and 328; see also discussion in Dreyfus, *Being-in-the-World*, 181–82.

34 Vigh, "Vigilance," 93, 98, 109.

35 Agamben, *Homo Sacer*, 96–97.

36 Price, *Prison and Social Death*; and Guenther, *Solitary Confinement*. Some Afro-pessimist scholars have argued that for Blacks, the institutional aspects of social death are insufficient to account for the banned character of being. See Chavez, "Intrusions of Violence"; and Warren, *Ontological Terror*.

37 Agamben, "What Is a Camp?," 39, 40.

38 Agamben, *Remnants of Auschwitz*, 128.

39 Agamben expands, "The werewolf . . . is, therefore, in its origin the figure of the man who has been banned from the city. That such a man is defined as a wolf-man and not simply as a wolf (the expression *caput lupinum* has the form of a juridical statute) is decisive here. The life of the bandit, like that of the sacred man, is not a piece of animal nature without any relation to law and the city. It is, rather, a threshold of indistinction and of passage between animal and man, *physis* and *nomos*, exclusion and inclusion: the life of the bandit is the life of the *loup garou*, the werewolf, who is precisely *neither man nor beast*, and who dwells paradoxically within both while belonging to neither." Agamben, *Homo Sacer*, 63. Agamben's observation of the hybridity of the werewolf also parallels his description of the monstrous *Muselmann* produced in Auschwitz. While a "living dead," the *Muselmann* transcends both life and death through a fusion with the witness: "*Muselmann* and witness, the inhuman and the human are coextensive and, at the same time, non-coincident; they are divided and nevertheless inseparable. And this in-divisible partition, this fractured and yet indissoluble life expresses itself through a double survival: the non-human is the one who can survive the human being and the human being is the one who can survive the non-human. Only because a *Muselmann* could be isolated in a human being, only because human life is essentially destructible and divisible can the witness survive the *Muselmann*. The witness' survival of the inhuman is a function of the *Muselmann*'s survival of the human. What can be infinitely destroyed is what can infinitely survive." Agamben, *Remnants of Auschwitz*, 41, 151; see also Torrano, "Politics over Monstrosity," 137–38.

40 Balke, "Derrida and Foucault," 77; see also Derrida, *Beast and the Sovereign*, 1:64.

41 Agamben, *Homo Sacer*, 63. On the curse, see Marryat, *Residence in Jutland*, 239; Deleuze and Guattari, *Thousand Plateaus*, 262; Beresford,

White Devil; and Baring-Gould, *Book of Were-Wolves*. Carlo Ginzburg
has argued that the werewolf transforms in another historical manner. In
parts of Italy, the werewolves were seen as the "hounds of God," preserving crops against the actions of witches. "Under pressure from the judges,
the original positive qualities of the werewolves began gradually to fade
away and become corrupted into the execrable image of the man-wolf,
ravager of livestock." Ginzburg, *Night Battles*, 31–32 (see also 29–30).

42 Heidegger argues that the dawn and the sun give Dasein the sight
through which to encounter the factical disclosedness of the world,
which culminates in a public agreement on objective time, and more:
"This dating of things in terms of the heavenly body giving forth light
and warmth, and in terms of its distinctive 'places' in the sky, is a way of
giving time which can be done in our being-with-one-another 'under the
same sky,' and which can be done for 'everyone' at any time in the same
way so that within certain limits everyone is initially agreed upon it."
Heidegger, *Being and Time*, 392–93.

43 Foucault notes the genealogy of this concern in Jeremy Bentham's reign
of opinion in the nineteenth century. Foucault, *Power/Knowledge*, 154.
Nevertheless, as Jonathan Bruno argues, Bentham's emphasis on "popular
vigilance" stumbles where the truth of political representation cannot
distinguish personal probity from the forces of constraint on otherwise-
unethical representatives. Bruno, "Vigilance and Confidence," 304.

44 Foucault, "Standing Vigil," 218.

45 See, for example, Honig, *Emergency Politics*; Rancière, *Proletarian Nights*;
and Deleuze, *Difference and Repetition*.

46 Foucault theorizes that darkness defeats the panoptic overseer's gaze,
affording "a sort of protection." Foucault, *Power/Knowledge*, 147.

47 In his discussion of the advent of disciplinary power in prisons, Foucault
writes an emphatic sentence: "Time, operator of punishment." Foucault,
Discipline and Punish, 108.

48 Foucault, *Discipline and Punish*, 223.

49 Eric Santner argues that this somatic sense is different from Schmitt's,
a fleshly extension of the power of the king. He quotes Foucault in
Discipline and Punish, 208, adding his own emphases: "'The body of the
king, with *its strange material and physical presence*, with the *force* that
he himself deploys or transmits to some few others, is at the opposite
extreme of *this new physics of power* . . . : a physics of a relational and
multiple power, which has its maximum intensity *not in the person of the
king, but in the bodies that can be individualized by these relations*.'" Santner adds, "What I believe Foucault has drawn attention to here without
being fully able to name it is, precisely, the mutation of the King's Two
Bodies into the People's Two Bodies: the migration of the *royal flesh* . . .
that supplants the merely mortal body of the king into the bodies and

lives of the citizens of modern nation states." Santner, *Royal Remains*, 10. Santner's reminder of these political theological origins connects us to earlier discussions in this book about the king's extraordinary vigilance over the bodies of his subjects at night. The curfew may, in this register, raise similar issues of the people's body at night.

50 Santner, *Royal Remains*, 24.

51 Arendt, *Eichmann in Jerusalem*, 148.

52 Theroux, "Paul Theroux Recalls."

53 "Willful nostalgia" also includes the boot camp, along with other forms of punishment, according to Simon. Simon, "They Died."

54 Foucault, *Essential Works*, 158. Consider what Jean-Paul Sartre says about this transgressive desire: "Remove the prohibition to circulate in the streets after the curfew, and what meaning can there be for me to have the freedom (which, for example, has been conferred on me by a pass) to take a walk at night?" Sartre, *Being and Nothingness*, 486.

55 Ordinances in France in the early eighteenth century, for example, required lighting as the nocturnal curfew was relaxed. Denys, *Police et sécurité*, 193. For a discussion of colonial American laws regarding lanterns (one from Albany, New York, in 1773 intended "to prevent Negro and Indian slaves from appearing in the streets after eight at night without a lantern with a lighted candle in it") see O. Williams, "Regimentation of Blacks," 333. Wolfgang Schivelbusch argues that there is, indeed, a connection between Enlightenment and its projects, such as science and law, that created the means and enforced necessary policies to illuminate the urban night. Schivelbusch, *Disenchanted Night*. Beaumont writes simply, "The Enlightenment proscribed the night." Beaumont, *Nightwalking*, 294.

56 Witches' assemblies forming a counterpower to early political assemblies were one form of magical crowd that medieval authorities feared. One charge against such gatherings was the prominence of ritualized child killing, which the curfew could possibly retard. Murray, "Medieval Origins," 72.

57 If we accept the force of Santner's reading that Foucault's disciplinary power is the inheritance by the people of the king's second body, then the crowd may be seen as another schism of that body. It reflects what Agamben has noted to be the essentially divided notion of a people: "What we call 'people' were in reality not a unitary subject but a dialectical oscillation between two opposite poles: on the one hand, the set of the People as a whole political body, and on the other, the subset of the people as a fragmentary multiplicity of needy and excluded bodies; or again, on the one hand, an inclusion that claims to be total, and on the other, an exclusion that is clearly hopeless; at one extreme, the total state of integrated and sovereign citizens, and at the other, the preserve—court of miracles or camp—of the wretched, the oppressed, and the defeated. . . . The

'people' thus always already carries the fundamental biopolitical fracture within itself." Agamben, *Homo Sacer*, 100. See also Rancière, *Disagreement*, 9: "The people are always more or less than the people."

58 Canetti, *Crowds and Power*, 18. On the inhibition of sociality and touch, Canetti brilliantly writes, "Any free or large gesture of approach towards another human being is inhibited. Impulse and counter impulse ooze away as in a desert. No man can get near another, nor reach his height. In every sphere of life, firmly established hierarchies prevent him touching anyone more exalted than himself, or descending, except in appearance, to anyone lower. In different societies the distances are differently balanced against each other, the stress in some lying on birth, in others on occupation or property" (18).

59 "Every form of social life established amongst men expresses itself in distances which allay the ceaseless fear of being seized and caught." Canetti, *Crowds and Power*, 207.

60 See Borch, "Body to Body"; and Ziarek, "Bare Life on Strike." Agamben does note that crowds may take forms other than *bios*: "It is curious that in the Gospel the multitude that surrounds Jesus is never present as a political entity (a people), but always in the terms of a crowd or a 'mob.' In the New Testament, we thus find three terms for 'people': *plēthos* (in Latin, *multitudo*) 31 times; *ochlos* (in Latin, *turba*) 131 times; and *laos* (in Latin, *plebs*) 142 times (in the subsequent vocabulary of the Church, the latter will become a veritable technical term: the people of God as *plebs Dei*). What is missing is the term with political value—*dēmos* (*populus*)—almost as if the messianic event had always already transformed the people into a *multitudo* or a formless mass. In an analogous manner, the constitution of the *mortalis Deus* in Hobbes's city results in the simultaneous dissolution of the body political into a multitude." Agamben, *Stasis*, 63–64.

61 In contexts as diverse as postcolonial Africa and medieval Europe, witches were imagined to fly and land at night. According to the historian Alexander Murray, night flights bound together diverse beliefs about evil (*maleficium*), demoniacal magic, and a secret society attributed to witches. Murray, "Medieval Origins," 68; see also Disalvo, "Fear of Flying"; and Geschiere, "Witchcraft," 232. The threat to social order posed by flight is analogous, I believe, to that of the night walker who flaunted the early European curfew and in modern times became the flaneur. Beaumont, *Nightwalking*, 21; and Carbonnier, *Flexible droit*, 65–66.

62 Grégoire Chamayou writes, "Cynegetic power is exercised over prey, living beings that escape and flee, with a double problem: how to catch them and how to retain them once they are caught." Chamayou, *Manhunts*, 15. In 1990 the African National Congress declared that an apartheid-era South African curfew gave "license to the police to hunt people as if they are game." Quoted in Brass, "Collective Violence," 325.

63   Walter Benjamin foreshadows this possibility in his "Theses on the Phi-
      losophy of History": "The tradition of the oppressed teaches us that the
      'state of emergency' in which we live is not the exception but the rule. We
      must attain to a conception of history that is in keeping with this insight.
      Then we shall clearly realize that it is our task to bring about a real state
      of emergency, and this will improve our position in the struggle against
      Fascism." Benjamin, *Illuminations*, 257.

64   Koslofsky, *Evening's Empire*, 142.

65   Hartford, "Curfew Laws."

66   Correia, *Police*, 3.

67   Chamayou, *Manhunts*, 90–91. On the pleasure of police power see
      Chamayou, *Manhunts*, 91.

68   Becker, *Jacob the Liar*, 4.

69   Becker, *Jacob the Liar*, 8.

70   Becker, *Jacob the Liar*, 12.

71   Becker, *Jacob the Liar*, 13–14.

72   Fine, "Mr. Justice Murphy," 200.

73   Hirabayashi v. United States, 320 U.S. 81, 95 (1943).

74   Hirabayashi, *Principled Stand*, 44, 56–57.

75   Hirabayashi, *Principled Stand*, 57.

76   By 1995 William Ruefle and Kenneth Reynolds found that fifty-nine of
      seventy-seven American cities with populations over 200,000 had youth
      curfews. Ruefle and Reynolds, "Keep Them at Home"; and Ruefle and
      Reynolds, "Curfews and Delinquency." See also the descriptions of how
      youth curfews fit into other racialized tactics in Los Angeles in M. Davis,
      City of Quartz, 258, 277–81.

77   Collins and Kearns, "Under Curfew," 401.

78   P. Baldwin, "'Nocturnal Habits,'" 593 (quoting "night child" from P. Davis
      and Kroll, *Street-Land*).

79   P. Davis and Kroll, *Street-Land*, 84.

80   Amsden, "Negotiating Liberalism and Bio-Politics," 410.

81   Quoted in Wildermuth, "Clinton Backs Youth Curfews."

82   In the context of policing, see the influential study by Phillip Goff et al.,
      "The Essence of Innocence." On racial disparities in school discipline, see
      Losen and Gillespie, "Opportunities Suspended." On the cultural connec-
      tion between whiteness and innocence, see R. Bernstein, *Racial Innocence*.
      In film, see the sentimental depiction of white youth violating curfew in
      Riot on Sunset Strip, Arthur Dreifuss, dir.

83   In a volume edited by Susan B. Anthony and Ida Husted Harper, curfews
      for girls were seen as an exemplar of responsible legislation enhanced by
      women's suffrage: "The bills introduced by women in the [Colorado] Leg-
      islature have been chiefly such as were designed to improve social condi-
      tions. The law raising the 'age of protection' for girls, the law giving the

mother an equal right in her children, and the law creating a State Home for Dependent Children were secured by women in 1895. In the next session they secured the Curfew Law and an appropriation for the State Home for Incorrigible Girls. By obtaining the removal of the emblems from the ballot, they enforced a measure of educational qualification. They have entirely answered the objection that the immature voter would be sure so to exaggerate the power of legislation that she would try to do everything at once." Anthony and Harper, *History of Woman Suffrage*, 526 (see also 1046).

Meda Chesney-Lind and Randall Shelden note, "One of the distinguishing characteristics of female delinquency is the role played by status offenses. Arrest statistics . . . consistently show that running away and curfew violation constitute a major portion of official female delinquency and that they are far less prominent in male delinquency. These two offenses alone generally account for approximately a fourth of all arrests of girls. . . . There are other uniquely juvenile offenses that . . . include truancy and offenses known variously as 'incorrigibility,' 'unmanageability,' and 'beyond control.'" Chesney-Lind and Shelden, *Girls*, 37.

84   Wacquant, *Punishing the Poor*, 68. On the ineffectiveness of curfews in reducing underage drinking, see Grossman, Jernigan, and Miller, "Do Juvenile Curfew Laws."

85   Murray, "Medieval Origins," 69.

86   Hartford, "Curfew Laws," 173.

87   Agamben, *Homo Sacer*, 18.

88   Foucault, *Abnormal*, 56.

89   Foucault, *Abnormal*, 313, 57–58; See also Foucault, Rabinow, and Hurley, *Ethics*, 52. Consider the title of the Children (Protection and Parental Responsibility) Act 1997 (in New South Wales, Australia), giving police augmented power to remove children from public places. This title fuses the background body (the family) and the child's body and, following this integration, forces parents to appear in court on behalf of their children. Chris Cunneen has demonstrated that in New South Wales and Western Australia, which implemented a similar "Northbridge Curfew," Indigenous youth and families absorb nearly 90 percent of the police attention. In light of the national apology for the forced removal of Indigenous children, the legal punishment of both child and parent for violating informal and formal curfews through legislation of this sort tends to rebuild some elements of the removal policy. See Cunneen, "Changing the Neo-Colonial Impacts," 44. See also Cooper and Love, "Youth Curfew."

90   Foucault, *Abnormal*, 59.

91   Foucault, *Abnormal*, 61.

92   Sharpe, *Foucault's Monsters*, 9; and Feder, "Dangerous Individual('s) Mother," 60. Foucault writes of racism that it is applicable to the abnormal

and can fuse with ethnic forms. Foucault, *Abnormal*, 317. See also Foucault, *Society Must Be Defended*, 258. In medieval Europe, Black people were also linked to demons and magic, which were the tools of witches. Murray, "Medieval Origins," 72 (also 67, 71).

93   One survey study at the time summed its own and other research as follows: "This contrast between black sympathy for the rioters and white condemnation of them, as reflected in explanations for the riot, has also been obtained in several more recent surveys made in other areas. . . . Negroes were about twice as likely as whites to attribute recent riots to grievances over jobs, education, housing, police and inequality. Whites were more likely than Negroes to blame outside agitation, lack of firmness by government authorities, the desire to loot, or a desire for violence. Negroes thought the riots were spontaneous; a vast majority of the whites thought they had been organized. Negroes thought the looted stores had been charging exorbitant prices; whites thought they had not. Among whites, 62 per cent felt looters should be shot; among Negroes, only 27 per cent felt that action was justifiable. In other post-riot surveys, Negroes in Detroit and in Watts have generally explained the rioting in terms of a response to grievances about housing, jobs, the police, and poverty. The most impressive difference of opinion about the rioters, then, is not between the law-abiders and the law-breakers in the Negro community, but between blacks and whites." Sears and Tomlinson, "Riot Ideology," 495–96.

94   Crenshaw et al., "Say Her Name"; Richie, *Arrested Justice*; and Brunson and Miller, "Gender, Race, and Urban Policing." In Rod Brunson and Jody Miller's ethnographic study of urban policing, one woman recounted, "My cousin, she a tomboy and she was sittin' on my grandma['s] front [porch] one night. . . . [The police] pulls up, tell her to put her hands up. . . . They take her, throw her into the wall. They check her, found nothin' on her, throw her on the ground and just start kicking her. Put a gun up and put it in her mouth. Tell her if she tell anybody, they'll blow her Black brains out. Or they'll take her away and rape her and she won't be found." Brunson and Miller, "Gender, Race, and Urban Policing," 546.

95   Meares and Kahan, "Law and (Norms of) Order," 821.

96   One poll taken in the District of Columbia in the mid-1990s found that 70 percent of Black youth supported curfews. Kahan, "Curfews Free Juveniles."

97   Mbembe, *On the Postcolony*, 33–34.

98   Fabian, *Time and the Other*, 15. See also McClintock, *Imperial Leather*; Povinelli, "Governance of the Prior"; and Povinelli, *Empire of Love*.

99   Giordano Nanni sees the value of Australian curfews early in the colonial era as engaging these various concerns: "The act of imposing the colonisers' idea of 'regularity' was another way of eliminating the presence of

an indigenous population, of making its 'irregular' presence less noticeable within colonial society. Given time's role as a marker of culture and identity, attempts to reform the fundamental rhythms of Aboriginal life were tantamount to a denial of Aboriginal identity. . . . Temporal reform complemented the process of territorial dispossession by helping to erase the cultural footprint of an Indigenous presence in Australia." Nanni, *Colonisation of Time*, 86.

100 Loewen, *Sundown Towns*; and Nugent, "Mapping Memories."

101 O. Williams, "Regimentation of Blacks." Oscar Williams points out that these ordinances were rarely enforced, in part because Blacks owned some and worked in many taverns popular with whites. "Crisis, and crisis alone, however, produced rigid enforcement of such regulations" (331).

102 O. Williams, "Regimentation of Blacks," 334.

103 O. Williams, "Regimentation of Blacks," 335.

104 The term is from Mbembe, *On the Postcolony*, 34.

105 Quoted in Njoh, "Colonial Philosophies," 587.

106 Njoh, "Colonial Philosophies," 589.

107 Fanon, *Wretched of the Earth*, 15. "The first thing the colonial subject learns is to remain in his place and not overstep its limits. Hence the dreams of the colonial subject are muscular dreams, dreams of action, dreams of aggressive vitality. I dream I am jumping, swimming, running, and climbing. I dream I burst out laughing, I am leaping across a river and chased by a pack of cars that never catches up with me. During colonization the colonized subject frees himself night after night between nine in the evening and six in the morning."

108 Njoh, "Colonial Philosophies," 597.

109 "In Dakar, Abidjan, Libreville, and Brazzaville, French residents took the highest land as their quarter and called it the Plateau. Did the name alone confer some protection? Niamey had a Plateau, but no plateau. In all their cities Europeans used topography—real or imagined—to symbolize the unequal distribution of wealth and power and the separation of ruler and ruled that characterized colonial urbanism." Winters, "Urban Morphogenesis," 141; see also Njoh, "Colonial Philosophies," 596.

110 Simatei, "Colonial Violence, Postcolonial Violations," 87. See also Fanon's connection between nocturnal movement and the conditions for revolution: "Constantly forced to remain on the move to elude the police, walking by night so as not to attract attention, they are able to travel the length and breadth of their country and get to know it." Fanon, *Wretched of the Earth*, 78.

111 On curfew as a trial of administration, see Brass, "Collective Violence," 327. As Lakhdar Ghettas notes in the case of the Egyptian Spring of 2011, a badly maintained curfew can destroy a regime's credibility:

"A night curfew was declared last Friday in the three main cities of Cairo, Alexandria, and Suez. The turning point in the protests came when the curfew was declared: it shattered what little remained of the regime's authority. Internationally it weakened the regime's credibility. A regime which cannot impose a curfew in its capital city conveys an image of weakness and, indeed, disintegration. Then the Egyptian Army was deployed nationally because the police forces had lost control of the situation." Ghettas, "What Next for Egypt?"

112   Stoler, *Along the Archival Grain*, 222.

113   Brass, "Collective Violence," 332. See also the novel exploring Hindu and Muslim curfew violence: Rāya, *Curfew in the City*.

114   Brass, "Collective Violence," 332–34.

115   Swigart, "Cultural Creolisation," 187n6.

116   Bahour, "Violence of Curfew."

117   On the link between "architectures of concentration and the spatial technologies of closure" in emergencies in Kenya and Palestine, see Pfingst, "Militarised Violence" (the quotation is from p. 21).

118   On population counting and state making, see B. Anderson, *Imagined Communities*; B. Cohn, *Colonialism*; T. Mitchell, *Colonising Egypt*; and Zureik, "Constructing Palestine."

119   Anat Liebler, quoted in Zureik, "Constructing Palestine," 214.

120   This terminology of manipulating and weaponizing time is from Peteet, "Closure's Temporality," 44.

121   Bahour, "Violence of Curfew," 29.

122   Similar effects of curfews were noted in Australia in the mid-nineteenth century. Nanni, *Colonisation of Time*, 102.

123   Peteet, "Closure's Temporality," 46. Ariella Azoulay and Adi Ophir reinforce this argument: "Because the rules that the subjects are supposed to follow change rapidly, it is impossible to rely on the validity of anything that is not accompanied by withheld violence. No order is worth the paper it is written on without the actual presence of the force that can implement it. The regime needs the massive presence of withheld violence in order to announce the rules and direct and dictate the behavior of its subjects with them. But the subjects, too, need this presence in order to be informed of the rules and to know how to calculate their everyday moves. In order to know which route to take to work, one must know where the checkpoint is placed; in order to decide whether even to bother going to work, one must know whether or not a curfew has been imposed during the night—and thus on and on, with every activity in every aspect of life." Azoulay and Ophir, *One-State Condition*, 142.

124   Anne Meneley, quoted in Peteet, "Closure's Temporality," 51. See also Peteet, *Space and Mobility*; and Weizman, *Hollow Land*.

125   McCracken, "Coercion and Control," 133; and Peteet, "Closure's Tempo-
        rality," 59.

126   Peteet, "Closure's Temporality," 60. As Hanna Baumann notes, "Mo-
        bility related to leisure, rather than to quotidian journeys, can also serve
        to undermine boundaries and Israeli control in Jerusalem's urban space.
        Activities such as walking, running, cycling or parkour resonate with
        notions of freedom of movement on both an affective and a political
        level." Baumann, "Enclaves," 176.

127   Abujidi, "Palestinian States of Exception," 283. Nurhan Abujidi includes
        this conversation: "Yesterday evening after *iftār* (the breaking of the
        fast) we wandered around the markets. The last time I was here the city
        centre streets were deserted at nine o'clock, but now they were bustling
        and noisy and people looked relaxed and happy. 'The Israelis do not come
        in so much during Ramadān,' said my friend as we were browsing for
        presents. Despite the apparent peace he did not let me out of his sight.
        'What will happen after Ramadān?' I asked him. He smiled. 'They will
        come in every night again like they do the rest of the year. It will go back
        to normal.' *Normal* in Nablus is that" (283).

128   Esteva, "Oaxaca Commune," 978.

129   See also this discussion of extensive vigilantism constituting the commu-
        nity in Nigeria: Pratten, "Politics of Vigilance," 724.

130   On the London plague, see Lord, *Great Plague*, 35.

131   Foucault, *Security, Territory, Population*, 10.

132   Esposito, *Immunitas*, 149.

133   Esposito, *Bios*, 139–45.

134   Thacker, "Shadows of Atheology," 135.

135   Thacker, "Shadows of Atheology," 137.

136   S. Cohn, "Pandemics"; S. Cohn, *Epidemics*; and Stevens, "How Asian-
        American Leaders."

137   Thucydides, *Peloponnesian War*, 99 (year 2, para. 53).

138   However, some political leaders apparently still pursued hedonism; Boris
        Johnson of the United Kingdom partied privately at the same time he
        ordered the public not to do the same. Elgot, "Boris Johnson."

139   Southall, "Virus's Toll"; D'Ambrosio and Wade, "Another Coronavirus
        Crisis"; Hardy, "Thief Who Stole Masks"; and Nakaso, "Personal Protec-
        tive Equipment Stolen."

140   Trump, quoted in Coll, "Donald Trump's Coronavirus Quackery."

141   Jeffrey Flier, quoted in M. Taylor and Roston, "Exclusive."

142   Pang, "End to Weekend Curfews."

143   Beckett and Herbert, *Banished*; and Feldman, *Citizens without Shelter*.

144   Bart and O'Brien, *Stopping Rape*, 2.

145   Beckett and Herbert, *Banished*, 122.

CHAPTER 4. TAKE BACK THE NIGHT

Epigraph 1: Peggy Seeger, "Reclaim the Night."

1   An early reference to a Take Back the Night march can be found in a Minneapolis newsletter. Newsletter, *National Lawyers Guild*, 7. There is some uncertainty over their origins, but American marches became prominent in 1978. Some European historians have claimed a separate origin in 1976 in Brussels, from where marches, often under the banner Reclaim the Night, quickly spread to the United Kingdom and across the continent. Mackay, "Mapping the Routes," 47.

2   Kant, "What Is Enlightenment?"

3   Beaumont, *Nightwalking*, 3–4.

4   Foucault, *Power/Knowledge*, 153.

5   Foucault, "Truth and Juridical Forms," 71; and Foucault, *Power/Knowledge*, 154.

6   Rich, "Afterword," 318.

7   R. Williams, "Night Spaces," 521–26.

8   The term is from a homeless woman, "Mary," quoted in Menih, "'Come Night-Time.'"

9   R. Shaw, "Pushed to the Margins," 121. See also Pickard and Bessant, "France's #Nuit Debout"; and Guichoux, "Nuit debout."

10 Jürgen Habermas has argued that the original development of bourgeois civil society depended on eighteenth-century institutions such as coffee houses that were active in the evening and leveled social hierarchies, suggesting a precedent for Nuit Debout. Habermas, *Structural Transformation*.

11 Eliza Daniel Stewart ("Mother Stewart") notes in her memoirs the many occasions in which prohibition and suffrage clasped hands. E. Stewart, *Memories of the Crusade*, 146; see also Masson, "Woman's Christian Temperance Union."

12 Stanton, quoted in Heen, "From Coverture to Contract," 363.

13 E. Stewart, *Memories of the Crusade*, 434; and Tickner, *Spectacle of Women*, 55. Lisa Tickner's book focuses on the British and not the American campaign. Ida B. Wells-Barnett, Sojourner Truth, and Frederick Douglass believed that Black women's suffrage "was inextricably connected to the power of photography." Lewis, "For Black Suffragists."

14 Dworkin, "Pornography and Grief," 291.

15 Locke manuscript notation, quoted in Balibar, *Identity and Difference*, 41.

16 Balibar, *Identity and Difference*, 101.

17 On Locke's arguments on Native ways of life, see Bhandar, *Colonial Lives of Property*, 163–71; and Arneil, "Wild Indian's Venison." On Locke's engagement with patriarchy, see the important scholarship of M. Butler, "Early Liberal Roots." Melissa Butler traces Locke's antipatriarchal

philosophy to his opposition to Sir Robert Filmer's entanglement of monarchy with patriarchy. Locke was "strangely indifferent" to racial slavery, giving it no philosophical justification even though he was mired in slavery and the slave trade in the Americas. Farr, "Locke, Natural Law," 516.

18 Locke, *Essay Concerning Human Understanding*, 57.

19 Petchesky, "Body as Property," 393–94.

20 Locke, *Second Treatise of Government*, 18.

21 Federici, *Caliban and the Witch*, 179–86.

22 Federici, *Caliban and the Witch*; and Federici, *Witches, Witch-Hunting, and Women*, 18. Federici found evidence of men opposing the witch hunts persecuting women only in the Basque lands in 1609. She concludes, "There is no doubt that years of propaganda and terror sowed among men the seeds of a deep psychological alienation from women, that broke class solidarity and undermined their own collective power." Federici, *Caliban and the Witch*, 89.

23 Moreton-Robinson, *White Possessive*; Petchesky, "Body as Property"; Nichols, *Theft Is Property!*; and P. Williams, *Alchemy of Race and Rights*.

24 See, notably, Pateman, "Self-Ownership and Property"; Pateman, *Sexual Contract*; Dickenson, *Property, Women and Politics*; and Petchesky, "Body as Property."

25 hooks, *Feminist Theory*, 10, quoted in Pateman and Mills, *Contract and Domination*, 197; and A. Harris, "Race and Essentialism."

26 Dworkin, *Letters from a War Zone*, 182–83.

27 Trinh, *Woman, Native, Other*, 40.

28 Petchesky, "Body as Property," 392.

29 Shanley, "Suffrage," 72. For the American case, see Siegel, "She the People," 980–87.

30 On petty treason, see Dolan, "Battered Women, Petty Traitors," 257. Regarding domestic violence under rules of coverture, Sir William Blackstone wrote, "Husband and wife, in the language of the law, are styled *baron* and *feme*. The word baron, or lord, attributes to the husband not a very courteous superiority. But we might be inclined to think this merely an unmeaning technical phrase, if we did not recollect that if the baron kills his feme it is the same as if he had killed a stranger, or any other person, but if the feme kills her baron, it is regarded by the laws as a much more atrocious crime, as she not only breaks through the restraints of humanity and conjugal affection, but throws off all subjection to the authority of her husband. And therefore the law denominates her crime a species of treason, and condemns her to the same punishment as if she had killed the king. And for every species of treason, (though in petit treason the punishment of men was only to be drawn and hanged,) till the 30 Geo. III. c. 48, the sentence of women was to be drawn and burnt

alive." Blackstone, *Commentaries*, 1:444n38. For more contemporary American analysis, see Heinzelman, "Women's Petty Treason."

31   I. Marcus, "Reframing 'Domestic Violence,'" 23, quoted in Dolan, "Battered Women, Petty Traitors," 272.

32   MacKinnon, "Agenda for Theory," 515.

33   MacKinnon, "Toward Feminist Jurisprudence," 644. See also Clark, *Rape*; and S. Marcus, "Fighting Bodies, Fighting Words."

34   MacKinnon, *Toward a Feminist Theory*, 172.

35   Pateman, "Self-Ownership and Property," 26–27.

36   Strathern, *Property, Substance, and Effect*, 165–75.

37   Fitzpatrick, *Mythology of Modern Law*, 50.

38   Davies, "Proper," 147. In another era James Madison argued that property also included those collective capacities that allowed the enjoyment of Davies's values. Property "included not only external objects and people's relationships to them, but also all of those human rights, liberties, powers, and immunities that are important for human well-being, including: freedom of expression, freedom of conscience, freedom from bodily harm, and free and equal opportunities to use personal faculties." Madison, quoted in C. Harris, "Whiteness as Property," 1726.

39   Rose, *Property and Persuasion*, 37. Because of this textual quality, theorists of property have always resorted to fictions such as apple gathering or civil contracting (e.g., Locke) or Robinson Crusoe (e.g., political economists), according to Rose.

40   Pateman, "Self-Ownership and Property," 24.

41   For Morris Cohen, property and sovereignty have as their essence the right to exclude others. "To the extent that . . . things are necessary to the life of my neighbor, the law thus confers on me a power, limited but real, to make him do what I want. . . . Dominion over things is also *imperium* over our fellow human beings." M. Cohen, "Property and Sovereignty," 12, 13. Cheryl Harris has argued that whiteness is a "status property" whose value depended on exclusivity. "Just as whiteness as property embraced the right to exclude, whiteness as a theoretical construct evolved for the very purpose of racial exclusion. Thus, the concept of whiteness is built on both exclusion and racial subjugation." C. Harris, "Whiteness as Property," 1737. See also Moreton-Robinson, *White Possessive*.

42   Petchesky, "Body as Property," 403.

43   Cover, "*Nomos* and Narrative," 11, 40.

44   Cover, "*Nomos* and Narrative," 40.

45   Wollstonecraft, *Vindication of the Rights*, 56.

46   Stanton, quoted in Ryan, "Sex Right," 949. See also Dolan, "Battered Women, Petty Traitors," 261.

47   Bröck-Sallah, *Gender*, 55.

48   Bröck-Sallah, *Gender*, 46; and Wilderson, "Grammar and Ghosts," 119.

49   Spillers, "Interstices," 76, 95.

50   The concept of parasitism is from Wilderson, *Red, White and Black*, 22, 45. Spillers writes, "In the historic outline of dominance, the respective subject-positions of 'female' and 'male' adhere to no symbolic integrity." Spillers, "Mama's Baby, Papa's Maybe," 66. See also Wynter, "Afterword"; and Bröck-Sallah, *Gender*.

51   Spillers, "Mama's Baby, Papa's Maybe," 73.

52   Spillers, "Interstices," 78.

53   Spillers, "Interstices," 74.

54   S. Hartman, *Scenes of Subjection*, 22.

55   This image is from Maurice Blanchot, who attributes this to a night to which we have access, distinguishing it from the "other night" in which "one is still outside." Blanchot, "Outside, the Night," 162.

56   Douglass, *Life and Times*, 96; and Beauvoir, *Ethics of Ambiguity*, 96.

57   Wilderson, *Red, White and Black*, 23.

58   Nichols, *Theft Is Property!*, 133. See Marx, "On the Jewish Question"; Nietzsche, *On the Genealogy of Morals*; and Foucault, *Discipline and Punish*. The Thirteenth Amendment to the US Constitution outlaws slavery and involuntary servitude, "except as a punishment for crime."

59   Bhandar, *Colonial Lives of Property*.

60   Epigraph: Dworkin, "Pornography and Grief," 291.

61   See Halley, *Split Decisions*, 50–57; Whittier, *Frenemies*; and Duggan and Hunter, *Sex Wars*.

62   Cameron, *Reconsidering Radical Feminism*. See also Serisier, "Who Was Andrea?"; and Fernflores, "Merciful Interpretation."

63   The FBI data suggest that the prevalence of estimated rape offenses in the United States moved from 30 per 100,000 people in 2001 to over 70 in 2017. Riccelli, "Historical Rape Trends," 14.

64   For statistics on sexual assault at home, see J. Jones et al., "Comparison of Sexual Assaults." On domestic violence during COVID, see Buccino, "Domestic Violence Cases Surge"; Fielding, "In Quarantine with an Abuser"; UN News, "UN Chief Urges End"; Rukmini, "Locked Down with Abusers"; and Taub and Bradley, "As Domestic Abuse Rises."

65   In 2014 there were more than twenty such marches in the United Kingdom. Take Back the Night marches have spread across the globe, sometimes organized in response to particular incidents; several large marches were quickly organized in Delhi, Mumbai, and other Indian cities, as well as Melbourne in 2012, after horrific rapes were publicized. Mackay, "Mapping the Routes," 46, 52. On the problems of unequal access to public space, see Sandberg and Coe, "Taking Back the Swedish Night"; Hubbard and Colosi, "Taking Back the Night?"; and Guenebeaud, Le Mat, and Verhaeghe, "Take Back the Night!" On men's roles in feminist organizing, see Kretschmer and Barber, "Men at the March."

66   For a theoretical genealogy of feminism, see Halley, *Split Decisions*; and
      Cameron, *Reconsidering Radical Feminism*. For a perspective on feminist
      legal theory, see West, "Women in the Legal Academy"; and Jaleel, *Work
      of Rape.*

67   Dworkin, "Pornography and Grief," 291.

68   Rooney, "Philosophy, Language, and Wizardry"; Heyes, *Line Draw-
      ings*; Tanesini, "Wittgenstein"; and Scheman and O'Connor, *Feminist
      Interpretations.*

69   Wittgenstein, *Philosophical Investigations*, 36.

70   Dworkin, "Night and Danger," 14.

71   Taussig, *Devil and Commodity Fetishism.*

72   Ginzburg, *Night Battles*, 40. See also Lecouteux, *Phantom Armies*. The
      characterization of the night as creepy is from Hutton, "Wild Hunt," 165.

73   Ginzburg, *Night Battles*, 43.

74   Ginzburg, *Ecstasies*; Ginzburg, *Night Battles*; and Federici, *Caliban and
      the Witch.*

75   Hutton, "Wild Hunt," 174. See also Federici, *Caliban and the Witch*, 169.

76   Underwood, "Witchcraft"; and Ekirch, *At Day's Close*, ch. 1. The Ku Klux
      Klan costume resembles the ghost, but the resurgence of the Klan in the
      1920s, which attracted many women into its fold, downplayed the signifi-
      cance of night that sustained this demonic symbolism. "Unlike the first
      Klan, which operated mainly at night, meeting in hard-to-find locations,
      the second operated in daylight and organized mass public events."
      Gordon, *Second Coming of the KKK*, 2. Witch hunts came to the new
      world as early as the middle of the sixteenth century, brought by Spanish
      conquistadors to defeat Indigenous resistance. See Federici, *Caliban and
      the Witch*, 198. Federici suggests that devil figures were plural until the
      gendering of the devil as male took place during the witch trials. Federici,
      Caliban and the Witch, 187.

77   Scott Morgensen tells of the 1990s San Francisco art happening, Homo-
      Hex, where queer feminists used "primitivist" rituals to reject heterosex-
      ual violence and celebrate liberation. One participant recounted, "We are
      queer witches and this is how we pray." Morgensen, *Spaces between Us*,
      171–72. On the terminology, community, and governance of "fairies," see
      Chauncey, *Gay New York*, 13–17.

78   Ginzburg and Lincoln, *Old Thiess.*

79   Dworkin, "Night and Danger," 14.

80   Dworkin, "Night and Danger," 13.

81   Hobsbawm, *Bandits*, 30; and Moten, "Case of Blackness," 179. Similarly,
      György Lukács wrote in 1920 that a revolutionary proletariat "must be
      able to slough off both the cretinism of legality and the romanticism of
      illegality." Lukács, *History and Class Consciousness*, 270.

82   Robson, *Lesbian (Out)Law.*

83   Dworkin, "Night and Danger," 14.

84   Dworkin, "Night and Danger," 14.

85   Haraway, *When Species Meet*, 4. See also Hallenbeck, "Toward a Post-human Perspective"; Deckha, "Postcolonial, Posthumanist Feminist Theory"; Quinlan, "Feminist Actor-Network Theory"; Corrigan and Mills, "Men on Board"; Puar, *Terrorist Assemblages*; and Puar, "I Would Rather Be a Cyborg."

86   Puar, "I Would Rather Be a Cyborg," 49. Jasbir Puar distinguishes the theoretical significance of posthumanist assemblage within feminist theory from intersectionality, in which difference is understood through historically sedimented categories, but she also argues for the value of a "positive conversation" between them. "While discipline works at the level of identity [thus, intersectionality], control works at the level of intensity; identity is a process involving an intensification of habituation, thus discipline and control are mutually intertwined, though not necessarily compatible" (62).

87   Dworkin, "Night and Danger," 13–14.

88   Agamben, *Means without End*, 104. Benjamin writes, "Police violence is . . . lawmaking, for its characteristic function is not the promulgation of laws but the assertion of legal claims for any decree, and law-preserving, because it is at the disposal of these ends. The assertion that the ends of police violence are always identical or even connected to those of general law is entirely untrue. Rather, the 'law' of the police really marks the point at which the state, whether from impotence or because of the immanent connections within any legal system, can no longer guarantee through the legal system the empirical ends that it desires at any price to attain." Benjamin, "Critique of Violence," 286–87; see also Derrida, "Force of Law," 1013. Note Grégoire Chamayou's discussion of the cynegetic power of the police, discussed in chapter 3.

89   Kraska and Kappeler, "To Serve and Pursue"; Stinson, Taylor, and Liederbach, "Police Sexual Violence"; Ross, "What the #MeToo Campaign"; Ostrowsky, "#MeToo's Unseen Frontier"; and Heil, "Fuzz(y) Lines of Consent."

90   On women and sanctuary, see Shoemaker, *Sanctuary and Crime*, 124. Norman Trenholme argues that women rarely used sanctuary since they were the victims rather than the perpetrators of most crime. However, in one case in 1225 a woman desiring divorce accused herself of a felony, sought sanctuary, and abjured the realm. Trenholme, *Right of Sanctuary*, 69.

91   Hobsbawm, *Bandits,* 14, cited in Chamayou, *Manhunts*, 27.

92   Chamayou, *Manhunts*, 27.

93   Chamayou notes that what haunts the power derived from the hunt is its inability to establish permanence. "What is peculiar to manhunting, what constitutes its danger but also its supreme aristocratic attraction,

is the constant possibility of a reversal of the relationship: the prey might become a predator, the hunted a hunter. Manhunting is characterized by this fundamental instability: when the prey, refusing to continue to be a prey and ceasing to run away, retaliates and tracks in turn, hunting becomes combat or a struggle." Chamayou, *Manhunts*, 74.

94 E. Bernstein, "Militarized Humanitarianism," 47.

95 Coker, "Crime Control"; and Kim, "Carceral Creep." See the general arguments about "governing through crime" in Simon, *Governing through Crime*; and Garland, *Culture of Control*. On the loss of sanctuary for women, see also Bumiller, *In an Abusive State*.

96 Kim, "Carceral Creep," 252.

97 A. Harris, "Race and Essentialism"; Russo, "'We Cannot Live'"; and Murphy and Livingstone, "Racism."

98 Dworkin, "Night and Danger," 15.

99 Freedman, *Redefining Rape*.

100 Gordon, *Second Coming of the KKK*; Fluri and Dowler, "Klanbake"; and Freedman, *Redefining Rape*, 56–60.

101 A. Davis, *Women, Race, and Class*, ch. 11. Davis is arguing against Russell, *Politics of Rape*; MacKellar, *Rape*; and Brownmiller, *Against Our Will*.

102 Hill Collins, *Black Sexual Politics*, 147. See also Razack, "Race, Space, and Prostitution."

103 hooks, *Black Looks*, 170.

104 Richard Ligon (ca. 1650) quoted in Handler, "Slave Revolts," 8.

105 Kelley, *Freedom Dreams*, 157–58.

106 R. Mitchell, "Les ombres noires de Saint Domingue," 14–15.

107 D. Cohen, "Social Injustice," 525. Daniel Cohen is responding to the revisionist historical work in Hodes, *White Women, Black Men*; Sommerville, "Rape Myth"; and Sommerville, "Rape, Race, and Castration."

108 Loewen, *Sundown Towns*.

109 A. Davis, *Blues Legacies*, 9–10.

110 Dworkin, "Night and Danger," 15.

111 Spillers, "Mama's Baby, Papa's Maybe," 80.

112 Mackay, "Mapping the Routes," 49. Finn Mackay traces the charges of racism to one influential but uninformed academic article that was re-cited several times. She laments "how easily issues of male violence against women can be hijacked by a racist media to fuel racism" (52).

113 Dworkin, "Night and Danger," 15. See also Dworkin, *Scapegoat*.

114 Interestingly, as Karl Shoemaker notes, under a Roman edict in 392, Jews were forbidden sanctuary, an enduring status of ineligibility that by the fifteenth century was shared with "ravishers of maidens" as well as heretics, traitors, blasphemers, homicides, exiles, and others. Shoemaker, *Sanctuary and Crime*, 36, 172.

115 K.-Y. Taylor, "How We Get Free," 20.

116   K.-Y. Taylor, "How We Get Free," 19; Crenshaw, "Mapping the Margins"; Hill Collins and Bilge, *Intersectionality*; and Grabham, *Intersectionality and Beyond*.

117   See, for instance, Wendy Brown's arguments. Cruz and Brown, "Feminism, Law, and Neoliberalism," 79.

118   Campkin and Marshall, "London's Nocturnal Queer Geographies," 82; and Hartal, "Fragile Subjectivities." See also Chauncey, *Gay New York*.

119   Ferguson, *Aberrations in Black*, 41 (and ch. 1 generally). See also Somerville, *Queering the Color Line*.

120   Ferguson, *Aberrations in Black*, 42. See also Razack, "Race, Space, and Prostitution."

121   Dworkin, "Night and Danger," 14.

122   Minkowski, *Lived Time*, 405; Merleau-Ponty, *Phenomenology of Perception*, 330.

123   Merleau-Ponty, *Phenomenology of Perception* 330–31.

124   Heyes, *Anaesthetics of Existence*, 22.

125   Heyes, *Anaesthetics of Existence*, 56.

126   As Gayle Salamon captures this, "In order to engage with the wider world, the self must be able to become lost to itself in the opaque thickness of the body." Salamon, "Place Where Life Hides Away," 107; see also Salamon, *Life and Death*, ch. 3.

127   Fanon, *Black Skin, White Masks*, 2.

128   Of course, in cases such as solitary confinement, which uses techniques of time distortion and surveillance to disrupt the rhythms of nonbeing and being, or night and day, the violence comes from excess rather than deprivation of this experience. Lisa Guenther finds this in the "experience of prisoners in prolonged solitary confinement: the strange feeling of death in life, in which one's body begins to 'communicate' with the cell, the outlines around things seem to melt, and the cell walls themselves begin to waver. Could the experience of endless day, as in the twenty-four-hour illumination of the supermax cell, be tantamount to an experience of night?" Guenther, *Solitary Confinement*, 172.

129   Epigraph: Dworkin, "Night and Danger," 16.

130   Levos and Zacchilli, "Nyctophobia."

131   Massumi, *Parables for the Virtual*, 60.

132   Deborah Talbot, for instance, writes that the fear of the dangerous working class and their urban districts dominated nineteenth-century London, while immigrants and their areas were the focus of the early twentieth century. Talbot, *Regulating the Night*, 8.

133   Massumi, *Parables for the Virtual*, 61.

134   Ahmed, *Cultural Politics of Emotion*, 69.

135   Ahmed, *Cultural Politics of Emotion*, 69.

136   Ahmed, *Cultural Politics of Emotion*, 68.

137   H. Lefebvre, *Production of Space*, 320.
138   Alec Brownlow's study shows that men, too, have fear in public space
        but that it is experienced as a generalized wariness that is contrary to
        hegemonic norms of masculinity and so often rhetorically suppressed.
        Brownlow, "Geography of Men's Fear." Women's fear is often focused on
        the threat of sexual violence signaled by the presence of even one man
        in public space. Men do have a greater statistical chance of experiencing
        violence in public spaces than women, while women have a greater chance
        of experiencing violence in the home. As Gill Valentine argues, "Women
        assume that the location of male violence is unevenly distributed through
        space and time. In particular women learn to perceive danger from strange
        men in public space despite the fact that statistics on rape and attack em-
        phasise clearly that they are more at risk at home and from men they know.
        This is because when in public the behaviour of any stranger encountered is
        potentially unpredictable and uncontrollable. (In this context my research
        suggests that women perceive only men as strangers)." G. Valentine, "Ge-
        ography of Women's Fear," 386. See also Day, "Strangers in the Night."
139   Pain, "Gender, Race, Age and Fear," 899–900.
140   Valentine calls, therefore, for reconciling the geography of violence and
        the geography of fear. G. Valentine, "Images of Danger."
141   Pain, "Gender, Race, Age and Fear," 901.
142   Ahmed, *Cultural Politics of Emotion*, 69. See also Bauman, *Liquid Fear*,
        3: "A person who has interiorized . . . insecurity and vulnerability will
        routinely, even in the absence of a genuine threat, resort to the responses
        proper to a point-blank meeting with danger; 'derivative fear' acquires a
        self-propelling capacity."
143   N. Duncan, "Renegotiating Gender," 132.
144   Koskela and Pain, "Revisiting Fear and Place."
145   "Underlying an attraction to and a marketing of the frisson of [pseud-
        onymous] Southview was fear—a fear of 'difference' but also of the
        experience of the end point of drugs, deprivation, discrimination and
        the violence it can engender. Incomers wanted to experience the distinct
        qualities of Southview without the reality that underlay it." Talbot, *Reg-
        ulating the Night*, 68. See also Hobbs, *Bouncers*; and R. Shaw, "Neoliberal
        Subjectivities."
146   M. Davis, *City of Quartz*, 196.
147   Listerborn, "Feminist Struggle," 252.
148   Tulloch and Jennett, "Women's Responses," 58.
149   Pain, "Gender, Race, Age and Fear."
150   Journalist interview in Swedish, translated in Sandberg and Coe, "Taking
        Back the Swedish Night," 1051.
151   Swedish activist, interview, in Sandberg and Coe, "Taking Back the
        Swedish Night," 1056.

152   Dworkin, "Pornography and Grief," 291.

153   "By the time she is a woman, fear and isolation are tangled into a hard, internal knot so that she cannot experience one without the other." Dworkin, *Our Blood*, 59.

154   Ahmed, *Cultural Politics of Emotion*, 64.

155   K. Stewart, *Ordinary Affects*, 128.

156   Canetti, *Crowds and Power*, 17.

157   Ahmed, *Cultural Politics of Emotion*, 70.

158   Quoted in Sandberg and Coe, "Taking Back the Swedish Night," 1051.

159   Dworkin, "Pornography and Grief," 291.

160   Darian-Smith, *Bridging Divides*, 178–79.

161   Sandberg and Coe, "Taking Back the Swedish Night," 1050.

162   Wooden, "Sexual Assault," 24.

163   "Every year, there's a fresh debate over whether men should be allowed to march. . . . There's no distinction between the sins of individual males and the male sex as a whole. Males are regularly denounced as the oppressor class, and rape is presented as white-male business-as-usual." R. Shalit, quoted in Wooden, "Sexual Assault," 81. See Kretschmer and Barber, "Men at the March."

164   On the origins of the march, see O'Reilly, "Slut Pride"; and McCormack and Prostran, "Asking for It."

165   Reger, "Micro-Cohorts," 51.

166   Quoted in Hill, "SlutWalk as Perifeminist Response," 24.

167   Carr, "SlutWalk Movement," 24–25; and Tuerkheimer, "Slutwalking." Joetta Carr has called SlutWalk a case of transnational feminist solidarity. On the significance of social media and the organization of a SlutWalk in Delhi in 2011, see Borah and Nandi, "Feminist Politics of 'SlutWalk,'" 415.

168   J. Butler, "Bodies in Alliance." Judith Butler, who elsewhere called SlutWalks a "public and courageous takeover of public space," also noted some Black feminist intellectuals' critique of the effort to reappropriate the term *slut*. J. Butler, *Performative Theory of Assembly*, 227n15.

169   From an open letter circulated on email, listservs, and Facebook, September 11, 2011, quoted in Reger, "Micro-Cohorts," 63–64. Patricia Hill Collins condenses this philosophy to this: "Black 'whores' make white 'virgins' possible. This race/gender nexus fostered a situation whereby white men could then differentiate between the sexualized woman-as-body who is dominated and 'screwed' and the asexual woman-as-pure-spirit who is idealized and brought home to mother. . . . The sexually denigrated woman, whether she was made a victim through her rape or a pet through her seduction, could be used as the yardstick against which the cult of true womanhood was measured. Moreover, this entire situation was profitable." Hill Collins, *Black Feminist Thought*, 145. In the early twentieth century, the revived Ku Klux Klan and purveyors

of etiquette books policed this racial distinction. See Fluri and Dowler, "Klanbake."

170   Borah and Nandi, "Feminist Politics of 'SlutWalk,'" 417.

171   Hill, "SlutWalk as Perifeminist Response," 27.

172   Dworkin, "Pornography and Grief," 289.

173   Quoted in Reger, "Micro-Cohorts," 57.

174   Reger, "Micro-Cohorts," 57.

175   Ahmed, *Cultural Politics of Emotion*, 107.

176   Nussbaum, *Hiding from Humanity*.

177   Monica Poziemski, SlutWalk organizer in Tasmania, quoted in Mendes, *SlutWalk*, 61.

178   Mendes, *SlutWalk*, 80.

179   Tuerkheimer, "Slutwalking," 1475.

180   Fischel, *Screw Consent*; West, "Sex, Law, and Consent"; M. Anderson, "Negotiating Sex"; A. Gruber, "Consent Confusion"; and Jaleel, *Work of Rape*, 177.

181   Crunk Feminist Collective, "I Saw the Sign."

182   Tuerkheimer, "Slutwalking," 1485.

183   Kapur, "Pink Chaddis," 11–12.

184   Bracewell, "Sex Wars," 73.

185   For a discussion of rape regulation using public law rather than an ineffective criminal law, see Kaplan, "Rape beyond Crime."

186   Bracewell, "Sex Wars," 75.

187   Tuerkheimer, "Slutwalking."

188   See, for example, the Australian experience with affirmative consent standards in Burgin, "Persistent Narratives."

189   Tuerkheimer, "Judging Sex," 1477.

190   Tuerkheimer, "Slutwalking," 1506.

191   MacKinnon, "Toward Feminist Jurisprudence," 639.

192   Epigraphs: Dworkin, "Night and Danger," 16–17, 16.

193   Van Allen, "'Sitting on a Man.'"

194   Van Allen, "'Sitting on a Man,'" 170.

195   Van Allen, "'Sitting on a Man,'" 174.

196   Peltier, "Banned Vigil"; Hinsliff, "Vigils"; and Taub, "Rage over Sarah Everard Killing."

197   Bloom, *Violent London*, 460.

CHAPTER 5. TRANSLATION IN THE DARK

Epigraph 1: Saramago, *Double*, 185.

Epigraph 2: Benjamin, "Task of the Translator," 261.

Epigraph 3: Derrida, "Force of Law," 951.

1   Holmes, "Path of the Law"; A. Lefebvre, *Image of Law*, 255; King, *Where Do We Go*; and J. Mensch, "What's Wrong."

2   Richards, *Identity*; and Heyer, *Rights Enabled*, esp. ch. 2. Cass Sunstein has argued that analogical reasoning in the law has four features: "principled consistency; a focus on particulars; incompletely theorized judgments; and principles operating at a low or intermediate level of abstraction," making it a form of bottom-up reasoning. Sunstein, "On Analogical Reasoning," 746. In this chapter I do not make a distinction between metaphorical and analogical reasoning. Although law often claims analogy as its own, reserving metaphor for "the dreamwork of language" (Brewer, "Exemplary Reasoning," 926), all metaphors are analogies (Itkonen, *Analogy*, 41), and "analogy is metaphor par excellence" (Derrida, "White Mythology," 42).

3   Halley, "'Like Race' Arguments."

4   Peter Schroth allows that something is always lost in legal translation ("usually neither the letter nor the spirit can be rendered with complete accuracy") but also acknowledges that legal language in part is designed to *prevent* understanding in a bid for its autonomy. Schroth, "Legal Translation," 48, 51.

5   Derrida, "Retrait of Metaphor," 48.

6   Hibbitts, "Making Sense of Metaphors"; Goodrich, "Law and Language"; Haverkamp, "Rhetoric, Law"; Winter, "'Color' of Law"; Thornburg, "Metaphors Matter"; M. Duncan, "In Slime and Darkness"; Sirico, "Failed Constitutional Metaphors"; Berger, "Lady, or the Tiger"; and Rideout, "Penumbral Thinking Revisited."

7   Derrida, *Writing and Difference*, 19.

8   Galanter, "Radiating Effects of Courts"; M. Shapiro, *Courts*; and Mnookin and Kornhauser, "Bargaining." Even the image of a field of law propounded by Pierre Bourdieu has, with a more vigorous idea of struggle, a centralized doxa emanating throughout the field of law. Bourdieu, "Force of Law." See, again, the epigraph by Jean Carbonnier in the introduction to this book.

9   Blumenberg, "Light as a Metaphor," 31.

10   Elizabeth Povinelli suggests that quasi-events be seen as "a form of occurring that never punctures the horizon of the here and now and there and then and yet forms the basis of forms of existence to stay in place or alter their place. The quasi-event is only ever *hereish* and *nowish* and thus asks us to focus our attention on forces of condensation, manifestation, and endurance rather than on the borders of objects." Povinelli, *Geontologies*, 21.

11   Ricoeur, "Metaphor," 102. The section epigraph is from Euripides, *Iphigenia in Tauris*, quoted in M. Duncan, "In Slime and Darkness," 732.

12   Ricoeur, "Metaphor," 107.

13   Berkey v. Third Ave. Ry. Co., 244 N.Y. 84, 94, 155 N.E. 58, 61 (1926). Benjamin Cardozo was appointed Associate Justice of the Supreme Court

in 1932. This quote was written while he sat on the New York Court of Appeals.

14   Goodrich, "Law and Language," 176.

15   Goodrich, "Law and Language," 175.

16   Thornburg, "Metaphors Matter," 228.

17   M. Duncan, "In Slime and Darkness," 727.

18   Sirico, "Failed Constitutional Metaphors," 461. Louis Sirico cites Richard Posner's dismissal that metaphors are "powerful though alogical modes of persuasion." Posner, *Problems of Jurisprudence*, 456.

19   Balkin, "Footnote," 316n100. Balkin continues, "Moreover, our attempts at excluding metaphor result in a dual impurity—first, because the figural can never be completely banished from discourse, only neglected or overlooked, and second, because any claim that legal thought can rest upon a wholly nonmetaphorical ground involves its own adulteration and deception." With regard to rhetoric, Anselm Haverkamp wryly suggests that "we find everyone—those in the legal profession as well as the poets, not to mention everybody else including the politicians—relying upon rhetoric only to deny rhetoric's substantial impact on what they do—or is it, rather, not what they do, but what is being done?" Haverkamp, "Rhetoric, Law," 1639.

20   Quoted in Cazeaux, *Metaphor and Continental Philosophy*, 176.

21   Nietzsche, *Philosophy and Truth*, 84, 86.

22   Nietzsche, "On Truth and Lie," 257. Sarah Kofman comments, "Metaphorical activity, always already 'forgotten,' is secondarily repressed by being deliberately abandoned in favour of the concept, of logic and science. It is as if there is an anticathexis of the originary forgetting by the creation of a 'social memory' which goes hand in hand with the creation of responsibility, self-consciousness, and moral conscience." Kofman, *Nietzsche and Metaphor*, 43.

23   It is worth observing not only that time may erode the vibrancy of metaphor but that modern legal institutions may intentionally aid this forgetting. For Stanley Fish, law hides its own commitment to rhetoric. Formalism, for example, depends on a certain—rhetorical, certainly—repulsion to interpretation. While this is impossible—formalism "cannot succeed in being formal because it is always *infected* [emphasis added] by interpretation," he writes—the institutional aspiration to formalism is what creates coherence: "The law is continually creating and recreating itself out of the very [nonlegal] materials and forces it is obliged, by the very desire to *be* law, to push away." Fish, "Law Wishes," 143–44, 156.

     While Fish metaphorically describes interpretation as "infection," Niklas Luhmann calls on an immunitary model to ultimately converge on a similar destination that is legal despite remaining rhetorical. For Luhmann, law uses metaphor (for example, the metaphorical idea of a "source" such as a social contract for law's legitimacy), but this rhetoric is metabolized and rendered harmless to the legal system. "The metaphor of sources of law has, as far as validity is concerned, the function of a formula of contingency—just like the concept of substantive justice from the perspective of a rule of reason. The concept transforms a tautology into a sequence of arguments and makes something that is seen as highly artificial and contingent from the outside appear quite natural and necessary from the inside." Luhmann, *Law as a Social System*, 445.

Both Fish and Luhmann project mechanisms, each in their own way, to reduce the dialogical character of law into a conception that ultimately appears oracular. Rather than measure the deviation of metaphor from some metaphysical reality, they find metaphor to be the self-eclipsing integuments of legal discourse.

24 Benjamin, "Critique of Violence."

25 The term is suggested by Jairus Grove, private communication. The "Negro law" discussed in chapter 2 is one example of what we might call a dark law: authoritative yet informal, based in violence and terror, and central to hierarchical projects such as the maintenance of white supremacy.

26 Cover, "*Nomos* and Narrative," 40–43.

27 Derrida, "White Mythology," 11. Bernard Harrison argues that the Western tradition in metaphysics against which Derrida argues includes the following dimensions: "We are asked, then, to focus on the argument, or knot of related arguments, which says (1) that 'ideas' or 'concepts' can be adequate or inadequate to reality; (2) that there must therefore be some one set of concepts which is metaphysically correct, faithful, as it were, to the way Being is; (3) that the most basic signs of a metaphysically adequate language would pick out such concepts in such a way that each sign would possess meaning independently of any other sign, since its meaning would simply be the concept for which it stood; (4) that such a language is, at least fragmentarily and in principle, achievable, and is thus a proper and, indeed, inevitable goal of philosophical theorising; (5) that everyday language is an inadequate tool for philosophy because (6) the interdependence of its signs makes it difficult to achieve the univocality, the clarity of reference which makes each basic sign in a logically perspicuous language." B. Harrison, "'White Mythology' Revisited," 512.

28 Maart, "When Black Consciousness Walks," 61–62; Peeters, *Derrida*, 445–48; and Malabou, *Counterpath*, 90–92. Derrida writes, "I am European, I am without doubt a European intellectual, I like to remember that, like to remind myself of that. . . . But I am not, nor do I feel, *completely* European." Quoted in Baring, *Young Derrida*, 19.

29 Ahluwalia, *Out of Africa*, 89.

30   Derrida, "White Mythology," 44. On metaphoricity preceding metaphor and concept, see Cools, "Gift and the Skin," 36.

31   Derrida, "Retrait of Metaphor," 49.

32   Derrida, "White Mythology," 18.

33   Derrida, "Retrait of Metaphor," 50.

34   Bennington, "Metaphor and Analogy," 94.

35   "Since the best metaphor is never absolutely good, since otherwise it would not be a metaphor, does not bad metaphor always provide the best example? Metaphor therefore means heliotrope, both movement turned to the sun, and the turning movement of the sun." Derrida, "White Mythology," 52.

36   Derrida, "White Mythology," 52.

37   Derrida, "White Mythology," 55.

38   Derrida, "White Mythology," 52. In a debate with Ricoeur, who in *The Rule of Metaphor* critiques an assumed relation between Heidegger's and Derrida's concerns with metaphor and metaphysics, Derrida clarifies that he is not simply attending to the collusive distinctions between the proper and figurative, and the visible and invisible, which Heidegger relies on, but that he is also asserting the deconstruction between the living and dead that fuels the idea that a metaphor passes from vibrant life to worn-out meaning found in a set of economic metaphors greater than the numismatic idea of the worn-out coin. One set of economic motifs that emerges from this economy, he argues, is home and light. Derrida, "Retrait of Metaphor," 61.

39   Derrida, "White Mythology," 53.

40   Derrida, "White Mythology," 74.

41   Derrida, "White Mythology," 70.

42   Derrida, "White Mythology," 45 (translation modified). Derrida's word *nocturne* in the original text is translated as "swathed in night," which I find too obscure. *Nocturne* as an adjective may be translated as "nocturnal," or as "belonging to the night."

43   Derrida writes about plurality in relation to Aristotle's disquisitions on the sun, "If the sun can 'sow,' it is because its name is written into a system of relations which constitute it. Its name is no longer the proper name of a unique thing on which the metaphor would supervene; that name has already begun to speak of the multiple and divided origin of all sowing, of the eye, of invisibility, of death, of the father, of the 'proper name,' and so on." Derrida, "White Mythology," 45.

        Gasché's understands Derrida's pathway as a quasi-transcendental opening to a text. He writes, "The notion of text in Derrida is a *sort of* transcendental concept. . . . The transcendental experience of the text is, indeed, neither the experience of a universal and eidetic object nor simply a repetition of a *transcendental* experience in either a Kantian or

Husserlian sense. The transcendental gesture in Derrida simultaneously serves to escape the danger of naïve objectivism and the value of transcendentality itself. . . . The text, like the trace, is to be understood as a pathway (*parcours*)." Gasché, "Joining the Text," 161.

    On Derrida's derision of vision, see Jay, *Downcast Eyes*, 511–16.

44   Hibbitts, "Making Sense of Metaphors," 230 (references omitted; bracketed phrase in original). In the case of bright-line tests, consider the ink with which they are written and the words of Derridean critic Geoffrey Hartman: "The blackness of ink or print suggests that écriture is a hymn to the Spirit of the Night." G. Hartman, *Saving the Text*, xix, quoted in Jay, *Downcast Eyes*, 510.

45   Hibbitts, "Making Sense of Metaphors," 264–65.

46   Hibbitts, "Making Sense of Metaphors," 291. By *differentiatory*, Hibbitts means the attribution of law's success to its "ability to make and maintain sharp distinctions between various situations, categories, and rules" (292), or its formalism.

47   Hibbitts, "Making Sense of Metaphors," 341.

48   Hibbitts, "Making Sense of Metaphors," 342–43.

49   Nietzsche, "Raids of an Untimely Man," ch. 10, in *Twilight of the Idols*, quoted in Kofman, *Nietzsche and Metaphor*, 11.

50   Nietzsche, *Daybreak*, 143.

51   Consider the way Elias Canetti opens his masterful work on crowds: "In the dark, the fear of an unexpected touch can mount to panic." Canetti, *Crowds and Power*, 15.

52   Genette, "Le jour, la nuit," 29 (translation mine).

53   Sirico, "Failed Constitutional Metaphors," 481–82. Christopher Rideout points out that the image of the penumbra was used several times in nineteenth-century American law, was written about by Justice Oliver Wendell Holmes before and after he was on the court, and could be seen as an implicit mode of reasoning as early as *McCulloch v. Maryland* (17 U.S. 316 [1819]), which found the federal bank to be constitutional despite a lack of direct constitutional language. Rideout, "Penumbral Thinking Revisited," 172, 178–81. See also the extensive doctrinal history of this metaphor in Sirico, "Failed Constitutional Metaphors"; Henly, "Penumbra"; and Greely, "Footnote to 'Penumbra.'"

54   Griswold v. Connecticut, 381 U.S. at 484 (1965).

55   Griswold v. Connecticut, 381 U.S. at 484 (1965). The historian A. Roger Ekirch writes, "'Shutting-in' emphasized the need for households to bolt portals against the advancing darkness. The fifteenth-century poet François Villon instructed, 'The house is safe but be sure it is shut tight.' Attested an English proverb, 'Men shut their doors against a setting sun.'" Ekirch, *At Day's Close*, 91–92. Certainly, the Fourth Amendment was inspired by royal prerogatives to enter and seize incriminating materials

for sedition. Nonetheless, some historians recognize the concern for nighttime integrity that also built up common law understandings of the basis for privacy. Cuddihy and Hardy, "Man's House," 375. The historian Amanda Vickery writes, "'The Englishman's home is his castle' was already a hoary cliché of English common law by 1700. The Westmorland JP Richard Burn, author of the most authoritative eighteenth century manual for magistrates, was rousing on the protections offered to the house in criminal law. 'Man's home or habitation is so far protected by the law, that if any person attempts to break open a house in the night time, and shall be killed in such attempt, the slayer shall be acquitted and discharged. And so tender is the law in respect of the immunity of a man's house, that it will never suffer it to be violated with impunity.'" Vickery, "Englishman's Home," 154–55, quoting Burn, *The Justice of the Peace*, 614–15.

56 Rideout, "Penumbral Thinking Revisited," 186.

57 Rideout, "Penumbral Thinking Revisited," 188. See also Sirico, "Failed Constitutional Metaphors," 484.

58 M. Duncan, "In Slime and Darkness," 739.

59 M. Duncan, "In Slime and Darkness," 733. Duncan quotes from Judge Leventhal's dissenting opinion in one of the cases stemming from the Watergate burglary: "I come back—again and again, in my mind—to the stark fact that we are dealing with a breaking and entering in the dead of night, both surreptitious and forcible, and a violation of civil rights statutes." United States v. Barker, 546 F.2d 940, 973 (D.C. Cir. 1976).

60 M. Duncan, "In Slime and Darkness," 735. Shakespeare, *Macbeth*, act III, scene 2, line 50.

61 "The other night" is a concept of Maurice Blanchot's. See Blanchot, "Outside, the Night," 162. Michael Newman explains, "By Blanchot's 'other night' we may understand the night which withdraws from the dialectical opposition of day and night and which, as the murmur of unnegatable being, is linked with the *il y a*." Newman, "Trace of Trauma," 157.

62 Epigraphs: Latour, *Making of Law*, 151–52; and Merleau-Ponty, *Visible and the Invisible*, 221.

63 Derrida, "Force of Law," 1009.

64 Derrida, "Force of Law," 1007.

65 Cover, "Bonds of Constitutional Interpretation," 832.

66 Roe v. Wade, 410 U.S. 113 (1973).

67 Žižek, "Superego by Default," 925. He adds, "From whence does this splitting of the law into the written public law and its underside, the 'unwritten,' obscene secret code, come? From the incomplete character of the public law. Explicit, public rules do not suffice; they must be supplemented by a clandestine 'unwritten' code aimed at those who, although

they violate no public rules, maintain a kind of inner distance and do not truly identify with the 'spirit of community'" (926).

68 This was one of Colorado's justifications for defending Amendment 2 (enacted in 1992), which denied cities and counties the power to extend antidiscrimination law to include sexual orientation. See Romer v. Evans, 517 U.S. 620, 630 (1996); and Goldberg-Hiller, "'Entitled to Be Hostile.'"

69 Bostock v. Clayton County, 590 U.S. __, 2 (2020) (Slip opinion).

70 See Salamon, *Life and Death*.

71 On transgender nightlife in the early twenty-first century, see D. Valentine, *Imagining Transgender*.

72 Freeman, *Time Binds*, 4.

73 Derrida, *Dissemination*, 258, quoted in Gasché, *Tain of the Mirror*, 310.

74 Derrida, *Margins of Philosophy*, 270–71, quoted in Gasché, *Tain of the Mirror*, 310.

75 Derrida, "White Mythology," 58. Derrida writes of catachresis, proposed by Pierre Fontanier's *Les Figures du discours* (1827) that it is "first of all concerned with the use of a sign by violence, force, or abuse, with the imposition of a sign on a sense not yet having a proper sign in the language. And so there is no substitution here, no transfer of proper signs, but an irruptive extension of a sign proper to one idea to a sense without a signifier." Derrida, "White Mythology," 57.

George Lakoff also uses the body but in a more transcendental fashion, likening metaphor to human thought. "Metaphor is pervasive in everyday life, not just in language but in thought and action. Our ordinary conceptual system, in terms of which we both think and act, is fundamentally metaphorical in nature." Lakoff and Johnson, *Metaphors We Live By*, 12. Lakoff's inability to account for the importance of metaphor when thought is impossible (e.g., during sleep) makes his argument that metaphor should not be separated from concepts less useful than the deconstructionist route I have taken in this journey of translation.

76 Derrida, "White Mythology," 59.

77 Cools, "Gift and the Skin," 40.

78 Derrida, *Gift of Death*, 63.

79 Cools, "Gift and the Skin," 42.

80 Derrida and Marion, "On the Gift," 59.

81 Boltanski, *Foetal Condition*, 21.

82 Cover, "*Nomos* and Narrative," 7n14.

83 Agamben, *Remnants of Auschwitz*, 151.

84 Freedman, *Redefining Rape*, 24–2; and Brendese, "Race."

85 Derrida, *Aporias*, 81 (emphasis mine).

86 Agamben uses the term *nightmare* in reference to the *Muselmann*: "Whether what survives is the human or the inhuman, the animal or the

organic, it seems that life bears within itself the dream—or the night-mare—of survival." *Remnants of Auschwitz*, 155.

87   Sarah Hammerschlag writes about Derrida's figure, "The Marrano's avowed betrayal of Judaism represents the strictest of loyalties." Hammer-schlag, *Figural Jew*, 246.

88   Derrida, "White Mythology," 43.

89   Gallan, "Becoming Crepuscular," 57.

90   Mohaghegh, *Night*, 2 (emphasis mine).

91   Deleuze and Guattari, *Kafka*, 22.

92   The words are from Casey, "Origin(s) in (of) Heidegger/Derrida," 605.

93   Derrida, "Speech and Phenomena," 52, quoted in Casey, "Origin(s) in (of) Heidegger/Derrida," 605.

Abujidi, Nurhan. "The Palestinian States of Exception and Agamben." *Contemporary Arab Affairs* 2, no. 2 (April–June 2009): 272–91.

Agamben, Giorgio. *Homo Sacer: Sovereign Power and Bare Life*. Stanford, CA: Stanford University Press, 1998.

Agamben, Giorgio. *Means without End: Notes on Politics*. Minneapolis: University of Minnesota Press, 2000.

Agamben, Giorgio. *The Omnibus Homo Sacer*. Stanford, CA: Stanford University Press, 2017.

Agamben, Giorgio. *Remnants of Auschwitz: The Witness and the Archive*. New York: Zone Books, 2000.

Agamben, Giorgio. *Stasis: Civil War as a Political Paradigm*. Edinburgh: Edinburgh University Press, 2015.

Agamben, Giorgio. *State of Exception*. Chicago: University of Chicago Press, 2005.

Agamben, Giorgio. *The Time That Remains: A Commentary on the Letter to the Romans*. Stanford, CA: Stanford University Press, 2005.

Agamben, Giorgio. *What Is an Apparatus? And Other Essays*. Edited by David Kishik and Stefan Pedatella. Stanford, CA: Stanford University Press, 2009.

Agamben, Giorgio. "What Is a Camp?" In *Means without End: Notes on Politics*, 37–45. Minneapolis: University of Minnesota Press, 2000.

Ahluwalia, Pal. *Out of Africa: Post-Structuralism's Colonial Roots*. London: Routledge, 2010.

Ahmed, Sara. *The Cultural Politics of Emotion*. New York: Routledge, 2004.

Alexovich, Ariel. "Clinton's National Security Ad." *The Caucus* (blog), *New York Times*, February 29, 2008. http://thecaucus.blogs.nytimes.com/2008/02/29/clintons-national-security-ad/.

Althusser, Louis. "The Underground Current of the Materialism of the Encounter." In *Philosophy of the Encounter: Later Writings, 1978–87*, edited by François Matheron and Olivier Corpet, 163–207. London: Verso, 2006.

Amodio, David M., Eddie Harmon-Jones, Patricia G. Devine, John J. Curtin, Sigan L. Hartley, and Alison E. Covert. "Neural Signals for the Detection of Unintentional Race Bias." *Psychological Science* 15, no. 2 (2004): 88–93.

Amsden, Brian. "Negotiating Liberalism and Bio-Politics: Stylizing Power in Defense of the Mall Curfew." *Quarterly Journal of Speech* 94, no. 4 (October 2008): 407–29.

Anderson, Benedict. *Imagined Communities: Reflections on the Origin and Spread of Nationalism*. London: Verso, 1983.

Anderson, Carol. *The Second: Race and Guns in a Fatally Unequal America*. New York: Bloomsbury, 2021.

Anderson, Michelle J. "Negotiating Sex." *Southern California Law Review* 78, no. 6 (September 2005): 1401–38.

Anghie, Antony. *Imperialism, Sovereignty and the Making of International Law*. Cambridge: Cambridge University Press, 2007.

Anker, Elisabeth R. *Ugly Freedoms*. Durham, NC: Duke University Press, 2022.

Anthony, Susan Brownell, and Ida Husted Harper, eds. *History of Woman Suffrage . . . : 1883–1900*. New York: Fowler and Wells, 1902.

Appleby, Joyce. "Republicanism and Ideology." *American Quarterly* 37, no. 4 (Autumn 1985): 461–73.

Aptheker, Herbert. *Nat Turner's Slave Rebellion: Including the 1831 "Confessions."* Mineola, NY: Dover, 2012.

Archer, Lu'ukia. "He Pou He'e I Ka Wawā: Slipping into the Tumult of Life and Politics." PhD diss., University of Hawai'i at Manoa, 2016.

Arendt, Hannah. *Eichmann in Jerusalem: A Report on the Banality of Evil*, revised and enlarged edition. New York: Penguin Books, 1994.

Arendt, Hannah. *On Revolution*. Boston: Penguin, 1990.

Aristotle. *Nicomachean Ethics*. Translated by Roger Crisp. Cambridge: Cambridge University Press, 2000.

Aristotle. *The Politics of Aristotle*. Translated by Benjamin Jowett. Oxford: Clarendon, 1885.

Arneil, Barbara. "The Wild Indian's Venison: Locke's Theory of Property and English Colonialism in America." *Political Studies* 44, no. 1 (March 1996): 60–74.

Askanius, Tina. "On Frogs, Monkeys, and Execution Memes: Exploring the Humor-Hate Nexus at the Intersection of Neo-Nazi and Alt-Right Movements in Sweden." *Television and New Media* 22, no. 2 (February 2021): 147–65.

Associated Press. "UN Chief Urges End to Domestic Violence, Citing Global Surge." *New York Times*, April 5, 2020. https://www.nytimes.com/aponline/2020/04/05/world/ap-un-virus-outbreak-un-domestic-violence.html.

Auden, W. H. "Law like Love." *University of Toledo Law Review* 14 (1982): viii.

Azoulay, Ariella, and Adi Ophir. *The One-State Condition: Occupation and Democracy in Israel/Palestine*. Stanford, CA: Stanford University Press, 2013.

Badiou, Alain. *Black: The Brilliance of a Non-Color*. Malden, MA: Polity, 2016.

Badiou, Alain. *Theory of the Subject*. London: Continuum, 2009.

Bahour, Sam. "The Violence of Curfew." *Tikkun* 17, no. 6 (December 2002): 29–31.

Bailyn, Bernard. *The Ideological Origins of the American Revolution*. Cambridge, MA: Harvard University Press, 1992.

Baldwin, James. *The Fire Next Time.* New York: Vintage International, 1993.

Baldwin, Peter C. *In the Watches of the Night: Life in the Nocturnal City, 1820–1930.* Chicago: University of Chicago Press, 2012.

Baldwin, Peter C. "'Nocturnal Habits and Dark Wisdom': The American Response to Children in the Streets at Night, 1880–1930." *Journal of Social History* 35, no. 3 (Spring 2002): 593–611.

Balibar, Étienne. "Citizen Subject." In *Who Comes after the Subject?*, edited by Eduardo Cadava, Peter Connor, and Jean-Luc Nancy, 33–57. New York: Routledge, 1991.

Balibar, Étienne. *Identity and Difference: John Locke and the Invention of Consciousness.* Brooklyn, NY: Verso Books, 2013.

Balke, Friedrich. "Derrida and Foucault on Sovereignty," *German Law Journal* 6, no. 1 (2005): 71–86.

Balkin, Jack M. "The Footnote." *Northwestern University Law Review* 83, nos. 1–2 (1989): 275–320.

Ball, Charles. *Slavery in the United States: A Narrative of the Life and Adventures of Charles Ball, a Black Man, Who Lived Forty Years in Maryland, South Carolina and Georgia, as a Slave.* New York: J. S. Taylor, 1837.

Baring, Edward. *The Young Derrida and French Philosophy, 1945–1968.* New York: Cambridge University Press, 2011.

Baring-Gould, Sabine. *The Book of Were-Wolves.* 1865. Hoboken, NJ: Start, 2013.

Barkan, Joshua. "Roberto Esposito's Political Biology and Corporate Forms of Life." *Law, Culture and the Humanities* 8, no. 1 (February 2012): 84–101.

Barnes, Christopher M., Sonia Ghumman, and Brent A. Scott. "Sleep and Organizational Citizenship Behavior: The Mediating Role of Job Satisfaction." *Journal of Occupational Health Psychology* 18, no. 1 (2013): 16–26.

Bart, Pauline, and Patricia H. O'Brien. *Stopping Rape: Successful Survival Strategies.* New York: Pergamon, 1985.

Bateson, Regina. "The Politics of Vigilantism." *Comparative Political Studies* 54, no. 6 (May 2021): 923–55.

Bauman, Zygmunt. *Liquid Fear.* Cambridge: Polity, 2006.

Baumann, Hanna. "Enclaves, Borders, and Everyday Movements: Palestinian Marginal Mobility in East Jerusalem." *Cities* 59 (November 2016): 173–82.

Bearak, Max, and Rael Ombuor. "Kenyan Police Shot Dead a Teenager on His Balcony during a Coronavirus Curfew Crackdown." *Washington Post*, March 31, 2020. https://www.washingtonpost.com/world/africa/kenyan-police-shot-dead-a-teenager-on-his-balcony-during-a-coronavirus-curfew-crackdown/2020/03/31/6344c70e-7350-11ea-ad9b-254ec99993bc_story.html.

Beaumont, Matthew. *Nightwalking: A Nocturnal History of London.* New York: Verso Books, 2015.

Beauvoir, Simone de. *The Ethics of Ambiguity.* Translated by Bernard Frechtman. New York: Citadel, 1948.

Beauvoir, Simone de. *The Second Sex.* Translated by H. M. Parshley. London: J. Cape, 1956.

Beck, Ulrich. *Risk Society: Towards a New Modernity.* Newbury Park, CA: Sage, 1992.

Beck, Ulrich. *World at Risk.* Hoboken, NJ: John Wiley and Sons, 2013.

Becker, Jurek. *Jacob the Liar.* Translated by Leila Vennewitz. New York: Arcade, 2012.

Beckett, Katherine. *Making Crime Pay: Law and Order in Contemporary American Politics.* New York: Oxford University Press, 1997.

Beckett, Katherine, and Steve Herbert. *Banished: The New Social Control in Urban America.* New York: Oxford University Press, 2011.

Benjamin, Walter. "Critique of Violence." In *Reflections,* 277–300. Translated by Edmund Jephcott. New York: Schocken Books, 1978.

Benjamin, Walter. *Illuminations.* Translated by Harry Zohn. New York: Random House, 2002.

Benjamin, Walter. "The Task of the Translator." In *Selected Writings,* vol. 1, *1913–1926,* edited by Marcus Paul Bullock and Michael William Jennings, 253–63. Cambridge, MA: Belknap Press of Harvard University Press, 1996.

Bennington, Geoffrey. "Metaphor and Analogy in Derrida." In *A Companion to Derrida,* edited by Zeynep Direk and Leonard Lawlor, 89–104. Chichester, UK: Wiley Blackwell, 2014.

Benveniste, Émile. *Problems in General Linguistics.* Miami, FL: University of Miami Press, 1971.

Beresford, Matthew. *The White Devil: The Werewolf in European Culture.* London: Reaktion Books, 2013.

Berger, Linda L. "The Lady, or the Tiger? A Field Guide to Metaphor and Narrative." *Washburn Law Journal* 50, no. 2 (Winter 2011): 275–317.

Berman, Mark. "What the Police Officer Who Shot Philando Castile Said about the Shooting." *Washington Post,* June 21, 2017. https://www .washingtonpost.com/news/post-nation/wp/2017/06/21/what-the -police-officer-who-shot-philando-castile-said-about-the-shooting/.

Bernhardt-House, Phillip A. "The Werewolf as Queer, the Queer as Werewolf, and Queer Werewolves." In *Queering the Non/Human,* edited by Noreen Giffney and Myra J. Hird, 187–212. Abingdon, UK: Routledge, 2016.

Bernstein, Elizabeth. "Militarized Humanitarianism Meets Carceral Feminism: The Politics of Sex, Rights, and Freedom in Contemporary Antitrafficking Campaigns." *Signs: Journal of Women in Culture and Society* 36, no. 1 (Autumn 2010): 45–71.

Bernstein, Robin. *Racial Innocence: Performing American Childhood from Slavery to Civil Rights.* New York: New York University Press, 2011.

Bernton, Hal. "Portland Allows Homeless to Camp Overnight on Streets." *Honolulu Star-Advertiser,* May 15, 2016. http://www.staradvertiser.com /breaking-news/portland-allows-homeless-to-camp-overnight-on-streets/.

Bhandar, Brenna. *Colonial Lives of Property: Law, Land, and Racial Regimes of Ownership.* Durham, NC: Duke University Press, 2018.

Black, Donald. *The Behavior of Law.* Cambridge, MA: Academic Press, 1980.

Blackstone, Sir William. *Commentaries on the Laws of England. In Four Books.* 2 vols. Philadelphia: J. B. Lippincott, 1893.

Blake, Aaron. "Trump's Eruption at an NBC Reporter Says It All about His Alternate Reality on Coronavirus." *Washington Post*, March 21, 2020. https://www.washingtonpost.com/politics/2020/03/20/trumps -eruption-an-nbc-reporter-says-it-all-about-his-alternate-reality -coronavirus/.

Blanchot, Maurice. "The Outside, the Night." In *The Space of Literature*, translated by Ann Smock, 163–70. Lincoln: University of Nebraska Press, 1989.

Blanchot, Maurice. "Sleep, Night." In *The Space of Literature*, translated by Ann Smock, 264–68. Lincoln: University of Nebraska Press, 1982.

Blassingame, John W., ed. *Slave Testimony: Two Centuries of Letters, Speeches, Interviews, and Autobiographies.* Baton Rouge: Louisiana State University Press, 1977.

Bloom, Clive. *Violent London: 2000 Years of Riots, Rebels and Revolts.* London: Palgrave Macmillan, 2010.

Blumenberg, Hans. "Light as a Metaphor for Truth: At the Preliminary Stage of Philosophical Concept Formation." In *Modernity and the Hegemony of Vision*, edited by David Michael Kleinberg-Levin, 30–62. Berkeley: University of California Press, 1993.

Bodei, Remo. *The Life of Things, the Love of Things.* Translated by Murtha Baca. New York: Fordham University Press, 2015.

Boltanski, Luc. *The Foetal Condition: A Sociology of Engendering and Abortion.* Cambridge: Polity, 2013.

Borah, Rituparna, and Subhalakshmi Nandi. "Reclaiming the Feminist Politics of 'SlutWalk.'" *International Feminist Journal of Politics* 14, no. 3 (September 2012): 415–21.

Borch, Christian. "Body to Body: On the Political Anatomy of Crowds." *Sociological Theory* 27, no. 3 (September 2009): 271–90.

Bosteels, Bruno. "Force of Nonlaw: Alain Badiou's Theory of Justice." *Cardozo Law Review* 29, no. 5 (April 2008): 1905–26.

Bourdieu, Pierre. "The Force of Law: Toward a Sociology of the Juridical Field." *Hastings Law Review* 38, no. 5 (1987): 814–53.

Boyett, Patricia Michelle. *Right to Revolt: The Crusade for Racial Justice in Mississippi's Central Piney Woods.* Jackson: University Press of Mississippi, 2015.

Bracewell, Lorna. "Sex Wars, SlutWalks, and Carceral Feminism." *Contemporary Political Theory* 19, no. 1 (March 2020): 61–82.

Brands, Jelle, Tim Schwanen, and Irina van Aalst. "Fear of Crime and Affective Ambiguities in the Night-Time Economy." *Urban Studies* 52, no. 3 (February 2015): 439–55.

Brandwein, Pamela. *Rethinking the Judicial Settlement of Reconstruction*. Cambridge Studies on the American Constitution. New York: Cambridge University Press, 2011.

Brass, Paul R. "Collective Violence, Human Rights, and the Politics of Curfew." *Journal of Human Rights* 5, no. 3 (September 2006): 323–40.

Brendese, Philip J. *The Power of Memory in Democratic Politics*. Rochester, NY: University of Rochester Press, 2014.

Brendese, Philip J. "The Race of a More Perfect Union: James Baldwin, Segregated Memory and the Presidential Race." *Theory and Event* 15, no. 1 (2012) https://doi.org/10.1353/tae.2012.0010.

Brendese, Philip J. "Worlds Neither New nor Brave: Racial Terror in America." In *Theory and Event* 20, no. 1 (2017): 24–43.

Brewer, Scott. "Exemplary Reasoning: Semantics, Pragmatics, and the Rational Force of Legal Argument by Analogy." *Harvard Law Review* 109, no. 5 (March 1996): 923–1028.

Bröck-Sallah, Sabine. *Gender and the Abjection of Blackness*. Albany: State University of New York Press, 2018.

Bronfen, Elisabeth. *Night Passages: Philosophy, Literature, and Film*. Translated by David Brenner. New York: Columbia University Press, 2013.

Brown, Daniel. "Sacramento Police Release Body Cam Footage of Officers Fatally Shooting Unarmed Black Man in His Own Backyard." *Business Insider*, March 22, 2018. https://www.businessinsider.com/stephon-clark -sacramento-police-shoot-unarmed-black-man-backyard-body-cam -2018-3.

Brown, Marie Alohalani. *Facing the Spears of Change: The Life and Legacy of John Papa ʻĪʻī*. Honolulu: University of Hawaiʻi Press, 2016.

Brown, Richard Maxwell. *No Duty to Retreat: Violence and Values in American History and Society*. New York: Oxford University Press, 1991.

Browne, Simone. *Dark Matters: On the Surveillance of Blackness*. Durham, NC: Duke University Press, 2015.

Brownlow, Alec. "A Geography of Men's Fear." *Geoforum* 36, no. 5 (September 2005): 581–92.

Brownmiller, Susan. *Against Our Will: Men, Women, and Rape*. New York: Simon and Schuster, 1975.

Bruce-Briggs, Barry. "The Great American Gun War." *Public Interest*, no. 45 (Fall 1976): 37–62.

Bruno, Jonathan R. "Vigilance and Confidence: Jeremy Bentham, Publicity, and the Dialectic of Political Trust and Distrust." *American Political Science Review* 111, no. 2 (May 2017): 295–307.

Brunson, Rod K., and Jody Miller. "Gender, Race, and Urban Policing: The Experience of African American Youths." *Gender and Society* 20, no. 4 (August 2006): 531–52.

Buccino, Rachel. "Domestic Violence Cases Surge amid Stay-at-Home Orders." *The Hill*, April 13, 2020. https://thehill.com/homenews/news/492506 -domestic-violence-cases-surge-amid-stay-at-home-orders.

Buman, Nathan A. "To Kill Whites: The 1811 Louisiana Slave Insurrection." Master's thesis, Louisiana State University and Agricultural and Mechanical College, 2008. https://digitalcommons.lsu.edu/gradschool_theses /1888.

Bumiller, Kristin. *In an Abusive State: How Neoliberalism Appropriated the Feminist Movement against Sexual Violence.* Durham, NC: Duke University Press, 2008.

Burgin, Rachael. "Persistent Narratives of Force and Resistance: Affirmative Consent as Law Reform." *British Journal of Criminology* 59, no. 2 (March 2019): 296–314.

Burn, Richard. *The Justice of the Peace, and Parish Officer,* 16th ed. 4 vols. London: Strahan and Woodfall, 1788.

Busby, Mattha. "London's Night Czar Criticised Following Strict New Hackney Nightlife Rules." *Independent*, July 20, 2018. https://www.independent.co .uk/news/uk/home-news/london-hackney-nightlife-curfew-rules-amy -lame-criticism-sadiq-khan-a8456666.html.

Butler, Judith. "Bodies in Alliance: Gender Theorist Judith Butler on the Occupy and SlutWalk Movements." Interview by Kyle Bella. *Truthout*, December 15, 2011. https://truthout.org/articles/bodies-in-alliance-gender -theorist-judith-butler-on-the-occupy-and-slutwalk-movements/.

Butler, Judith. *Notes toward a Performative Theory of Assembly.* Cambridge, MA: Harvard University Press, 2015.

Butler, Melissa A. "Early Liberal Roots of Feminism: John Locke and the Attack on Patriarchy." *American Political Science Review* 72, no. 1 (March 1978): 135–50.

Byman, Daniel. "White Supremacy, Terrorism, and the Failure of Reconstruction in the United States." *International Security* 46, no. 1 (Summer 2021): 53–103.

Cabantous, Alain. *Histoire de la nuit: XVIIe–XVIIIe siècle.* Paris: Fayard, 2009.

Calavita, Kitty. *Invitation to Law and Society: An Introduction to the Study of Real Law.* Chicago: University of Chicago Press, 2010.

Cameron, Jessica Joy. *Reconsidering Radical Feminism: Affect and the Politics of Heterosexuality.* Vancouver: University of British Columbia Press, 2018.

Camp, Stephanie M. H. "The Pleasures of Resistance: Enslaved Women and Body Politics in the Plantation South, 1830–1861." *Journal of Southern History* 68, no. 3 (August 2002): 533–72.

Campbell, James. *Crime and Punishment in African American History.* London: Palgrave Macmillan, 2012.

Campkin, Ben, and Laura Marshall. "London's Nocturnal Queer Geographies." *Soundings* 2018, no. 70 (Autumn 2018): 82–96.

Canetti, Elias. *Crowds and Power*. Translated by Carol Stewart. New York: Viking, 1966.

Cao, Sheng-gao. "Relaxation of the Curfew Rule in the Late Tang Dynasty and Its Cultural Influence." *Academic Research* 2007, no. 7 (2007). http://en.cnki.com.cn/Article_en/CJFDTOTAL-XSYJ200707019.htm.

Carbonnier, Jean. *Flexible droit: Pour une sociologie du droit sans rigueur*. Paris: L. G. D. J., 2001.

Cardozo, Benjamin N. *The Nature of the Judicial Process*. New Haven, CT: Yale University Press, 1921.

Cardyn, Lisa. "Sexualized Racism/Gendered Violence: Outraging the Body Politic in the Reconstruction South." *Michigan Law Review* 100, no. 4 (February 2002): 675–867.

Carlson, Jennifer D. *Policing the Second Amendment: Guns, Law Enforcement, and the Politics of Race*. Princeton, NJ: Princeton University Press, 2020.

Carlson, Jennifer D. "States, Subjects and Sovereign Power: Lessons from Global Gun Cultures." *Theoretical Criminology* 18, no. 3 (August 2014): 335–53.

Carr, Joetta. "The SlutWalk Movement: A Study in Transnational Feminist Activism." *Journal of Feminist Scholarship* 4, no. 4 (Spring 2013): 24–38.

Carro, Jorge L. "Sanctuary: The Resurgence of an Age-Old Right or Dangerous Misinterpretation of an Abandoned Ancient Privilege." *University of Cincinnati Law Review* 54, no. 3 (1985): 747–78.

Carter Jackson, Kellie. *Force and Freedom: Black Abolitionists and the Politics of Violence*. Philadelphia: University of Pennsylvania Press, 2019.

Casey, Edward S. "Origin(s) in (of) Heidegger/Derrida." *Journal of Philosophy* 81, no. 10 (October 1984): 601–10.

Cazeaux, Clive. *Metaphor and Continental Philosophy: From Kant to Derrida*. 2nd ed. Oxfordshire, UK: Routledge, 2007.

Certeau, Michel de. *The Practice of Everyday Life*. Berkeley: University of California Press, 1984.

Chamayou, Grégoire. *Manhunts: A Philosophical History*. Princeton, NJ: Princeton University Press, 2012.

Chamayou, Grégoire. *A Theory of the Drone*. New York: New Press, 2015.

Chamayou, Grégoire. "Fichte's Passport—A Philosophy of the Police." *Theory and Event* 16, no. 2 (2013). https://muse.jhu.edu/article/509902.

Chauncey, George. *Gay New York: Gender, Urban Culture, and the Makings of the Gay Male World, 1890–1940*. New York: Basic Books, 1994.

Chavez, Ernest K. "Intrusions of Violence: Afro-Pessimism and Reading Social Death beyond Solitary Confinement." *Theoretical Criminology* 25, no. 1 (February 2021): 3–22.

Chen-Edinboro, Lenis P., Christopher N. Kaufmann, Jura L. Augustinavicius, Ramin Mojtabai, Jeanine M. Parisi, Alexandra M. V. Wennberg, Michael T. Smith, and Adam P. Spira. "Neighborhood Physical Disorder,

Social Cohesion, and Insomnia: Results from Participants over Age 50 in the Health and Retirement Study." *International Psychogeriatrics* 27, no. 2 (February 2015): 289–96.

Cheng, Cheng, and Mark Hoekstra. "Does Strengthening Self-Defense Law Deter Crime or Escalate Violence? Evidence from Expansions to Castle Doctrine." *Journal of Human Resources* 48, no. 3 (Summer 2013): 821–53.

Chesney-Lind, Meda, and Randall G. Shelden. *Girls, Delinquency, and Juvenile Justice.* 4th ed. Chichester, UK: John Wiley and Sons, 2014.

Chicago Police Torture Archive. Accessed September 24, 2021. https://chicagopolicetorturearchive.com.

Cixous, Hélène. *Stigmata: Escaping Texts.* London: Routledge, 2005.

Clark, Lorenne M. G. *Rape: The Price of Coercive Sexuality.* Toronto: Women's Press, 1977.

Clavin, Matthew J. "American Toussaints: Symbol, Subversion, and the Black Atlantic Tradition in the American Civil War." In *African Americans and the Haitian Revolution: Selected Essays and Historical Documents*, edited by Maurice Jackson and Jacqueline Bacon, 107–20. New York: Routledge, 2010.

Codrea-Rado, Anna. "What Europe's 'Night Mayors' Can Teach New York." *New York Times*, August 30, 2017. https://www.nytimes.com/2017/08/30/arts/new-york-night-mayor-europe.html.

Cohen, Daniel A. "Social Injustice, Sexual Violence, Spiritual Transcendence: Constructions of Interracial Rape in Early American Crime Literature, 1767–1817." *William and Mary Quarterly* 56, no. 3 (July 1999): 481–526.

Cohen, Morris R. "Property and Sovereignty." *Cornell Law Quarterly* 13, no. 1 (December 1927): 8–30.

Cohn, Bernard S. *Colonialism and Its Forms of Knowledge: The British in India.* Princeton, NJ: Princeton University Press, 1996.

Cohn, Samuel K. *Epidemics: Hate and Compassion from the Plague of Athens to AIDS.* Oxford: Oxford University Press, 2018.

Cohn, Samuel K. "Pandemics: Waves of Disease, Waves of Hate from the Plague of Athens to A.I.D.S." *Historical Research* 85, no. 230 (2012): 535–55.

Coker, Donna. "Crime Control and Feminist Law Reform in Domestic Violence Law: A Critical Review." *Buffalo Criminal Law Review* 4, no. 2 (2001): 801–60.

Coll, Steve. "The Meaning of Donald Trump's Coronavirus Quackery." *New Yorker*, April 6, 2020. https://www.newyorker.com/magazine/2020/04/06/the-meaning-of-donald-trumps-coronavirus-quackery.

Collins, Damian C. A., and Robin A. Kearns. "Under Curfew and under Siege? Legal Geographies of Young People." *Geoforum* 32, no. 3 (August 2001): 389–403.

"Condition of the South—Recommitted to the Select Committee on That Portion of the President's Message Relating to the Condition of the South and Ordered to Be Printed." H.R. Rep. No. 261, 43rd Congress, 2nd session, February 23, 1875.

Cools, Arthur. "The Gift and the Skin: Derrida and Levinas on Language, Metaphor and Subjectivity." In *Heidegger, Levinas, Derrida: The Question of Difference*, edited by Lisa Foran and Rozemund Uljée, 31–43. New York: Springer, 2016.

Cooper, Trudi, and Terence Love. "A Youth Curfew: A Retrospective View of the Rise, Fall and Legacy of the Northbridge Policy." *Australian Journal of Social Issues* 52, no. 3 (September 2017): 204–21.

Cornell, Saul. "The Early American Origins of the Modern Gun Control Debate: The Right to Bear Arms, Firearms Regulations, and the Lessons of History Symposium—Gun Control: Old Problems, New Paradigms." *Stanford Law and Policy Review* 17, no. 3 (2006): 571–96.

Correia, David. *Police: A Field Guide*. La Vergne: Verso, 2018.

Corrigan, Lawrence T., and Albert J. Mills. "Men on Board: Actor-Network Theory, Feminism and Gendering the Past." *Management and Organizational History* 7, no. 3 (2012): 251–65.

Coto, Danica. "ACLU Files 1st Coronavirus Curfew Lawsuit in Puerto Rico." *Washington Post*, April 5, 2020. https://www.washingtonpost.com/world /the_americas/aclu-files-1st-coronavirus-curfew-lawsuit-in-puerto-rico /2020/04/05/70ea2c68-777a-11ea-a311-adb1344719a9_story.html.

Cottrol, Robert J., and Raymond T. Diamond. "Never Intended to Be Applied to the White Population: Firearms Regulation and Racial Disparity—The Redeemed South's Legacy to a National Jurisprudence." *Chicago-Kent Law Review* 70, no. 3 (April 1995): 1307–38.

Cottrol, Robert J., and Raymond T. Diamond. "The Second Amendment: Toward an Afro-Americanist Reconsideration." *Georgetown Law Journal* 80 (1991): 309–61.

Cover, Robert M. "The Bonds of Constitutional Interpretation: Of the Word, the Deed, and the Role." *Georgia Law Review* 20 (1986): 815.

Cover, Robert M. "*Nomos* and Narrative." *Harvard Law Review* 97, no. 1 (November 1983): 4–68.

Cover, Robert M. "Violence and the Word." *Yale Law Journal* 95, no. 8 (July 1986): 1601–29.

Crane, Michael J. "Controlling the Night: Perceptions of the Slave Patrol System in Mississippi." *Journal of Mississippi History* 61, no. 1 (Summer 1999): 119–36.

Crary, Jonathan. *24/7: Late Capitalism and the Ends of Sleep*. London: Verso, 2013.

Crenshaw, Kimberlé. "Mapping the Margins: Intersectionality, Identity Politics, and Violence against Women of Color." *Stanford Law Review* 43, no. 6 (July 1991): 1241–99.

Crenshaw, Kimberlé, Andrea Ritchie, Rachel Anspach, Rachel Gilmer, and Luke Harris. "Say Her Name: Resisting Police Brutality against Black

Women." New York: African American Policy Forum, 2015. https://ncvc
.dspacedirect.org/handle/20.500.11990/1926.

Cross, Donald. "The *Vigil* of Philosophy: Derrida on Anachrony." *Derrida Today* 8, no. 2 (2015): 175–92.

Crunk Feminist Collective. "I Saw the Sign but Did We Really Need a Sign? SlutWalk and Racism." Facebook, October 6, 2011. https://www
.facebook.com/notes/crunk-feminist-collective/i-saw-the-sign-but-did
-we-really-need-a-sign-slutwalk-and-racism/10150310214381750/.

Cruz, Katie, and Wendy Brown. "Feminism, Law, and Neoliberalism: An Interview and Discussion with Wendy Brown." *Feminist Legal Studies* 24, no. 1 (April 2016): 69–89.

Cuddihy, William, and B. Carmon Hardy. "A Man's House Was Not His Castle: Origins of the Fourth Amendment to the United States Constitution." *William and Mary Quarterly* 37, no. 3 (July 1980): 372–400.

Cunneen, Chris. "Changing the Neo-Colonial Impacts of Juvenile Justice." *Current Issues in Criminal Justice* 20, no. 1 (July 2008): 43–58.

D'Amato, Anthony. "The Speluncean Explorers—Further Proceedings." *Stanford Law Review* 32 (1980): 467–86.

D'Ambrosio, Michael, and Terry Wade. "There's Another Coronavirus Crisis Brewing: Fraud." *Washington Post*, April 14, 2020. https://
www.washingtonpost.com/opinions/2020/04/14/theres-another
-coronavirus-crisis-brewing-fraud/.

Darian-Smith, Eve. *Bridging Divides: The Channel Tunnel and English Legal Identity in the New Europe.* Berkeley: University of California Press, 1999.

Davies, Margaret. "Pluralism and Legal Philosophy." *Northern Ireland Legal Quarterly* 57, no. 4 (Winter 2006): 577–96.

Davies, Margaret. "The Proper: Discourses of Purity." *Law and Critique* 9, no. 2 (September 1998): 147–73.

Davis, Angela Y. *Blues Legacies and Black Feminism: Gertrude "Ma" Rainey, Bessie Smith, and Billie Holiday.* New York: Vintage, 1999.

Davis, Angela Y. *Women, Race, and Class.* New York: Vintage, 1983.

Davis, Kathleen. *Periodization and Sovereignty: How Ideas of Feudalism and Secularization Govern the Politics of Time.* Philadelphia: University of Pennsylvania Press, 2008.

Davis, Mike. *City of Quartz.* New York: Verso, 1990.

Davis, Philip, and Grace Kroll. *Street-Land: Its Little People and Big Problems.* Boston: Small, Maynard, 1915.

Davison, Walter Phillips. "Some Observations on Viet Cong Operations in the Villages." Santa Monica, CA: Rand Corporation, 1968.

Day, Kristen. "Strangers in the Night: Women's Fear of Sexual Assault on Urban College Campuses." *Journal of Architectural and Planning Research* 16, no. 4 (Winter 1999): 289–312.

Dayan, Colin. *The Law Is a White Dog: How Legal Rituals Make and Unmake Persons*. Princeton, NJ: Princeton University Press, 2011.

Deckha, Maneesha. "Toward a Postcolonial, Posthumanist Feminist Theory: Centralizing Race and Culture in Feminist Work on Nonhuman Animals." *Hypatia* 27, no. 3 (August 2012): 527–45.

Delattre, Simone. *Les douzes heures noires: La nuit à Paris au XIXe siècle*. Paris: Albin Michel, 2004.

Deleixhe, Martin. "Biopolitical Sovereignty and Borderlands." *Journal of Borderlands Studies* 34, no. 5 (March 2019): 649–64.

Deleuze, Gilles. *Difference and Repetition*. New York: Columbia University Press, 1994.

Deleuze, Gilles. "Postscript on Control Societies." In *Negotiations, 1972–1990*, 177–82. New York: Columbia University Press, 1995.

Deleuze, Gilles. "Society of Control." *L'autre Journal*, no. 1 (May 1990).

Deleuze, Gilles. "What Is a Dispositif?" In *Michel Foucault, Philosopher*, edited by Timothy J. Armstrong, 159–68. London: Harvester Wheatsheaf, 1992.

Deleuze, Gilles, and Félix Guattari. *Kafka: Toward a Minor Literature*. Translated by Dana Polan. Minneapolis: University of Minnesota Press, 1986.

Deleuze, Gilles, and Félix Guattari. *A Thousand Plateaus: Capitalism and Schizophrenia*. Translated by Brian Massumi. Minneapolis: University of Minnesota Press, 1987.

Delgadillo, Natalie. "The Rise of the 'Night Mayor' in America." Governing: The Future of States and Localities, August 9, 2017. http://www.governing.com/topics/urban/gov-night-mayor-economy-america.html.

Dement, William C. *The Promise of Sleep: A Pioneer in Sleep Medicine Explores the Vital Connection between Health, Happiness, and a Good Night's Sleep*. New York: Delacorte, 1999.

Denys, Catherine. "The Development of Police Forces in Urban Europe in the Eighteenth Century." *Journal of Urban History* 36, no. 3 (May 2010): 332–44.

Denys, Catherine. *Police et sécurité au XVIIIe siècle dans les villes de la frontière franco-belge*. Paris: Harmattan, 2002.

Derickson, Alan. *Dangerously Sleepy: Overworked Americans and the Cult of Manly Wakefulness*. Philadelphia: University of Pennsylvania Press, 2014.

Derrida, Jacques. *Aporias: Dying–Awaiting (One Another at) the "Limits of Truth" (Mourir–s'attendre aux "limites de la vérité")*. Stanford, CA: Stanford University Press, 1993.

Derrida, Jacques. "Autoimmunity: Real and Symbolic Suicides—A Dialogue with Jacques Derrida." Translated by Pascale-Anne Brault and Michael Naas. In *Philosophy in a Time of Terror: Dialogues with Jurgen Habermas and Jacques Derrida*, 85–136. Chicago: University of Chicago Press, 2003.

Derrida, Jacques. *The Beast and the Sovereign*. Vols. 1 and 2. Chicago: University of Chicago Press, 2009–11.

Derrida, Jacques. "Before the Law." In *Acts of Literature*, 181–220. New York: Routledge, 1992.

Derrida, Jacques. *The Death Penalty*. Translated by Elizabeth Rottenberg. Chicago: University of Chicago Press, 2013.

Derrida, Jacques. *Dissemination*. Translated by Barbara Johnson. Chicago: University of Chicago Press, 1981.

Derrida, Jacques. "Force of Law: The 'Mystical Foundation of Authority.'" Translated by Mary Quaintance. *Cardozo Law Review* 11, nos. 5–6 (July/August 1990): 919–1046.

Derrida, Jacques. *The Gift of Death*. Translated by David Wills. Chicago: University of Chicago Press, 1996.

Derrida, Jacques. *Margins of Philosophy*. Translated by Alan Bass. Chicago: University of Chicago Press, 1982.

Derrida, Jacques. "The Retrait of Metaphor." In *Psyche: Inventions of the Other*, Translated by Peggy Kamuf, 48–80. Stanford, CA: Stanford University Press, 2007.

Derrida, Jacques. *Rogues: Two Essays on Reason*. Translated by Pascale-Anne Brault and Michael Naas. Stanford, CA: Stanford University Press, 2005.

Derrida, Jacques. "Speech and Phenomena, and Other Essays on Husserl's Theory of Signs." In *Northwestern University Studies in Phenomenology and Existential Philosophy*. Translated by David B. Allison. Evanston, IL: Northwestern University Press, 1973.

Derrida, Jacques. "White Mythology: Metaphor in the Text of Philosophy." Translated by F. C. T. Moore. *New Literary History* 6, no. 1 (Autumn 1974): 5–74.

Derrida, Jacques. *Writing and Difference*. Translated by Alan Bass. Chicago: University of Chicago Press, 1978.

Derrida, Jacques, and Jean-Luc Marion. "On the Gift: A Discussion between Jacques Derrida and Jean-Luc Marion, Moderated by Richard Kearney." Translated by Alan Bass. In *God, the Gift, and Postmodernism*, edited by John D. Caputo and Michael J. Scanlon, 54–78. Bloomington: Indiana University Press, 1999.

Dickenson, Donna Lee. *Property, Women and Politics: Subjects or Objects?* Oxford: Polity, 1997.

Dickerson, Donna Lee, ed. *The Reconstruction Era: Primary Documents on Events from 1865 to 1877*. Westport, CT: Greenwood, 2003.

Dirlam, Jonathan, Trent Steidley, and David Jacobs. "A Link to the Past: Race, Lynchings, and the Passage of Stand-Your-Ground Laws." *Sociological Quarterly* 62, no. 4 (October 2021): 690–711.

Disalvo, Jacqueline. "Fear of Flying: Milton on the Boundaries between Witchcraft and Inspiration." *English Literary Renaissance* 18, no. 1 (January 1988): 114–37.

Dolan, Frances E. "Battered Women, Petty Traitors, and the Legacy of Coverture." *Feminist Studies* 29, no. 2 (Summer 2003): 249–77.

Douglass, Frederick. "Change of Opinion Announced." In *Frederick Douglass: Selected Speeches and Writings*, edited by Philip Sheldon Foner and Yuval Taylor, 173–74. Chicago: Lawrence Hill Books, 1999.

Douglass, Frederick. *The Life and Times of Frederick Douglass: From 1817–1882.* London: Christian Age Office, 1882.

Douglass, Frederick. "The Meaning of July Fourth for the Negro (1852)." In *Frederick Douglass: Selected Speeches and Writings*, edited by Philip Sheldon Foner and Yuval Taylor, 188–206. Chicago: Lawrence Hill Books, 1999.

Dowd, Marion, and Robert Hensey, eds. *The Archaeology of Darkness.* Oxford: Oxbow Books, 2016.

Dreyfus, Hubert L. *Being-in-the-World: A Commentary on Heidegger's Being and Time, Division I.* Cambridge, MA: MIT Press, 1991.

Du Bois, William Edward Burghardt. *Black Reconstruction in America: An Essay toward a History of the Part Which Black Folk Played in the Attempt to Reconstruct Democracy in America, 1860–1880.* London: Atheneum, 1969.

Duggan, Lisa, and Nan D. Hunter. *Sex Wars: Sexual Dissent and Political Culture.* New York: Routledge, 2006.

Duncan, Martha Grace. "In Slime and Darkness: The Metaphor of Filth in Criminal Justice." *Tulane Law Review* 68, no. 4 (1993): 725–802.

Duncan, Nancy. "Renegotiating Gender and Sexuality in Public and Private Spaces." In *BodySpace: Destabilising Geographies of Gender and Sexuality*, 127–44. London: Routledge, 1996.

Dunn, Nick. *Dark Matters: A Manifesto for the Nocturnal City.* Winchester: John Hunt, 2016.

Dunn, Nick, and Tim Edensor. *Rethinking Darkness: Cultures, Histories, Practices.* London: Routledge, 2020.

du Plessis, Gitte. "Hunting as Techniques of Governing: Chamayou's *Manhunts*, and Fassin's *Enforcing Order*." *Theory and Event* 18, no. 2 (2015). http://muse.jhu.edu/article/578642.

Durkheim, Émile. *Professional Ethics and Civic Morals.* Translated by Cornelia Brookfield. Glencoe, IL: Free Press, 1958.

Duval, Raymond. *Temps et vigilance.* Paris: Librairie Philosophique Vrin, 2000.

Dworkin, Andrea. *Letters from a War Zone.* Brooklyn, NY: Lawrence Hill Books, 1993.

Dworkin, Andrea. "The Night and Danger." In *Letters from a War Zone*, 13–18. Brooklyn, NY: Lawrence Hill Books, 1993.

Dworkin, Andrea. *Our Blood: Prophecies and Discourses on Sexual Politics.* New York: Perigee Books, 1981.

Dworkin, Andrea. "Pornography and Grief." In *Take Back the Night: Women on Pornography*, edited by Laura Lederer, 286–91. New York: William Morrow, 1980.

Dworkin, Andrea. *Scapegoat: The Jews, Israel, and Women's Liberation.* New York: Free Press, 2000.

Edensor, Tim. "The Gloomy City: Rethinking the Relationship between Light and Dark." *Urban Studies* 52, no. 3 (February 2015): 422–38.

Edensor, Tim. "Reconnecting with Darkness: Gloomy Landscapes, Lightless Places." *Social and Cultural Geography* 14, no. 4 (June 2013): 446–65.

Ekirch, A. Roger. *At Day's Close: Night in Times Past.* New York: W. W. Norton, 2005.

Ekirch, A. Roger. "Sleep We Have Lost: Pre-industrial Slumber in the British Isles." *American Historical Review* 106, no. 2 (April 2001): 343–86.

Elgot, Jessica. "Boris Johnson 'Had Birthday Party Indoors during Lockdown.'" *Guardian*, January 24, 2022. https://www.theguardian.com/politics /2022/jan/24/boris-johnson-had-birthday-party-indoors-during -lockdown.

Ellison, Louise. "Cities Aflame . . . Young Imaginations on Fire." *Young Children* 23, no. 5 (May 1968): 261–64.

Elster, Jon. *Sour Grapes: Studies in the Subversion of Rationality.* Cambridge: Cambridge University Press, 1983.

Engel, David M. "Law, Time and Community." *Law and Society Review* 21, no. 4 (1987): 605–37.

Engel, David M., and Jaruwan Engel. *Tort, Custom, and Karma: Globalization and Legal Consciousness in Thailand.* Palo Alto, CA: Stanford University Press, 2010.

Engel, David M., and Frank W. Munger. *Rights of Inclusion: Law and Identity in the Life Stories of Americans with Disabilities.* Chicago: University of Chicago Press, 2003.

Enright, Brian. "The Constitutional 'Terra Incognita' of Discretionary Concealed Carry Laws." *University of Illinois Law Review* 2015, no. 2 (2015): 909–58.

Eskridge, William N., Jr. "Case of the Speluncean Explorers: Twentieth-Century Statutory Interpretation in a Nutshell." *George Washington Law Review* 61, no. 6 (August 1993): 1731–53.

Esposito, Roberto. *Bios: Biopolitics and Philosophy.* Minneapolis: University of Minnesota Press, 2008.

Esposito, Roberto. *Communitas: The Origin and Destiny of Community.* Stanford, CA: Stanford University Press, 2010.

Esposito, Roberto. "Community, Immunity, Biopolitics." Translated by Zakiya Hanafi. *Angelaki: Journal of the Theoretical Humanities* 18, no. 3 (September 2013): 83–90.

Esposito, Roberto. "The *Dispositif* of the Person." *Law, Culture and the Humanities* 8, no. 1 (February 2012): 17–30.

Esposito, Roberto. *Immunitas: The Protection and Negation of Life.* Cambridge: Polity, 2011.

Esposito, Roberto. "Interview: Roberto Esposito." Interview by Timothy Campbell. *Diacritics* 36, no. 2 (2006): 49–56.

Esposito, Roberto. *Persons and Things: From the Body's Point of View.* Cambridge: Polity, 2015.

Esposito, Roberto. *Third Person: Politics of Life and Philosophy of the Impersonal.* Translated by Zakiya Hanafi. Cambridge: Polity, 2012.

Esposito, Roberto. *Two: The Machine of Political Theology and the Place of Thought.* New York: Fordham University Press, 2015.

Esposito, Roberto, and Jean-Luc Nancy. "Dialogue on the Philosophy to Come." Translated by Timothy Campbell. *Minnesota Review* 2010, no. 75 (Fall 2010): 71–88.

Esteva, Gustavo. "The Oaxaca Commune and Mexico's Coming Insurrection." *Antipode* 42, no. 4 (September 2010): 978–93.

Ewick, Patricia, and Susan Silbey. *The Common Place of Law: Stories from Everyday Life.* Chicago: University of Chicago Press, 1998.

Fabian, Johannes. *Time and the Other: How Anthropology Makes Its Object.* New York: Columbia University Press, 1983.

Fanning, Sara C. "The Roots of Early Black Nationalism: Northern African Americans' Invocations of Haiti in the Early Nineteenth Century." In *African Americans and the Haitian Revolution: Selected Essays and Historical Documents,* edited by Maurice Jackson and Jacqueline Bacon, 39–55. New York: Routledge, 2010.

Fanon, Frantz. *Black Skin, White Masks.* Translated by Charles Lam Markmann. London: Pluto, 2008.

Fanon, Frantz. *The Wretched of the Earth.* Translated by Richard Philcox. New York: Grove, 2004.

Farbman, Herschel. *The Other Night: Dreaming, Writing, and Restlessness in Twentieth-Century Literature.* New York: Fordham University Press, 2008.

Farr, James. "Locke, Natural Law, and New World Slavery." *Political Theory* 36, no. 4 (August 2008): 495–522.

Fassin, Didier. *Enforcing Order: An Ethnography of Urban Policing.* Translated by Rachel Gomme. Cambridge: Polity, 2013.

"Fatal Police Violence by Race and State in the USA, 1980–2019: A Network Meta-Regression." *Lancet* 398, no. 10307 (October 2021): P1239–P1255.

Feder, Ellen K. "The Dangerous Individual('s) Mother: Biopower, Family, and the Production of Race." *Hypatia* 22, no. 2 (May 2007): 60–78.

Federici, Silvia. *Caliban and the Witch.* 2nd, rev. ed. New York: Autonomedia, 2014.

Federici, Silvia. *Witches, Witch-Hunting, and Women.* Binghamton, NY: PM, 2018.

Feerick, John D. "The Problem of Presidential Inability—Will Congress Ever Solve It?" *Fordham Law Review* 83 (2010): 1097–160.

Feldman, Leonard C. *Citizens without Shelter: Homelessness, Democracy, and Political Exclusion.* Ithaca, NY: Cornell University Press, 2004.

Fellman, Michael. *In the Name of God and Country: Reconsidering Terrorism in American History.* New Haven, CT: Yale University Press, 2010.

Fentress, James, and Chris Wickham. *Social Memory.* Oxford: Blackwell, 1992.

Ferguson, Roderick A. *Aberrations in Black: Toward a Queer of Color Critique.* Minneapolis: University of Minnesota Press, 2004.

Fernflores, Rachel. "Merciful Interpretation." *Women's Studies* 38, no. 3 (May 2009): 253–72.

Fielding, Sarah. "In Quarantine with an Abuser: Surge in Domestic Violence Reports Linked to Coronavirus." *Guardian*, April 3, 2020. https://www.theguardian.com/us-news/2020/apr/03/coronavirus-quarantine-abuse -domestic-violence.

Fine, Sidney. "Mr. Justice Murphy and the Hirabayashi Case." *Pacific Historical Review* 33, no. 2 (May 1964): 195–209.

Fischel, Joseph J. *Screw Consent: A Better Politics of Sexual Justice.* Oakland: University of California Press, 2019.

Fish, Stanley. "The Law Wishes to Have a Formal Existence." In *There's No Such Thing as Free Speech: And It's a Good Thing, Too*, ch. 11, 144–79. Oxford: Oxford University Press, 1994.

Fitzgerald, Michael W. "Ex-Slaveholders and the Ku Klux Klan." In *After Slavery: Race, Labor, and Citizenship in the Reconstruction South*, edited by Bruce E. Baker and Brian Kelly, 143–58. Gainesville: University Press of Florida, 2013.

Fitzgerald, Michael W. "The Ku Klux Klan: Property Crime and the Plantation System in Reconstruction Alabama." *Agricultural History* 71, no. 2 (Spring 1997): 186–206.

Fitzpatrick, Peter. "Bare Sovereignty." In *Politics, Metaphysics, and Death: Essays on Giorgio Agamben's Homo Sacer*, edited by Andrew Norris, 49–73. Durham, NC: Duke University Press, 2005.

Fitzpatrick, Peter. *Modernism and the Grounds of Law.* Cambridge: Cambridge University Press, 2001.

Fitzpatrick, Peter. *The Mythology of Modern Law.* London: Routledge, 1992.

Fluri, Jennifer, and Lorraine Dowler. "Klanbake: Gender, Etiquette, and White Supremacy in America, 1913–30." *Historical Geography* 29 (2002): 139–53.

Flynn, Meagan. "'I Accept It': DOJ Lawyer Defends Herself over Viral Video about Providing Migrants with Soap, Toothbrushes." *Washington Post*, June 26, 2019. https://www.washingtonpost.com/nation/2019/06/26/i -accept-it-doj-lawyer-defends-herself-over-viral-video-about-providing -migrants-with-soap-toothbrushes/.

Foner, Eric. *A Short History of Reconstruction, 1863–1877*. New York: Harper and Row, 1990.

Fontanier, Pierre. *Des figures du discours autres que les tropes*. Paris: Maire-Nyon, 1827.

Forbes, Ella. "'By My Own Right Arm': Redemptive Violence and the 1851 Christiana, Pennsylvania Resistance." *Journal of Negro History* 83, no. 3 (Summer 1998): 159–67.

Forman, James. *Locking Up Our Own: Crime and Punishment in Black America*. New York: Farrar, Straus and Giroux, 2018.

Forsyth, Miranda. "The Regulation of Witchcraft and Sorcery Practices and Beliefs." *Annual Review of Law and Social Science* 12 (October 2016): 331–51.

Foucault, Michel. *Abnormal: Lectures at the College de France 1974–1975*. Translated by Graham Burchell. New York: Picador USA, 2004.

Foucault, Michel. *The Birth of Biopolitics: Lectures at the Collège de France, 1978–79*. Translated by Graham Burchell. New York: Palgrave Macmillan, 2008.

Foucault, Michel. "The Confession of the Flesh." Translated by Graham Burchell. In *Power/Knowledge: Selected Writings and Other Interviews, 1972–1977*, 194–228. New York: Pantheon, 1980.

Foucault, Michel. *Discipline and Punish: The Birth of the Prison*. Translated by Alan Sheridan. New York: Vintage, 1995.

Foucault, Michel. *Essential Works of Foucault: 1954–1984*. Vol. 2. New York: New Press, 1997.

Foucault, Michel. *History of Madness*. Translated by Jonathan Murphy and Jean Khalfa. Edited by Jean Khalfa. London: Routledge, 2006.

Foucault, Michel. *The History of Sexuality: An Introduction*. Translated by Robert Hurley. New York: Vintage, 1990.

Foucault, Michel. *Power*. Translated by Robert Hurley. New York: New Press, 2000.

Foucault, Michel. *Power/Knowledge: Selected Writings and Other Interviews, 1972–1977*. Translated by Colin Gordon and Leo Marshall. New York: Pantheon, 1980.

Foucault, Michel. *Security, Territory, Population: Lectures at the Collège de France, 1977–78*. Translated by Graham Burchell. New York: Palgrave Macmillan, 2007.

Foucault, Michel. *Society Must Be Defended: Lectures at the Collège de France, 1975–76*. Translated by Graham Burchell. New York: Saint Martin's, 2003.

Foucault, Michel. "Standing Vigil for the Day to Come." Translated by Elise Woodard and Robert Harvey. *Foucault Studies* no. 19 (June 2015): 217–23.

Foucault, Michel. "Truth and Juridical Forms." In *Power*, edited by James D. Faubion, translated by Robert Hurley, 1–89. New York: New Press, 2001.

Foucault, Michel, and Maurice Blanchot. *Maurice Blanchot: The Thought from Outside*. Translated by Brian Massumi. New York: Zone Books, 1989.

Foucault, Michel, Paul Rabinow, and Robert Hurley. *Ethics: Subjectivity and Truth*. New York: New Press, 1997.

France, Anatole. *Le lys rouge*. Paris: Ancienne Maison Michel Lévy Frères, 1894.

Frank, Jason. "The Living Image of the People." *Theory and Event* 18, no. 1 (2015). https://muse-jhu-edu/pub/1/article/566086.

Freedman, Estelle B. *Redefining Rape: Sexual Violence in the Era of Suffrage and Segregation*. Cambridge, MA: Harvard University Press, 2013.

Freeman, Elizabeth. *Time Binds: Queer Temporalities, Queer Histories*. Durham, NC: Duke University Press, 2010.

Freud, Sigmund. *The Interpretation of Dreams*. Translated by James Strachey. New York: Basic Books, 2010.

Freud, Sigmund. "Some Character-Types Met with in Psycho-Analytic Work." In *Writings on Art and Literature*, 151–73. Translated by Neil Hertz. Stanford, CA: Stanford University Press, 1997.

Freud, Sigmund. *Three Essays on the Theory of Sexuality*. Translated by James Strachey. New York: Basic Books, 1975.

Freud, Sigmund. *Totem and Taboo: Some Points of Agreement between the Mental Lives of Savages and Neurotics*. Translated by James Strachey. New York: Norton, 1952.

Fry, Gladys-Marie. *Night Riders in Black Folk History*. Knoxville: University of Tennessee Press, 1975.

Fuller, Lon L. "The Case of the Speluncean Explorers." *Harvard Law Review* 62, no. 4 (February 1949): 616–45.

Fuller, Lon L. *The Morality of Law*. Storrs Lectures on Jurisprudence 1963. New Haven, CT: Yale University Press, 1964.

Fuller, Lon L. "Positivism and Fidelity to Law: A Reply to Professor Hart." *Harvard Law Review* 71, no. 4 (February 1958): 630–72.

Galanter, Marc. "Legal Torpor: Why So Little Has Happened in India after the Bhopal Tragedy Symposium: The Bhopal Tragedy: Social and Legal Issues." *Texas International Law Journal* 20, no. 2 (Spring 1985): 273–94.

Galanter, Marc. "The Radiating Effects of Courts." In *Empirical Theories about Courts*, edited by Keith Boyum and Lynn Mather, 117–42. New York: Longman, 1983.

Galanter, Marc. "Why the 'Haves' Come Out Ahead: Speculations on the Limits of Legal Change." *Law and Society Review* 9, no. 1 (Autumn 1974): 95–160.

Galinier, Jacques, Aurore Monod Becquelin, Guy Bordin, Laurent Fontaine, Francine Fourmaux, Juliette Roullet Ponce, Piero Salzarulo, Philippe Simonnot, Michèle Therrien, and Iole Zilli. "Anthropology of the Night: Cross-Disciplinary Investigations." *Current Anthropology* 51, no. 6 (December 2010): 819–47.

Gallan, Ben. "Becoming Crepuscular: Rethinking the Human Relationship to Day and Night." PhD diss., University of Wollongong, 2014. https://ro.uow.edu.au/theses/4187.

Gallan, Ben. "Night Lives: Heterotopia, Youth Transitions and Cultural Infrastructure in the Urban Night." *Urban Studies* 52, no. 3 (February 2015): 555–70.

Gallan, Ben, and Chris Gibson. "New Dawn or New Dusk? Beyond the Binary of Day and Night." *Environment and Planning A* 43, no. 11 (November 2011): 2509–15.

Garland, David. *The Culture of Control: Crime and Social Order in Contemporary Society*. Chicago: University of Chicago Press, 2002.

Gasché, Rodolphe. "Joining the Text: From Heidegger to Derrida." In *The Yale Critics: Deconstruction in America*, edited by Jonathan Arac, Wlad Godzich, and Wallace Martin, 156–75. Minneapolis: University of Minnesota Press, 1983.

Gasché, Rodolphe. *The Tain of the Mirror: Derrida and the Philosophy of Reflection*. Cambridge, MA: Harvard University Press, 1986.

Genette, Gérard. "Le jour, la nuit." *Languages* 3, no. 12 (1968): 28–42.

Genovese, Eugene D. *From Rebellion to Revolution: Afro-American Slave Revolts in the Making of the Modern World*. Baton Rouge: Louisiana State University Press, 1992.

Genovese, Eugene D. *Roll, Jordan, Roll: The World the Slaves Made*. New York: Pantheon Books, 1974.

Geschiere, Peter. "Witchcraft and the Limits of the Law." In *Law and Disorder in the Postcolony*, edited by Jean Comaroff and John Comaroff, 219–46. Chicago: University of Chicago Press, 2006.

Ghettas, Lakhdar. "What Next for Egypt?" Situation analysis, International Affairs, Diplomacy and Strategy LSE, February 2011. http://eprints.lse.ac.uk/43543/1/SA009.pdf.

Gilson, Erinn C. *The Ethics of Vulnerability: A Feminist Analysis of Social Life and Practice*. New York: Routledge, 2014.

Ginzburg, Carlo. *Ecstasies: Deciphering the Witches' Sabbath*. New York: Pantheon Books, 1991.

Ginzburg, Carlo. *The Night Battles: Witchcraft and Agrarian Cults in the Sixteenth and Seventeenth Centuries*. Baltimore: Johns Hopkins University Press, 1983.

Ginzburg, Carlo, and Bruce Lincoln. *Old Thiess, a Livonian Werewolf: A Classic Case in Comparative Perspective*. Chicago: University of Chicago Press, 2020.

Glasbeek, Amanda, Mariful Alam, and Katrin Roots. "Seeing and Not-Seeing: Race and Body-Worn Cameras in Canada." *Surveillance and Society* 18, no. 3 (September 2020): 328–42.

Goff, Phillip Atiba, Matthew Christian Jackson, Brooke Allison Lewis Di Leone, Carmen Marie Culotta, and Natalie Ann DiTomasso. "The Essence of Innocence: Consequences of Dehumanizing Black Children." *Journal of Personality and Social Psychology* 106, no. 4 (2014): 526–45.

Goldberg-Hiller, Jonathan. "'Entitled to Be Hostile': Narrating the Political Economy of Civil Rights." *Social and Legal Studies* 7, no. 4 (1998): 517–38.

Goldberg-Hiller, Jonathan. "Prison and Place: Carceral Reform and Indigenous Dispossession in Hawai'i." *Darkmatter* 14, no. 14 (2016).

Golder, Ben. *Foucault and the Politics of Rights.* Stanford, CA: Stanford University Press, 2015.

Goldstein, Jared A. "The Klan's Constitution." *Alabama Civil Rights and Civil Liberties Law Review* 9, no. 2 (2018): 285–378.

Goldstein, Leslie Friedman. "The Second Amendment, the Slaughter-House Cases (1873), and *United States v. Cruikshank* (1876)." *Albany Government Law Review* 1, no. 365 (2008): 365–418.

Gonlin, Nancy, and April Nowell, eds. *Archaeology of the Night: Life after Dark in the Ancient World.* Boulder: University Press of Colorado, 2017.

Gonzales, Alberto R., and Donald Q. Cochran. "Police-Worn Body Cameras: An Antidote to the Ferguson Effect." *Missouri Law Review* 82, no. 2 (2017): 299–338.

Goodman, Kevis. "Introduction." In *The Weight of All Flesh: On the Subject-Matter of Political Economy*, by Eric Santner, edited by Kevin Goodman, 1–29. Oxford: Oxford University Press, 2015.

Goodrich, Peter. "The Judge's Two Bodies: The Case of Daniel Paul Schreber." *Law and Critique* 26, no. 2 (July 2015): 117–33.

Goodrich, Peter. *Languages of Law: From Logics of Memory to Nomadic Masks.* Littleton, CO: Fred B. Rothman, 1990.

Goodrich, Peter. "Law and Language: An Historical and Critical Introduction." *Journal of Law and Society* 11, no. 2 (Summer 1984): 173–206.

Goodrich, Peter. *Oedipus Lex: Psychoanalysis, History, Law.* Berkeley: University of California Press, 1995.

Goodrich, Peter. "The Theatre of Emblems: On the Optical Apparatus and the Investiture of Persons." *Law, Culture and the Humanities* 8, no. 1 (February 2012): 47–67.

Gordon, Linda. *The Second Coming of the KKK: The Ku Klux Klan of the 1920s and the American Political Tradition.* New York: Liveright, 2017.

Gorup, Michael. "The Strange Fruit of the Tree of Liberty: Lynch Law and Popular Sovereignty in the United States." *Perspectives on Politics* 18, no. 3 (September 2020): 819–34.

Gourevitch, Alexander. *From Slavery to the Cooperative Commonwealth: Labor and Republican Liberty in the Nineteenth Century.* New York: Cambridge University Press, 2015.

Grabham, Emily. *Intersectionality and Beyond: Law, Power and the Politics of Location.* Abingdon: Routledge-Cavendish, 2008.

Greely, Henry T. "A Footnote to 'Penumbra' in *Griswold v. Connecticut.*" *Constitutional Commentary* 6 (1989): 251–66.

Greenhouse, Carol J. "Just in Time: Temporality and the Cultural Legitimation of Law." *Yale Law Journal* 98, no. 8 (June 1989): 1631–51.

Griffiths, John. "What Is Legal Pluralism?" *Journal of Legal Pluralism and Unofficial Law* 18, no. 24 (1986): 1–55.

Grogger, Jeffrey, and Greg Ridgeway. "Testing for Racial Profiling in Traffic Stops from behind a Veil of Darkness." *Journal of the American Statistical Association* 101, no. 475 (September 2006): 878–87.

Grossman, Elyse R., David H. Jernigan, and Nancy A. Miller. "Do Juvenile Curfew Laws Reduce Underage Drinking?" *Journal of Studies on Alcohol and Drugs* 77, no. 4 (July 2016): 589–95.

Grovogui, Siba N'Zatioula. *Sovereigns, Quasi Sovereigns, and Africans: Race and Self-Determination in International Law.* Minneapolis: University of Minnesota Press, 1996.

Gruber, Aya. "Consent Confusion." *Cardozo Law Review* 38, no. 2 (December 2016): 415–58.

Gruber, Reut. "Short Sleep Duration Is Associated with Teacher-Reported Inattention and Cognitive Problems in Healthy School-Aged Children." *Nature and Science of Sleep* 4 (March 2012): 33–40.

Guenebeaud, Camille, Aurore Le Mat, and Sidohie Verhaeghe. "Take Back the Night! Une exposition pour combattre les violences sexistes dans l'espace public." Métropolitiques, October 11, 2018. https://www.metropolitiques .eu/Take-back-the-night-Une-exposition-pour-combattre-les-violences -sexistes-dans-l.html.

Guenther, Lisa. *Solitary Confinement: Social Death and Its Afterlives.* Minneapolis: University of Minnesota Press, 2013.

Guichoux, Arthur. "Nuit debout et les 'mouvements des places': Désenchantement et ensauvagement de la démocratie." *Les Temps Modernes*, no. 5 (2016): 30–60.

Gulasekaram, Pratheepan. "'The People' of the Second Amendment: Citizenship and the Right to Bear Arms." *NYU Law Review* 85, no. 5 (November 2010): 1521–80.

Habermas, Jürgen. *The Structural Transformation of the Public Sphere: An Inquiry into a Category of Bourgeois Society.* Cambridge, MA: MIT Press, 1989.

Hall, Kim F. *Things of Darkness: Economies of Race and Gender in Early Modern England.* Ithaca, NY: Cornell University Press, 2018.

Hallenbeck, Sarah. "Toward a Posthuman Perspective: Feminist Rhetorical Methodologies and Everyday Practices." *Advances in the History of Rhetoric* 15, no. 1 (January 2012): 9–27.

Halley, Janet E. "'Like Race' Arguments." In *What's Left of Theory? New Work on the Politics of Literary Theory*, edited by Judith Butler, John Guillory, and Kendall Thomas, 40–74. New York: Routledge, 2000.

Halley, Janet E. *Split Decisions: How and Why to Take a Break from Feminism.* Princeton, NJ: Princeton University Press, 2008.

Hamilton, Alexander, John Jay, James Madison, George W. Carey, and James McClellan, eds. *The Federalist.* Indianapolis: Liberty Fund, 2001.

Hammerschlag, Sarah. *The Figural Jew: Politics and Identity in Postwar French Thought.* Chicago: University of Chicago Press, 2010.

Handler, Jerome S. "Slave Revolts and Conspiracies in Seventeenth-Century Barbados." *Nieuwe West-Indische Gids/New West Indian Guide* 56, nos. 1–2 (1982): 5–42.

Hanieh, Adam. "The Politics of Curfew in the Occupied Territories." In *The Struggle for Sovereignty: Palestine and Israel, 1993–2005*, edited by Joel Beinin and Rebecca L. Stein, 324–37. Stanford, CA: Stanford University Press, 2006.

Haraway, Donna Jeanne. "The Biopolitics of Postmodern Bodies: Constitutions of Self in Immune System Discourse." In *Simians, Cyborgs, and Women: The Reinvention of Nature*, 203–30. New York: Routledge, 1991.

Haraway, Donna Jeanne. *When Species Meet.* Minneapolis: University of Minnesota Press, 2008.

Haraway, Donna Jeanne, and Cary Wolfe. *Manifestly Haraway.* Minneapolis: University of Minnesota Press, 2016.

Hardt, Michael, and Antonio Negri. *Multitude: War and Democracy in the Age of Empire.* New York: Penguin, 2004.

Hardy, Jack. "Thief Who Stole Masks from Hospital Jailed for 12 Weeks." *Telegraph*, April 7, 2020. https://www.telegraph.co.uk/news/2020/04/07/thief-stole-masks-hospital-jailed-12-weeks/.

Harford, Barbara, and Sarah Hopkins, eds. *Greenham Common: Women at the Wire.* London: Women's Press, 1984.

Harris, Angela. "Race and Essentialism in Feminist Legal Theory." *Stanford Law Review* 42, no. 3 (February 1990): 581–616.

Harris, Cheryl. "Whiteness as Property." *Harvard Law Review* 106, no. 8 (June 1993): 1707–91.

Harrison, Bernard. "'White Mythology' Revisited: Derrida and His Critics on Reason and Rhetoric." *Critical Inquiry* 25, no. 3 (1999): 505–34.

Harrison, Conor. "Extending the 'White Way': Municipal Streetlighting and Race, 1900–1930." *Social and Cultural Geography* 16, no. 8 (December 2015): 950–73.

Hart, Herbert Lionel Adolphus. *The Concept of Law.* Oxford: Clarendon, 1961.

Hart, Herbert Lionel Adolphus. "Positivism and the Separation of Law and Morals." *Harvard Law Review* (1958): 593–629.

Hartal, Gilly. "Fragile Subjectivities: Constructing Queer Safe Spaces." *Social and Cultural Geography* 19, no. 8 (2018): 1053–72.

Hartford, Clare. "Curfew Laws: White by Night." *South African Journal on Human Rights* 1, pt. 2 (August 1985): 173–74.

Hartman, Geoffrey H. *Saving the Text: Literature/Derrida/Philosophy*. Baltimore: Johns Hopkins University Press, 1982.

Hartman, Saidiya V. *Lose Your Mother: A Journey along the Atlantic Slave Route*. New York: Farrar, Straus and Giroux, 2008.

Hartman, Saidiya V. *Scenes of Subjection: Terror, Slavery, and Self-Making in Nineteenth-Century America*. New York: Oxford University Press, 1997.

Hartman, Saidiya V. "Seduction and the Ruses of Power." *Callaloo* 19, no. 2 (Spring 1996): 537–60.

Haverkamp, Anselm. "Rhetoric, Law, and the Poetics of Memory." *Cardozo Law Review* 13, no. 5 (March 1992): 1639–54.

Hawaii Tribune-Herald. "Mauna Kea Rules Nullified." October 11, 2015. http://hawaiitribune-herald.com/news/local-news/mauna-kea-rules -nullified.

Hawkins, Homer, and Richard Thomas. "White Policing of Black Populations: A History of Race and Social Control in America." In *Out of Order? Policing Black People*, edited by Ellis Cashmore and Eugene McLaughlin, 65–86. London: Routledge, 2013.

Hay, Douglas. "Property, Authority and the Criminal Law." In *Albion's Fatal Tree: Crime and Society in Eighteenth-Century England*, 17–63. New York: Pantheon, 1976.

Hayes-Jonkers, Charmaine, Adele Wright, Lisa Golding, and Cliff Singer. "Hidden Racism and Systematic Racism: Is It Contributing to the Decreased Health and Well-Being of Aboriginal Homeless Persons in the Inner City of Cairns?" In *Proceedings of the Third International Conference on Racisms in the New World Order: Realities of Culture, Colour and Identity*, edited by Narayan Gopalkrishnan and Hurriyet Babacan, 117–28. Cairns: Cairns Institute, 2013. http://researchonline.jcu.edu.au/30073/.

Haygood, Wil. "The Police No Longer Need the Cover of Darkness to Kill Innocent Black People." *Washington Post*, June 3, 2020. https://www .washingtonpost.com/opinions/2020/06/03/police-no-longer-need -cover-darkness-kill-innocent-black-people/.

Heen, Mary L. "From Coverture to Contract: Engendering Insurance on Lives." *Yale Journal of Law and Feminism* 23, no. 2 (2011): 335–84.

Hegel, Georg Wilhelm Friedrich. *Elements of the Philosophy of Right*. Edited by Allen W. Wood. Translated by Hugh Barr Nisbet. Cambridge: Cambridge University Press, 1991.

Heidegger, Martin. *Being and Time*. Albany: State University of New York Press, 2010.

Heidegger, Martin. *Heraclitus: The Inception of Occidental Thinking and Logic: Heraclitus's Doctrine of the Logos*. Translated by Julia Goesser Assaiante and S. Montgomery Ewegen. New York: Bloomsbury Academic, 2018.

Heidegger, Martin. *On Time and Being.* New York: Harper and Row, 1972.

Heil, Katherine A. "The Fuzz(y) Lines of Consent: Police Sexual Misconduct with Detainees Criminal Law." *South Carolina Law Review* 70, no. 4 (Summer 2019): 941–76.

Heinzelman, Susan Sage. "Women's Petty Treason: Feminism, Narrative, and the Law." *Journal of Narrative Technique* 20, no. 2 (Spring 1990): 89–106.

Helms, Mary W. "Before the Dawn: Monks and the Night in Late Antiquity and Early Medieval Europe." *Anthropos* 99, no. 1 (2004): 177–91.

Hening, William Walter, ed. *Hening's Statutes at Large.* Vol. 2. New York: R. and W. and G. Bartow, 1823.

Henly, Burr. "Penumbra: The Roots of a Legal Metaphor." *Hastings Constitutional Law Quarterly* 15, no. 1 (Fall 1987): 81–100.

Henshall, Kenneth. *A History of Japan: From Stone Age to Superpower.* New York: Springer, 2012.

Herman, Daniel Justin. "Hunting and American Identity: The Rise, Fall, Rise and Fall of an American Pastime." *International Journal of the History of Sport* 31, nos. 1–2 (January 2014): 55–71.

Hershey, O. F. "Lynch Law." *Green Bag* 12, no. 9 (1900): 466–69.

Herzogenrath, Bernd. *An American Body-Politic: A Deleuzian Approach.* Hanover, NH: Dartmouth College Press, published by University Press of New England, 2010.

Heyer, Katharina. *Rights Enabled: The Disability Revolution, from the US, to Germany and Japan, to the United Nations.* Ann Arbor: University of Michigan Press, 2015.

Heyes, Cressida J. *Anaesthetics of Existence: Essays on Experience at the Edge.* Durham, NC: Duke University Press, 2020.

Heyes, Cressida J. *Line Drawings: Defining Women through Feminist Practice.* Ithaca, NY: Cornell University Press, 2000.

Hibbitts, Bernard. "Making Sense of Metaphors: Visuality, Aurality, and the Reconfiguration of American Legal Discourse." *Cardozo Law Review* 16, no. 2 (December 1994): 229–356.

Hildreth, Richard. *Despotism in America: An Inquiry into the Nature, Results, and Legal Basis on the Slave-Holding System in the United States.* Boston: John P. Jewett, 1854.

Hill, Annie. "SlutWalk as Perifeminist Response to Rape Logic: The Politics of Reclaiming a Name." *Communication and Critical/Cultural Studies* 13, no. 1 (2016): 23–39.

Hill Collins, Patricia. *Black Feminist Thought: Knowledge, Consciousness, and the Politics of Empowerment.* Rev. 10th anniv. ed. New York: Routledge, 2000.

Hill Collins, Patricia. *Black Sexual Politics: African Americans, Gender, and the New Racism.* New York: Routledge, 2004.

Hill Collins, Patricia, and Sirma Bilge. *Intersectionality.* Cambridge: Polity, 2016.

"Hillary Clinton Ad—3 AM White House Ringing Phone." YouTube, uploaded May 15, 2008. https://www.youtube.com/watch?v=7yr7odFUARg.

Hinsliff, Gaby. "The Vigils Were Not Just about Sarah Everard, but about the Whole Justice System." *Guardian*, March 15, 2021. http://www.theguardian.com/commentisfree/2021/mar/15/vigils-sarah-everard-women.

Hirabayashi, Gordon K. *A Principled Stand: The Story of Hirabayashi v. United States.* Seattle: University of Washington Press, 2013.

Hobbes, Thomas. *Leviathan.* Edited by G. A. J. Rogers and Karl Schuhmann. London: Continuum, 2005.

Hobbs, Dick. *Bouncers: Violence and Governance in the Night-Time Economy.* Oxford: Oxford University Press, 2003.

Hobsbawm, Eric. *Bandits.* London: Weidenfeld & Nicolson, 2000.

Hodes, Martha. *White Women, Black Men: Illicit Sex in the Nineteenth-Century South.* New Haven, CT: Yale University Press, 1999.

Hogue, James K. "The 1873 Battle of Colfax: Paramilitarism and Counterrevolution in Louisiana." Unpublished paper, 2006.

Holmes, Oliver Wendell. "The Path of the Law." *Harvard Law Review* 10, no. 8 (March 1897): 457–78.

Honig, Bonnie. "Charged: Debt, Power, and the Politics of the Flesh in Shakespeare's *Merchant*, Melville's *Moby-Dick*, and Eric Santner's *The Weight of All Flesh*." In *The Weight of All Flesh: On the Subject-Matter of Political Economy*, by Eric Santner, edited by Kevis Goodman, 1–182. Oxford: Oxford University Press, 2015.

Honig, Bonnie. *Emergency Politics: Paradox, Law, Democracy.* Princeton, NJ: Princeton University Press, 2009.

hooks, bell. *Black Looks: Race and Representation.* New York: Routledge, 2015.

hooks, bell. *Feminist Theory: From Margin to Center.* 3rd ed. New York: Routledge, 2014.

Horwitz, Morton J. "Republicanism and Liberalism in American Constitutional Thought." *William and Mary Law Review* 29, no. 1 (Fall 1987): 57–74.

Hubbard, Phil, and Rachela Colosi. "Taking Back the Night? Gender and the Contestation of Sexual Entertainment in England and Wales." *Urban Studies* 52, no. 3 (February 2015): 589–605.

Hughes, Langston. *The Collected Poems of Langston Hughes*, edited by Arnold Rampersad and David Roessel. New York: Vintage Books, 1995.

Husserl, Edmund. *The Phenomenology of Internal Time-Consciousness.* Bloomington: Indiana University Press, 1964.

Hutton, Ronald. "The Wild Hunt and the Witches' Sabbath." *Folklore* 125, no. 2 (August 2014): 161–78.

Ignatiev, Noel. *How the Irish Became White.* New York: Routledge, 1995.

Itkonen, Esa. *Analogy as Structure and Process: Approaches in Linguistics, Cognitive Psychology, and Philosophy of Science.* Amsterdam: John Benjamins, 2005.

Jackson, Maurice, and Jacqueline Bacon, eds. *African Americans and the Haitian Revolution: Selected Essays and Historical Documents*. New York: Routledge, 2010.

Jackson, Richard A. "The Sleeping King." *Bibliothèque d'Humanisme et Renaissance* 31, no. 3 (1969): 525–51.

Jaleel, Rana M. *The Work of Rape*. Durham, NC: Duke University Press, 2021.

James, C. L. R. *The Black Jacobins: Toussaint L'Ouverture and the San Domingo Revolution*. 2nd ed. New York: Vintage, 1989.

James, William. "The One and the Many." In *Some Problems of Philosophy: A Beginning of an Introduction to Philosophy*, 113–34. London: Longmans, Green, 1911.

Jay, Martin. *Downcast Eyes: The Denigration of Vision in Twentieth-Century French Thought*. Berkeley: University of California Press, 1993.

Jefferson, Thomas. *Notes on the State of Virginia*. Boston: Lilly and Wait, 1832.

Johnson, David A. "Vigilance and the Law: The Moral Authority of Popular Justice in the Far West." *American Quarterly* 33, no. 5 (Winter 1981): 558–86.

Johnson, David T., and Franklin E. Zimring. *The Next Frontier: National Development, Political Change, and the Death Penalty in Asia*. Oxford: Oxford University Press, 2009.

Johnson, Dayna A., Devin L. Brown, Lewis B. Morgenstern, William J. Meurer, and Lynda D. Lisabeth. "The Association of Neighborhood Characteristics with Sleep Duration and Daytime Sleepiness." *Sleep Health* 1, no. 3 (September 2015): 148–55.

Johnson, Manie White. "The Colfax Riot of April, 1873." *Louisiana Historical Quarterly* 13 (July 1930): 391–427.

Johnson, Nicholas J. "Firearms Policy and the Black Community: An Assessment of the Modern Orthodoxy." *Connecticut Law Review* 45, no. 5 (July 2013): 1491–1604.

Johnson, Nicholas J. *Negroes and the Gun: The Black Tradition of Arms*. Amherst, NY: Prometheus Books, 2014.

Johnson, Nicholas J., David B. Kopel, George A. Mocsary, and Michael P. O'Shea. *Firearms Law and the Second Amendment: Regulation, Rights, and Policy*. New York: Wolters Kluwer, 2017.

Johnson, Noel D., and Mark Koyama. "Taxes, Lawyers, and the Decline of Witch Trials in France." *Journal of Law and Economics* 57, no. 1 (February 2014): 77–112.

Johnson, Sarah Lindstrom, Barry S. Solomon, Wendy C. Shields, Eileen M. McDonald, Lara B. McKenzie, and Andrea C. Gielen. "Neighborhood Violence and Its Association with Mothers' Health: Assessing the Relative Importance of Perceived Safety and Exposure to Violence." *Journal of Urban Health* 86, no. 4 (July 2009): 538–50.

Johnston, Les. "What Is Vigilantism?" *British Journal of Criminology* 36, no. 2 (Spring 1996): 220–36.

Johnston, Wm. F. "Fugitive Slave Riot in Lancaster Co., Pa." *New York Times*, September 18, 1851.

Jones, Christopher B., Jillian Dorrian, and Shanthakumar M. W. Rajaratnam. "Fatigue and the Criminal Law." *Industrial Health* 43, no. 1 (January 2005): 63–70.

Jones, Jeffrey S., Barbara N. Wynn, Boyd Kroeze, Chris Dunnuck, and Linda Rossman. "Comparison of Sexual Assaults by Strangers versus Known Assailants in a Community-Based Population." *American Journal of Emergency Medicine* 22, no. 6 (October 2004): 454–59.

Justice Kozinski, Justice Sunstein, Justice West, Justice Easterbrook, and Stupidest Housemaid. "The Case of the Speluncean Explorers: Revisited." *Harvard Law Review* 112, no. 8 (June 1999): 1876–923.

Kafka, Franz. "The Judgment," "The Metamorphosis." In *Franz Kafka: The Complete Stories*, 101–13 and 114–64. New York: Schocken Books, 1971.

Kahan, Dan M. "Curfews Free Juveniles." *Washington Post*, November 14, 1996. https://www.washingtonpost.com/archive/opinions/1996/11/14/curfews-free-juveniles/9920d059-7c8e-498a-ad09-58e05bdb04cd/.

Kamakau, Samuel Manaiakalani. *Ruling Chiefs of Hawaii.* Rev. ed. Honolulu, HI: Kamehameha Schools Press, 1992.

Kamakau, Samuel Manaiakalani. *Ka Poʻe Kahiko = The People of Old.* Honolulu: Bishop Museum Press, 1992.

Kameʻeleihiwa, Lilikalā. *Native Land and Foreign Desires: How Shall We Live in Harmony? (Ko Hawaiʻi ʻĀina a Me Nā Koi Puʻumake a Ka Poʻe Haole: Pehea Lā E Pono Ai?).* Honolulu, HI: Bishop Museum Press, 1992.

Kameʻeleihiwa, Lilikalā. "Nā Wāhine Kapu: Divine Hawaiian Women." In *Women's Rights and Human Rights: International Historical Perspectives*, edited by Patricia Grimshaw, Katie Holmes, and Marilyn Lake, 71–87. Basingstoke, UK: Palgrave, 2001.

Kamir, Orit. "Honor and Dignity in the Film *Unforgiven*: Implications for Sociolegal Theory." *Law and Society Review* 40, no. 1 (March 2006): 193–234.

Kant, Immanuel. "What Is Enlightenment?" In *The Enlightenment: A Comprehensive Anthology*, edited by Peter Gay, 383–89. New York: Simon and Schuster, 1973.

Kantorowicz, Ernst Hartwig. *The King's Two Bodies: A Study in Mediaeval Political Theology.* Princeton, NJ: Princeton University Press, 1957.

Kantorowicz, Ernst Hartwig. "Oriens Augusti. Lever du roi." *Dumbarton Oaks Papers* 17 (January 1963): 117–77.

Kaplan, Margo. "Rape beyond Crime." *Duke Law Journal* 66, no. 5 (February 2017): 1045–112.

Kapur, Ratna. "Pink Chaddis and SlutWalk Couture: The Postcolonial Politics of Feminism Lite." *Feminist Legal Studies* 20, no. 1 (April 2012): 1–20.

Karandinos, George, Laurie Kain Hart, Fernando Montero Castrillo, and Philippe Bourgois. "The Moral Economy of Violence in the US Inner City." *Current Anthropology* 55, no. 1 (February 2014): 1–22.

Katyal, Neal Kumar. "Architecture as Crime Control." *Yale Law Journal* 111, no. 5 (March 2002): 1039–139.

Katz, Charles M., David E. Choate, Justin R. Ready, and Lidia Nuño. "Evaluating the Impact of Officer Worn Body Cameras in the Phoenix Police Department." Phoenix, AZ: Center for Violence Prevention and Community Safety, Arizona State University, Evaluating the Impact, 2014.

Katz, Jonathan. *Resistance at Christiana: The Fugitive Slave Rebellion, Christiana, Pennsylvania, September 11, 1851: A Documentary Account.* New York: Crowell, 1974.

Kauanui, J. Kēhaulani. *Hawaiian Blood: Colonialism and the Politics of Sovereignty and Indigeneity.* Durham, NC: Duke University Press, 2008.

Kautzer, Chad. "The Self-Defeating Notion of the Sovereign Subject in US Gun Culture." *Lateral* 9, no. 1 (Spring 2020). https://csalateral.org/forum /gun-culture/self-defeating-notion-sovereign-subject-kautzer/.

Keith, LeeAnna. *The Colfax Massacre: The Untold Story of Black Power, White Terror, and the Death of Reconstruction.* Oxford: Oxford University Press, 2008.

Kelley, Robin D.G. *Freedom Dreams: The Black Radical Imagination.* Boston: Beacon, 2002.

Kellogg, Joshua. "District Attorneys Rule Shooting of Frankie Anchondo by Farmington Officer Justified." *Daily Times*, October 5, 2019. https:// www.daily-times.com/story/news/local/farmington/2019/10/05 /das-rule-shooting-frankie-anchondo-farmington-police-justified /3867922002/.

Khanna, Ranjana. *Dark Continents: Psychoanalysis and Colonialism.* Durham, NC: Duke University Press, 2003.

Khanna, Ranjana. "On the Right to Sleep, Perchance to Dream." In *A Concise Companion to Psychoanalysis, Literature, and Culture,* edited by Laura Marcus and Ankhi Mukherjee, 351–65. Chichester, UK: John Wiley and Sons, 2014.

Kierkegaard, Søren. *Gospel of Sufferings.* London: J. Clarke, 1955.

Kim, Mimi E. "The Carceral Creep: Gender-Based Violence, Race, and the Expansion of the Punitive State, 1973–1983." *Social Problems* 67, no. 2 (May 2020): 251–69.

King, Martin Luther, Jr. 1967. "Where Do We Go from Here?" Transcript of speech delivered at 11th Annual Student Christian Leadership Congress. Atlanta, Georgia. August 16, 1967. https://kinginstitute.stanford.edu/ where-do-we-go-here.

Kiplagat, Sam. "Court Declines to Declare Curfew Illegal, Exempts LSK and Ipoa." *Nation,* May 13, 2020. https://www.nation.co.ke/news/Court -declines-to-declare-curfew-illegal/1056-5526296-auuw9xz/index .html.

Kipling, Rudyard. *The Second Jungle Book.* New York: The Century Company, 1895.

Kirk, William. "Town and Country Planning in Ancient India According to Kautilya's Arthasastra." *Scottish Geographical Magazine* 94, no. 2 (September 1978): 67–75.

Kofman, Sarah. *Nietzsche and Metaphor.* Translated by Duncan Large. Stanford, CA: Stanford University Press, 1993.

Kopel, David B. "The Self-Defense Cases: How the United States Supreme Court Confronted a Hanging Judge in the Nineteenth Century and Taught Some Lessons for Jurisprudence in the Twenty-First." *American Journal of Criminal Law* 27, no. 3 (Summer 2000): 293–328.

Kopel, David B. "The Torah and Self-Defense." *Penn State Law Review* 109, no. 1 (Summer 2004): 17–42.

Koskela, Hille, and Rachel Pain. "Revisiting Fear and Place: Women's Fear of Attack and the Built Environment." *Geoforum* 31, no. 2 (May 2000): 269–80.

Koslofsky, Craig. *Evening's Empire: A History of the Night in Early Modern Europe.* Cambridge: Cambridge University Press, 2011.

Kraska, Peter B., and Victor E. Kappeler. "To Serve and Pursue: Exploring Police Sexual Violence against Women." *Justice Quarterly* 12, no. 1 (1995): 85–112.

Kretschmer, Kelsy, and Kristen Barber. "Men at the March: Feminist Movement Boundaries and Men's Participation in Take Back the Night and Slutwalk." *Mobilization: An International Quarterly* 21, no. 3 (September 2016): 283–300.

Krieger, Linda Hamilton. "The Content of Our Categories: A Cognitive Bias Approach to Discrimination and Equal Employment Opportunity." *Stanford Law Review* 47, no. 6 (July 1995): 1161–1248.

Lacey, Nicola. "In Search of the Responsible Subject: History, Philosophy and Social Sciences in Criminal Law Theory." *Modern Law Review* 64, no. 3 (May 2001): 350–71.

Lakoff, George, and Mark Johnson. *Metaphors We Live By.* Chicago: University of Chicago Press, 2008.

Lane, Charles. *The Day Freedom Died: The Colfax Massacre, the Supreme Court, and the Betrayal of Reconstruction.* New York: Holt, 2009.

Laporte, Roger. *La veille.* Paris: Gallimard, 1963.

Laporte, Roger, and Bernard Noël. *Deux lectures de Maurice Blanchot.* Paris: Fata morgana, 1973.

Laruelle, François. "Du noir univers: Dans les fondations humaines de la couleur." *La Décision Philosophique* 5 (1988): 107–12.

Laruelle, François. "On the Black Universe: In the Human Foundations of Color." In *Dark Nights of the Universe*, edited by Eugene Thacker, Daniel Colucciello Barber, Nicola Masciandaro, Alexander Galloway, François Laruelle, and Aaron Metté, 102–10. New York: [NAME] NAME Publications, 2013.

Latour, Bruno. *The Making of Law: An Ethnography of the Conseil d'Etat.* Cambridge: Polity, 2010.

Lawrence, Charles R., III. "The Id, the Ego, and Equal Protection: Reckoning with Unconscious Racism." *Stanford Law Review* 39, no. 2 (January 1987): 317–88.

Lawrence, Charles R., III. "Implicit Bias in the Age of Trump." *Harvard Law Review* 133, no. 7 (May 2020): 2304–57.

Lawrence, Charles R., III. "Unconscious Racism Revisited: Reflections on the Impact and Origins of 'The Id, the Ego, and Equal Protection.'" *Connecticut Law Review* 40, no. 4 (May 2008): 931–77.

Lecouteux, Claude. *Phantom Armies of the Night: The Wild Hunt and the Ghostly Processions of the Undead.* Rochester, VT: Inner Traditions, 2011.

Lee, Cynthia. "Making Race Salient: Trayvon Martin and Implicit Bias in a Not Yet Post-Racial Society." *North Carolina Law Review* 91, no. 5 (June 2013): 1555–817.

Lee, Marcus. "Originating Stand Your Ground: Racial Violence and Neoliberal Reason." *Du Bois Review: Social Science Research on Race* 16, no. 1 (Spring 2019): 107–29.

Lefebvre, Alexandre. *The Image of Law: Deleuze, Bergson, Spinoza.* Stanford, CA: Stanford University Press, 2008.

Lefebvre, Henri. *The Production of Space.* Oxford: Blackwell, 1991.

Legewie, Joscha, and Jeffrey Fagan. "Group Threat, Police Officer Diversity and the Deadly Use of Police Force." Social Science Research Network, December 6, 2016. https://papers.ssrn.com/abstract=2778692.

Lepore, Jill. *The Name of War: King Philip's War and the Origins of American Identity.* New York: Vintage, 2013.

Levack, Brian P. "Possession, Witchcraft, and the Law in Jacobean England." *Washington and Lee Law Review* 52, no. 5 (1995): 1613–40.

Levack, Brian P. *The Witch-Hunt in Early Modern Europe.* 3rd ed. Harlow, UK: Pearson Longman, 2006.

Levin, Benjamin. "A Defensible Defense: Reexamining Castle Doctrine Statutes Note." *Harvard Journal on Legislation* 47, no. 2 (2010): 523–54.

Lévinas, Emmanuel. *Existence and Existents.* Pittsburgh, PA: Duquesne University Press, 2001.

Lévinas, Emmanuel. *Otherwise Than Being, or Beyond Essence.* Pittsburgh, PA: Duquesne University Press, 1998.

Lévinas, Emmanuel. *Proper Names.* Stanford, CA: Stanford University Press, 1996.

Levinson, Justin D. "Forgotten Racial Equality: Implicit Bias, Decision-Making and Misremembering." Working paper, Bepress Legal Series, August 2006, 1630. https://law.bepress.com/expresso/eps/1630/.

Levinson, Justin D., Huajian Cai, and Danielle Young. "Guilty by Implicit Racial Bias: The Guilty/Not Guilty Implicit Association Test." *Ohio State Journal of Criminal Law* 8, no. 1 (Fall 2010): 187–208.

Levinson, Justin D., and Robert J. Smith. *Implicit Racial Bias across the Law.* Cambridge: Cambridge University Press, 2012.

Lévi-Strauss, Claude. *The Elementary Structures of Kinship*. Rev. ed. Boston: Beacon, 1969.

Levos, Joshua, and Tammy Lowery Zacchilli. "Nyctophobia: From Imagined to Realistic Fears of the Dark." *Psi Chi Journal of Psychological Research* 20, no. 2 (Summer 2015): 102–10.

Lewis, Sarah Elizabeth. "For Black Suffragists, the Lens Was a Mighty Sword." *New York Times*, August 12, 2020. https://www.nytimes.com/2020/08/12/arts/19th-amendment-black-womens-suffrage-photos.html.

Light, Caroline. *Stand Your Ground: A History of America's Love Affair with Lethal Self-Defense*. Boston: Beacon, 2017.

Lindsey, R. Hōkūlei. "Native Hawaiians and the Ceded Lands Trust: Applying Self-Determination as an Alternative to the Equal Protection Analysis." *American Indian Law Review* 34, no. 2 (January 2010): 223–57.

Linnemann, Travis, and Corina Medley. "Black Sites, 'Dark Sides': War Power, Police Power, and the Violence of the (Un)Known." *Crime, Media, Culture* 15, no. 2 (August 2019): 341–58.

Lippert, Randy. "Sanctuary Practices, Rationalities, and Sovereignties." *Alternatives: Global, Local, Political* 29, no. 5 (November–December 2004): 535–55.

Listerborn, Carina. "Feminist Struggle over Urban Safety and the Politics of Space." *European Journal of Women's Studies* 23, no. 3 (August 2016): 251–64.

Locke, John. *An Essay Concerning Human Understanding*. London: Penguin Books, 1997.

Locke, John. *Second Treatise of Government*. Edited by Richard Howard Cox. Arlington Heights, IL: H. Davidson, 1982.

Loewen, James W. *Sundown Towns: A Hidden Dimension of American Racism*. New York: Touchstone, 2006.

Londoño, Ernesto, Manuela Andreoni, and Letícia Casado. "Bolsonaro, Isolated and Defiant, Dismisses Coronavirus Threat to Brazil." *New York Times*, April 1, 2020. https://www.nytimes.com/2020/04/01/world/americas/brazil-bolsonaro-coronavirus.html.

Lord, Evelyn. *The Great Plague: A People's History*. New Haven, CT: Yale University Press, 2014.

Losen, Daniel J., and Jonathan Gillespie. "Opportunities Suspended: The Disparate Impact of Disciplinary Exclusion from School." K–12 Racial Disparities in School Discipline, Civil Rights Project, UCLA, August 7, 2012. https://escholarship.org/uc/item/3g36n0c3.

L'Ouverture, Toussaint. *The Haitian Revolution*. London: Verso Books, 2019.

Lowe, Pam, Cathy Humphreys, and Simon J. Williams. "Night Terrors: Women's Experiences of (Not) Sleeping Where There Is Domestic Violence." *Violence against Women* 13, no. 6 (June 2007): 549–61.

Lucretius. *On the Nature of Things.* Translated by H. A. J. Munro. With an introduction by J. D. Duff. London: George Bell and Sons, 1908.

Luhmann, Niklas. *Law as a Social System.* Translated by Klaus A. Ziegert and Fatima Kastner. Oxford: Oxford University Press, 2009.

Luhmann, Niklas. *Social Systems.* Stanford, CA: Stanford University Press, 1995.

Lukács, György. *History and Class Consciousness: Studies in Marxist Dialectics.* Cambridge, MA: MIT Press, 1971.

Luke, Timothy W. "Counting Up AR-15s: The Subject of Assault Rifles and the Assault Rifle as Subject." In *The Lives of Guns*, edited by Jonathan Obert, Andrew Poe, and Austin Sarat, 70–92. New York: Oxford University Press, 2019.

Maart, Rozena. "When Black Consciousness Walks Arm-in-Arm with Critical Race Theory to Meet Racism and White Consciousness in the Humanities." *Alternation* 21, no. 2 (2014): 54–82.

Macey, David. *Lacan in Contexts.* London: Verso, 1988.

Mackay, Finn. "Mapping the Routes: An Exploration of Charges of Racism Made against the 1970s UK Reclaim the Night Marches." *Women's Studies International Forum* 44, no. 1 (May 2014): 46–54.

MacKellar, Jean Scott. *Rape: The Bait and the Trap; A Balanced, Humane, Up-to-Date Analysis of Its Causes and Control.* New York: Crown, 1975.

MacKenzie, Melody Kapilialoha. "Ka Lama Ku O Ka No'eau: The Standing Torch of Wisdom." *University of Hawai'i Law Review* 33, no. 1 (Winter 2010): 3–16.

MacKinnon, Catharine A. "Feminism, Marxism, Method, and the State: An Agenda for Theory." *Signs: Journal of Women in Culture and Society* 7, no. 3 (Spring 1982): 515–44.

MacKinnon, Catharine A. "Feminism, Marxism, Method, and the State: Toward Feminist Jurisprudence." *Signs: Journal of Women in Culture and Society* 8, no. 4 (Summer 1983): 635–58.

MacKinnon, Catharine A. *Toward a Feminist Theory of the State.* Cambridge, MA: Harvard University Press, 1989.

Maine, Sir Henry. *Ancient Law.* Everyman's Library. London: J. M. Dent and Sons, 1917.

Malabou, Catherine. *Counterpath: Traveling with Jacques Derrida.* Stanford, CA: Stanford University Press, 2004.

Malcolm, Joyce Lee. "The Right of the People to Keep and Bear Arms: The Common Law Tradition." *Hastings Constitutional Law Quarterly* 10, no. 2 (Winter 1983): 285–314.

Malo, Davida. *Hawaiian Antiquities: (Moolelo Hawaii).* Honolulu, HI: Hawaiian Gazette Company, 1903.

Manderson, Desmond. *Songs without Music: Aesthetic Dimensions of Law and Justice.* Berkeley: University of California Press, 2000.

Marcus, Isabel. "Reframing 'Domestic Violence': Terrorism in the Home." In *The Public Nature of Private Violence: The Discovery of Domestic Abuse*, edited by Martha Albertson Fineman and Roxanne Mykituk, 25–49. New York: Routledge, 1994.

Marcus, Sharon. "Fighting Bodies, Fighting Words: A Theory and Politics of Rape Prevention." In *Feminists Theorize the Political*, edited by Judith Butler and Joan Wallach Scott, 385–403. New York: Routledge, 1992.

Marryat, Horace. *A Residence in Jutland, the Danish Isles, and Copenhagen.* London: J. Murray, 1860.

Martí, José Luis, and Philip Pettit. *A Political Philosophy in Public Life: Civic Republicanism in Zapatero's Spain.* Princeton, NJ: Princeton University Press, 2010.

Martin, Emily. *Flexible Bodies: Tracking Immunity in American Culture from the Days of Polio to the Age of AIDS.* Boston: Beacon, 1994.

Marx, Karl. "On the Jewish Question." In *The Marx-Engels Reader*, 2nd ed., edited by Robert Tucker, 26–52. New York: W. W. Norton, 1978.

Masciandaro, Nicola. "Secret: No Light Has Ever Seen the Black Universe." In *Dark Nights of the Universe*, edited by Eugene Thacker, Daniel Colucciello Barber, Nicola Masciandaro, Alexander Galloway, François Laruelle, and Aaron Metté, 45–87. New York: NAME Publications, 2013.

Masson, Erin M. "The Woman's Christian Temperance Union, 1874–1898: Combating Domestic Violence." *William and Mary Journal of Women and the Law* 3, no. 1 (April 1997): 163–88.

Massumi, Brian. *Parables for the Virtual: Movement, Affect, Sensation.* Durham, NC: Duke University Press, 2007.

Matricciani, Lisa, Timothy Olds, and John Petkov. "In Search of Lost Sleep: Secular Trends in the Sleep Time of School-Aged Children and Adolescents." *Sleep Medicine Reviews* 16, no. 3 (June 2012): 203–11.

Mauss, Marcel. *Seasonal Variations of the Eskimo: A Study in Social Morphology.* Translated by James J. Fox. London: Routledge, 2004.

Mawani, Renisa. "The Times of Law." In "Symposium: Parker's *Common Law, History, and Democracy in America*." *Law and Social Inquiry* 40, no. 1 (Winter 2015): 253–63.

Mayali, Laurent. "Lex animata: Rationalisation du pouvoir politique et science juridique (XIIeme–XIVeme siecles)." In *Renaissance du pouvoir législatif et genese de l'état*, edited by André Gouron and Albert Rigaudière, 155–64. Montpellier: Société d'histoire du droit et des institutions des anciens pays de droit écrit, 1988.

Mbembe, Achille. *Critique of Black Reason.* Translated by Laurent Dubois. Durham, NC: Duke University Press, 2017.

Mbembe, Achille. "Domaines de la nuit et autorité onirique dans les Maquis du Sud-Cameroun (1955–1958)." *Journal of African History* 32, no. 1 (March 1991): 89–121.

Mbembe, Achille. *Necropolitics*. Durham, NC: Duke University Press, 2019.
Mbembe, Achille. *On the Postcolony*. Berkeley: University of California Press, 2001.
McCann, Michael. *Rights at Work: Pay Equity Reform and the Politics of Legal Mobilization*. Chicago: University of Chicago Press, 1994.
McCann, Michael. "The Unbearable Lightness of Rights: On Sociolegal Inquiry in the Global Era." *Law and Society Review* 48, no. 2 (June 2014): 245–73.
McClintock, Anne. *Imperial Leather: Race, Gender and Sexuality in the Colonial Contest*. New York: Routledge, 1995.
McCormack, Clare, and Nevena Prostran. "Asking for It: A First-Hand Account from SlutWalk." *International Feminist Journal of Politics* 14, no. 3 (September 2012): 410–14.
McCracken, John. "Coercion and Control in Nyasaland: Aspects of the History of a Colonial Police Force." *Journal of African History* 27, no. 1 (March 1986): 127–47.
McKittrick, Katherine. "On Plantations, Prisons, and a Black Sense of Place/ Sobre plantaciones, cárceles, y un negro sentido de lugar." *Social and Cultural Geography* 12, no. 8 (December 2011): 947–63.
McMillen, Neil R. *Dark Journey: Black Mississippians in the Age of Jim Crow*. Urbana: University of Illinois Press, 1990.
Meares, Tracey L., and Dan M. Kahan. "Law and (Norms of) Order in the Inner City." *Law and Society Review* 32, no. 4 (1998): 805–38.
Meier, Josiane, Ute Hasenöhrl, Katharina Krause, and Merle Pottharst. *Urban Lighting, Light Pollution and Society*. New York: Routledge, 2014.
Melbin, Murray. "Night as Frontier." *American Sociological Review* 43, no. 1 (February 1978): 3–22.
Melbin, Murray. *Night as Frontier: Colonizing the World after Dark*. New York: Free Press, 1987.
Meltzer, Jonathan. "Open Carry for All: Heller and Our Nineteenth-Century Second Amendment Note." *Yale Law Journal* 123, no. 5 (March 2014): 1486–531.
Melville, Herman. *Billy Budd, Sailor, and Other Stories*. New York: Random House, 2006.
Melzer, Sara E., and Kathryn Norberg, eds. *From the Royal to the Republican Body: Incorporating the Political in Seventeenth- and Eighteenth-Century France*. Berkeley: University of California Press, 1998.
Ménager, Daniel. *La renaissance et la nuit*. Geneva: Librairie Droz, 2005.
Mendes, Kaitlynn. *SlutWalk*. London: Palgrave Macmillan, 2015.
Menih, Helena. "'Come Night-Time, It's a War Zone': Women's Experiences of Homelessness, Risk and Public Space." *British Journal of Criminology* 60, no. 5 (September 2020): 1136–54.
Mensch, Elizabeth. "The History of Mainstream Legal Thought." In *The Politics of Law: A Progressive Critique*, edited by David Kairys, 13–37. New York: Pantheon, 1982.

Mensch, Jennifer. "What's Wrong with Inevitable Progress? Notes on Kant's Anthropology Today." *Cogent Arts and Humanities* 4, no. 1 (2017): 1390917.

Merleau-Ponty, Maurice. *Phénoménologie de la perception*. Paris: Gallimard, 2009.

Merleau-Ponty, Maurice. *Phenomenology of Perception: An Introduction*. Translated by Colin Smith. London: Routledge, 1995.

Merleau-Ponty, Maurice. *The Visible and the Invisible*. Evanston, IL: Northwestern University Press, 1968.

Merry, Sally Engle. *Colonizing Hawai'i: The Cultural Power of Law*. Princeton, NJ: Princeton University Press, 2000.

Merry, Sally Engle. "Legal Pluralism." *Law and Society Review* 22, no. 5 (1988): 869–96.

Messerschmidt, Cristina Georgiana. "A Victim of Abuse Should Still Have a Castle: The Applicability of the Castle Doctrine to Instances of Domestic Violence Comments." *Journal of Criminal Law and Criminology* 106, no. 3 (Summer 2016): 593–626.

Mills, Charles W. *The Racial Contract*. Ithaca, NY: Cornell University Press, 1997.

Minkowski, Eugène. *Lived Time: Phenomenological and Psychopathological Studies*. Evanston, IL: Northwestern University Press, 1970.

Mitchell, Robin. "Les ombres noires de Saint Domingue: The Impact of Black Women on Gender and Racial Boundaries in Eighteenth- and Nineteenth-Century France." PhD diss., University of California, Berkeley, 2010. https://escholarship.org/uc/item/4277f7zb.

Mitchell, Timothy. *Colonising Egypt*. Berkeley: University of California Press, 1991.

Mnookin, Robert H., and Lewis Kornhauser. "Bargaining in the Shadow of the Law: The Case of Divorce." *Yale Law Review* 88, no. 5 (April 1979): 950–97.

Mohaghegh, Jason Bahbak. *Night*. Ridgefield, CT: Zero Books, 2019.

Montag, Warren. "Between Interpellation and Immunization: Althusser, Balibar, Esposito." *Postmodern Culture* 22, no. 3 (May 2012) https://doi.org/DOI_10.1353/pmc.2012.0016.

Moore, Matthew J. "The Nature of Sleep." *Comparative Studies in Society and History* 53, no. 4 (October 2011): 945–70.

Moreton-Robinson, Aileen. *The White Possessive: Property, Power, and Indigenous Sovereignty*. Minneapolis: University of Minnesota Press, 2015.

Morgan, Edmund S. "Slavery and Freedom: The American Paradox." *Journal of American History* 59, no. 1 (June 1972): 5–29.

Morgensen, Scott Lauria. *Spaces between Us: Queer Settler Colonialism and Indigenous Decolonization*. Minneapolis: University of Minnesota Press, 2011.

Morris, Thomas D. *Southern Slavery and the Law, 1619–1860*. Chapel Hill: University of North Carolina Press, 1996.

Morrison, Toni. *Playing in the Dark*. New York. Random House, 2007.

Moten, Fred. "The Case of Blackness." *Criticism* 50, no. 2 (Spring 2008): 177–218.

Moten, Fred. "The Touring Machine (Flesh Thought Inside Out)." In *Plastic Materialities: Politics, Legality, and Metamorphosis in the Work of Catherine Malabou*, edited by Brenna Bhandar and Jonathan Goldberg-Hiller, 265–86. Durham, NC: Duke University Press, 2015.

Moye, J. Todd. *Let the People Decide: Black Freedom and White Resistance Movements in Sunflower County, Mississippi, 1945–1986*. Chapel Hill: University of North Carolina Press, 2004.

Muhammad, Khalil Gibran. *The Condemnation of Blackness: Race, Crime, and the Making of Modern Urban America*. Cambridge, MA: Harvard University Press, 2010.

Murakawa, Naomi. *The First Civil Right: How Liberals Built Prison America*. Oxford: Oxford University Press, 2014.

Murphy, Lindsay, and Jonathan Livingstone. "Racism and the Limits of Radical Feminism." *Race and Class* 26, no. 4 (April 1985): 61–70.

Murray, Alexander. "Medieval Origins of the Witch Hunt." *Cambridge Quarterly* 7, no. 1 (January 1976): 63–74.

Musharbash, Yasmine. "Night, Sight, and Feeling Safe: An Exploration of Aspects of Warlpiri and Western Sleep." *Australian Journal of Anthropology* 24, no. 1 (April 2013): 48–63.

Naffine, Ngaire. "Who Are Law's Persons? From Cheshire Cats to Responsible Subjects." *Modern Law Review* 66, no. 3 (May 2003): 346–67.

Nakaso, Dan. "$250,000 Worth of Personal Protective Equipment Stolen from Oahu Health Care Company." *Honolulu Star-Advertiser*, April 7, 2020. https://www.staradvertiser.com/2020/04/07/hawaii-news/250000 -worth-of-personal-protective-equipment-stolen-from-oahu-health-care -company-2/.

Nancy, Jean-Luc. *The Fall of Sleep*. Translated by Charlotte Mandell. New York: Fordham University Press, 2009.

Nanni, Giordano. *The Colonisation of Time: Ritual, Routine and Resistance in the British Empire*. Manchester: Manchester University Press, 2012.

Nash, Roderick W. *The Christiana Riot: An Evaluation of Its National Significance*. Lancaster, PA: Lancaster County Historical Society, 1961.

National Commission on Sleep Disorders Research, United States, and Department of Health and Human Services. *Wake Up America: A National Sleep Alert; Report of the National Commission on Sleep Disorders Research*. Washington, DC: The Commission, 1993.

National Lawyers Guild. *Newsletter, Twin Cities Chapter*. Minneapolis: National Lawyers Guild, Twin Cities Chapter, 1973.

Naudé, Gabriel. *Political Considerations upon Refin'd Politicks: And the Master-Strokes of State, as Practis'd by the Ancients and Moderns*. London: H. Clements, 1711.

Newman, Michael. "The Trace of Trauma: Blindness, Testimony and the Gaze in Blanchot and Derrida." In *Maurice Blanchot: The Demand of Writing*, edited by Carolyn Bailey Gill, 152–73. London: Routledge, 1996.

New York Times. "Protest Groups Defy Curfew, and Police Act Quickly to Enforce It: Live Updates." June 5, 2020. https://www.nytimes.com/2020/06/03/nyregion/nyc-protests-george-floyd.html.

Ngũgĩ wa Thiong'o. *Weep Not, Child*. New York: Penguin, 2012.

Nichols, Robert. *Theft Is Property! Dispossession and Critical Theory*. Durham, NC: Duke University Press, 2020.

Nicholson-Crotty, Sean, Jill Nicholson-Crotty, and Sergio Fernandez. "Will More Black Cops Matter? Officer Race and Police-Involved Homicides of Black Citizens." *Public Administration Review* 77, no. 2 (March–April 2017): 206–16.

Nielsen, Laura Beth. "Situating Legal Consciousness: Experiences and Attitudes of Ordinary Citizens about Law and Street Harassment." *Law and Society Review* 34, no. 4 (January 2000): 1055–90.

Nietzsche, Friedrich. *Daybreak: Thoughts on the Prejudices of Morality*. Edited by Maudemarie Clark and Brian Leiter. Translated by R. J. Hollingdale. Cambridge: Cambridge University Press, 1997.

Nietzsche, Friedrich. *On the Genealogy of Morals*. Translated by Walter Arnold Kaufmann. New York: Vintage Books, 2011.

Nietzsche, Friedrich. "On Truth and Lie in an Extra-Moral Sense." In *Friedrich Nietzsche: Writings from the Early Notebooks*, edited by Raymond Geuss and Alexander Nehamas, translated by Ladislaus Löb, 253–64. Cambridge: Cambridge University Press, 2009.

Nietzsche, Friedrich. *Philosophy and Truth: Selections from Nietzsche's Notebooks of the Early 1870's*. Translated by Daniel Breazeale. Atlantic Highlands, NJ: Humanities Press, 1979.

Nietzsche, Friedrich. *Thus Spoke Zarathustra: A Book for All and None*. Translated by Adrian Del Caro. Cambridge: Cambridge University Press, 2006.

Nietzsche, Friedrich. *Twilight of the Idols, or, How to Philosophize with the Hammer*. Translated by Richard Polt. Indianapolis: Hackett Publishing Company, 1997.

Njoh, Ambe J. "Colonial Philosophies, Urban Space, and Racial Segregation in British and French Colonial Africa." *Journal of Black Studies* 38, no. 4 (March 2008): 579–99.

Nozick, Robert. *Anarchy, State, and Utopia*. New York: Basic Books, 1974.

Nugent, Maria. "Mapping Memories: Oral History for Aboriginal Cultural Heritage in New South Wales, Australia." In *Oral History and Public Memories*, edited by Paula Hamilton and Linda Shopes, 47–65. Philadelphia: Temple University Press, 2008.

Nussbaum, Martha C. *Hiding from Humanity: Disgust, Shame, and the Law*. Princeton, NJ: Princeton University Press, 2004.

Obasogie, Osagie K. "Do Blind People See Race? Social, Legal, and Theoretical Considerations." *Law and Society Review* 44, nos. 3–4 (September–December 2010): 585–616.

Obert, Jonathan, Andrew Poe, and Austin Sarat, eds. *The Lives of Guns.* New York: Oxford University Press, 2019.

Olsen, Otto H. "The Ku Klux Klan: A Study in Reconstruction Politics and Propaganda." *North Carolina Historical Review* 39, no. 3 (July 1962): 340–62.

Ombuor, Rael, and Max Bearak. "'Killing in the Name of Corona': Death Toll Soars from Kenya's Curfew Crackdown." *Washington Post*, April 16, 2020. https://www.washingtonpost.com/world/africa/kenya-coronavirus -curfew-crackdown-death-toll/2020/04/15/740a8c4e-79be-11ea-a311 -adb1344719a9_story.html.

O'Reilly, Andrea. "Slut Pride: A Tribute to SlutWalk Toronto." *Feminist Studies* 38, no. 1 (Spring 2012): 245–50.

Osse, Anneke, and Ignacio Cano. "Police Deadly Use of Firearms: An International Comparison." *International Journal of Human Rights* 21, no. 5 (June 2017): 629–49.

Ostrowsky, Jonathan. "#MeToo's Unseen Frontier: Law Enforcement Sexual Misconduct and the Fourth Amendment Response Comment." UCLA *Law Review* 67, no. 1 (2020): 258–314.

Pain, Rachel. "Gender, Race, Age and Fear in the City." *Urban Studies* 38, nos. 5–6 (May 2001): 899–913.

Palmer, Bryan D. *Cultures of Darkness: Night Travels in the Histories of Transgression.* New York: Monthly Review Press, 2000.

Panagia, Davide. "On the Political Ontology of the Dispositif." *Critical Inquiry* 45, no. 3 (March 2019): 714–46.

Pandian, Anand. "Pastoral Power in the Postcolony: On the Biopolitics of the Criminal Animal in South India." *Cultural Anthropology* 23, no. 1 (February 2008): 85–117.

Pang, Gordon Y. K. "Caldwell, Ballard Put an End to Weekend Curfews." *Honolulu Star-Advertiser*, April 14, 2020. https://www.staradvertiser.com /2020/04/14/hawaii-news/caldwell-ballard-put-an-end-to-weekend -curfews/.

Paquette, Robert L. "'A Horde of Brigands?' The Great Louisiana Slave Revolt of 1811 Reconsidered." *Historical Reflections/Réflexions Historiques* 35, no. 1 (Spring 2009): 72–96.

Parker, John. "Northern Gothic: Witches, Ghosts and Werewolves in the Savanna Hinterland of the Gold Coast, 1900s–1950s." *Africa* 76, no. 3 (2006): 352–80.

Parker, John Howard. "The Life and Works of James Howell Street." PhD diss., University of Tennessee, 1978. http://www.proquest.com/docview /302883908/citation/93664813589342C9PQ/1.

Parker, Kim, Juliana Menasce Horowitz, Ruth Igielnik, J. Baxter Oliphant, and Anna Brown. "The Demographics of Gun Ownership." Chapter 1 of *America's Complex Relationship with Guns*. Report, Social and Demographic Trends Project, Pew Research Center, June 22, 2017. https://www.pewresearch.org/social-trends/2017/06/22/the-demographics-of-gun-ownership/.

Parker, Kunal Madhukar. *Common Law, History, and Democracy in America, 1790–1900: Legal Thought before Modernism*. New York: Cambridge University Press, 2011.

Parker, William. "The Freedman's Story." *Atlantic Monthly*, February 1866, 152–66; and March 1866, 276–95.

Parris, Benjamin. "'The Body Is with the King, but the King Is Not with the Body': Sovereign Sleep in *Hamlet* and *Macbeth*." *Shakespeare Studies* 40 (2012): 101–42.

Parsons, Elaine Frantz. *Ku-Klux: The Birth of the Klan during Reconstruction*. Chapel Hill: University of North Carolina Press, 2015.

Pateman, Carole. "Self-Ownership and Property in the Person: Democratization and a Tale of Two Concepts." *Journal of Political Philosophy* 10, no. 1 (March 2002): 20–53.

Pateman, Carole. *The Sexual Contract*. Stanford, CA: Stanford University Press, 1988.

Pateman, Carole, and Charles W. Mills. *Contract and Domination*. Cambridge: Polity, 2007.

Patterson, Orlando. *Rituals of Blood: The Consequences of Slavery in Two American Centuries*. Rev. ed. New York: Civitas Books, 1999.

Patterson, Orlando. *Slavery and Social Death: A Comparative Study*. Cambridge, MA: Harvard University Press, 1982.

Payne, B. Keith. "Prejudice and Perception: The Role of Automatic and Controlled Processes in Misperceiving a Weapon." *Journal of Personality and Social Psychology* 81, no. 2 (August 2001): 181–92.

Peeters, Benoît. *Derrida: A Biography*. Translated by Andrew Brown. Cambridge: Polity, 2013.

Peltier, Elian. "Banned Vigil for Sarah Everard Becomes Large Anti-Violence Rally Instead." *New York Times*, March 13, 2021. https://www.nytimes.com/2021/03/13/world/europe/sarah-everard-vigil-rally.html.

Perkins, Chloe, Rebecca Steinbach, Lisa Tompson, Judith Green, Shane Johnson, Chris Grundy, Paul Wilkinson, and Phil Edwards. "What Is the Effect of Reduced Street Lighting on Crime and Road Traffic Injuries at Night? A Mixed-Methods Study." *Public Health Research* 3, no. 11 (September 2015). https://www.ncbi.nlm.nih.gov/books/NBK316503/pdf/Bookshelf_NBK316503.pdf.

Petchesky, Rosalind Pollack. "The Body as Property: A Feminist Re-Vision." In *Conceiving the New World Order: The Global Politics of Reproduction*, edited by Faye D. Ginsburg and Rayna Rapp, 387–406. Berkeley: University of California Press, 1995.

Peteet, Julie. "Closure's Temporality: The Cultural Politics of Time and Waiting." *South Atlantic Quarterly* 117, no. 1 (January 2018): 43–64.

Peteet, Julie. *Space and Mobility in Palestine.* Bloomington: Indiana University Press, 2017.

Peters, Douglas, and Robert Rubin. "How We Handled a Sexsomnia Case." *Champion*, April 2013, 18.

Peters, Edward. *The Magician, the Witch, and the Law.* Philadelphia: University of Pennsylvania Press, 1978.

Pfeifer, Geoff. *The New Materialism: Althusser, Badiou, Žižek.* New York: Routledge, 2015.

Pfingst, Annie. "Militarised Violence in the Service of State-Imposed Emergencies over Palestine and Kenya." *Cosmopolitan Civil Societies: An Interdisciplinary Journal* 6, no. 3 (February 2015): 6–37.

Pickard, Sarah, and Judith Bessant. "France's #Nuit Debout Social Movement: Young People Rising Up and Moral Emotions." *Societies* 8, no. 4 (2018): 100–21.

Plato. *Republic.* Translated by C. D. C Reeve. Indianapolis: Hackett, 2004.

Pocock, J. G. A. *The Machiavellian Moment: Florentine Political Thought and the Atlantic Republican Tradition.* Princeton, NJ: Princeton University Press, 1975.

Poe, Edgar Allan. "The Man of the Crowd." In *The Works of Edgar Allan Poe*, vol. 5, 175–88. New York: Funk and Wagnalls, 1904.

Pope, James Gray. "Snubbed Landmark: Why *United States v. Cruikshank* (1876) Belongs at the Heart of the American Constitutional Canon." *Harvard Civil Rights-Civil Liberties Law Review* 49, no. 2 (2014): 385–448.

Posner, Richard A. *The Problems of Jurisprudence.* Cambridge, MA: Harvard University Press, 1990.

Post, Gaines. *Studies in Medieval Legal Thought: Public Law and the State, 1100–1322.* Princeton, NJ: Princeton University Press, 1964.

Post, Harry. "The Judgment of the Grand Chamber in *Hatton and Others v. the United Kingdom* or: What Is Left of the 'Indirect' Right to a Healthy Environment." *Non-State Actors and International Law* 4, no. 2 (January 2004): 135–57.

Pound, Roscoe. "The Work of the American Law School." *West Virginia Law Quarterly* 30, no. 1 (November 1923): 1–17.

Povinelli, Elizabeth A. *The Empire of Love: Toward a Theory of Intimacy, Genealogy, and Carnality.* Durham, NC: Duke University Press, 2006.

Povinelli, Elizabeth A. *Geontologies: A Requiem to Late Liberalism.* Durham, NC: Duke University Press, 2016.

Povinelli, Elizabeth A. "The Governance of the Prior." *Interventions* 13, no. 1 (March 2011): 13–30.

Pratten, David. "The Politics of Vigilance in Southeastern Nigeria." *Development and Change* 37, no. 4 (July 2006): 707–34.

Price, Joshua M. *Prison and Social Death*. New Brunswick, NJ: Rutgers University Press, 2015.

Prison Policy Initiative. "Not Just 'a Few Bad Apples': U.S. Police Kill Civilians at Much Higher Rates Than Other Countries." Accessed October 1, 2021. https://www.prisonpolicy.org/blog/2020/06/05/policekillings/.

Pualani Warren, Joyce Lindsay. "Theorizing Pō: Embodied Cosmogony and Polynesian National Narratives." PhD diss., University of California, Los Angeles, 2017. https://www.proquest.com/docview/1983541442/abstract/321E1426D0A44F8CPQ/1.

Puar, Jasbir K. "'I Would Rather Be a Cyborg Than a Goddess': Becoming-Intersectional in Assemblage Theory." *philoSOPHIA: A Journal of Continental Feminism* 2, no. 1 (2012): 49–66.

Puar, Jasbir K. *Terrorist Assemblages: Homonationalism in Queer Times.* Durham, NC: Duke University Press, 2008.

Pukui, Mary Kawena. *Hawaiian Dictionary: Hawaiian-English, English-Hawaiian.* Rev. enl. ed. Honolulu: University of Hawai'i Press, 1986.

Quinlan, Andrea. "Imagining a Feminist Actor-Network Theory." *International Journal of Actor-Network Theory and Technological Innovation (IJANTTI)* 4, no. 2 (April–June 2012): 1–9.

Radun, Igor, Jussi Ohisalo, Jenni Radun, Mattias Wahde, and Göran Kecklund. "Driver Fatigue and the Law from the Perspective of Police Officers and Prosecutors." *Transportation Research Part F: Traffic Psychology and Behaviour* 18 (May 2013): 159–67.

Raiford, Leigh. "Lynching, Visuality, and the Un/Making of Blackness." *Nka: Journal of Contemporary African Art*, no. 20 (Fall 2006): 22–31.

Rancière, Jacques. *Disagreement: Politics and Philosophy.* Minneapolis: University of Minnesota Press, 1999.

Rancière, Jacques. *Proletarian Nights: The Workers' Dream in Nineteenth-Century France.* London: Verso Books, 2012.

Rancière, Jacques. "The Thinking of Dissensus: Politics and Aesthetics." Goldsmith's College, 2003.

Rawls, John. *A Theory of Justice.* Rev. ed. Cambridge, MA: Belknap Press of Harvard University Press, 1999.

Rāya, Vibhūtinārāyaṇa. *Curfew in the City: A Novella.* Gugaon, India: Penguin Books, 2016.

Razack, Sherene. "Race, Space, and Prostitution: The Making of the Bourgeois Subject." *Canadian Journal of Women and the Law* 10, no. 2 (December 1998): 338–79.

Reger, Jo. "Micro-Cohorts, Feminist Discourse, and the Emergence of the Toronto SlutWalk." *Feminist Formations* 26, no. 1 (Spring 2014): 49–69.

Reiss, Benjamin. *Wild Nights: How Taming Sleep Created Our Restless World.* New York: Basic Books, 2017.

"Report of the Joint Select Committee Appointed to Inquire into the Condition of Affairs in the Late Insurrectionary States, So Far as Regards the Execution of Laws, and the Safety of the Lives and Property of the Citizens of the United States and Testimony Taken." H.R. Rep. No. 22, pt. 1, 42nd Congress, 2nd session. February 19, 1872. https://lccn.loc.gov /35031867.

Riccelli, Catherine. "United States Historical Rape Trends and Multi-Country Comparison." Master's thesis, University of Pittsburgh, 2019. http://d -scholarship.pitt.edu/36618/.

Rice, Anthony. "A Legacy Transformed: The Christiana Riot in Historical Memory." PhD diss., Lehigh University, 2012.

Rich, Adrienne. Afterword to *Take Back the Night: Women on Pornography*, edited by Laura Lederer, 313–20. New York: William Morrow, 1980.

Richards, David. *Identity and the Case for Gay Rights: Race, Gender, Religion as Analogies.* Chicago: University of Chicago Press, 1999.

Richardson, Joe M. "Florida Black Codes." *Florida Historical Quarterly* 47, no. 4 (1968): 365–79.

Richie, Beth. *Arrested Justice: Black Women, Violence, and America's Prison Nation.* New York: New York University Press, 2012.

Richter, Antje. "Sleeping Time in Early Chinese Literature." In *Night-Time and Sleep in Asia and the West: Exploring the Dark Side of Life*, edited by Brigitte Steger and Lodewijk Brunt, 25–42. London: RoutledgeCurzon, 2003.

Ricoeur, Paul. "Metaphor and the Main Problem of Hermeneutics." *New Literary History* 6, no. 1 (Autumn 1974): 95–110.

Ricoeur, Paul. *The Rule of Metaphor: The Creation of Meaning in Language.* London: Routledge, 2004.

Rideout, J. Christopher. "Penumbral Thinking Revisited: Metaphor in Legal Argumentation." *Journal of the Association of Legal Writing Directors* 7, no. 1 (2010): 155–92.

Dreifuss, Arthur, Director. American International Pictures: Hollywood, CA. *Riot on Sunset Strip.* 1967.

Roberts, Marion. "'A Big Night Out': Young People's Drinking, Social Practice and Spatial Experience in the 'Liminoid' Zones of English Night-Time Cities." *Urban Studies* 52, no. 3 (February 2015): 571–88.

Robson, Ruthann. *Lesbian (Out)Law: Survival under the Rule of Law.* Ithaca, NY: Firebrand Books, 1992.

Rolnick, Addie C. "Defending White Space: Part I: Policing, Race and Incarceration." *Cardozo Law Review* 40, no. 4 (June 2019): 1639–722.

Roman, John. "Race, Justifiable Homicide, and Stand Your Ground Laws: Analysis of FBI Supplementary Homicide Report Data." Urban Insti-

tute, July 26, 2013. https://www.urban.org/research/publication/race
-justifiable-homicide-and-stand-your-ground-laws.

Rooney, Phyllis. "Philosophy, Language, and Wizardry." In *Feminist Interpretations of Ludwig Wittgenstein*, edited by Naomi Scheman and Peg O'Connor, 25–47. University Park: Pennsylvania State University Press, 2002.

Rose, Carol M. *Property and Persuasion: Essays on the History, Theory, and Rhetoric of Ownership*. New York: Routledge, 2019.

Ross, Josephine. "What the #MeToo Campaign Teaches about Stop and Frisk." *Idaho Law Review* 54, no. 2 (September 2018): 543–62.

Rousseau, Jean-Jacques. *The Social Contract*. Baltimore: Penguin Books, 1968.

Roux, Jacques. *Être vigilant: L'opérativité discrète de la société du risque*. Paris: Université de Saint-Etienne, 2006.

Ruefle, William, and Kenneth Reynolds. "Curfews and Delinquency in Major American Cities." *Crime and Delinquency* 41, no. 3 (July 1995): 347–63.

Ruefle, William, and Kenneth Reynolds. "Keep Them at Home: Juvenile Curfew Ordinances in 200 American Cities." *American Journal of Police* 15, no. 1 (March 1996): 63–84.

Rukmini, S. "Locked Down with Abusers: India Sees Surge in Domestic Violence." *Al Jazeera*, April 17, 2020. https://www.aljazeera.com/news/2020/04/locked-abusers-india-domestic-violence-surge-200415092014621.html.

Russell, Diana E. H. *The Politics of Rape: The Victim's Perspective*. New York: Stein and Day, 1975.

Russo, Ann. "'We Cannot Live without Our Lives': White Women, Antiracism, and Feminism." In *Third World Women and the Politics of Feminism*, edited by Chandra Talpade Mohanty, Ann Russo, and Lourdes Torres, 297–313. Bloomington: Indiana University Press, 1991.

Ryan, Rebecca M. "The Sex Right: A Legal History of the Marital Rape Exemption." *Law and Social Inquiry* 20, no. 4 (Autumn 1995): 941–1004.

Salamon, Gayle. *The Life and Death of Latisha King: A Critical Phenomenology of Transphobia*. New York: New York University Press, 2018.

Salamon, Gayle. "'The Place Where Life Hides Away': Merleau-Ponty, Fanon, and the Location of Bodily Being." *Differences* 17, no. 2 (September 2006): 96–112.

Sandberg, Linda, and Anna-Britt Coe. "Taking Back the Swedish Night: Making and Reclaiming Space." *Gender, Place and Culture* 27, no. 7 (2020): 1044–62.

Santner, Eric L. *On the Psychotheology of Everyday Life: Reflections on Freud and Rosenzweig*. Chicago: University of Chicago Press, 2001.

Santner, Eric L. *The Royal Remains: The People's Two Bodies and the Endgames of Sovereignty*. Chicago: University of Chicago Press, 2011.

Santner, Eric L. *The Weight of All Flesh: On the Subject-Matter of Political Economy*. Edited by Kevis Goodman. Oxford: Oxford University Press, 2015.

Saramago, José. *The Double.* Translated by Margaret Jull Costa. Orlando, FL: Houghton Mifflin Harcourt, 2005.

Sarat, Austin. *Pain, Death, and the Law.* Ann Arbor: University of Michigan Press, 2001.

Sartre, Jean-Paul. *Being and Nothingness: An Essay on Phenomenological Ontology.* New York: Philosophical Library, 1956.

Scahill, Jeremy. "Killed in the Darkness." *Intercepted* (podcast), June 9, 2021. https://theintercept.com/2021/06/09/intercepted-st-louis-cortez -bufford/.

Scalia, Antonin. "Originalism: The Lesser Evil." *University of Cincinnati Law Review* 57, no. 3 (1988): 849–66.

Scheingold, Stuart A. *The Politics of Rights: Lawyers, Public Policy, and Political Change.* 2nd ed. Ann Arbor: University of Michigan Press, 2004.

Scheman, Naomi, and Peg O'Connor, eds. *Feminist Interpretations of Ludwig Wittgenstein.* University Park: Pennsylvania State University Press, 2002.

Schivelbusch, Wolfgang. *Disenchanted Night: The Industrialization of Light in the Nineteenth Century.* Berkeley: University of California Press, 1995.

Schlumbohm, Jürgen. "Gesetze, die nicht durchgesetzt werden: Ein Struktur- merkmal des frühneuzeitlichen Staates?" *Geschichte und Gesellschaft* 23, no. 4 (October–December 1997): 647–63.

Schmitt, Carl. *The Concept of the Political.* Chicago: University of Chicago Press, 2007.

Schmitt, Carl. *Political Theology: Four Chapters on the Concept of Sovereignty.* Cambridge, MA: MIT Press, 1985.

Schmitt, Carl. *Political Theology II.* Cambridge: Polity, 2008.

Schroeder, Jeanne L. "Totem, Taboo and the Concept of Law: Myth in Hart and Freud." *Washington University Jurisprudence Review* 1, no. 1 (2009): 139–92.

Schroth, Peter W. "Legal Translation." *American Journal of Comparative Law* 34, no. s1 (1986): 47–65.

Scott, James C. *The Art of Not Being Governed: An Anarchist History of Upland Southeast Asia.* New Haven, CT: Yale University Press, 2009.

Scott, James C. *Seeing like a State: How Certain Schemes to Improve the Human Condition Have Failed.* New Haven, CT: Yale University Press, 1998.

Sears, David O., and T. M. Tomlinson. "Riot Ideology in Los Angeles: A Study of Negro Attitudes." *Social Science Quarterly* 49, no. 3 (December 1968): 485–503.

Seeger, Peggy. "Reclaim the Night." Track 2 on *Different Therefore Equal.* Folkway Recordings, 1979. Vinyl LP. Lyrics retrieved from Genius Lyrics. https://genius.com/Peggy-seeger-reclaim-the-night-lyrics.

Serisier, Tanya. "Who Was Andrea? Writing Oneself as a Feminist Icon." *Women: A Cultural Review* 24, no. 1 (2013): 26–44.

Serres, Michel. *The Five Senses: A Philosophy of Mingled Bodies (I).* London: Continuum, 2009.

Shakespeare, William. *Shakespeare: Complete Works.* Edited by W. J. Craig. Oxford: Oxford University Press, 1980.

Shalhope, Robert E. "Toward a Republican Synthesis: The Emergence of an Understanding of Republicanism in American Historiography." *William and Mary Quarterly* 29, no. 1 (January 1972): 49–80.

Shanley, Mary Lyndon. "Suffrage, Protective Labor Legislation, and Married Women's Property Laws in England." *Signs: Journal of Women in Culture and Society* 12, no. 1 (Autumn 1986): 62–77.

Shannon, Sarah K. S., Christopher Uggen, Jason Schnittker, Melissa Thompson, Sara Wakefield, and Michael Massoglia. "The Growth, Scope, and Spatial Distribution of People with Felony Records in the United States, 1948–2010." *Demography* 54, no. 5 (October 2017): 1795–818.

Shapiro, David L. "The Case of the Speluncean Explorers: A Fiftieth Anniversary Symposium—Foreword: A Cave Drawing for the Ages." *Harvard Law Review* 112 (1999): 1834–2025.

Shapiro, Harvey. "When the Exception Is the Rule: School Shootings, Bare Life, and the Sovereign Self." *Educational Theory* 65, no. 4 (August 2015): 423–40.

Shapiro, Herbert. "The Ku Klux Klan during Reconstruction: The South Carolina Episode." *Journal of Negro History* 49, no. 1 (January 1964): 34–55.

Shapiro, Martin M. *Courts, a Comparative and Political Analysis.* Chicago: University of Chicago Press, 1981.

Sharpe, Andrew. *Foucault's Monsters and the Challenge of Law.* New York: Routledge, 2010.

Shaw, Karena. *Indigeneity and Political Theory: Sovereignty and the Limits of the Political.* London: Routledge, 2008.

Shaw, Robert. "Neoliberal Subjectivities and the Development of the Night-Time Economy in British Cities." *Geography Compass* 4, no. 7 (July 2010): 893–903.

Shaw, Robert. "Pushed to the Margins of the City: The Urban Night as a Time-space of Protest at Nuit Debout, Paris." *Political Geography* 59 (July 2017): 117–25.

Sherwin, Richard K. "Law in the Flesh: Tracing Legitimation's Origin to *The Act of Killing.*" *No Foundations: An Interdisciplinary Journal of Law and Justice*, no. 11 (2014): 38–60.

Shoemaker, Karl. *Sanctuary and Crime in the Middle Ages, 400–1500.* New York: Fordham University Press, 2011.

Shors, Teri, and Susan H. McFadden. "1918 Influenza: A Winnebago County, Wisconsin Perspective." *Clinical Medicine and Research* 7, no. 4 (December 2009): 147–56.

Siegel, Reva B. "She the People: The Nineteenth Amendment, Sex Equality, Federalism, and the Family." *Harvard Law Review* 115, no. 4 (February 2002): 947–1046.

Silva, Noenoe K. *Aloha Betrayed: Native Hawaiian Resistance to American Colonialism.* Durham, NC: Duke University Press, 2004.

Silva, Noenoe K. "Mana Hawai'i: An Examination of Political Uses of the Word Mana in Hawaiian." In *New Mana: Transformations of a Classic Concept in Pacific Languages and Cultures,* edited by Matt Tomlinson and Ty P. Kāwika Tengan, 39–56. Canberra: Australia National University Press, 2016.

Simatei, Tirop. "Colonial Violence, Postcolonial Violations: Violence, Landscape, and Memory in Kenyan Fiction." *Research in African Literatures* 36, no. 2 (Summer 2005): 85–94.

Simon, Jonathan. "Fear and Loathing in Late Modernity: Reflections on the Cultural Sources of Mass Imprisonment in the United States." *Punishment and Society* 3, no. 1 (January 2001): 21–33.

Simon, Jonathan. *Governing through Crime: How the War on Crime Transformed American Democracy and Created a Culture of Fear.* Oxford: Oxford University Press, 2007.

Simon, Jonathan. "They Died with Their Boots On: The Boot Camp and the Limits of Modern Penalty." *Social Justice* 22, no. 2 (Summer 1995): 25–48.

Simonelli, Guido. "Perceived Neighborhood Safety and Sleep, Commentary on 'The Association of Neighborhood Characteristics with Sleep Duration and Daytime Sleepiness.'" *Sleep Health* 1, no. 3 (September 2015): 156–57.

Simonelli, Guido, Sanjay R. Patel, Solange Rodríguez-Espínola, Daniel Pérez-Chada, Agustín Salvia, Daniel P. Cardinali, and Daniel E. Vigo. "The Impact of Home Safety on Sleep in a Latin American Country." *Sleep Health* 1, no. 2 (June 2015): 98–103.

Sirico, Louis J., Jr. "Failed Constitutional Metaphors: The Wall of Separation and the Penumbra." *University of Richmond Law Review* 45, no. 2 (January 2011): 459–90.

Skinner, Quentin. *Liberty before Liberalism.* Cambridge: Cambridge University Press, 1998.

Slabaugh, Seth. "Klan Leaflets Left around Indiana City." *Indianapolis Star,* October 10, 2014. http://www.indystar.com/story/news/2014/10/10/ku -klux-klan-winchester-indiana-recruiting/17028771/.

Smith, Adam. *The Theory of Moral Sentiments.* Indianapolis: Liberty Classics, 1976.

Smith, Oliver Hampton. *Early Indiana Trials and Sketches: Reminiscences.* Cincinnati: Moore, Wilstach, Keys, 1858.

Snedker, Karen A. "Explaining the Gender Gap in Fear of Crime." *Feminist Criminology* 7, no. 2 (April 2012): 75–111.

Soifer, Avi. *Law and the Company We Keep.* Cambridge, MA: Harvard University Press, 1995.

Somerville, Siobhan B. *Queering the Color Line: Race and the Invention of Homosexuality in American Culture.* Durham, NC: Duke University Press, 2000.

Sommerville, Diane Miller. "The Rape Myth in the Old South Reconsidered." *Journal of Southern History* 61, no. 3 (August 1995): 481–518.

Sommerville, Diane Miller. "Rape, Race, and Castration in Slave Law in the Colonial and Early South." In *The Devil's Lane: Sex and Race in the Early South*, edited by Catherine Clinton and Michele Gillespie, 74–89. Oxford: Oxford University Press, 1997.

Southall, Ashley. "Virus's Toll on N.Y. Police: 1 in 6 Officers Is Out Sick." *New York Times*, April 3, 2020. https://www.nytimes.com/2020/04/03/nyregion/coronavirus-nypd.html.

Spadoni, Robert. "Strange Botany in *Werewolf of London*." *Horror Studies* 1, no. 1 (January 2010): 49–71.

Spillers, Hortense J. "Interstices: A Small Drama of Words." In *Pleasure and Danger: Exploring Female Sexuality*, edited by Carole Vance, 73–100. Boston: Routledge and K. Paul, 1984.

Spillers, Hortense J. "Mama's Baby, Papa's Maybe: An American Grammar Book." *Diacritics* 17, no. 2 (Summer 1987): 64–81.

Stacey, Michele, and Heidi S. Bonner. "Veil of Darkness and Investigating Disproportionate Impact in Policing: When Researchers Disagree." *Police Quarterly* 24, no. 1 (March 2021): 55–73.

Stampp, Kenneth M. *The Peculiar Institution: Slavery in the Ante-Bellum South.* New York: Vintage Books, 1989.

Steger, Brigitte, and Lodewijk Brunt, eds. *Night-Time and Sleep in Asia and the West: Exploring the Dark Side of Life.* London: RoutledgeCurzon, 2003.

Stevens, Matt. "How Asian-American Leaders Are Grappling with Xenophobia amid Coronavirus." *New York Times*, March 29, 2020. https://www.nytimes.com/2020/03/29/us/politics/coronavirus-asian-americans.html.

Stewart, Eliza Daniel. *Memories of the Crusade: A Thrilling Account of the Great Uprising of the Women of Ohio in 1873, against the Liquor Crime.* Chicago: H. J. Smith, 1890.

Stewart, Kathleen. *Ordinary Affects.* Durham, NC: Duke University Press, 2007.

Still, William. *The Underground Railroad: A Record of Facts, Authentic Narratives, Letters, &c., Narrating the Hardships, Hair-Breadth Escapes and Death Struggles of the Slaves in Their Efforts for Freedom, as Related by Themselves and Others, or Witnessed by the Author; Together with Sketches of Some of the Largest Stockholders, and Most Liberal Aiders and Advisers, of the Road.* Philadelphia: People's Publishing Company, 1871.

Stinson, Philip Matthew, Robert W. Taylor, and John Liederbach. "The Situational Context of Police Sexual Violence: Data and Policy Implications."

Family and Intimate Partner Violence Quarterly 12, no. 4 (Spring 2020): 59–68.

St. Louis, Ermus, Alana Saulnier, and Kevin Walby. "Police Use of Body-Worn Cameras: Challenges of Visibility, Procedural Justice, and Legitimacy." *Surveillance and Society* 17, nos. 3–44 (September 2019): 305–21.

Stoler, Ann. *Along the Archival Grain: Thinking through Colonial Ontologies.* Princeton, NJ: Princeton University Press, 2008.

Stone, Taylor. "The Value of Darkness: A Moral Framework for Urban Nighttime Lighting." *Science and Engineering Ethics* 24, no. 2 (April 2018): 607–28.

Stramignoni, Igor. "Badiou's Nocturnal Jurisprudence." *Cardozo Law Review* 29, no. 5 (April 2008): 2361–94.

Strathern, Marilyn. *Property, Substance, and Effect: Anthropological Essays on Persons and Things.* London: Athlone, 1999.

Suk, Jeannie. *At Home in the Law: How the Domestic Violence Revolution Is Transforming Privacy.* New Haven, CT: Yale University Press, 2009.

Sukarieh, Mayssoun, and Stuart Tannock. "The Global Securitisation of Youth." *Third World Quarterly* 39, no. 5 (May 4, 2018): 854–70.

Sunstein, Cass R. "On Analogical Reasoning." *Harvard Law Review* 106, no. 3 (January 1993): 741–91.

Swigart, Leigh. "Cultural Creolisation and Language Use in Post-Colonial Africa: The Case of Senegal." *Africa* 64, no. 2 (1994): 175–89.

Tahmassebi, Stefan B. "Gun Control and Racism." *George Mason University Civil Rights Law Journal* 2, no. 1 (Summer 1991): 67–100.

Talbot, Deborah. *Regulating the Night: Race, Culture and Exclusion in the Making of the Night-Time Economy.* London: Ashgate, 2007.

Tanesini, Alessandra. "Wittgenstein: A Feminist Interpretation." Malden, MA: Polity Press, 2004.

Taub, Amanda. "In Rage over Sarah Everard Killing, 'Women's Bargain' Is Put on Notice." *New York Times*, March 14, 2021. https://www.nytimes.com /2021/03/14/world/europe/sarah-everard-women-protest.html.

Taub, Amanda, and Jane Bradley. "As Domestic Abuse Rises, U.K. Failings Leave Victims in Peril." *New York Times*, July 2, 2020. https://www .nytimes.com/interactive/2020/07/02/world/europe/uk-coronavirus -domestic-abuse.html.

Taussig, Michael. *The Devil and Commodity Fetishism in South America.* Chapel Hill: University of North Carolina Press, 1980.

Taylor, G. Flint. "The Long Path to Reparations for the Survivors of Chicago Police Torture." *Northwestern Journal of Law and Social Policy* 11, no. 3 (Spring 2016): 330–53.

Taylor, Keeanga-Yamahtta, ed. *How We Get Free: Black Feminism and the Combahee River Collective.* Chicago: Haymarket Books, 2017.

Taylor, Marisa, and Aram Roston. "Exclusive: Pressed by Trump, U.S. Pushed Unproven Coronavirus Treatment Guidance." *Reuters*, April 5, 2020.

https://www.reuters.com/article/us-health-coronavirus-usa-guidance
-exclu-idUSKBN21M0R2.

Teacher, Beth E. "Sleepwalking Used as a Defense in Criminal Cases and the
Evolution of the Ambien Defense." *Duquesne Criminal Law Journal* 2,
no. 2 (2009): 127–38.

Thacker, Eugene. "Necrologies; or, The Death of the Body Politic." In *Beyond
Biopolitics: Essays on the Governance of Life and Death*, edited by Patricia
Ticineto Clough and Craig Willse, 139–62. Durham, NC: Duke Univer-
sity Press, 2011.

Thacker, Eugene. "The Shadows of Atheology: Epidemics, Power and Life
after Foucault." *Theory, Culture and Society* 26, no. 6 (November 2009):
134–52.

Thacker, Eugene. *Starry Speculative Corpse: Horror of Philosophy*. Winchester,
UK: Zero Books, 2015.

Theroux, Paul. "Paul Theroux Recalls a Fear-Filled Lockdown." *New York
Times*, March 30, 2020. https://www.nytimes.com/2020/03/30/travel
/coronavirus-travel-theroux-essay.html.

Thomas, Colin J., and Rosemary D. F. Bromley. "City-Centre Revitalisation:
Problems of Fragmentation and Fear in the Evening and Night-Time
City." *Urban Studies* 37, no. 8 (July 2000): 1403–29.

Thornburg, Elizabeth G. "Metaphors Matter: How Images of Battle, Sports,
and Sex Shape the Adversary System." *Wisconsin Women's Law Journal* 10,
no. 2 (Fall 1995): 225–82.

Thucydides. *The Peloponnesian War*. Translated by Martin Hammond. Oxford:
Oxford University Press, 2009.

Tickner, Lisa. *The Spectacle of Women: Imagery of the Suffrage Campaign,
1907–14*. Chicago: University of Chicago Press, 1988.

Tipton, Cory. "FAA Measures to Prevent Night Time Flying Accidents
Transportation Law." *Preventive Law Reporter* 21, no. 2: 6–8.

Tocqueville, Alexis de. *Democracy in America*. Vols. 1 and 2. Translated by
Henry Reeve. Auckland, NZ: Floating Press, 2009.

Tomlins, Christopher. *In the Matter of Nat Turner: A Speculative History*.
Princeton, NJ: Princeton University Press, 2020.

Torrano, Andrea. "Politics over Monstrosity and Politics of Monstrosity: The
Difference between Negative and Positive Consideration about Monsters." In *Monsters, Monstrosities, and the Monstrous in Culture and Society*,
edited by Diego Compagna and Stefanie Steinhart, 131–55. Wilmington,
DE : Vernon, 2020.

Tregle, Joseph G., Jr. "Early New Orleans Society: A Reappraisal," *The Journal of
Southern History*, 18, no. 1 (February 1952): 20–36.

Trelease, Allen W. *White Terror: The Ku Klux Klan Conspiracy and Southern
Reconstruction*. Westport, CT: Praeger, 1979.

Trenholme, Norman Maclaren. *The Right of Sanctuary in England: A Study in Institutional History.* Columbia, MO: E. W. Stephens, 1903.

Trigg, Dylan. *The Thing: A Phenomenology of Horror.* Alresford, UK: Zero Books, 2014.

Trinh, T. Minh-Ha. *Woman, Native, Other: Writing Postcoloniality and Feminism.* Bloomington: Indiana University Press, 1989.

Tuerkheimer, Deborah. "Judging Sex." *Cornell Law Review* 97, no. 6 (September 2012): 1461–504.

Tuerkheimer, Deborah. "Slutwalking in the Shadow of the Law." *Minnesota Law Review* 98, no. 4 (2014): 1453–511.

Tulloch, Marian, and Christine Jennett. "Women's Responses to Fear of Crime." *Security Journal* 14, no. 2 (April 2001): 53–62.

Turner, Nat, and Thomas R. Gray. *The Confessions of Nat Turner, the Leader of the Late Insurrection in Southampton, Va., as Fully and Voluntarily Made to Thomas R. Gray, in the Prison Where He Was Confined, and Acknowledged by Him to Be Such, When Read before the Court of Southampton: With the Certificate, under Seal of the Court Convened at Jerusalem, Nov. 5, 1831, for His Trial.* Baltimore: T. R. Gray, 1832.

Umlauf, Mary Grace, John M. Bolland, and Brad E. Lian. "Sleep Disturbance and Risk Behaviors among Inner-City African-American Adolescents." *Journal of Urban Health* 88, no. 6 (December 2011): 1130–42.

Underwood, Amanda. "Witchcraft in the American Colonies beyond the Limits of Salem." *Fairmount Folio: Journal of History* 19 (2019): https://journals.wichita.edu/index.php/ff/article/view/216/214.

Valentine, David. *Imagining Transgender: An Ethnography of a Category.* Durham, NC: Duke University Press, 2007.

Valentine, Gill. "The Geography of Women's Fear." *Area* 21, no. 4 (December 1989): 385–90.

Valentine, Gill. "Images of Danger: Women's Sources of Information about the Spatial Distribution of Male Violence." *Area* 24, no. 1 (March 1992): 22–29.

Valentine, Gill. "Women's Fear of Male Violence in Public Space: A Spatial Expression of Patriarchy." PhD diss., University of Reading, UK, 1989.

Van Allen, Judith. "'Sitting on a Man': Colonialism and the Lost Political Institutions of Igbo Women." *Canadian Journal of African Studies/Revue Canadienne des Études Africaines* 6, no. 2 (1972): 165–81.

Van Liempt, Ilse. "Safe Nightlife Collaborations: Multiple Actors, Conflicting Interests and Different Power Distributions." *Urban Studies* 52, no. 3 (February 2015): 486–500.

Van Liempt, Ilse, Irina van Aalst, and Tim Schwanen. "Introduction: Geographies of the Urban Night." *Urban Studies* 52, no. 3 (February 2015): 407–21.

Verdon, Jean. *Night in the Middle Ages.* Notre Dame, IN: University of Notre Dame Press, 2002.

Vickery, Amanda. "An Englishman's Home Is His Castle? Thresholds, Boundaries and Privacies in the Eighteenth-Century London House." *Past and Present*, no. 199 (May 2008): 147–73.

Vigh, Henrik. "Vigilance: On Conflict, Social Invisibility, and Negative Potentiality." *Social Analysis* 55, no. 3 (December 2011): 93–114.

Vito, Anthony G., Vanessa Woodward Griffin, Gennaro F. Vito, and George E. Higgins. "'Does Daylight Matter'? An Examination of Racial Bias in Traffic Stops by Police." *Policing: An International Journal* 43, no. 4 (August 2020): 675–88.

Wacquant, Loïc. *Punishing the Poor: The Neoliberal Government of Social Insecurity.* Durham, NC: Duke University Press, 2009.

Wade, Richard C. *Slavery in the Cities: The South, 1820–1860.* Cary, NC: Oxford University Press, 1967.

Wagner, Kevin M., Dukhong Kim, and Jeremy C. Hagler. "Stand Your Ground in Florida: The Effect of Race, Location and Weapons on Convictions." *Ralph Bunche Journal of Public Affairs* 5, no. 1 (Spring 2016): article 2.

Waldrep, Christopher. *The Many Faces of Judge Lynch: Extralegal Violence and Punishment in America.* New York: Palgrave Macmillan, 2002.

Walker, David. *Appeal.* Boston: Printed for the author. 1829.

Wang, Hai-na. "Research on the Communication Regulations Recorded in Zhou Li." *Journal of Ancient Books Collation and Studies* 2007, no. 4 (2007). http://en.cnki.com.cn/Article_en/CJFDTOTAL -GJZL200704026.htm.

Warren, Calvin L. *Ontological Terror: Blackness, Nihilism, and Emancipation.* Durham, NC: Duke University Press, 2018.

Washington Post. "Thailand Imposes 6-Hour Nightly Curfew to Combat Virus." April 2, 2020. https://www.washingtonpost.com/business /thailand-imposes-6-hour-nightly-curfew-to-combat-virus/2020/04/02 /820654ae-74dc-11ea-ad9b-254ec99993bc_story.html.

Weheliye, Alexander G. *Habeas Viscus: Racializing Assemblages, Biopolitics, and Black Feminist Theories of the Human.* Durham, NC: Duke University Press, 2014.

Weiss, Kenneth J., Clarence Watson, Dimitri Markov, and Elena Del Busto. "Parasomnias, Violence and the Law." In "Program in Psychiatry and the Law (Part I)." Special issue, *Journal of Psychiatry and Law* 39, no. 2 (June 2011): 249–86.

Weizman, Eyal. *Hollow Land: Israel's Architecture of Occupation.* London: Verso, 2007.

Wells, H. G. *The Island of Doctor Moreau.* London: W. Heinemann, 1896.

Wells-Barnett, Ida B. *The Red Record: Tabulated Statistics and Alleged Causes of Lynching in the United States.* CreateSpace, 2015.

Wells-Barnett, Ida B. *Southern Horrors: Lynch Law in All Its Phases*. New York, 1892. Project Gutenberg, 2005. http://www.gutenberg.org/ebooks /14975.

Wendling, Mike. *Alt-Right: From 4chan to the White House*. London: Pluto, 2018.

West, Robin. "Sex, Law, and Consent." In *Ethics of Consent: Theory and Practice*, edited by Franklin G. Miller and Alan Wertheimer, 221–47. Oxford: Oxford University Press, 2009.

West, Robin. "Women in the Legal Academy: A Brief History of Feminist Legal Theory." *Fordham Law Review* 87, no. 3 (2018): 977–1004.

White, Edward Joseph. *The Law in the Scriptures: With Explanations of the Law Terms and Legal References in Both the Old and the New Testaments*. Union, NJ: Lawbook Exchange, 2000.

Whittier, Nancy. *Frenemies: Feminists, Conservatives, and Sexual Violence*. New York: Oxford University Press, 2018.

Wildermuth, John. "Clinton Backs Youth Curfews/He Proposes Teens Be Home by 8 P.M." *San Francisco Chronicle*, May 31, 1996. https://www. sfgate.com/news/article/Clinton-Backs-Youth-Curfews-He-proposes -teens-2979504.php.

Wilderson, Frank B., III. "Grammar and Ghosts: The Performative Limits of African Freedom." *Theatre Survey* 50, no. 1 (May 2009): 119–25.

Wilderson, Frank B., III. *Red, White and Black: Cinema and the Structure of U.S. Antagonisms*. Durham, NC: Duke University Press, 2010.

Williams, Kidada E. "Never Get over It: Night-Riding's Imprint on African American Victims." In *Reconstruction and the Arc of Racial (In)Justice*, edited by Julian M. Hayter and George R. Goethals, 59–83. Cheltenham, UK: Edward Elgar, 2018.

Williams, Kidada E. *They Left Great Marks on Me: African American Testimonies of Racial Violence from Emancipation to World War I*. New York: New York University Press, 2012.

Williams, Oscar R. "The Regimentation of Blacks on the Urban Frontier in Co- lonial Albany, New York City and Philadelphia." *Journal of Negro History* 63, no. 4 (Fall 1978): 329–38.

Williams, Patricia J. "Alchemical Notes: Reconstructing Ideals from Decon- structed Rights." *Harvard Civil Rights–Civil Liberties Law Review* 22, no. 2 (Spring 1987): 401–34.

Williams, Patricia J. *Alchemy of Race and Rights: Diary of a Law Professor*. Rev. ed. Cambridge, MA: Harvard University Press, 1992.

Williams, Robert. "Night Spaces: Darkness, Deterritorialization, and Social Control." *Space and Culture* 11, no. 4 (November 2008): 514–32.

Williams, Simon Johnson. *The Politics of Sleep: Governing (Un)Consciousness in the Late Modern Age*. New York: Palgrave Macmillan, 2011.

Williams, Simon Johnson. *Sleep and Society: Sociological Ventures into the (Un) Known.* London: Routledge, 2005.

Wilson, Jason. "Hiding in Plain Sight: How the 'Alt-Right' Is Weaponizing Irony to Spread Fascism." *Guardian,* May 23, 2017. http://www.theguardian.com /technology/2017/may/23/alt-right-online-humor-as-a-weapon-facism.

Winter, Steven L. "What Is the 'Color' of Law?" In *The Cambridge Handbook of Metaphor and Thought,* edited by Raymond W. Gibbs, 363–79. New York: Cambridge University Press, 2008.

Winters, Christopher. "Urban Morphogenesis in Francophone Black Africa." *Geographical Review* 72, no. 2 (April 1982): 139–54.

Wittgenstein, Ludwig. *Philosophical Investigations.* New York: Macmillan, 1958.

Wolff, Martin. "On the Nature of Legal Persons." *Law Quarterly Review* 54 (October 1938): 494–521.

Wolf-Meyer, Matthew J. "Myths of Modern American Sleep: Naturalizing Primordial Sleep, Blaming Technological Distractions, and Pathologizing Children." *Science as Culture* 24, no. 2 (2015): 205–26.

Wollstonecraft, Mary. *A Vindication of the Rights of Woman: With Strictures on Political and Moral Subjects.* T. F. Unwin, 1891.

Wood, Gordon S. *The Creation of the American Republic, 1776–1787.* Chapel Hill: University of North Carolina Press, 1998.

Wooden, Julie Marie. "Sexual Assault in Our Society: Women (and Men) Take Back the Night." Master's thesis, Iowa State University, 2000.

Woodward, C. Vann. *The Strange Career of Jim Crow.* 2nd rev. ed. New York: Oxford University Press, 1966.

Wortham, Simon. *The Poetics of Sleep: From Aristotle to Nancy.* London: Bloomsbury, 2013.

Wynter, Sylvia. "Afterword: Beyond Miranda's Meanings: Un/Silencing the 'Demonic Ground' of Caliban's 'Woman.'" In *Out of the Kumbla: Caribbean Women and Literature,* edited by Carole Boyce Davies and Elaine Savory, 355–68. Trenton, NJ: Africa World Press, 1990.

Xu, Mingzhao. "Sexsomnia: A Valid Defense to Sexual Assault." *Journal of Gender, Race and Justice* 12, no. 3 (Spring 2009): 687–712.

Yankah, Ekow N. "Republican Responsibility in Criminal Law." *Criminal Law and Philosophy* 9, no. 3 (September 2015): 457–75.

Young, Iris Marion. *Throwing like a Girl and Other Essays in Feminist Philosophy and Social Theory.* Bloomington: Indiana University Press, 1990.

Yuhas, Alan. "Honolulu Upholds Ban: Don't Sit or Lie Down Where a Tourist Might See You." *Guardian,* June 4, 2015. https://www.theguardian.com /us-news/2015/jun/04/honolulu-upholds-ban-dont-sit-or-lay-down -where-a-tourist-might-see-you.

Zaveri, Mihir. "Washington Wants to Hire a Night Mayor. So What Is That?" *New York Times,* October 10, 2018. https://www.nytimes.com/2018/10 /10/us/night-mayor-washington-dc.html.

Ziarek, Ewa Płonowska. "Bare Life on Strike: Notes on the Biopolitics of Race and Gender." *South Atlantic Quarterly* 107, no. 1 (Winter 2008): 89–105.

Zimring, Franklin E. *When Police Kill.* Cambridge, MA: Harvard University Press, 2017.

Zimring, Franklin E., and Brittany Arsiniega. "Trends in Killing of and by Police: A Preliminary Analysis." *Ohio State Journal of Criminal Law* 13, no. 1 (Fall 2015): 247–64.

Žižek, Slavoj. *The Plague of Fantasies.* 2nd ed. London: Verso, 2009.

Žižek, Slavoj. *The Sublime Object of Ideology.* London: Verso, 1989.

Žižek, Slavoj. "Superego by Default." *Cardozo Law Review* 16, nos. 3–4 (January 1995): 925–42.

Zourabichvili, François. *Deleuze: A Philosophy of the Event; Together with the Vocabulary of Deleuze.* Edinburgh: Edinburgh University Press, 2012.

Zureik, Elia. "Constructing Palestine through Surveillance Practices." *British Journal of Middle Eastern Studies* 28, no. 2 (November 2001): 205–27.

INDEX

Boltanski, Luc 192

Boone, Daniel, 67

Bostock v. Clayton County, 188

Bourdieu, Pierre, 255n8

Bracewell, Lorna, 169–70

Bradley, Joseph (justice), 80–81

Brass, Paul, 125

Bröck-Sallah, Sabine, 142–43

Bronfen, Elisabeth, 208–9n8, 230n214

Brotherhood (militia), 224n114

Brown v. Board of Education, 9

Brown v. United States, 229n198

Brown, Michael, 58

Brownlow, Alec, 252n138

Brundage, W. Fitzhugh, 227n169

Bruno, Jonathan, 235n43

Brunson, Rod, 240n94

Buber, Martin, 46

Bufford, Cortez, 58, 217n5

Burge, Jon, 84

Burn, Richard (justice of the peace), 259–60n55

Butler, Judith, 55, 165–66, 253n168

Butler, Melissa, 244–45n17

Byman, Daniel, 226n150

Cabantous, Alain, 13

Cameron, Jessica Joy, 146

Camp, Stephanie, 218n19, 219n33

Canetti, Elias, 16, 111–12, 163, 237nn58–59, 259n51

Carbonnier, Jean, 1

Cardozo, Benjamin, 9, 177, 255–56n13

Carlson, Jennifer, 58, 73, 82

Carr, Joetta, 253n167

Carter Jackson, Kellie, 62

Castile Philando, 57–58, 74, 94

Certeau, Michel de, 16, 38, 212n46

Chamayou, Grégoire, 32, 67–68, 90, 94, 113, 151, 221n70, 237–38n62, 249n88; 249–50n93

Chauhan, B. S. (justice), 53–54

Chauvin, Derek, 58

Christiana incident, 69–72, 74, 88, 195; nocturnal symbolism of, 72

Cicero, 178

civil death, 54

civil sleep, 54–55, 190–91

Cixous, Hélène, 18

Clapham Common, 173

Clark, Stephon, 94, 230n213

Clarke, Lewis, 69

Clinton, Hillary Rodham, 38, 212n47

Clinton, William Jefferson, 119

Cohen, Morris, 246n41

Colfax massacre, 79–80, 224n111; and *United States v. Cruikshank*, 80, 86

Combahee River Collective, 157

consciousness-raising, 138–39, 157, 171

Cools, Arthur, 190–91

Cooper, Davina, 200n10

Cooper, Eli, 86–87

coronavirus. *See* COVID-19

Cottrol, Robert, 222–23n100

Cover, Robert, 3, 24–25, 142, 179, 187, 193

coverture, 139–40, 245–46n30

COVID-19, 99, 104, 128, 130–31, 146

Crary, Jonathan, 42, 51

Crockett, Davy, 67

crowds, 16, 36, 111–13, 137, 163, 236n57, 237n58, 237n60, 259n51; magical, 236n56; sleeping, 53–54

Crunk Feminist Collective, 168

Cunneen, Chris, 239n89

curfew, 4, 12–13, 15, 25–26, 31, 99–101, 132–33, 192–95, 231n6, 232n10, 232n13; colonialism and, 98, 122–28, 237n61, 239n89, 240–41n99, 242n123; crowds and, 111–13; epidemics and, 99, 128–32; exception and, 101–4; incitement to law and, 107–111; legitimacy and, 241–42n.111; lighting and, 111, 236n55; magic and, 236n56; rape and, 132; sanctuary and, 107, 116, 132; subjectivity and, 113–18; transgression and, 236n54; vigilance and, 104–7; werewolf and, 108; youth and, 118–22, 238n76, 238n82, 238–39n83, 240n96

Curry, James, 218n14

Darian-Smith, Eve, 163

dark law, 179, 257n25

David, Jacques-Louis, 17

Davies, Margaret, 10, 141

Davis, Angela, 152, 154

Davis, Mike, 162

Davis, Sidney Fant (judge), 227n166

Dayan, Colin, 54, 56

De-Occupy Honolulu v. City and County of Honolulu, 210n15

Dekker, Thomas, 203n62

Deleuze, Gilles, 5, 196; *dispositif* and, 6–8, 201n36

Denby, Bill, 88–89

Derickson, Alan, 42

Derrida, Jacques, 3; catachresis and, 261n75; gift and, 190–91; heliotrope and, 26, 181–83, 186, 195, 197, 258n35; law and, 185–86, 199n6; Marrano and, 194, 262n87; metaphor and, 174–75, 179–82, 185, 190, 195, 197, 255n2, 258n35, 258n38; plurality and, 183, 186, 258–59n43; sleep and, 35–36, 190; the sun, on, 258–59n43; vigilance and, 233–4n32; werewolf and, 203n60; whiteness and, 180, 257n28; witnessing and, 194

Diamond, Raymond, 222–23n100

Diggers, 137

Diouf, Abdou, 125

dispositif, 6–8, 11, 201n36; biopolitics and, 128–29; curfew and, 193; gender and, 169; Hawaiian, 30–31; immunity and, 41–43, 50, 213n66; legal consciousness and, 7; legal mobilization and, 7; legal person and, 40–43, 46; legal violence and, 187; masculinity and, 149; metaphor and, 175; nocturnal, 11, 13, 15, 25, 135, 155, 175, 198; power and, 129; racial violence and, 59; sexual rights and, 169, 189; sociolegal studies and, 7–8; sovereignty and, 17; vigilantes and, 186

District of Columbia v. Heller, 227n178

Douglas, William O. (justice), 184

Douglass, Frederick, 67, 70–72, 85, 88–89, 143, 225n138, 228n190

Dred Scott v. Sandford, 85, 228n181

Du Bois, W. E. B., 77, 224n118

Duncan, Martha Grace, 185, 260n59

Duncan, Nancy 162

Durkheim, Émile, 65

Duval, Raymond, 105–6

Dworkin, Andrea, 1, 26, 135, 144, 173; activism and, 137–38, 145, 196; antipornography and, 145, 172; demonism and magic and, 147–52, 196; Enlightenment and, 145, 171; fear and, 160–64; feminist theory and, 146–47; legality and, 172–73; property and, 141; race and, 152–59; SlutWalk and, 166–67, 170

Eichmann, Adolf, 110

Ekirch, A. Roger, 5, 13; curfew and, 231n6; shutting in and, 259–60n55; sleep and, 17, 211n41

Elster, Jon, 213n59

emergency, 15, 25–26, 99, 110, 123; Benjamin, Walter and, 238n63; colonialism and, 125; COVID-19 and, 131; crowd and, 112; curfew as, 112–13, 116–17, 125; law and, 113, 116, 136, 193, 215n106; protest and, 136; sovereignty and, 131, 232n16; vigilance and, 104

endarkenment, 139

Engel, David, 7

Enlightenment, 2, 9, 20, 23, 26, 63, 111, 134–38, 142–43; consent and, 167; critique of, 26, 135, 138–39, 143–45, 147, 159, 171–73, 180; Hawaiian thought and, 208n8; law and, 4, 9, 111, 140, 142, 145, 147, 176, 182; light and, 145, 176, 236n55; metaphor and, 20, 27; night and, 195, 198, 236n55; property and, 172; race and, 143–44, 153; republicanism and, 63; SlutWalk and, 167

epidemic, 99, 128–32, 135

equality: crowd and, 111–12; curfew and, 101, 132; law and, 80, 87, 116–17, 174, 176, 246n38; night and, 12, 15–19, 132, 157, 172, 179, 188; sleep and, 29, 32, 53, 216n115; state and, 38, 41, 112; urban access and, 146, 164, 247n65; women's activism and, 157

Erwin v. State, 229n191

Esposito, Roberto, 6, 40–41, 43–44, 46; affirmative biopolitics and, 47, 49; flesh and, 49; immunity and, 50, 52, 129, 213n69

Esteva, Gustavo, 128

Grant, Ulysses S. (president), 81

Greenham Common Women's Peace Camp, 215n108

Griswold v. Connecticut, 184, 192, 199n5, 214n79

Gross, Tabb, 218n16

Grove, Jairus, 257n25

Guenther, Lisa, 38, 251n128

guns, 58–59, 74, 95–96, 189; concealed carry of, 66–67; confiscation of, 62, 69, 73, 77, 89, 189; control, 63, 73, 85, 222–23n100; law and, 63, 89–90; liberalism and, 85–86; night and, 58–59, 73, 77, 90, 220–21n62; open carry of, 66; police and, 92, 95; populism and, 82; race and, 59, 62, 73–74, 77, 87–88, 91–92, 218n8; representation of, 95; republicanism and, 63, 66–67, 85; Saturday night special, 73; self-defense and, 86, 89–90; slavery and, 61–64, 69, 73, 219n36; sovereignty and, 59, 87. *See also* Amendment, Second

Habermas, Jürgen, 232n8, 244n10

Haiti: constitution of, 4–5; revolution and, 62, 74, 154, 219n26

Hall, Kim, 22

Hamilton, Alexander, 59

Hammerschlag, Sarah, 262n87

Haraway, Donna, 150, 213n69

Harper, Ida Husted, 238–39n83

Harris, Cheryl, 246n41

Harrison, Bernard, 257n27

Hart, Herbert Lionel Adolphus, 29

Hartman, Geoffrey, 259n44

Hartman, Saidiya, 143, 228n184

Hatton case, 43–45, 49, 53–54, 191

Haverkamp, Anselm, 256n19

Hawai'i, 30–31, 43, 45, 54, 116, 131–32, 208n5, 208–9n8, 209nn11–12, 209–10n13, 210n15, 215n105

Hay, Douglas, 209n12

Haygood, Wil, 205n91

Hegel, Georg Wilhelm Friedrich. 96; influence of, 8, 39

Heidegger, Martin, 6; anxiety and, 106; light and, 21, 235n42; metaphor and, 178, 258n38; temporality and, 105; vigilance and, 233n31

heliotrope, 26–27, 179, 181–86, 189, 192–93, 195–97, 258n35

Herbert, Steve, 207–8n3

Heyes, Cressida, 158–59

Hibbitts, Bernard, 182–83, 259n46

Hill Collins, Patricia, 153, 253–54n169

Hill, Annie, 166

Hirabayashi v. United States, 238n73

Hirabayashi, Gordon, 116–18, 120, 127

Hobbes, Thomas, 47–48; influence of, 43, 102, 237n60

Hobsbawm, Eric, 149, 151

Hogue, James, 225n139

Holmes, Oliver Wendell, 9, 90, 202n50, 259n53

homo sacer, 108, 112, 234n39

Homrn, John, 218n13

Honig, Bonnie, 51, 54–55, 214n91, 215n106

hooks, bell, 138, 153

Hughes, Langston, 15–16

hunting 67; curfew and, 112, 114, 116, 133; night and, 74, 94, 158, 170; people as prey, 67–68, 70–74, 112, 114, 237n62, 249–50n93; police and, 15, 69, 95, 113–14, 221n70; race and, 63, 96; republicanism and, 67; reversal and, 68, 72, 249–50n93; slavery and, 32, 61, 67–69; werewolf and, 151; witches of, 138, 245n22, 248n76; women and, 141, 145, 147, 151, 158–59, 170. *See also* Chamayou, Grégoire

Husserl, Edmund, 105, 233–34n32

immunity, 4, 41–45, 47–52, 59, 117, 129–30, 174, 190, 213n66, 213n69, 256–57n23, 259–60n55; sleep and, 45

incitement: biopower and, 103; legal, 107–11, 113, 126, 132, 192–93

Innocents (militia), 224n114

Jackson, Richard, 35

Jackson, Robert (justice), 199n5

James, William, 202n49

Jankélévitch, Vladimir, 46

Jaruzelski, Wojciech, 104

Jay, Martin, 17, 181

Jefferson, Thomas, 63, 65

Jim Crow laws, 81–82, 166, 220n54, 227n170

Naudé, Gabriel, 15

Negro law, 83, 257n25

neoliberalism, 42–43; austerity and, 136, 151; curfews and, 120; nocturnal activism and, 136, 146; nocturnal economy and, 162, 252n145; nocturnal danger and, 162; property and, 147; sleep and, 42–43, 46, 210n23; Take Back the Night and, 146; vigilance and, 104. *See also* liberalism

New Jersey v. Delaware, 199n5

Newman, Michael, 260n61

Ngũgĩ wa Thiong'o, 98, 103–4, 112

Nichols, Robert, 144

Nietzsche, Friedrich, 14, 32, 144, 202n56, 210n17; metaphor on, 178–180, 183

night child, 118

Night Czar, 19, 206n115

night riding, 68, 78–79, 86

nightwalking: *See* walking

nightmare, 261–62n86

nocturnalization. 13

Nuit Debout, 136, 244n9

Nussbaum, Martha, 167

Obasogie, Osagie, 199n5

Ophir, Adi, 242n123

Opondo, Samson, 228n190

other night, 21, 185, 206–7n128, 247n55, 260n61

outlawry, 128, 149–51

Pain, Rachel, 161

Pale Faces (militia), 223n110, 224n114

Palestine, 100, 110, 126–27, 243n127

Panagia, Davide, 6

Parker, Kunal, 9

Parker, William, 70–71, 222n80

Parris, Benjamin, 212n55

Parsons, Elaine, 76

Pateman, Carole, 140

Patterson, Orlando, 226n154

Peaden, Durell (senator), 90–91

Pence, Mike (vice president), 104

penumbra: *See* metaphor

Pepe the Frog, 224n121

Petchesky, Rosalind, 137, 139, 142

Pettit, Philip, 65

phenomenology, 24, 33, 47–48, 104–5, 113; feminism and, 158–59, 196; law and, 105–6, 108–11, 182–83; night and, 158; sleep and, 48, 54; vigilance and, 233–34n32

pleasure: consent and, 168, 170; curfew and, 122; darkness and, 20, 161; equality and, 19; feminism and, 146, 159, 167, 170–71; lynching and, 82; night and, 18–20, 122, 153–54, 161, 197; police power and, 113, 238n67; slave patrols and, 69; sleep and, 159, 189–90; vigilantism and, 77–78, 82, 225n127

pluralism, legal, 7–11, 99, 132, 182–83, 198, 202n50; temporal, 99, 132, 157, 198, 202n45

Pocock, J. G. A., 63–64

Poe, Edgar Allen, 14

police, 15–16, 121, 187, 227n170; Black women and, 122; body cameras and, 231n218; children and, 239n89; colonialism and, 100, 113, 241n110; curfew and, 99–100, 110, 113–14, 119, 130, 132, 241–42n111; cynegetic power and, 15, 113–14, 221n70; fear and, 162; killings by, 14, 25, 36, 52–53, 57–59, 68, 74, 87, 91–95, 99, 112–13, 173, 188, 194, 205n91, 217n3, 217n5, 229nn206–7, 230nn208–10, 230n213, 237–38n62; law and, 25, 114, 150, 186, 196, 229n206, 249n88; night raids and, 52–53, 215n108; night watch and, 31–32, 110; power and pleasure, 113–14, 238n67; race and 14, 23, 25, 58, 84, 87, 91–94, 100, 112–13, 119, 121–22, 151, 187, 240nn93–94; reform and, 113; self-defense and, 88; sexual minorities and, 157; slavery and, 16, 205n97; sleep and, 29, 207–8n3; SlutWalk and, 165–67, 169–70; sousveillance and, 36; vigilantism and, 4, 84–85, 186–88, 227n170, 227n177; vision and, 23, 231n218; women and, 122, 134, 136, 150–51, 162, 170, 173, 196, 215n108

pornography, 145, 147, 164, 166–67, 169; anti-pornography ordinances, 145, 172

Posner, Richard, 256n18

Post, Gaines, 211n35

Post, Louis, 215n106

Pound, Roscoe, 2

Rawls, John, 65

Reclaim the Night, 134, 155, 173, 196, 244n1. *See also* Take Back the Night

Reclaim These Streets, 173

Reconstruction, 74–75, 79–81, 85, 96; gun control and, 222–23n100

Regents of the University of California v. Bakke, 228n180

Reger, Jo, 167

Reiss, Benjamin, 219n29

representation: biopolitics and, 43; body politic and, 50; darkness and, 25; law and, 25, 50; lynching and, 84; nocturnal activism and, 26, 164, 167, 196; pornography and, 146, 172; public opinion and, 235n43; radical feminism and, 146, 164, 166, 171–72, 196; republicanism and, 65–66, 74; SlutWalk and, 166–71; suffrage and, 137; temporality and, 105, 189

republicanism 59, 63–67, 81, 86, 186, 220n49; abolition and, 74; aristocracy and, 63–64; concealed firearms and, 66; darkness and, 66–67, 69, 71, 74, 78, 95; guns and, 63, 66–67, 85, 94; hunting and, 67, 69, 71; law and, 70, 77–78, 81–82, 85, 220n54; liberal rights and, 85, 87; lynching and, 82–85; open carry of firearms and, 66; night and, 25, 66–67, 72, 86, 221n63; nondependency and, 64, 67; people (the) and, 64–66, 82, 221n63; race and, 67, 77, 94; slavery and, 64–65, 67, 70–71, 74; standing army and, 59, 64; vigilantism and, 67, 69, 77–78, 82–85, 186, 226–27n165; visibility and, 65. *See also* militia

Reynolds, Kenneth, 238n76

Rich, Adrienne, 135

Ricoeur, Paul, 177, 186, 195, 258n38

Rideout, Christopher, 184, 259n53

Robson, Ruthann, 149

Roe v. Wade, 187

Roethlisberger, Lucas, 217n5

Romer v. Evans, 261n68

Rose, Carole, 141, 246n39

Rousseau, Jean-Jacques, 63, 220n49

Roux, Jacques, 106

Ruefle, William, 238n76

Salamon, Gayle, 251n126

sanctuary, 4, 26, 30–31; body and, 160; curfew and, 107, 116, 132; Hawaiian law and, 209n11, 215n105; Jews and, 250n114; police and, 150; *pu'uhonua* as, 209nn10–11, 215n105; sleep as, 52, 54; women and, 146, 149–151, 156–158, 162, 249n90, 250n95

Santner, Eric, 5, 34, 50–52, 109, 214–15 n94, 236–37n57; flesh and, 50–52, 215n100, 235–36n49; political theology and, 211–12n42, 236–37n57

Saramago, José, 174–77; 179, 188

Sartre, Jean-Paul, 236n54

Schivelbusch, Wolfgang, 236n55

Schmitt, Carl, 3, 102–3, 109, 200n8, 232n16

Schroth, Peter, 255n4

Scott, James, 202n47, 207n132

Seeger, Peggy, 134–35

self-defense, 4, 20, 78, 87, 200n11, 229n193; guns and, 86, 90, 95; law and, 89–90, 229nn193–94; race and, 57–58, 70–72, 75, 86

Serres, Michel, 24

Seurat, Georges, 8

sexual violence: commodification of, 162; coverture and, 140; night and, 132–33, 149; prevalence of, 149, 252n138; property and, 140–41; queer feminism and, 284n77; race and, 143, 152, 154; reform and, 154; SlutWalk and, 165–172; Take Back the Night and, 149, 152–54, 165, 170–71; unconsciousness and, 158–59. *See also* rape

Shakespeare, William, 14, 71, 185

Shanley, Mary, 139

Sharpe, Andrew, 121

Shaw, Robert, 14

Sherwin, Richard, 52, 56, 59

Shoah (Holocaust), 102, 110; Crystal Night [Kristallnacht] and, 156

Shoemaker, Karl, 250n114

shutting in, 38, 100, 158, 184, 259–60n55

Simatei, Tirop, 125

Simon, Jonathan, 110, 236n53

Sirico, Louis, 256n18

Slaughterhouse Cases, 80, 85

wild hunt, 148

Wilderson, Frank, 143–44, 247n50

William the Conqueror, 231n6

Williams, Kidada, 86

Williams, Oscar, 241n101

Williams, Patricia, 22

Williams, Robert, 6, 136, 162

Williams, Simon, 212n50

witches and witch hunts, 12, 13, 99–101,
106, 112, 138, 148–49, 151, 203n60, 231n6,
234–35n41; 236n56, 237n61, 245n22,
248n77; sabbath, 148–49; trials, 120, 149,
173, 203n61, 248n76

Wittgenstein, Ludwig, 147, 177

Wollstonecraft, Mary 142–43

Wood, Gordon, 63, 220–21n62

Wortham, Simon, 40

Yanez, Jeronimo, 57

Yankah, Ekow, 65, 220n54

Youngstown Sheet and Tube v. Sawyer, 199n5

Zimmerman, George, 56–57, 68, 88, 91,
188

Zimring, Franklin, 94, 230n210, 230–31n215

Žižek, Slavoj, 3, 104–5, 107, 188, 260–61n67